Creating Documents

with

Scientific WorkPlace®

and

Scientific Word®

Version 5

Creating Documents with Scientific WorkPlace® and Scientific Word®

Version 5

Susan Bagby
MacKichan Software, Inc.

Printed in the United States of America

10   9   8   7   6   5   4   3   2   1

Trademarks

Scientific WorkPlace, Scientific Word, Scientific Notebook, and EasyMath are registered trademarks of MacKichan Software, Inc. EasyMath is the sophisticated parsing and translating system included in *Scientific WorkPlace, Scientific Word,* and *Scientific Notebook* that allows the user to work in standard mathematical notation, request computations from the underlying computational system (MuPAD in this version) based on the implied commands embedded in the mathematical syntax or via menu, and receive the response in typeset standard notation or graphic form in the current document. MuPAD is a registered trademark of SciFace GmbH. Acrobat is the registered trademark of Adobe Systems, Inc. TEX is a trademark of the American Mathematical Society. TrueTEX is a registered trademark of Richard J. Kinch. PDFTEX is the copyright of Hàn Thế Thành and is available under the GNU public license. Windows is a registered trademark of Microsoft Corporation. MathType is a trademark of Design Science, Inc. ImageStream Graphics Filters and ImageStream are registered trademarks of Inso Kansas City Corporation:

> ImageStream Graphic Filters
> Copyright 1991-1999
> Inso Kansas City Corporation
> All Rights Reserved

All other brand and product names are trademarks of their respective companies. The spelling portion of this product utilizes the Proximity Linguistic Technology. Words are checked against one or more of the following Proximity Linguibase® products:

Linguibase Name	Publisher	Number of Words	Proximity Copyright
American English	Merriam-Webster, Inc.	144,000	1997
British English	William Collins Sons & Co. Ltd.	80,000	1997
Catalan	Lluis de Yzaguirre i Maura	484,000	1993
Danish	IDE a.s	169,000	1990
Dutch	Van Dale Lexicografie bv	223,000	1996
Finnish	IDE a.s	191,000	1991
French	Hachette	288,909	1997
French Canadian	Hachette	288,909	1997
German	Bertelsmann Lexikon Verlag	500,000	1999
German (Swiss)	Bertelsmann Lexikon Verlag	500,000	1999
Italian	William Collins Sons & Co. Ltd.	185,000	1997
Norwegian (Bokmal)	IDE a.s	150,000	1990
Norwegian (Nynorsk)	IDE a.s	145,000	1992
Polish	MorphoLogic, Inc.		1997
Portuguese (Brazilian)	William Collins Sons & Co. Ltd.	210,000	1990
Portuguese (Continental)	William Collins Sons & Co. Ltd.	218,000	1990
Russian	Russicon		1997
Spanish	William Collins Sons & Co. Ltd.	215,000	1997
Swedish	IDE a.s	900,000	1990

This document was produced with *Scientific WorkPlace.*

Author: *Susan Bagby*
Manuscript Editors: *John MacKendrick and George Pearson*
Compositor: *MacKichan Software Inc.*
Printing and Binding: *Malloy Lithographing, Inc.*

Contents

What's New in Version 5

Welcome to Version 5 of *Scientific WorkPlace*, *Scientific Word*, *Scientific Notebook*, and the free *Scientific Viewer*. Version 5 enhances the family of MacKichan Software products with new features including typeset PDF output, improved RTF import and export with MathType support, improved HTML and MathML export, and an improved user interface. *Scientific WorkPlace* and *Scientific Notebook* contain the MuPAD computer algebra engine.

Together, MacKichan Software products bring to your workplace the ease of entering text and mathematics in natural notation, the power of symbolic and numeric computation, the flexibility and beauty of printed or typeset output, and the convenience of direct Internet access. Individually, the products offer combinations of capabilities and features that meet a range of user needs and make creating technical documents easier than ever.

This manual is your guide to working with Version 5. The manual begins with this overview of the program. It then provides information about basic tasks—those things you need to do for nearly every document you write—and continues with information about more advanced tasks. The appendixes summarize information about the program tools: the toolbars, shortcuts, and commands.

About Our Products

All four products—which we refer to individually by their initials—share the same easy-to-learn, easy-to-use scientific word processor. Text appears on the same screen as mathematics, which you create using familiar mathematical notation. Also, all four products use styles and tags to simplify document formatting. Other capabilities and features differ from product to product:

Capabilities and Features	SWP	SW	SNB	SV
Document creation and printing	•	•	•	
Typesetting with LaTeXand PDFLaTeX	•	•		
Computation and plotting	•		•	
Internet browsing and printing	•	•	•	•
HTML output with MathML	•	•	•	
RTF output with MathType	•	•	•	
Creation of interactive course materials with Exam Builder	•		•	

Each time you print in *SWP* or *SW*, you can choose whether or not to typeset your documents with LaTeX or PDFLaTeX. When you don't need to typeset, you can easily create the page appearance you want using improved document formatting features. You can exchange documents more easily with colleagues at other LaTeX installations when you save documents using the Portable LaTeX filter, and you can provide documents to colleagues at non-LaTeX installations when you export files with the Rich Text Format (RTF) filter or create a typeset PDF file with PDFLaTeX. And with the Style Editor, you can create printed documents that meet your formatting requirements.

SWP and *SNB* also support a wide range of symbolic and numeric mathematical computations with MuPAD including plotting of various two- and three-dimensional expressions. You can perform computations with named physical units and you can convert from unit to unit. You can perform dynamic calculations with formula objects and you can even import and compute with data from your graphing calculator. With the Exam Builder, you can create algorithmically-generated course materials from your *SWP* and *SNB* source files.

If you have an Internet connection, you can access the Internet directly from within your Version 5 installation, and you can post your documents on the Web in TeX, HTML, or PDF form. Getting help when you need it is easy with the updated online Help system.

Available at no charge, *SV* provides an easy way to explore many of these features. Those who haven't yet purchased *SWP*, *SW*, or *SNB* can use *SV* to view and print documents you create with the program, whether those documents are available on your local system or on the Internet.

New Features

Version 5 operates under Windows XP, 2000, NT, Me, 98, and 95. It uses a licensing system that requires you to register the software and obtain a license file to activate the main program features. Please refer to *Getting Started with Scientific WorkPlace, Scientific Word, and Scientific Notebook* or to the online Help system for instructions. The following features are new in Version 5.

Compatibility

You can interact with colleagues more easily and distribute your documents in different formats when you take advantage of new and enhanced export filters in Version 5. Chapter 2 "Creating Documents" and Chapter 10 "Creating Documents for Online Use" have more information about these new features:

- **Export your documents as RTF files.** You can now export your *SWP*, *SW*, and *SNB* documents as Rich Text Format (RTF) files, so that interactions with colleagues in non-TeX environments are simplified. The RTF export preserves the formatting you see in the document window. Any mathematics in your document can be represented with MathType 3 (Equation Editor) or MathType 5 objects. The resulting RTF file can be viewed in Microsoft Word even if an Equation Editor is not part of the Word installation. If the Microsoft Word installation includes the appropriate Equation Editor, any MathType 3 or MathType 5 mathematical objects in the RTF file can be edited. The file can also be displayed in outline mode.

- **Read MathType mathematics in RTF files.** In Version 5, you can open and read the MathType equations in RTF files when you import the RTF files in *SWP*, *SW*, or *SNB*. The equations are converted to LaTeX.

- **Create more accurate HTML files.** When you export your *SWP*, *SW*, or *SNB* documents to HTML, the program now places any graphics generated during the process in a subdirectory. Version 5 successfully exports fixed-width tables to HTML and saves the screen format to a Cascading Style Sheet (.css file). With HTML exports, you can make your mathematics available on various platforms over the Internet and in applications that can read HTML files.

- **Export mathematics as MathML.** When you export HTML files, you can output mathematics as MathML or graphics. Not all HTML browsers support MathML.

Typesetting

Version 5 provides new typesetting capabilities and many new document shells, some intended for international use. Chapter 2 "Creating Documents" and Chapter 9 "Structuring Documents for Typesetting" contain more information about these new typesetting features. See also *A Gallery of Document Shells for Scientific WorkPlace and Scientific Word*, provided on the program CD.

- **Create typeset PDF files.** Now you can share your work in PDF format by typesetting your *SWP* and *SW* documents with PDFLaTeX. No extra software is necessary to generate PDF files. The program automatically embeds fonts and graphics in the PDF file.

- **Use PDFTeX to process files that contain graphics.** Until now, using PDFTeX with most graphics file formats has been tedious or impossible. Version 5 of *SWP* and *SW* converts the graphics in your document to formats that can be processed by PDFLaTeX before typesetting.

- **Preserve LaTeX cross-references in PDF files.** If you add the *hyperref* package to your document, any cross-references in your *SWP* or *SW* document are converted to hypertext links when you typeset with PDFLaTeX. The package extends hypertext capabilities with hypertext targets and references. Additionally, PDFLaTeX fully links the table of contents in the resulting PDF file and includes in the file hierarchical markers and thumbnail pictures of all the pages in the document.

- **Use LaTeX PostScript packages.** If you create PDF files from your *SWP* and *SW* documents, you can take advantage of LaTeX packages, such as the *rotating* package.

- **Use expanded typesetting documentation.** A new edition of *Typesetting Documents in Scientific WorkPlace and Scientific Word* provides more typesetting tips and tricks and information about more LaTeX packages. Learn how to tailor the typesetting specifications from inside your document to achieve the typeset document appearance you require.

- **Examine an expanded gallery of shells.** View images of sample documents for each shell provided with the program in *A Gallery of Document Shells for Scientific WorkPlace and Scientific Word*, provided on the program CD as a PDF file. Use the documentation to choose document shells appropriately.

- **Choose shells tailored for international documents.** Version 5 includes new shells for documents created in non-English languages, including German, Japanese, Chinese, and Russian. *SWP* and *SW*, in combination with TrueTeX, support international typesetting with the Lambda system.

Computation

Complex computational capability makes *SWP* and *SNB* indispensable tools. *Doing Mathematics with Scientific WorkPlace and Scientific Notebook* explains how to use the built-in computer algebra system to do mathematics without dealing directly with the syntax of the computer algebra system.

- **Compute with MuPAD.** In *SWP* and *SNB*, compute right in your document with the MuPAD computer algebra engine.

- **Use enhanced MuPAD capabilities.** The new MuPAD kernel is an upgrade from the MuPAD 2.0 kernel included in Version 4.0. New features include improved 2D and 3D plotting, expanded ODE capabilities, an expanded Rewrite submenu, and an improved Simplify operation.

- **Compute with MathType mathematics in RTF files.** If you open an RTF file containing MathType equations, the program converts the equations to LaTeX. In *SWP* and *SNB*, you can compute with the mathematics just like any other mathematics in *SWP* and *SW* documents.

- **Use an improved Exam Builder.** The Version 5 Exam Builder is fully functional with MuPAD. Printed quizzes can be reloaded without losing their math definitions, just like other documents. Exam Builder materials generated with earlier versions using either MuPAD or Maple work successfully in Version 5.

Basic Features

The new program features introduced in this version enhance the important features present in earlier versions of the program: the logical separation of content and appearance; a rich interface for the natural entry of text and mathematics; the ability to perform mathematical computations inside your *SWP* and *SNB* documents; compatibility with other software and systems; the production of beautiful printed documents; and the easy creation of complex documents.

Logical Design

The most important feature of *SWP, SW,* and *SNB* is the separation of content and appearance. The content of your work results from the creative process of forming ideas and putting them into words. The appearance of your work results from the mechanical process of formatting: displaying the document on the screen and on the printed page in the most readable way.

Our approach, known as *logical design,* separates the creative process of writing from the mechanical process of formatting. Logical design frees you to focus on creating the content instead of formatting it and results in greatly increased productivity. Logical design also leads to a more consistent and higher-quality document appearance, because choices of fonts, spacing, emphasis, and countless other aspects of format are applied automatically. An alternative approach to word processing, called *visual design* or WYSIWYG (for What You See Is What You Get), focuses on making the screen look as much like the printed page as possible.

Understanding the difference between the two approaches is important, because a logical system requires a very different interface from a visual system. If you've used only visual systems before now, you may at first be surprised by some of the differences.

One major difference is in document formatting. When you use a visual system, you constantly apply commands that affect the appearance of the content—you select text and then choose a font, a font size, or a typeface, or you apply alignment commands such as center, left justify, or right justify. To center a title or an equation, for example, you select it and choose the center alignment.

When you use a logical system, you focus on how the content relates logically to other parts of the document rather than on the appearance of the content. Commands that define the logical structure of the content replace commands that define its appearance. Thus, instead of applying a centering command to create a centered title, you apply a title tag to the title information. The *properties* of the tag you use determine the format and alignment of the title.

In *SNB*, tag properties are determined by the *style*, a collection of commands that define the way the document appears when you display it on the screen and when you produce it without typesetting. In *SWP* and *SW*, tag properties are determined in two ways: by the style and by the document's *typesetting specifications*—a collection of commands that define the way the document appears when you typeset it.

Another difference between visual and logical systems is in the display of page divisions. On the screen, visual systems divide documents into pages according to their anticipated appearance in print. To see an entire line, you often have to scroll horizontally because the screen dimensions and page dimensions don't match. In a logical system, working with pages is unnecessary, because the division of a document into pages has no connection to the document's logical structure. Thus, on the screen lines are broken to fit the window. If you resize the window, the program reshapes the text to fit it. The program displays page divisions when you preview the document.

Our emphasis on logical structure doesn't ignore the fact that documents must still be printed in a readable, organized, and visually pleasing format, nor does it ignore the fact that you may not always need publication-quality output. With *SWP* and *SW*, you can preview and print your documents in two ways. You can compile, preview, and print your documents with LaTeX or PDFLaTeX to obtain a high-quality, typeset appearance, or you can preview and print without typesetting when a fine appearance is less important.

Separating the processes of creating and formatting a document combines the best of the online and print worlds. You do the work of creating a good document; the program does the work of creating a beautiful one.

Rich Interface

- **Apply what you already know** about using Windows applications. First, you can find the available commands in menus, bars, buttons, and popup lists on the screen. Second, you can enter commands using standard keyboard and mouse techniques, and you can speed your work with drag-and-drop editing, speed scrolling, and expanded toolbar operations. Third, you can use many standard Windows keyboard conventions, such as using CTRL+X to cut a selection to the clipboard or SHIFT to extend a selection. For a review of these conventions, see your Windows documentation.

- **Customize your workplace.** Dock or float the toolbars where you want them; hide the toolbars you don't need; and display the symbol panels while you work. The program retains the toolbar and panel placement from session to session. Use the User Setup dialog box to set the defaults for mouse button uses, start-up document shell, placement and size of new graphics, automatic saving, and many other aspects of the environment.

- **Configure the Symbol Cache toolbar and the expanded symbol panels.** Customize the Symbol Cache toolbar by removing the symbols you don't need and adding any symbols you want from the expanded symbol panels. Customize the symbol panels by removing the symbols that you don't use. Revert easily to the original configuration of the cache and the panels. A brief, mouse-activated tooltip gives the name of each toolbar button and panel symbol.

- **Work faster with a comprehensive set of keyboard shortcuts.** These special key combinations for performing basic operations and entering symbols, characters, and the most common mathematical objects are often faster to use than the mouse.

- **Navigate easily with toolbars.** Use the Link toolbar and the History toolbar as external navigation tools to speed moving around in other documents. Use the Navigate toolbar as an internal navigation tool to speed moving around in the active document. You can control the number of heading levels displayed in the Navigate toolbar, which significantly increases its usefulness as an online table of contents for your document.

- **Open several windows at once.** Open several documents and several views of the same document at the same time. The changes you make in one view of a document are recorded in all views of the same document.

- **Work with pleasing on-screen mathematics and italics** created with TrueType outline fonts. The program uses Windows TrueType fonts. Some of the required fonts are supplied with Windows and others are supplied with the program.

- **Find help online.** Documentation available online includes extensive information about creating documents and performing mathematical computations. Use the Help search feature to find information quickly when you need it. The online Help also includes tutorial exercises to help you learn to use the software. In addition to the main online Help system, separate Help information is available for the Style Editor, Exam Builder, and Document Manager.

- **Magnify your printed document.** Set the zoom factor used when you print without typesetting. The print zoom factor simplifies the creation of overhead transparencies for meetings and classroom use.

- **Load documents quickly with the quick-load feature.** Speed document loading by turning on the quick-load feature. This feature is especially useful for large documents used as interactive texts.

Natural Entry of Text and Mathematics

- **Enter text and mathematics in the same paragraph.** The screen default is to show text in black and mathematics in red so you can easily distinguish them. The Math/Text button on the Standard toolbar indicates whether the insertion point is in text or in mathematics:

 The insertion point is in text.

 The insertion point is in mathematics.

Everything you enter is assumed to be text unless you specify otherwise. You can toggle between text and mathematics easily with the mouse or the keyboard.

- **Use templates to enter mathematical objects** such as fractions, radicals, enclosures, and matrices by inserting and filling the template for the object you want. For example, if you insert a fraction, the program places this template into your document

and positions the insertion point in the small input box that appears in the numerator so you can complete the fraction. You can enter individual mathematical symbols and characters directly into your expression via the menus, buttons, or keyboard shortcuts.

- **Define automatic substitution sequences** to speed the entry of the mathematical expressions you use most often. When the insertion point is in mathematics and you type the substitution sequence, the sequence is replaced with the corresponding expression. You can turn automatic substitution off or on at any time.

- **Use the full set of American Mathematical Society symbols.** Incorporate in your *SWP* and *SW* documents all the symbols in the $\mathcal{A}_{\mathcal{M}}\mathcal{S}$ fonts. The program supports the full set of $\mathcal{A}_{\mathcal{M}}\mathcal{S}$ fonts, both on the screen and in print.

- **Create multiline displays quickly** and add numbers selectively to each line of the display for easy cross-referencing throughout your document. You can override the automatically generated numbers with your own labels.

Mathematical Computations in SWP and SNB Documents

- **Use MuPAD** to perform numeric and symbolic mathematical computations directly from the *SWP* or *SNB* program window. You can use a separate computation space for each open document.

- **Execute mathematical operations.** Apply Evaluate to display the result of operations written in the document, from basic arithmetic operations to computations in calculus and linear algebra.

- **Apply mathematical operations.** The Compute menu provides many operations you can apply to solve mathematical problems. You can solve systems of linear equations or differential equations, fit curves to data, experiment with graphs, and perform Fourier and Laplace transforms. You can perform mathematical computations intuitively with substitution in expressions, deferred evaluation, subscript variables, and other features of the computational interface. The Stop button halts computations.

- **Obtain mathematical results separately or in place.** Select a piece of mathematics and apply an operation to obtain the result directly in your document. Press the CTRL key during the operation to replace the original expression with the result of the computation.

- **Use formula objects for dynamic calculations.** Enter a mathematical expression together with a computational operation with the formula object in *SWP* and *SNB*. The value you see on the screen is the result of the operation.

- **Compute with equations containing named physical units.** Whether your problem is stated in feet, meters, kilograms, or seconds, the program provides the correct unit for answers and can even convert among units.

- **Import data from your calculator.** You can import a list, vector, matrix, expression, or number to a document from your Casio, Texas Instruments, or Hewlett Packard graphing calculator. Once imported, the data can be used in computations like any other data created with *SWP* or *SNB*.

- **Create plots.** Create two- and three-dimensional plots with Plot 2D and Plot 3D Rectangular, or use the many other options provided on the Plot 2D and Plot 3D submenus. Use convenient plot tools to zoom and pan two-dimensional plots and rotate three-dimensional plots to obtain optimal views. Use drag-and-drop mouse techniques to add new functions to a graph quickly and easily. Modify the plot properties to adjust the color, line thickness, axes, and view of plots.

- **Create and operate on matrices.** Build matrices quickly with Fill Matrix. Carry out implied operations simply by applying Evaluate to a sum, product, or power. Apply the numerous mathematical operations displayed on the Matrices submenu.

- **Operate with the names of functions,** after defining them by expressions. Define generic functions and use them to illustrate rules for differentiation or use the names of generic functions in defining new functions.

- **Make use of user-defined functions.** Use the Define Name dialog box to access and take advantage of functions that have been programmed in MuPAD or that reside in the standard computational engine libraries, or to create custom programmed functions.

- **Create online tests.** Use the Exam Builder to construct online multiple-choice tests and other algorithmically-generated course materials from your *SWP* and *SNB* source files. The software takes advantage of formula objects, several special commands for generating random numbers, and the equivalents of several HTML input objects including radio buttons and check boxes. Online exams and homework can be graded automatically by computer, so students receive instant feedback and solutions. Save the Exam Builder database in a format that can be opened in Microsoft Excel.

Compatibility

- **Export your documents to HTML.** Create an accurate HTML version of your document using the new HTML output filter. The HTML filter provides a way to make representations of mathematics available on various platforms over the Internet and also in applications that can read HTML files. The filter saves the screen format to a Cascading Style Sheet (.css) file and exports mathematics as graphic images. You can customize HTML exports.

- **Work with online files.** If you have Internet access, you can open *SWP, SW,* and *SNB* files over the Web and can launch your browser to open the file at any URL address. When you save online *SWP, SW,* and *SNB* files locally, you can use the information they contain in your own documents. You can also perform computations on the mathematics they contain.

- **Export mathematics as MathML.** When you export HTML files, output your mathematics as MathML or as graphics. Note that not all HTML browsers currently support MathML.

- **Copy selections more accurately to other applications.** Preserve the appearance of information in your document when you use the enhanced copy operation to copy selections to other applications. The copy operation writes your selection to the clipboard using a filtered Unicode format as well as the program's internal format used previously. The new format is more easily recognized by other applications.

- **Tailor graphics copied or exported from your document.** You can set the defaults for the appearance of selected information that you want to copy or export as graphics. Independent of the display settings for your document, you can set export and copy defaults for the View settings (including the zoom factor), the page and paragraph background, and the appearance of gray boxes.

- **Import and export RTF files.** Use the rtf2latex2e converter to open RTF documents and export documents as RTF files for use in other installations.

Beautiful Printed Documents

With *SWP* and *SW* you can produce beautiful documents with or without typesetting. The two production processes are different, as are their printed results. Understanding the distinction is important; please read Chapter 8 "Formatting Documents" and Chapter 9 "Structuring Documents for Typesetting" for more information.

- **Produce your document with or without typesetting.** Choose whether to produce your *SWP* or *SW* document with or without typesetting. When you need the beautiful document formatting that LaTeX provides, typeset your document from the Typeset menu. When fine formatting doesn't matter and you don't need automatically generated document elements, produce your document from the File menu. The software prints your document using the Page Setup specifications and many of the same routines it uses to display the document in the program window. Regardless of how you produce your document, the program saves it as a LaTeX file.

- **Produce typeset-quality printed documents automatically.** *SWP* and *SW* documents can be typeset using LaTeX, a set of macros designed by Leslie Lamport to enhance TeX with document-structuring features such as tables of contents and bibliographies. TeX is the extraordinary mathematics typesetting program and language designed by Donald Knuth. Typesetting provides hyphenation, kerning, ligatures, and many other precise typeset formatting features. Typesetting also involves the automatic generation of document elements such as footnotes, margin notes, tables of contents, and indexes. Because typesetting is automatic, you don't have to know TeX or LaTeX to typeset your documents effectively. The Windows implementation of TeX and LaTeX that is supplied with the program is TrueTeX, a product of TrueTeX Software.

- **Choose a document shell that meets your requirements.** Select the typeset and non-typeset appearance of your document by choosing from among numerous shells, or sets of specifications, for producing books, articles, reports, and other types of documents. View typeset images of sample documents for each shell provided with the program in *A Gallery of Document Shells for Scientific WorkPlace and Scientific Word,* provided on the program CD. Because the specifications contain complete document formatting instructions, you can concentrate on writing your document instead of on formatting its appearance.

- **Tailor the typesetting documentation.** Learn how to tailor the typesetting specifications from inside your document to achieve the typeset document appearance you require. *SWP* and *SW* include *Typesetting Documents in Scientific WorkPlace and Scientific Word,* which provides significant documentation for LaTeX typesetting.

- **Develop your own typesetting specifications with the Style Editor.** Set the specifications for fonts, paragraphs, and other elements of typesetting and preview your specifications from the Style Editor.

- **Format documents easily.** Use the Tag Appearance dialog box to change the screen and print appearance—but not the typeset appearance—of tagged document elements such as line spacing, font size, and justification. You can modify all style properties of all tags available for the document shell, including default and front matter tags. You can specify which properties are *inherited* from the surrounding text and which use the style default values. You can also *clone* new body and text tags. The properties shown in the dialog box are stored in a .cst file. They affect the appearance of the document when you display it in the program window and when you use the Preview or Print commands from the File menu. *SWP* and *SW* ignore these settings when you typeset your document.

- **Take advantage of the latest in TeXnology.** Use TeX and LaTeX to create documents with a wide variety of scalable fonts. The software supports the New Font Selection Scheme (NFSS). TrueTeX features a previewer that uses TrueType fonts, supports a wide range of graphics formats, and enables you to print on any Windows-supported device including fax boards. With *SWP* and *SW*, use a version of TrueTeX that supports the newest versions of TeX, Omega, BibTeX, MakeIndex, and other TeX tools. The program includes the latest version of LaTeX and $\mathcal{AMS}$ macros.

- **Create $\mathcal{AMS}$-LaTeX documents.** Create documents in $\mathcal{AMS}$-LaTeX format automatically by choosing a shell that uses $\mathcal{AMS}$-LaTeX typesetting specifications.

- **Produce documents using REVTₑX,** a package of LᴬTₑX macros designed for preparing physics manuscripts. The software includes a shell with typesetting specifications for producing documents in REVTₑX formats for several different publications.

- **Use improved fonts.** The program uses Unicode and associated extended Unicode TrueType fonts. The software uses its own font for non-typeset mathematics, called *tci1–4,* and includes font packages that set mathematics in Times. The packages yield ligatures and improved kerning in Times text when documents are typeset, and both use the widely accepted PostScript New Font Selection Scheme (PSNFSS) for LᴬTₑX.

- **Preview the typeset appearance of your documents with more than one previewer.** Use the previewer installed with your system when you're ready to see your document as it will appear when typeset. You can also compile your document to create a typeset file without previewing or printing until you're ready to see the finished document. If you have other TₑX systems or preview drivers installed, choose the previewer you want.

Easy Creation of Complex Documents

- **Format with tags.** Use tags to add structural elements such as lists, sections, or theorems to your document and to emphasize words or phrases in the text. Each paragraph has an associated tag that determines whether it is a section heading or part of the body of your document. Use the Body Math tag for performing scratchpad computations anywhere within a document.

- **Manage large typeset documents with ease.** In *SWP* and *SW,* create a master document that incorporates several smaller, more manageable subdocuments. When you print the master document, the program creates all surrounding front and back matter required by the typesetting specifications and resolves all cross-references internal to all subdocuments.

- **Take advantage of file management and file editing features.** Maintain your View settings for all documents, save and restore your user preferences, and return easily to read-only documents when you open the program. Several features make editing your documents easy and intuitive: a Context menu defines operations available for the text and mathematics elements that are selected; the default action for the spacebar, ENTER key, and TAB key has been set to enter additional space; and the Status area gives information about linked objects.

- **Create dynamic documents with hypertext links and linked documents.** Use the links to jump to documents, paragraphs, sections, or objects with an identifying key, and then retrace your steps with the History feature. Use drop-down lists of defined markers for fast entry of links. Use document links to connect online documents in a logical structure without having to include hypertext links in the text of your document.

- **Enhance online documents with notes.** Create popup notes in online documents to provide readers with additional information, tips, hints, and problem solutions.

- **Produce LaTeX files for Internet use.** If you have Internet access, you can open *SWP, SW,* and *SNB* files over the Web and can launch your browser to open the file at any URL address. When you save online *SWP, SW,* and *SNB* files locally, you can use the information they contain in your own documents. You can also perform computations on the mathematics they contain.

- **Import files directly into an active document** to speed document creation. Use the Import Contents feature to copy the contents of other files into your active document. The program imports the body of the document but not the typesetting specifications, style, or front matter.

- **Illustrate your ideas with graphics** created in popular software applications and imported to your document. Enhance your documents with graphics generated in many formats.

- **Display program code.** Use the *verbatim* environment to include portions of programs in your document or to display computational input lines.

- **Create graphic images of text and mathematics.** Duplicate text and mathematics in a different location, such as on the Internet or in another application, by creating a graphic image of the information just as you see it in the document window. The careful formatting of your information is maintained when you paste a picture of it to the clipboard in Windows Enhanced Metafile format or export a picture of it to a file created in one of several widely used graphics formats.

- **Create indexes and bibliographies easily** in *SWP* and *SW*. Simplify the generation of back matter for your document with a streamlined procedure for creating indexes and the ability to create either manual or BIBTeX bibliographies.

- **Resolve all document cross-references automatically** when you typeset. Create cross-references to sections, pages, and other markers in your *SWP* or *SW* document, and then let LaTeX or PDFLaTeX do the work of resolving the references when you compile your document.

- **Produce Portable LaTeX output.** Open your *SWP* or *SW* documents successfully on other LaTeX installations by saving them with the Portable LaTeX output filter. When you save with the Portable LaTeX filter, the program doesn't include the special set of macros called `tcilatex` in your document. It includes only those LaTeX packages, such as *amsmath* and *graphicx,* that are standard on modern LaTeX installations.

- **Use the program with non-English languages.** The program provides fonts and hyphenation support for European languages other than English. If you typeset, you can switch languages in the same document by using *babel,* the multilingual LaTeX package, and you can enter your documents from non-U.S. keyboards. *SWP* and *SW,* in combination with TrueTeX, supports international typesetting with the Lambda system.

Before You Begin

Before you attempt to install and use the program, make sure your personal computer or network client computer meets the hardware and software requirements shown in the following table. Additional information and installation and registration instructions appear in the booklet *Getting Started with Scientific WorkPlace, Scientific Word, and Scientific Notebook,* supplied with the program.

System Requirements	SWP **or** SW	SNB	SV
Available disk space	70–250 MB*	15–150 MB*	5–25 MB*
Windows XP, 2000, NT, Me, 98, or 95**	●	●	●
CD-ROM drive	●	●	

* Depending on the type of hard drive and installation options

** Windows Me, 98, and 95 require Windows Multilanguage Support

Conventions

Understanding the notation and the terms we use in our documentation will help you understand the instructions in this manual. We assume you are familiar with basic Windows procedures and terminology. If necessary, review your Windows documentation. In this manual, we use the notation and terms listed below.

General Notation

- Text like this indicates the name of a menu, program command, or dialog box.
- TEXT LIKE THIS indicates the name of a keyboard key.
- **Text like this** indicates text you should type exactly as it is shown.
- ***Text like this*** is a placeholder for information that you must supply.
- `Text like this` indicates the name of a file or directory, a LATEX command, or other code.
- *Text like this* indicates a term that has special meaning in the context of the program.
- *Typeset your file* means to process your document with either LATEX or PDFLATEX.
- *Choose* means to designate a command for the program to carry out. As with all Windows applications, you can choose a command with the mouse or with the keyboard. Commands may be listed on a menu or shown on a button in a dialog box. For example, the instruction "From the File menu, choose Open" means you should first choose the File menu and then from that menu, choose the Open command. The instruction "choose OK" means to click the OK button with the mouse or press TAB to move the attention to the OK button and then press the ENTER key on the keyboard.
- *Select* means to highlight the part of the document that you want your next action to affect or to highlight a specific option in a dialog box or list.
- *Check* means to turn on an option in a dialog box.

Keyboard Conventions

We also use standard Windows conventions to give keyboard instructions.

- The names of keys in the instructions match the names shown on most keyboards. They appear like this: ENTER, F4, SHIFT.

- A plus sign (+) between the names of two keys indicates that you must press the first key and hold it down while you press the second key. For example, CTRL+G means that you press and hold down the CTRL key, press G, and then release both keys.

- The notation CTRL+**word** means that you must hold down the CTRL key, type the word that appears in bold type after the +, then release the CTRL key. Note that if a letter appears capitalized, you should type that letter as a capital.

Mouse Conventions

The program uses these mouse pointers:

Pointer	Indication
I	The pointer is over text
	The pointer is over mathematics
	A selection is being dragged
	A selection is being copied
	A selection is being copied or dragged with the right mouse button
	A graphic is being panned
+	A graphic is being resized
	The pointer is over a hypertext link

Additionally, *SWP* and *SNB* display a pointer for the computational engine when a computation is in progress.

In this manual we give mouse instructions using standard Windows conventions. The instructions assume you haven't changed the mouse button defaults.

- *Point* means to move the mouse pointer to a specific position.

- *Click* means to position the mouse pointer, then press and immediately release the left or right mouse button without moving the mouse.

- *Double-click* means to position the mouse pointer, then click the left mouse button twice in rapid succession without moving the mouse.

- *Drag* means to position the mouse pointer, press the left mouse button and hold it down while you move the mouse, then release the button.

As in most Windows applications, you can use the right mouse button to display a Context menu for the current selection or the item under the mouse pointer. Pressing the Context Menu key [icon] also displays the menu.

Getting Help

The program comes with a set of tutorial exercises to help you learn to use the program. While you're working, you can get information quickly from the online Help system, the library of reference materials about mathematics and science, and, if you have an Internet connection, the MacKichan Software web site. If these resources don't contain the information you need, technical support is available. We also regularly make additional information available on our unmoderated discussion forum and email list. You can find an errata sheet for this book, as well as all other manuals published by MacKichan Software, Inc., at this URL:

http://www.mackichan.com/techtalk/errata.html

Learning the Program

You can learn a great deal about the program just by working with it. Start by opening the program, typing a few sentences, entering some mathematics, and then previewing and printing your document. Chapter 1 "Understanding the Workplace" explains how to use the features available in the program window.

We also urge you to work through the step-by-step tutorial exercises. The exercises will guide you as you create several increasingly complex documents and learn how to enter a variety of mathematical expressions, how to compute while working in your document, and how to print with and without typesetting.

▶ **To open the tutorial exercises**

1. From the Help menu, choose Contents.

2. Choose Learn the Basics.

3. Choose the exercise you want:
   - "Before You Start" provides information about the notation, terminology, and instructions used in the exercises.
   - "Creating a Simple Document" provides basic document instructions.
   - "Printing and Typesetting" explains two ways to produce your document.
   - "Creating an Advanced Document" gives instructions for creating and typesetting a somewhat more complex SWP or SW document. The exercise, which takes about 90 minutes to complete, focuses on document structuring, guiding you step-by-step through the unique procedures for creating titles, headings, and theorem statements. Because the document you create contains equations, the exercise also illustrates the straightforward entry and editing of mathematics.
   - "Creating Mathematics" presents a series of mathematical examples. The exercises give step-by-step instructions for entering a variety of mathematical expressions using the mouse and the keyboard.
   - "Sharing Your Work" presents information about creating documents for use across platforms, installations, and systems; on a network; or on the Web.
   - "Performing Computations" presents a series of mathematical computation exercises. The step-by-step instructions guide you through basic computational procedures for SWP and SNB.

Online Help

While you're working, you can get information quickly from the online Help system. Without leaving the application, you can search Help to find basic and advanced information about all program commands and operations, including those related to numeric, symbolic, and graphic computations. In particular, you can find additional material regarding TEX, LATEX, LATEX packages, and other related topics. The Help system remembers the last search you made. If you save copies of the Help documents in *SWP* or *SNB*, you can interact with the mathematics they contain, experimenting with or reworking the included examples. In addition, two programs—the Style Editor and the Document Manager—have their own online Help systems.

▶ **To get help from the** Help **menu**

Choose	To
Contents	See a list of online information
Search...	Find a Help topic
Index	Access the online index to General Information, Computing Techniques, or the Reference Library
MacKichan Software Website	Open the link to the MacKichan Software website
Register...	Register your software and obtain a license
System Features...	See a list of available features; change the serial number for your installation
License Information	Obtain information about registering your system
About...	Obtain information about your installation

▶ **To go directly to the Help Contents, press** F1.

Supplemental Technical Documents

We urge you to open, view, and print the supplemental technical documents supplied with the program. In particular, we urge you to read the following documents:

- In the Help\general directory, the document 50techref.tex, which contains technical information on the features in Version 5.

- In the Play directory, the sample documents, which demonstrate the use of computation in *SWP* and *SNB*.

- In the SWSamples directory,

  - The sample documents, which illustrate the use of LATEX packages in *SWP* and *SW*.

  - The file OptionsPackagesLaTeX.tex, which describes and contains links to information about the options, packages, and other TEX-related items provided with the program.

  - The file BibTeXBibliographyStyles.tex, which lists and describes the BIBTEX style (.bst) files installed with the program.

- In the SNSamples directory, the documents that are examples of online documents created with the program.

Obtaining Technical Support

If you can't find the answer to your questions in the manuals or the online Help, you can obtain technical support from our website at

http://www.mackichan.com/techtalk/knowledgebase.html

or at our Web-based Technical Support forum at

http://www.mackichan.com/techtalk/UserForums.htm

You can also contact our Technical Support staff by email, telephone, or fax. We urge you to submit questions by email whenever possible in case our technical staff needs to obtain your file to diagnose and solve the problem.

When you contact us by email or fax, please provide complete information about the problem you're trying to solve. We must be able to reproduce the problem exactly from your instructions. When you contact us by telephone, you should be sitting at your computer with the program running. Please provide the following information any time you contact Technical Support:

- The MacKichan Software product you have installed.

- The version and build numbers of your installation (see Help / About).

- The serial number of your installation (see Help / System Features).

- The version of the Windows system you're using.

- The type of hardware you're using, including network hardware.

- What happened and what you were doing when the problem occurred.

- The exact wording of any messages that appeared on your computer screen.

▶ **To contact technical support**

- Contact Technical Support by email, fax, or telephone between 8 AM and 5 PM Pacific Time:

Internet email address: support@mackichan.com
Fax number: 360-394-6039
Telephone number: 360-394-6033
Toll-free telephone: 877-SCI-WORD (877-724-9673)

Additional Information

You can learn more about *SWP, SW,* and *SNB* on our website, which we update regularly to provide the latest technical information about the program. The site also houses links to other $\TeX$ and $\LaTeX$ resources. We maintain an unmoderated discussion forum and an unmoderated email list so our users can share information, discuss common problems, and contribute technical tips and solutions. You can link to these valuable resources from our home page at **http://www.mackichan.com**.

1 Understanding the Workplace

The program window is your workplace. This chapter explains how to use the commands available through the menus, dialog boxes, tab sheets, and toolbars, and how to move around in the workplace. To display the program window, start the program.

▶ To start the program

- Double-click the program icon on the desktop.

  or

1. From the Windows **Start** menu, choose **Programs**.

2. From the **Programs** menu, choose your product.

3. From the product submenu, choose your product to display the program window:

Title bar — Menu bar — Standard toolbar—   Stop toolbar —

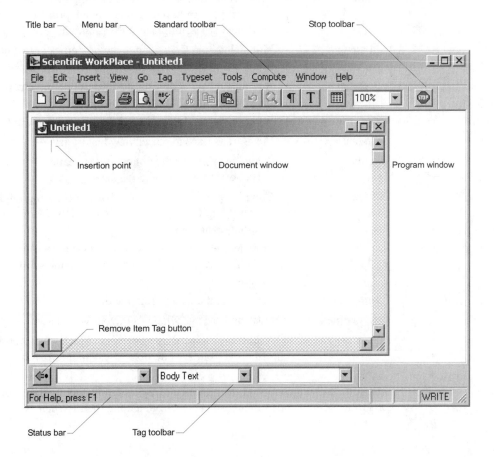

Insertion point   Document window   Program window

Remove Item Tag button

Status bar —   Tag toolbar —

The window has a Menu bar at the top, a Status bar at the bottom, and several basic toolbars elsewhere in the window. Many other toolbars are available, as described later in this chapter. The blinking vertical bar in the document window is the *insertion point,* which indicates where the program will insert the next character you type or where the next command you choose will take effect.

The program commands are available through the menus, toolbar buttons, and lists shown in the program window, and also from the keyboard. Some commands have associated dialog boxes from which you can choose additional options.

Using the Menus

File   Edit   Insert   View   Go   Tag   Typeset   Tools   Compute   Window   Help

The Menu bar lists the menus shown above. In *SW,* the **Compute** menu doesn't appear. In *SNB,* the **Typeset** menu doesn't appear. When you choose one of the menus, the program displays a pull-down list of available commands.

Commands on	Have this effect
File menu	Open, close, and save new and existing files; import and export files; import graphics; layout, print, and preview without typesetting; leave the program
Edit menu	Edit, delete, move, or change the properties of text or mathematics; undo the last deletion
Insert menu	Add mathematical objects; add typeset objects, markers, hypertext links, notes, and formulas
View menu	Arrange the window and toolbars the way you want them
Go menu	Move from place to place; view history list
Tag menu	Apply tags; change the nontypeset appearance of tagged text; assign tags to function keys
Typeset menu	Compile, preview, or print your document using LaTeX or PDFLaTeX typesetting; work with LaTeX packages and settings
Tools menu	Provide user setup and system settings; access tools; spell check; execute jumps; set automatic substitution sequences
Compute menu	Perform mathematical computations
Window menu	Open and arrange windows in your workplace
Help menu	Access the online Help system and MacKichan website; register your system; obtain system information

When you choose a command that is followed by an arrow, the program displays a list of associated commands so you can choose from among them. When you choose a command that is followed by ellipses (dots), the program displays a dialog box so you can choose from among additional associated options. Some commands are available only in certain environments. For example, if you haven't made a deletion, the Undo command on the Edit or Context menu is not available.

As with any Windows application, you can use the mouse or the keyboard to make selections from the menus, dialog boxes, and lists. Appendix C "Commands in Version 5" lists all commands in the program.

▶ **To choose a command with the mouse**

1. Point to a menu name and click the left mouse button to open the menu.

2. Point to a menu command and click the left mouse button.

▶ **To choose a command with the keyboard**

1. Press the ALT key to activate the menu bar.

2. Press the underlined letter for the menu you want.

   or

   Press the RIGHT ARROW or LEFT ARROW key to select the command you want and then press ENTER.

3. Press the underlined letter for the command you want. (If several commands on the menu have the same underlined letter, press the letter repeatedly to move the highlight to the command you want and then press ENTER.)

   or

   Press the UP ARROW or DOWN ARROW key to select the command you want and then press ENTER.

▶ **To cancel a menu**

- Click any point in the window that is off the menu.
  or

- Press ESC twice.
  The menu vanishes when you press ESC the first time. However, the Menu bar remains active until you press ESC the second time.

Using the Dialog Boxes

A dialog box is a special window from which you can choose additional options for certain commands. Dialog boxes contain various kinds of controls—option and command buttons, lists, check boxes, and fields for entering text and mathematics.

A darkened control indicates that the option is currently active. A dimmed control indicates that it is currently unavailable. In some dialog boxes, the insertion point appears as a blinking vertical line. In others, a small dotted box indicates where your next action will take place.

You can use standard typing and editing commands to enter text in a dialog box. Additionally, in a program dialog box, you can use program commands, buttons, and popup lists to enter text, mathematics, and tags. In dialog boxes, the TAB and ENTER keys function differently, and keyboard shortcuts apply to items in the dialog box itself rather than to the menus.

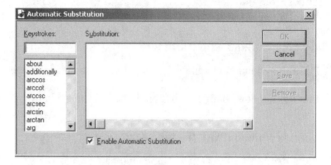

Some dialog boxes group together related commands on a series of *tab sheets*. The controls on tab sheets behave like those in dialog boxes, with one important difference: *When you choose to accept or discard the new selections on one tab sheet in a dialog box, you accept or discard any new selections on all tab sheets in the dialog box.*

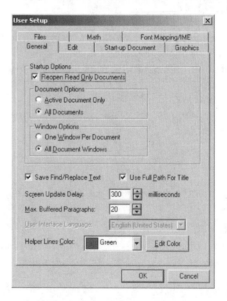

For example, if you choose the settings shown above in the General tab sheet of the User Setup dialog box, move to the Edit tab sheet to change settings and then choose Cancel, the program will discard the changes you made on the General tab sheet as well as those you made on the Edit tab sheet.

You can make selections in dialog boxes with the mouse or, using the keys in the following table, with the keyboard.

To	Press
Move the insertion point:	
to the next control	TAB or ARROW*
to the previous control	SHIFT+TAB
to the next option	ARROW
directly to a command	ALT+underlined letter in the command name
Display a drop-down list	ALT+underlined letter in the name, F4
Select from a list	UP ARROW or DOWN ARROW, then ALT+DOWN ARROW to close the list
Close a list	ALT+DOWN ARROW
Adjust a number up or down	UP ARROW or DOWN ARROW
Check or uncheck a box	The spacebar
See the start of a range of numbers	CTRL+HOME
See the end of a range of numbers	CTRL+END
Move to a different tab sheet	CTRL+TAB, or TAB to highlight the current tab sheet name, then RIGHT ARROW or LEFT ARROW
Choose OK	TAB to the OK button, then ENTER
Choose Cancel	ESC, or TAB to the Cancel button, then ENTER

*If you're entering a mathematical object in a dialog box, use the arrow keys instead of the TAB key to move within the object template. Using the TAB key moves the insertion point to the next control in the dialog box.

▶ To select an item from a list

1. Scroll the list or click the arrow to the right of the list box to display the list items.

2. Select the item you want from the list.

Use the OK or Cancel buttons in the dialog boxes to indicate that you have finished making selections. (Some dialog boxes have Open and Close or Save buttons instead of OK and Cancel.) In a dialog box with tab sheets, choose OK to accept or Cancel to discard the selections you have made not only in the active tab sheet but also in any other tab sheets in the dialog box.

▶ To complete selections in a dialog box

- Choose OK to have the program accept and act on any choices you have made anywhere in the dialog box and then return to the document.

- Choose Cancel to discard any choices you have made anywhere in the dialog box and then return to the document.

Using the Toolbars

When you start the program, only a few of the available toolbars appear in the program window, but you can display as many others as you need. With the Toolbars command on the View menu you can hide or show the toolbars. You can further customize the window so that the toolbars are placed in locations that are convenient for you. For more information about arranging the window, refer to Chapter 12 "Customizing the Program."

▶ **To show or hide a toolbar**

1. From the View menu, choose Toolbars.

2. In the Toolbars dialog box, check the box next to each toolbar you want to display and uncheck the box next to each toolbar you want to hide.

3. Choose Close.

The buttons on the toolbars are identical in function to commands on the File, Edit, Insert, View, Tools, Go, Tag, Compute, and Typeset menus. Point the mouse at each toolbar button for a few seconds to display a brief *tooltip* that identifies the button; the Status bar displays a fuller description. Appendix A "Toolbar Buttons and Menu Commands" lists the equivalent menu commands for each button.

▶ **To choose a toolbar button**

- Click it with the mouse.

The operations associated with buttons that appear dimmed are currently unavailable.

The Standard Toolbar

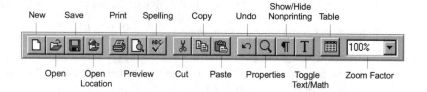

The buttons on the Standard toolbar invoke common file, document, and editing operations and change the screen appearance of the document in the active window. These operations are also available from commands on one of these menus: File, Edit, Insert, View, or Tools. The Open Location button opens a document over the network or, if you have Internet access, on the Web. The Standard toolbar includes a special tool, the Math/Text toggle.

The Preview and Print buttons on the Standard toolbar invoke the same operations as the Preview and Print commands on the File menu: they produce your document without typesetting it, using many of the same output routines that are used to display documents in the program window. Unlike the commands on the Typeset toolbar in *SWP* and *SW*, they don't use LaTeX to produce your document.

The Math Toolbars

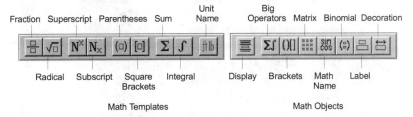

Math Templates   Math Objects

Most of the buttons on the Math Templates toolbar insert mathematical objects directly into your document. The Unit Name button and the buttons on the Math Objects toolbar open dialog boxes for mathematical objects that can't be inserted into your document without more information. These commands are also available from the Insert menu.

The Symbol Panels Toolbar

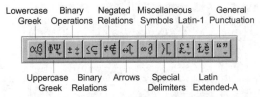

Each Symbol Panels toolbar button has a popup panel of mathematical, Greek, or Unicode symbols or characters, as shown on page 8. You can remove from the panels any symbol you don't want. You can reset the panels to the full complement of characters at any time. Most symbols are identified with a tooltip indicating the LaTeX name of the symbol. A fuller description appears on the Status bar. You can use the keyboard to enter any symbol that has a LaTeX name.

▶ **To insert a symbol or character from a panel into your document**

- Click the button for the panel with the symbol you want and then click the symbol.

▶ **To remove a symbol from a panel**

- Hold down the SHIFT key, select the symbol, and drag it off the panel.

▶ **To restore a symbol panel to its original configuration**

- Click the right mouse button in the panel and choose Reset to Defaults.

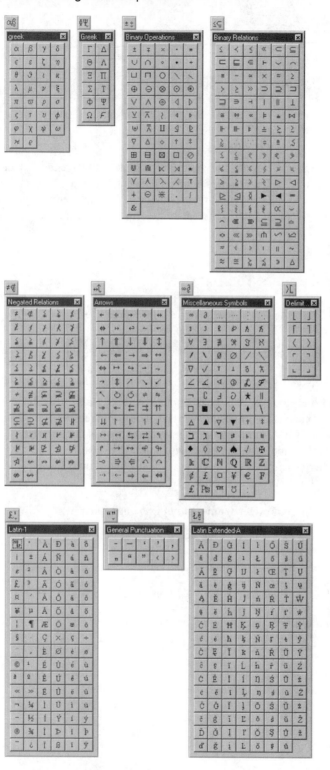

The Symbol Cache Toolbar

The Symbol Cache toolbar contains buttons for frequently used symbols. The toolbar is completely customizable: you can add as many symbols from the symbol panels as you need and you can remove any symbols you don't need. As with the symbol panels, most symbols are identified in two ways: with a tooltip indicating the LaTeX name of the symbol and with a fuller description on the Status bar.

▶ **To add a symbol to the Symbol Cache toolbar**

1. Open the symbol panel containing the symbol.

2. Select the symbol and drag it to any location on the Symbol Cache toolbar.

▶ **To remove a symbol from the Symbol Cache toolbar**

- Hold down the SHIFT key, select the symbol, and drag it off the toolbar.

You can also add and remove symbols by clicking the right mouse button in the toolbar, choosing Customize, and adding or removing symbols from the Customize Toolbar dialog box.

▶ **To restore the Symbol Cache toolbar to its original configuration**

- Click the right mouse button in the toolbar and choose Reset to Defaults.

The Compute Toolbar

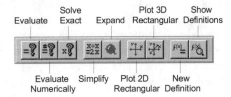

The Compute toolbar appears in *SWP* and *SNB*. The buttons on the toolbar invoke the most common computational operations.

▶ **To perform a computation**

1. Select the expression on which you want to perform an operation, or place the insertion point to its right.

2. Click the button for the operation you want to perform.

While the computation takes place, the program displays the Compute pointer. Then, the program inserts the result in your document. Most computations are fast, but some take several minutes. You can stop a computation with the Stop toolbar button. Refer to *Doing Mathematics with Scientific WorkPlace and Scientific Notebook* and to Computing Techniques in the Help system for more information about using commands to perform mathematical computations. The toolbar doesn't appear in *SW*.

The Stop Toolbar

Stop Operation

The Stop Operation button stops two operations: linking to the Internet and, in *SWP* or *SNB*, performing computations. You can also stop these operations by pressing CTRL+BREAK. The stop operation is not available from a menu.

The Tag Toolbar

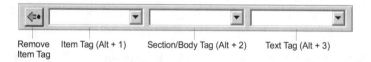

Remove   Item Tag (Alt + 1)   Section/Body Tag (Alt + 2)   Text Tag (Alt + 3)
Item Tag

The Tag toolbar contains lists of available *tags* that add structure, content, or formatting to a paragraph or text selection. The program has item tags, section tags, body tags, and text tags. The Remove Item Tag button at the left end of the toolbar removes the item tag most recently inserted in the paragraph currently containing the insertion point.

When you apply a tag to information in your document, the program applies the properties of the tag to that information. The tags that appear in each popup list depend on the *shell,* or template, you use to create your document. The boxes in the Tag toolbar name the item, section, body, and text tags in effect at the insertion point. Chapter 8 "Formatting Documents" contains more information about using tags.

- Item Tags—Apply item tags to whole paragraphs to create lists, bibliography items, statements of theorems, and front matter elements. You can apply up to four list item tags to a paragraph, thus setting up lists within lists. The Tag toolbar shows the last tag in effect for the paragraph containing the insertion point.

- Section Tags—Apply section tags to whole paragraphs to create section headings and provide the structure of your document. Paragraphs tagged as chapter, part, and section headings can be numbered automatically when you typeset the document, depending on the shell you choose.

- Body Tags—Apply body tags to add structure to the main text of your document. The main text of the document carries the **Body Text** tag. For most shells, the first paragraph of a new document is automatically tagged as **Body Text** unless you change it. The program has several other body tags for text displays that are set off from the main part of a paragraph.

- Text Tags—Apply text tags to emphasize or differentiate words or phrases within a paragraph. Some tags have special meaning within mathematics. You might use the Bold tag to indicate symbols for vectors, matrices, and other special constructs, and you can use the Calligraphic tag to indicate sets. Some document shells provide additional mathematics tags such as Fraktur and Blackboard Bold.

▶ **To apply a tag from a popup list**

- Press the popup list shortcut or click the box for the tag list you want and then click the tag.

The Editing Toolbar

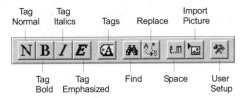

The buttons on the Editing toolbar give you fast access to frequently used tools for developing and editing the content of your document. The buttons invoke operations available on the Tag popup lists and on the **File, Edit, Insert, Tag,** and **Tools** menus.

The Fragments Toolbar

A *fragment* is information saved in a separate file for later recall. The program provides you with a wide assortment of predefined fragments, many of which are constant values commonly used in mathematics and science. In addition, you can create your own fragments by saving portions of text or mathematics. Fragments are available from the popup list on the Fragments toolbar and from the **Import Fragment** command on the **File** menu.

▶ **To import a fragment from the popup list**

- Press ALT+4 or click the Fragments box and then click the fragment, or use the arrow keys to select the fragment and press ENTER.

The Navigate Toolbar

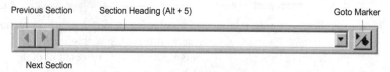

The buttons on the Navigate toolbar help you move quickly through your document by jumping from section to section and marker to marker. The buttons invoke some of the operations that appear on the Go menu. The wide box displays the heading of the section containing the insertion point. You can display a list of the headings in your document with the arrow to the right of the Section Heading box, and then jump to a specific heading by selecting it.

The Link Toolbar

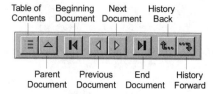

With the buttons on the Link toolbar, you can move quickly through a series of related documents with a minimum of scrolling. These buttons invoke some of the operations that appear on the Go menu and the Go / Links menu.

The History Toolbar

The three buttons on the History toolbar move you to markers or back and forward through the History list, which is a record of the jumps you make. History buttons also appear on the Link toolbar, and a Goto Marker button also appears on the Navigate toolbar. The operations are available from the Go menu.

The Exam Toolbar

With the buttons on the Exam toolbar, you can open the Exam Builder and view .qiz files in *SWP* and *SNB*. The toolbar isn't available in *SW*.

The Typeset Toolbar

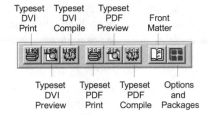

The buttons on the Typeset toolbar are related to typesetting in *SWP* and *SW*. The buttons on the left invoke the preview, print, and compile operations associated with typesetting your document with LaTeX or PDFLaTeX. These commands, which are also available from the **Typeset** menu, produce documents with a finely controlled, publication-quality appearance. The two buttons on the right provide quick access to the **Front Matter** and **Options and Packages** dialog boxes, with which you can modify the typeset appearance of your document. Chapter 9 "Structuring Documents for Typesetting" contains more information. The toolbar doesn't appear in *SNB*.

The Field Toolbar

The Field toolbar contains buttons for enhancing your document with notes, markers, and links to other parts of the document or to subdocuments, other documents, and Internet addresses. If you have *SWP* or *SNB*, you can insert a formula consisting of a mathematical expression and a computational operation. The operations on this toolbar are available from the **Insert** menu.

The Typeset Object Toolbar

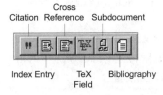

The Typeset Object toolbar contains buttons for enhancing the structure of your *SWP* or *SW* document with subdocuments, BIBTeX bibliographies, and internal references such as bibliography citations, cross-references, and index entries. With the TeX button, you can insert TeX commands into your document. These operations are all available from the **Insert / Typeset Object** menu. The toolbar doesn't appear in *SNB*.

Moving Around

In your document, actions take place at the insertion point, unless you have marked, or *selected,* a part of your document by highlighting it. The insertion point or selection is where the program will insert the next character you type or execute the next command you choose.

While you're working, you may need to move the insertion point from place to place, see another part of the current document, or jump to a different document. With the available scrolling and navigation techniques, you can move within and among documents easily.

Moving the Insertion Point

Depending on how you move around in your document, you may also need to move the insertion point. To move the insertion point, you can use the mouse, the keyboard, or, if NUM LOCK is off, the directional arrows on the numeric keypad. Navigational commands also move the insertion point.

▶ **To use the mouse to move the insertion point in the document window**

- Point the mouse where you want the insertion point to be and click.

▶ **To use the keyboard to move the insertion point**

- Use the commands in the following table:

To move the insertion point	Press
To the left	LEFT ARROW
To the right	RIGHT ARROW (and SPACEBAR in math)
Up	UP ARROW
Down	DOWN ARROW
To the start of the line	HOME
To the end of the line	END
To the start of the next word or object	CTRL+RIGHT ARROW
To the start of the previous or current word or object	CTRL+LEFT ARROW
To the next field inside a template	TAB or INSERT
To the previous field inside a template	SHIFT+TAB
To the outside of a template	RIGHT or LEFT ARROW or SPACEBAR
Next screen	PAGE DOWN
Previous screen	PAGE UP
To the beginning of the document	CTRL+HOME
To the end of the document	CTRL+END
To a different document window	CTRL+TAB

Scrolling

You can scroll rapidly through the length of your document with the mouse or the keyboard. Because the program automatically fits your document to the width of the window, you need to scroll horizontally only when your document contains an unbreakable object that is wider than the window.

To scroll with the mouse, you drag the shaded box on the vertical *scroll bar* of the document window. The box on the bar indicates the approximate location in the document of the text displayed in the window. When you scroll with the mouse, the program doesn't automatically move the insertion point. Instead, it remains in the location it was when you began to scroll.

To scroll with the keyboard, you press certain keys or combinations of keys. When you scroll with the keyboard, the program automatically moves the insertion point to the part of the document displayed on the screen.

To scroll	With the mouse	With the keyboard
Up	Drag the shaded scroll box up on the scroll bar	Press UP ARROW repeatedly
Down	Drag the shaded scroll box down on the scroll bar	Press DOWN ARROW repeatedly
To the top of a document	Drag the shaded scroll box to the top of the scroll bar	Press CTRL+HOME
To the bottom of a document	Drag the shaded scroll box to the bottom of the scroll bar	Press CTRL+END
One screen up	Click the scroll bar above the shaded scroll box	Press PAGE UP
One screen down	Click the scroll bar below the shaded scroll box	Press PAGE DOWN
One line up	Click the arrow at the top of the scroll bar	Press UP ARROW until the line appears
One line down	Click the arrow at the bottom of the scroll bar	Press DOWN ARROW until the line appears

Navigating

Within your document, you can use the commands on the Navigate, History, and Link toolbars and the Go menu to move quickly to a particular section, to a particular marker, or to the beginning of a particular paragraph. (Note that the program considers section headings to be paragraphs for this purpose.) The Section Headings box on the Navigate toolbar serves as an online table of contents for your document, reflecting the section headings you create. See Chapters 3 "Creating Text" and 9 "Structuring Documents for Typesetting" for more information about section headings.

Also, you can navigate from one document to another or through an established string of linked documents. You can make jumps to specific hypertext targets in the same document, in other documents, or on the Internet. The program records your jumps on the History list. Chapter 10 "Creating Documents for Online Use" contains more information about working with hypertext links and related documents.

▶ **To move to a particular section in the current document**

1. On the Navigate toolbar, click the Section Heading popup list.

   The Section Heading box lists the headings in the document and highlights the heading of the section that contains the insertion point.

2. On the list, click the section heading you want.

   The program moves to that section and places the insertion point at the beginning of the heading.

▶ **To move to the previous section in the current document**

- On the Navigate toolbar, click the Previous Section button ◀ or, from the Go menu, choose Previous Section.

▶ **To move to the next section in the current document**

- On the Navigate toolbar, click the Next Section button ▶ or, from the Go menu, choose Next Section.

▶ **To move to the paragraph or object containing a particular marker in the current document**

1. On the Navigate toolbar, click the Goto Marker button ▶ or, from the Go menu, choose To Marker.

2. From the list in the dialog box, select the marker to which you want to move the insertion point and choose OK.

▶ **To move to a particular paragraph**

1. From the Go menu, choose To Paragraph.

   The Goto Paragraph dialog box displays the number of the paragraph containing the insertion point.

2. In the dialog box, type the number of the target paragraph and then choose OK.

▶ **To jump to a hypertext target**

- Place the insertion point in the link and, from the Tools menu, choose Action.
  or

- Hold down the CTRL key and click the link.
  or

- In a document saved as read-only, click the link.

▶ **To return to the source of the most recent jump or move back through jumps**

- On the History toolbar or the Link toolbar, click the History Back button or, from the Go menu, choose History Back.

▶ **To undo a move backwards**

- On the History toolbar or Link toolbar, click the History Forward button or, from the Go menu, choose History Forward.

The History Forward command isn't active unless you've moved through the History list with the History Back command.

Using the History List

The program records all jumps you make on the History list. Each time you jump to a marker, open a document created with the program on your system or network, or open a .tex file located on the Internet, the program adds an entry for the target to the top of the History list. You can view the list to see the sequence of the jumps you've made. Also, you can use the list for navigation, moving back and forth through targets on the list with the commands on the Go menu and the buttons on the History and Link toolbars.

▶ **To view the History list**

- From the Go menu, choose View History.
  The program opens the list, which shows the record of the jumps you've made and the documents you've opened, beginning with the most recent.

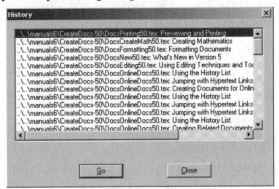

▶ **To return to an entry on the History list**

- Open the History list and double-click the entry you want.

Making Selections

The program executes the commands you give it at the insertion point unless you have selected part of your document. If you have made a selection, the next action you take will affect the entire selection. You can select part of a document with the mouse or with the directional arrows in combination with other keys on the keyboard. For more information about using the keyboard, see Appendix B "Keyboard Shortcuts."

▶ **To select an individual word or mathematical object**

- Double-click the word or object.

▶ **To select part of a document with the mouse**

1. Point to where you want the selection to begin and hold down the left mouse button.

2. Drag the mouse pointer to where you want the selection to end, and then release the mouse button.

▶ **To select a large part of a document with the mouse**

1. Point to where you want the selection to begin and click the mouse.

2. Move the mouse pointer to where you want the selection to end.

3. Press and hold SHIFT.

4. Click the mouse and then release SHIFT.

You may need to scroll to place the mouse pointer where you want the selection to end.

▶ **To make a selection with the keyboard**

1. Place the insertion point where you want the selection to begin.

2. Make the selection you want using the keyboard commands below. Note that the keyboard commands for selecting information correspond to the keyboard commands for moving the insertion point. That is, selecting information is the same as moving with the SHIFT key down.

To select	Press
The character to the left	SHIFT+LEFT ARROW
The character to the right	SHIFT+RIGHT ARROW
The word to the left	CTRL+SHIFT+LEFT ARROW
The word to the right	CTRL+SHIFT+RIGHT ARROW
To the end of the line	SHIFT+END
To the start of the line	SHIFT+HOME
One line down	SHIFT+DOWN ARROW
One line up	SHIFT+UP ARROW
One screen down	SHIFT+PAGE DOWN
One screen up	SHIFT+PAGE UP
To the end of the document	CTRL+SHIFT+END
To the start of the document	CTRL+SHIFT+HOME

2 Creating Documents

Before you can take advantage of the many program features in *SWP, SW,* and *SNB,* you must either create a new document or open an existing one. This chapter explains how to create new documents using document shells and how to open existing files in various file formats on your system or network or on the Internet.

To preserve the work you do, you must save your documents. By default, the program saves all files as LaTeX files and gives them a `.tex` file extension. You can also save files as wrapped (`.rap`) files and, in *SWP* and *SW,* in a Portable LaTeX format that simplifies the transfer of documents to other LaTeX systems. In addition to explaining how to save your documents, this chapter explains how to export them in HTML, RTF, and other formats for use on other installations and platforms. In Version 5 of *SWP* and *SW,* you can also create typeset PDF files; see Chapter 7 "Previewing and Printing" for more information about typesetting. Finally, the chapter explains how to prevent accidental changes to your documents, create document backups, close documents, and leave the program.

Opening Documents

When you start the program, it automatically opens a new, empty *start-up document* created with a default template called a *document shell.* You can use the start-up document, open a new document with a different shell, or open a document that already exists.

Understanding Document Shells

Every new document is created from a document shell. The program includes over 200 shells that produce both general purpose documents and documents designed to meet the specific typesetting requirements of many universities and scholarly journals. You can create your own shells by exporting any document as a shell file; see page 42. Shells have a file extension of `.shl` and are installed in one of the subdirectories of the `Shells` directory in your program installation. Although many shells are similar, no two are exactly alike. The online manual, *A Gallery of Document Shells for Scientific WorkPlace and Scientific Word,* explains the characteristics of the shells provided with the program. Available on your program CD as a PDF file, the manual contains brief discussions and illustrations of typeset documents created with each shell (except those created with *SNB,* which are not intended for typesetting).

As their names indicate, some shells have been designed to create articles, and others have been designed to create books, reports, or other types of documents. The features available for document structuring and formatting differ from shell to shell, as do the resulting documents. The features are determined by several sets of specifications that determine the initial appearance of the shell when you display it in the document window, print it, or, in *SWP* and *SW*, typeset it. These specifications extend to each new document you create with the shell. Some shells also contain predefined information that you can use or modify.

To create a document, you first select a shell appropriate for the type of document you want to create. The program then opens a new document and copies into it the shell you selected and its associated specifications. The program uses some of the specifications when you display the document or print it without typesetting. These include the *page setup specifications,* the *print options,* and the *style specifications* that are stored in the style (.cst) file for the shell. When you typeset your document, the program uses the *typesetting specifications.*

The way you produce the document—displaying it in the document window, printing it, or typesetting it—determines which specifications are used. Because the specifications differ, the way you produce your document also affects the appearance of the document. Remember that typesetting is a feature of *SWP* and *SW,* but not of *SNB.*

When the document is	The document appearance depends on
Displayed in the document window	Style (.cst file)
Produced without typesetting	Style, Page setup, Print options
Produced with typesetting	Typesetting specifications

Please see Chapter 8 "Formatting Documents" and Chapter 9 "Structuring Documents for Typesetting" for more information about how typesetting specifications, styles, page setup specifications, and print options affect the appearance of your document.

If you expect to open your documents on other platforms or installations, you should create them with one of the standard LaTeX document shells, which provide the greatest flexibility and portability. You can achieve almost any typesetting effect by beginning with a standard shell and adding LaTeX packages as necessary. Chapter 8 "Formatting Documents" contains more information about LaTeX and about choosing fonts that increase the portability of your documents. Chapter 5 "Using Graphics and Tables" contains information about creating more portable graphics.

Important   If you're using *SWP* or *SW,* we strongly recommend that you begin all new documents using one of the standard LaTeX shells, unless you have a compelling reason (such as publisher's instructions) to do otherwise.

Occasionally, you may want to use a shell that isn't provided as part of your program installation. Instructions for using shells from outside sources appear in *Typesetting Documents in Scientific WorkPlace and Scientific Word* and on our website at **http://www.mackichan.com**. Please note that although you may be able to create documents using a shell from another source, the program supports only those documents created with typesetting specifications that are provided with the program.

Working in the Start-up Document

Starting the program opens an empty start-up document using a default shell. If the start-up document is appropriate for the document you want to create, you can start entering text and mathematics immediately. Otherwise, you can open a new document with a different shell. Until you save it, the new document carries the temporary name Untitled1. If you open a new document immediately after starting the program and without modifying the start-up document, the program discards the start-up document.

Note   You can specify a different default shell for start-up documents. See Chapter 12 "Customizing the Program" for instructions.

Opening New Documents

You create a new document by choosing the shell for the kind of document you want to create. Choosing a shell carefully can save both time and frustration, especially if you expect your document to be complex.

If you plan to typeset your document, keep your typesetting requirements in mind when you choose a shell. Be sure you choose the type of shell that is appropriate for the type of document you want to write. Also, make sure that the shell contains the document elements you need. You may need front matter elements or theorem environments that aren't universally available. Instead of using one of the provided shells, you can use any document created with the program as a shell. The closer the shell fits your typesetting requirements, the easier your typesetting task. Refer to the online manual *A Gallery of Document Shells for Scientific WorkPlace and Scientific Word* for more information about the characteristics of available shells.

Note   Choose the new document type with care. Not all document types have the same elements. Converting to a different document type later can cause unpredictable results.

If you're unsure of your typesetting requirements or you expect to open your document on another platform or LaTeX installation, we urge you to choose one of the standard LaTeX shells for greater flexibility and portability.

When you open a new document, the program copies the shell you select, along with its style, page setup, print options, and typesetting specifications, into a new document. Until you save the document and give it the name you want, it carries the temporary name Untitled, followed by a number, as in Untitled2. If you have other open unnamed documents, the program gives the new document the name Untitled plus the next sequential number, as in Untitled3.

▶ **To open a new document**

1. On the Standard toolbar, click the New button 　□　 or, from the File menu, choose New. The program displays the New dialog box shown on the next page.

2. From the Shell Directories list, select the shell directory for the type of document you want to create.

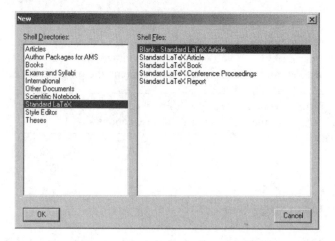

3. From the **Shell Files** list, select the shell file you want and then choose **OK**.

The program opens a new file based on the shell document and its style and type-setting specifications. Depending on the shell, the new file may be blank or it may contain predefined information that you can modify or delete. The program places the insertion point in the entry area so that you can start entering text and mathematics right away.

Opening Existing Documents

In *SW, SWP,* and *SNB,* you can open .tex files created with the program. The files can be located on your computer or, if you have network access, on a network. On the **File** menu, the program maintains a short numbered list of recently opened files, from which you can quickly open a document.

▶ **To open an existing document**

1. On the Standard toolbar, click the Open button 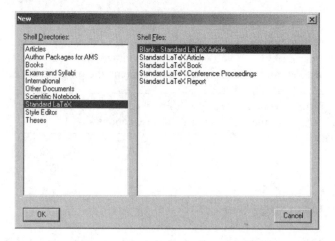; from the **File** menu, choose **Open**; or press CTRL+O.

2. From the **Open** dialog box, select the correct drive and directory.

3. Type the document name in the **File name** box.

   or

   Scroll through the list of documents to select the one you want to open. To display a list of all available files, specify ***.*** in the **File name** box.

   or

   If you want to select more than one document, hold down the CTRL key while you make the selections.

4. Choose **Open**.

▶ **To open a recently opened document**

1. Choose the File menu.

2. From the Recent List at the bottom of the menu, select the document you want or type the number to its left.

The program opens the document you selected and, if you've just started the program, discards the start-up document if it hasn't been modified.

Opening Documents with a Different Format

In addition to opening any .tex file created with the program, you can use the built-in input filters to open existing documents in these file formats:

- Wrapped files created by *SNB* or by *SW* or *SWP* Version 3 or higher (.rap).

- Wrapped files created by *SW* or *SWP* Version 2.5 (.msg).

- Quiz (.qiz).

- LaTeX (.tex).

- ANSI and ASCII (.txt).

- Rich Text Format (.rtf).

- TI, HP, and Casio files (.txt).

- T^3 files (.tex).

Wrapped files gather together in a single text file all the files that must accompany your primary document file when you send it to another location. See Chapter 11 "Managing Documents" for more information about wrapping and unwrapping files in *SWP*, *SW*, and *SNB*.

Quiz (.qiz) files are algorithmically generated by the Exam Builder from .tex documents. When a .qiz file is opened, the Exam Builder reads the file and creates an instance of the exam, which can be taken and graded online. For more information about the Exam Builder and working with .qiz files, see the online Help.

ANSI, ASCII, and RTF files are automatically converted to LaTeX when you open them in *SWP*, *SW*, or *SNB*, although some files may require attention before you can open them, as described below. Files from your graphing calculator and documents created in T^3 require special processing before you can open them.

You may also be able to open documents in other formats as .tex, .qiz, or .rap files. Regardless of the original file format of a document, the program stores it as a LaTeX file when you save the document.

▶ **To open a document with a different format**

1. On the Standard toolbar, click the Open button 📂; from the File menu, choose Open; or press CTRL+O.

2. In the Files of type box, select the format of the document you want to open.

3. Select the location of the document.

4. In the File name box, type or select the name of the document.

   To display the names of all files in the current directory, regardless of format, type *.* in the File name box, and then select the document you want.

5. Choose Open.

Opening Existing LaTeX Files

Some existing LaTeX documents can be opened directly by the program. However, some LaTeX constructs need modification with an ASCII editor before they can be opened. In particular, statements of the form \newcommand and \def often cause problems, and macro definitions that contain unknown environment changes (signaled by \begin and \end statements) always do. In general, constructs that differ from Plain TeX (such as array versus matrix) should be modified to use the LaTeX construct.

If you successfully read and modify a LaTeX document in the program and then save it as an *SWP, SW,* or *SNB* (.tex) document, the program inserts the command \input{tcilatex} in the document preamble and uses in the file macros defined in tcilatex, a special set of macros. (The command isn't inserted in the preamble if you save the document as a Portable LaTeX file. See Saving Documents as Portable LaTeX Files on page 33 for more information.)

Opening ASCII and ANSI Files

The program has ASCII and ANSI filters for reading arbitrary files. The filters remove characters that aren't valid in LaTeX and deal correctly with characters that need special handling:

$$\{ \quad \} \quad \$ \quad \# \quad @ \quad \% \quad \& \quad \backslash \quad | \quad < \quad > \quad \sim$$

The ANSI filter converts the upper ANSI characters to the appropriate LaTeX characters. Be sure to choose the ANSI file format if the file you want to read contains characters from the upper ANSI set and you want to preserve them.

Caution   Don't use the ASCII and ANSI filters to open a LaTeX document. Damage to your document may result.

If you open a LaTeX document using the ASCII and ANSI filters, the program opens the file and displays the LaTeX code underlying any mathematics and objects contained in the document, rather than displaying the mathematics and objects themselves. If you then save the document, the program saves the LaTeX code. The mathematics and other objects in the document won't be available the next time you open the file. Further, if you have saved the document with the same name, thus overwriting the original LaTeX document, you can't recover the mathematics or objects.

Opening Rich Text Format (RTF) Files

Many word processing systems can export documents in the Microsoft RTF format. The program includes the rtf2latex2e RTF conversion program for reading RTF files. The program converts text with reasonable accuracy, but some retagging and reformatting of RTF files opened in *SWP, SW,* and *SNB* may be necessary. The program also accurately converts mathematics created with MathType 3 (Equation Editor) or MathType 5. The program usually reads Windows Metafile (WMF) and Windows Bitmap (BMP) graphics, but graphics in other formats may not be converted successfully. Be sure to proofread RTF documents carefully after you open them in *SWP, SW,* and *SNB.* Note that opening large RTF files can be time-consuming.

Opening Files from Graphing Calculators

You can open files created on certain models of Casio, Hewlett Packard, and Texas Instruments graphing calculators:

- Casio fx-9700GE graphing calculators.

- Hewlett Packard 48G and 48GX graphing calculators.

- TI-82, TI-83, TI-85 and TI-92 graphing calculators.

You can also import data from these calculators; see page 31. Calculator data behave just like any other data created with the program. If you have *SWP* or *SNB,* you can perform calculations with the data.

Before you can open the files, you must move the file from your calculator to your computer and then export the data to an ASCII text (`.txt`) file. This process requires some special hardware and software:

- Communications software designed specifically for your calculator.

- Appropriate hardware and software, as specified by the communications software.

- Cables and adapters to link your calculator to your computer. Cables are sometimes provided with the communications software.

The specific processes for moving data from a calculator to an ASCII file differ for each type of calculator and are thus outside the scope of this manual. For details, please consult the online Help system and the documentation for your calculator. Once you've created the ASCII file, you can open it in the program just like any other file. When you select the file to open, be sure to choose the correct file type for your calculator.

Opening T^3 Files

The program has a special filter for opening documents created with the T^3 Scientific Word Processing System, which is a DOS product. Before you can open a T^3 document, you must first convert the document to a special, restricted form of Plain TeX using a file conversion utility, `T3toTeX`, which is found in T^3 Version 2.3. See your T^3 documentation for more details. The utility is included with a complete installation of *SWP, SW,* or *SNB;* you can also install the utility by modifying a typical installation.

▶ **To install the T^3 conversion utility**

1. Place your program CD-ROM in your CD-ROM drive.

2. From the Windows Start menu, choose Run.

3. Type ***drive:\location\setup.exe*** where ***drive*** is the letter of your CD-ROM drive, ***location*** is the directory for your product, and ***setup.exe*** is the setup program for your product.

4. Follow the instructions on the screen to enter your license information and select **Modify**.

5. When the program displays the **Select Features** dialog box, check **T3 Utilities**.

   Do not uncheck any other items or the installation program will remove them.

6. Follow the instructions on the screen to complete the installation.

   The installation creates the `T3Utilities` directory in your program installation and places the T^3 conversion utility in it.

7. When the program asks whether you want to restart your computer, choose **Yes**.

▶ **To transfer a T^3 document to the specialized Plain TEX form of the file**

1. Transfer the document from T^3 to DOS:

   a. From the T^3 **Main** menu, accept **Document**.
   b. Select the document you want to convert.
   c. From the **Operations** menu, accept **DOS Transfer** to open the **Transfer Document** form.
   d. Complete the **Transfer Document** form, using `T3Utilities` as the directory for the DOS file and `convert.cnv` as the control file. Enter the complete path of the DOS transfer file. Use **.t3** as the file extension.
   e. Highlight all parts of the document in the bottom field of the form.
   f. Accept the form.
      When the transfer process is complete, T^3 returns to the **Main** menu.

2. Exit T^3.

3. At the DOS prompt in the `T3Utilities` directory, type

   t3totex   *name*

   where ***name*** is the name of your document (not including the file extension). The program completes the conversion of the file to a T3toTeX file.

▶ **To open the specialized Plain TEX file**

1. Start *SWP, SW,* or *SNB.*

2. On the Standard toolbar, click the Open button 📂 ; from the **File** menu, choose **Open**; or press CTRL+O.

3. Select the `T3Utilities` directory in the program installation.

4. In the **Files of type** box, select **T3 (*.tex)**.

5. Enter the name of the converted T^3 file and choose **Open**.

6. Save the file.

If the source T^3 document contains built-up mathematical expressions that cannot be converted to TeX, the converter outputs a column of characters using the macro \tcol. The program places the \tcols in TeX fields, which are easy to see in the document. To recreate the expression, edit the document to replace the \tcols by the correct mathematical construct. We suggest you have a T^3 printout of your document at hand when you perform this editing, as the most effective approach is to delete the \tcols and replace them. There is no effective way to use the text in the \tcol fields.

Some T^3 documents can produce strange results when converted to TeX and opened in the program. For example, T^3 allows the placement of a superscript character in the subscript position, producing the following in TeX:

```
\hfill $x_{^2}$\hfill
```

Although this prints correctly in T^3, it doesn't look good in TeX and you must change it to a simple subscript. More detailed information about what the conversion does can be found in the notes for the T^3 Conversion Programs included with the T^3 documentation.

Opening Files in Other Formats as .tex, .qiz, or .rap Files

When you jump to a non-.tex document located on the Web or link to a document created in a different format, the program ordinarily activates your Web browser to open the file. By using specially constructed targets in Open Location commands and hypertext links, you can attempt to open a LaTeX file that doesn't have a .tex or .qiz extension as a .tex or .qiz file, or a wrapped file that doesn't have a .rap extension as a .rap file. The program opens as much of the file as possible using the file format you specify.

Although this feature is perhaps most useful when working with documents generated by Internet applications, it isn't limited to those documents. See Chapter 10 "Creating Documents for Online Use" for more information about using hypertext and working with online information.

▶ **To open a file in a program file format**

1. On the Standard toolbar, click the Open Location button ![button] or, from the File menu, choose Open Location.

2. In the Open URL box, enter the complete path name or Uniform Resource Locator (URL) for the document.

3. Press the spacebar, type **as**, press the spacebar, and type the file format you want to use: **.tex, .qiz,** or **.rap**.

4. Choose Open to open the Internet location in *SWP, SW,* or *SNB*.

▶ **To build a hypertext link to open as a program file**

1. On the Field toolbar, click the Hypertext Link button ![button] or, from the Insert menu, choose Hypertext Link.

2. In the Text area, enter the text of the link as you want it to appear on the screen.

3. In the URL box, enter the complete URL for the document.

4. Press the spacebar, type **as**, press the spacebar, and type the file format you want to use: **.tex**, **.qiz**, or **.rap**.

5. Choose Open to complete the hypertext link and return to your document.

6. If you want to jump to the linked document, hold down the CTRL key and click the link.

See page 281 for additional instructions about jumping with hypertext links.

Opening Several Documents at Once

You can open several different documents or several views of the same document at the same time using different windows. Each document window has a title bar, scroll bars, and minimize and maximize buttons. When you have several windows open, the title bar of the active window is displayed in the same color as the program title bar. You can move easily from window to window, and you can copy and move information from document to document.

If you open multiple views of the same document, you can view different parts of the document at the same time, one part in each window. Also, you can change the way you view the document in each window by changing the options on the View menu. The content changes you make in one view are recorded in all views.

From the Window menu, you can arrange the open windows any way you want, cascading or tiling them, or minimizing them so they appear as icons in the program window. Chapter 12 "Customizing the Program" has more details about arranging windows.

▶ **To open several existing documents at once**

1. On the Standard toolbar, click the Open button 🖼 ; from the File menu, choose Open; or press CTRL+O.

2. Hold down the CTRL key while selecting the documents you want to open from the file list.

3. Choose Open.

The program opens each document into a new window and places the insertion point at the beginning of the first document you specified. All other open windows remain open.

▶ **To open a new document in a new window**

1. On the Standard toolbar, click the New button 🗋 or, from the File menu, choose New.

2. From the New dialog box, select the shell you want and choose OK.

The program opens a new window and places the insertion point in it. All other open windows remain open.

▶ **To open another view of the active document**

- From the Window menu, choose New Window.

    The program opens another window containing the active document and places the insertion point at the beginning of the document in the new window.

▶ **To move from window to window**

- On the Window menu, click the window you want or type the number next to the window you want.

    or

- Click the mouse on the title bar of the document you want.

    or

- Press CTRL+TAB.

Opening Internet Locations

The program can take you directly to the Internet. If you have Internet access, you can open Uniform Resource Locator (URL) locations on the web from within *SWP, SW,* or *SNB.* You can also open any URL location specified in a hypertext link in an active *SWP, SW,* or *SNB* document.

The URL locations can be documents created with the program or documents in other formats, such as HTML or PDF. If the information is in an *SWP, SW,* or *SNB* document (with a file extension of .tex or .rap) on the current system or network or on the Web, the program opens it as a read-only document in a new document window. If the information is in a document with a different format, the program activates the appropriate software on your computer, such as your Web browser or PDF viewer, to access the location. Read more about hypertext and working with online documents in Chapter 10 "Creating Documents for Online Use."

▶ **To open an Internet location**

1. On the Standard toolbar, click ![icon] or, from the File menu, choose Open Location.

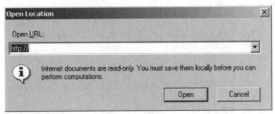

2. In the Open Location dialog box, enter the URL of the location.

    Click the arrow to the right of the box to display a list of recently opened URLs.

3. Choose Open.

    If an attempt to open an online .rap file is unsuccessful, delete the temporary Internet files on your computer and try again.

Remember that any document created with *SWP, SW,* or *SNB* and having a .tex or .rap extension is available on the Internet as a read-only document. That is, you must save a copy of the document locally if you want to work with any information it contains or typeset it in *SWP* or *SW.* You must also save a copy locally to be able to use *SWP* or *SNB* to perform computations with any mathematics in the document.

▶ **To open an Internet location specified in a hypertext link**

- Place the insertion point in the link so that the pointer appears as ☝ and then, from the Tools or Context menu, choose Action.
    or

- In a document saved as read-only (such as those provided with the program), click the link.
    or

- In a document not saved as read-only, hold down the CTRL key and click the link. The document remains open while you browse.

    Linking to the Internet can occasionally take a long time. You can cancel an attempt to link to the Internet.

▶ **To cancel an attempt to link to the Internet**

- On the Stop toolbar, click the Stop Operation button [STOP] or press CTRL+BREAK.

Importing Information

In addition to opening files in other formats, you can import information to your document from other documents or from your graphing calculator.

Importing One Document into Another

If you want to create a document using an existing document, you can preserve the existing document by importing its contents into the body of an open document. The import process copies the body of the specified file but not the front matter, typesetting specifications, or style.

▶ **To import the contents of one document into another**

1. Open the document into which you want to import the contents of another document.

2. Place the insertion point where you want to insert the contents.

3. From the File menu, choose Import Contents.

4. In the Import Contents dialog box, select the name, location, and file type of the document you want to import.

5. Choose Open.

    The program copies the body of the specified document into the active document, beginning at the insertion point.

Importing Data from Graphing Calculators

Lists, vectors, matrices, or numbers that are stored on these models of Casio, Hewlett Packard, and Texas Instruments graphing calculators can be imported to your document:

- Casio fx-9700GE graphing calculators.

- Hewlett Packard 48G and 48GX graphing calculators.

- TI-82, TI-83, TI-85 and TI-92 graphing calculators.

Imported data behave just like any other data created with the program. In *SWP* or *SNB,* you can compute with the data from your calculator.

Before you can import the data, you must move the file from your calculator to your computer and then export the data to an ASCII text (.txt) file. This process requires some special hardware and software, as described in Opening Files From Graphing Calculators on page 25. The specific processes for moving data from a calculator to an ASCII file differ for each type of calculator and are thus outside the scope of this manual. For details, please consult the documentation for your calculator. Additional information appears in the online Help. Once you've created the ASCII text file, you can import its contents into your document.

▶ **To import calculator data into a document**

1. Open the document in *SWP, SW,* or *SNB.*

2. From the File menu, choose Import Contents.

3. In the Files of type box, select the file format for your calculator.

4. Specify the location and name of the text file containing the data exported from your calculator and then choose OK.

   The calculator import filter reads the data file and converts it to a list, matrix, or value, then imports the data into your document beginning at the insertion point.

Saving Documents

To preserve your latest work, save your document regularly. Saving your document regularly means that you lose very little work if you experience problems. We suggest that you save your document every 10 to 20 minutes and also before you print, before you make a large change (such as a global replace), and after you enter any work that would be difficult to redo. To ensure that your work is saved routinely, you can have the program back up your documents as frequently as you want. See Backing Up at Regular Intervals on page 44. When you save a document, it remains open so you can keep working. Each time you leave the program, save and close all active documents.

By default, the program saves all files as LaTeX files and gives them a .tex file extension. However, if you have *SWP* or *SW,* you can save most files as Portable LaTeX (.tex) files to make them more portable to other LaTeX installations. You can save files in a quick-load (.cdx) format for faster opening and, if you need to send your documents to a different location, you can also save them as wrapped (.rap) files. In addition to saving your files, you can *export* them for use on the Internet, on different platforms, and on other systems and LaTeX installations. See Exporting Documents on page 39.

Besides saving and exporting your documents in different formats, in Version 5 of *SWP* or *SW* you can create typeset PDF files for use on different platforms. See Chapter 7 "Previewing and Printing" for more information.

Saving New, Untitled Documents

When you save an untitled document, the program automatically opens the Save As dialog box so you can name the document. You can assign to your document any Windows file name that is acceptable for your installation. Avoid using a DOS command name as a file name. Otherwise, the name can include any characters except the following:

$$* \quad ? \quad \backslash \quad / \quad : \quad | \quad < \quad > \quad \$ \quad \wedge$$

Note that if the file name or the name of the directory containing the file includes characters that have special meaning to TeX, such as a space or ~, you may not be able to typeset your document. In particular, documents that you intend to typeset shouldn't be saved in the My Documents directory. If the file or directory name includes one of these characters or an underscore, the program displays a warning when you attempt to typeset your document. You can turn the warning off; see Chapter 7 "Previewing and Printing." Spaces are acceptable in *SNB* document and directory names.

We suggest that you also avoid the use of characters that have special meanings on other platforms. For example, $ and # have special meanings (as do many other nonalphanumeric characters) in certain UNIX shells. You can use a period only to separate the file name from the extension.

The file name you assign is followed by an optional period and an extension of one to three characters, which indicates the type of file. The program automatically adds a .tex extension to the file name unless you type another extension. You can use a different extension by typing a period and the extension you want, such as article.ltx. However, if you use other extensions, you must include the extension every time you type the file name. If you don't want any extension, type the file name and end it with a period. Regardless of the extension, the program saves all documents as LaTeX files.

Note   You may be able to use the ASCII import feature in other word processors to import LaTeX files. However, when you do this, mathematics appears in LaTeX code form. For example, $\alpha^2 + \beta^2$ appears as $\alpha^2+\beta^2$.

▶ **To save a new, untitled document**

1. On the Standard toolbar, click the Save button ⊞ or, from the File menu, choose Save or Save As.

2. In the Save as type box, select the file format you want.

3. Select the drive and folder in which you want to save the document.

4. In the File name box, type a name for your document.

5. Choose **Save**.

6. If you type a file name that already exists in the chosen directory, the program asks whether you want to replace the existing document with the new document.

   - Choose **No** to preserve the old document and then type another file name.

   or

   - Choose **Yes** to replace the old document with the open document.

Saving Existing Documents

When you choose the **Save** command, the program saves your active document with the same name, in the same format, and in the same directory you used the last time you saved the document. If you want to save the document with a new name or in another location, save a copy of the document according to the instructions on page 37.

▶ **To save an existing document under its current name**

   - On the Standard toolbar, click the Save button ⊞ or, from the **File** menu, choose **Save**.

▶ **To save all open existing documents under their current names**

   - From the **File** menu, choose **Save All**.

Saving Documents as Portable LATEX Files

SWP and *SW* contain a Portable LATEX output filter designed to create .tex documents that are more easily read by standard LATEX installations. Portable LATEX files don't include tcilatex, a special set of macros, so the line \input{tcilatex} doesn't appear in the document preamble. They don't include additional LATEX macros in the .tex file nor any LATEX packages that aren't part of a standard LATEX installation. Portable LATEX isn't available in *SNB* or for documents created with Style Editor styles or styles created using LATEX 2.09.

When you save your document as a Portable LATEX file, the program removes the \input{tcilatex} line from the preamble and saves the body of the document as described above. It then closes the original file and keeps the Portable LATEX file open. Any subsequent changes are made to the Portable LATEX file but not to the original file.

If your document contains graphics or, in *SWP*, plots, you can leave them unchanged in the original format, choose not to export them, or export them in a format you designate. If you want to export them as .eps graphics, which are supported by commonly used LATEX DVI drivers, you must install and configure the wfm2eps print driver, according to the instructions in the online Help.

Although you will probably specify a single format for all graphics, you can specify different formats for different types of graphics, such as raster or vector graphics, or for types of graphics that you group together in sets. A graphics file type can appear in more than one set. The program applies the selected export formats to the sets in the order in which the sets are listed in the **Portable LaTeX Graphics Export Options** dialog; you can change the order.

If you choose to export plots as graphics, the program applies a single format to all plots. In addition to choosing the export formats, you can choose a naming scheme for exported graphics. The program usually exports graphics to a subdirectory of the directory containing the document, but you can designate a different subdirectory if you prefer.

If you want the Portable LaTeX filter to be your default output filter, customize your installation as described in Chapter 12 "Customizing the Program."

▶ **To save a document as a portable LaTeX file using the default export settings**

1. On the Standard toolbar, click the Save button ![save] or, from the File menu, choose Save or Save As.

2. In the box labeled Save as type, select Portable LaTeX (*.tex).

3. Select the drive and folder in which you want to save the document.

4. In the File name box, type a name for your document.

5. Choose Save.

▶ **To specify graphics export settings for a portable LaTeX file**

1. From the Typeset menu, choose General Settings.

2. From the General Settings dialog box, choose Portable LaTeX Graphics Settings.

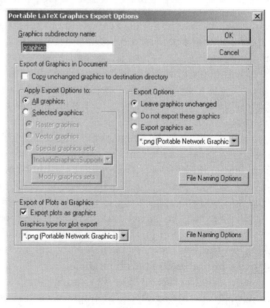

3. If you want to change the directory used for exported graphics and plots, enter the name of the subdirectory you want to use.

4. In the **Apply Export Options to** area, select **All graphics** or select a type or set of graphics.

5. If you want to modify, add, or remove a set of graphics,

   a. Choose **Modify Graphics Sets** to open the dialog box.

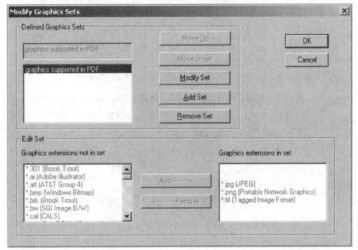

   b. If you want to remove an existing set, select it and choose **Remove Set**.

   c. If you want to add a set, enter a name for it in the **Defined Graphics Sets** edit box, choose **Add Set**, and then, in the **Edit Set** area, select the extensions to add to the set.

   d. If you want to modify an existing set, select it, choose **Modify Set**, and then, in the **Edit Set** area, select the extensions to add to or remove from the set.

   e. If you need to move a set to a new position in the list, select the set, and use the **Move Up** or **Move Down** controls to place it in the correct position.

   f. When your selections are complete, choose **OK**.

6. In the **Export Options** area, select a formatting option for the selected type or set of graphics. The default is to leave the graphics unchanged.

Option	Use
Leave graphics unchanged	Use the current format of the selected graphics type or set
Do not export these graphics	Do not export the selected graphics type or set
Export graphics as	Select a format for the selected graphics type or set

7. Repeat steps 4–6 as necessary.

8. If you want to designate a naming scheme for all exported graphics,

   a. Choose **Graphics File Naming Options** to open the **Naming Options** dialog box shown on the next page.

   b. Select a naming scheme.

   c. Choose **OK**.

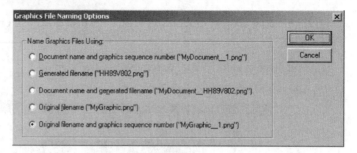

9. If you're using *SWP* and you want to export plots as graphics,

   a. Check **Export plots as graphics** and select a graphics format.
   b. If you want to designate a naming scheme for all exported plots,
      i Choose **Plot File Naming Options**.
      ii Select the scheme you want.
      iii Choose **OK**.

10. When all selections are complete, choose **OK**.

11. Choose **OK** to return to your document.

Saving Documents as Quick-Load Files

When you open a document that has been saved with the quick-load feature, the program uses a special form of the file that opens faster than usual. The feature is especially useful for opening large documents. (Subdocuments can't be saved with the quick-load feature. See Chapter 9 "Structuring Documents for Typesetting" for information about subdocuments.) No special process is required to open a quick-load file. When a quick-load file is being opened, the paragraph numbers don't appear in the Status bar.

You must save a document for quick loading before you can open it with the quick-load feature. When you save for quick loading, the program creates a fast-loading companion file, leaving the .tex file unchanged. The new file has the same name as the document file but has a file extension of .cdx instead of .tex. You can save your document in both forms; see Setting the Save Options on page 38.

Quick-load files created with earlier versions of the program can't be opened in the current version. Instead, the program notifies you that the quick-load file format is outdated and opens the corresponding .tex file instead.

Important   A quick-load file is typically two to three times larger than its original LaTeX document.

▶ **To save a document for quick loading**

   1. From the File menu, choose **Document Info**.

   2. Choose the **Save Options** tab.

3. Check the Save for Quick Load box.

4. Check Export TeX File On Save.to save the .tex form of your document as well as the quick-load form.

   We recommend that you save the file in both forms.

5. Choose OK.

6. Save the document.

Saving Documents as Wrapped Files

Use wrapped files when you want to send a document and all its associated files to another location. You can either save or export your document as a wrapped (.rap) file. The program handles the files differently for each method. If you save your document as a wrapped file, the program saves your original .tex document and creates a new .rap file using the same file name. The program closes the .tex file and opens the .rap file. Any subsequent changes you make occur in the .rap file. When you save again, the program saves the .rap file and also updates your original .tex file.

If you export your document as a .rap file, as described on page 43, the program creates but doesn't open a .rap file using the file name you choose. If the file name is the same as that of the .tex document, the program also updates the .tex file. The program leaves the .tex file open so you can continue working in it. Any subsequent changes you make occur only in the .tex file. When you save again, the program updates the .tex file but not the exported .rap file.

You can wrap documents more precisely with the Document Manager. Chapter 11 "Managing Documents" describes the process.

Saving All Open Documents

When you have multiple documents open, you can save them all with a single command. The documents are saved in the same names, formats, and locations in which they were last saved. If an open document hasn't yet been saved for the first time, the program displays a dialog box so you can name the file.

▶ **To save all open documents**

- From the File menu, choose Save All.

Saving a Copy of an Open Document

If you want to create a copy of the document with a new name, save the document in a different location, or save the document in a different format, use the Save As command.

▶ **To save a copy of an open document**

1. From the File menu, choose Save As.

2. If you want to save the document under another name, type a new name in the File Name box.

3. If you want to save the document in another directory or on another drive, select the new drive and folder in the Save in box.

4. If you want to save the document in a different format, select the new format from the list in the Save as type box.

5. Choose Save.

6. If you type a file name that already exists in the chosen directory, the program asks whether you want to replace the existing document with the new document.
   - Choose No to preserve the old document and then type another file name.
     or
   - Choose Yes to replace the old document with the open document.

Setting the Save Options

You can save your document with certain options in effect. For example, by default the program saves any graphics in the file with absolute path names. You can change the default to save the graphics with relative path names instead. You can also save the settings on the View menu and the current magnification setting. The next time you open the document, the program uses the saved settings. These save options are available:

Check	To
Save for Quick Load	Save the quick-load form of your document
Export TeX File On Save	Save the .tex file as well as a quick-load file
Store Relative Graphics Paths	Save graphics with relative instead of absolute path names (default)
Store View Settings in File	Save the current settings on the View menu
Store View Percent in File	Save the current magnification setting
Store Notes View Settings in File	Save the current settings on the View menu for notes
Store Notes View Percent in File	Save the current magnification setting for notes

If you're using *SWP* or *SW*, you can also set output options for creating DVI or PDF files. See Chapter 7 "Previewing and Printing."

▶ **To set the save options**

1. From the File menu, choose Document Info, then choose the Save Options tab.

2. Check those options you want to set.

3. Choose OK.

Exporting Documents

In addition to saving your documents in various ways, you can export them for use on the Web; on other platforms, installations, or systems; or as document shells. Version 5 has filters for exporting HTML files, RTF files, shell files, and wrapped files.

When you export documents as HTML or RTF files, the program uses default formats for mathematics, plots, and graphics. The defaults are adequate for nearly all documents, but you can change them before you export, if necessary, as described on the next pages.

SWP and *SNB* can also export Exam Builder quiz (.qiz) files, which are algorithmically generated by the Exam Builder from .tex documents. For information about .qiz files, see the Exam Builder documentation available from the online Help system. The program can also produce graphic images of your text and mathematics; page 124 presents information about exporting pictures.

▶ To export a document

1. Open the document.

2. From the File menu, choose Export Document.

3. Select a location and name for the file.

   We suggest avoiding these characters in the file name as they may have special meanings in certain circumstances: * ? \ / : | < > $ ^.

4. In the box labeled Save as type, specify the file format you want and choose Save.

Note that in Version 5, creating files for use across platforms isn't limited to exporting files. In *SWP* and *SW,* you can create typeset PDF files. See Chapter 7 "Previewing and Printing" for details.

Exporting Documents as HTML Files

Exporting your documents as HTML files provides a way for your documents—and the mathematics and graphics they contain—to be viewed on a variety of platforms via the Internet, even if *SWP, SW,* and *SNB* aren't available. The HTML export filter creates accurate HTML documents that can be viewed with recent versions of the most popular browsers. Several export formats are available.

The HTML filter includes any graphics contained in your document, exporting them as PNG files by default. Other graphics formats are available. The programs saves the exported graphics to a subdirectory of the directory containing the HTML file. Also by default, the filter converts any instances of mathematics and mathematics plots in your document to PNG graphics. Alternatively, you can export any mathematics as MathML. Note, however, that currently not all browsers support MathML.

By default, the filter creates a Cascading Style Sheet (.css file) that reflects the appearance of your document in the document window; that is, its appearance without typesetting. To make certain that the content of your document converts correctly to HTML, develop the document without regard for its typeset form and appearance.

Chapter 10 "Creating Documents for Online Use" and Chapter 12 "Customizing the Program" contain instructions for creating HTML files and changing export defaults.

Exporting Documents as RTF Files

Exporting your documents as RTF files provides another way for you to share your work with people who don't have *SWP, SW,* or *SNB.* The RTF export filter preserves most of the formatting that you see in the document window. Note that when document elements have no equivalents in RTF, they may be discarded by the filter.

For exporting RTF files, the system uses default formats for mathematics, plots, and graphics. The defaults are adequate for nearly all documents, but you can change them if necessary. When you export to RTF, any mathematics in your document is exported as an embedded graphic, by default. You can choose to export mathematics as both embedded graphics and embedded MathType 3 (Equation Editor) or MathType 5 objects. Also, you can select a MathType 5 preference file for generating mathematical objects or you can choose to have the size of mathematics be inherited from its context, which is the default. If the font size is inherited, the mathematics is sized appropriately for its surroundings when the object is rendered by MathType 5.

The export process embeds any plots in your document as graphics files; various formats are available. If you choose to export plots as graphics, the program applies a single format to all plots. You can leave graphics in the original format, choose not to export them, or choose the default graphics export format or a different format. Although you will probably specify a single format for all graphics, you can specify different formats for different types of graphics, such as raster or vector graphics, or for types of graphics that you group together in sets. A graphics file type can appear in more than one set. The program applies the selected export formats to the sets in the order in which the sets are listed in the **RTF Graphics Export Options** dialog; you can change the order.

The RTF files you export from *SWP, SW,* and *SNB* can be opened in Microsoft Word. If the Microsoft Word installation includes the appropriate Equation Editor, MathType 3 or MathType 5 mathematical objects can be edited. If the installation doesn't include an Equation Editor, mathematical objects can still be displayed but they can't be edited. RTF files can be viewed with the Microsoft Word outline feature.

Working with RTF files can be somewhat difficult and time consuming. If you export mathematics using a bitmap format, you will increase the portability of your document because bitmaps aren't font dependent. However, fonts may remain an issue. In order to ensure that your exported RTF documents display correctly on systems that don't have *SWP, SW,* or *SNB,* a group of 16 program font files must be installed on the system. Those files, which are freely redistributable, are `tci1.ttf` through `tci4.ttf`, and their corresponding bold, italic, and bold italic files:

Base Font	Bold	Italic	Bold Italic
tci1.ttf	tci1b.ttf	tci1i.ttf	tci1bi.ttf
tci2.ttf	tci2b.ttf	tci2i.ttf	tci2bi.ttf
tci3.ttf	tci3b.ttf	tci3i.ttf	tci3bi.ttf
tci4.ttf	tci4b.ttf	tci4i.ttf	tci4bi.ttf

Certain document shells may also require special fonts. If the system has the Equation Editor, these fonts may not be needed, but other font issues may arise and you may need additional Equation Editor fonts.

Also, exported RTF files that contain graphics and mathematical objects are very large in comparison to their original .tex documents. If the RTF files are saved in Microsoft Word, the resulting .doc files are also quite large. For example, one sample .tex file with 1 MB of text and 24 MB of graphics produced a 160-MB RTF file. Microsoft Word can fail to load large, complex files. The large size of RTF files containing many embedded graphics and mathematical objects causes them to open slowly in Microsoft Word. Consider dividing large files into several smaller files before exporting them to RTF. Note too that particularly long mathematical objects may open with difficulty in Microsoft Word. Finally, the export process itself can be time consuming. You can cancel it if necessary.

Because of these considerations, you may prefer to use typeset PDF files for sharing work with people who don't have *SWP, SW,* or *SNB.* See Chapter 7 "Previewing and Printing" for information about typesetting PDF files.

▶ **To specify export settings for an RTF file**

1. From the Tools menu, choose Export Settings and choose the RTF Document Export Options tab.

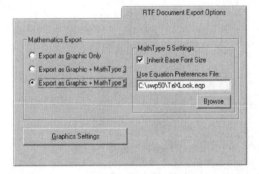

2. Select the format for exporting any mathematics in your document. The default is to export as graphics only.

3. If you select MathType 5, change the MathType 5 settings as necessary:

   a. Specify an equation preferences file for use with MathType 5.
   b. If you want the mathematics base font to inherit its size from surrounding text, as in footers or section headings, check Inherit base font size.
      This control overrides the equation preferences file.

4. If you want to change the export settings for graphics, choose Graphics Settings and change the settings as necessary:

   a. In the Apply Export Options to area, select All graphics or select a type or set of graphics.
   b. If you want to modify, add, or remove a set of graphics,
      i Choose Modify Graphics Sets.
      ii If you want to remove an existing set, select it and choose Remove Set.

iii If you want to add a set, enter a name for it in the **Defined Graphics Sets** edit box, choose **Add Set**, and then, in the **Edit Set** area, select the extensions to add to the set.

iv If you want to modify an existing set, select it, choose **Modify Set**, and then, in the **Edit Set** area, select the extensions to add to or remove from the set.

v If you need to move a set to a new position in the list, select the set, and use the **Move Up** or **Move Down** controls to place it in the correct position.

vi When your selections are complete, choose **OK**.

c. In the **Export Options** area, select a formatting option for the selected type or set of graphics. The default is to leave the graphics unchanged.

d. Repeat steps a–c as necessary.

5. If you're using *SWP* and you want to export plots as graphics, check **Export of plots as graphics** and select a graphics format.

6. If you want to export mathematics as graphics, check **Export of mathematics as graphics** and select a graphics format.

7. When your selections are complete, choose **OK**.

8. Choose **OK** to return to your document.

▶ **To stop the RTF export process**

- Press ESC.

Exporting Document as Shells

You can use any document as a shell for a new document. In particular, if you have modified a document so that it meets your requirements, you may want to export it as a shell so that you can use it repeatedly. You should export the document as a shell to one of the Shells subdirectories in your program installation. If you export it to some other directory, the name won't appear in the list of available shells when you start a new document. You can create new shell subdirectories as necessary.

▶ **To save a document as a shell**

1. Open the document.

2. From the **File** menu, choose **Export Document**.

3. Select a location for the new shell:

a. In the box labeled **Save in**, select the Shells directory in your program installation.

b. Select or create the appropriate subdirectory for the new shell.

4. In the box labeled File name, type a name for the shell.

The name can include spaces and nonalphabetic characters.

5. In the box labeled Save as type, specify Shell (*.shl) and choose Save.

The next time you open a new document, the shell name appears on the Shell Files list corresponding to the shell subdirectory you specified.

Exporting Documents as Wrapped Files

When you want to send a document and all its associated files to another location, you can export or save the document as a wrapped (.rap) file. The results of the two methods differ. If you export your document as a .rap file, the program creates but doesn't open a .rap file using the file name you choose. If the file name is the same as that of the .tex document, the program also updates the .tex file. The program leaves the .tex file open so you can continue working in it. Any subsequent changes you make occur only in the .tex file. When you save again, the program updates the .tex file but not the exported .rap file. The .rap file exists as a snapshot of the document at the time of the export; it reflects no subsequent changes.

See page 37 for information about saving .rap files. You can wrap documents more precisely with the Document Manager. Chapter 11 "Managing Documents" describes the process.

Preserving Documents

You can enhance the safety of your documents by saving them with the read-only option, by using the quick-load backup feature, and by creating automatic backup files. The program provides an additional safety feature if a system problem occurs while you're working in a document: the program automatically attempts to save as much information about the open document as possible in a special file. The program names the file with the same name as the original document but with a file extension of .dmp, and places the .dmp file in the same directory as the document file. The program then displays a message that a serious error has occurred. It closes all files and exits.

These safety features protect your documents while you work, but they don't provide long-term safety, because the program saves the files in the same directory and on the same drive as the original file. Any problems with the disk can damage all the files. Therefore, you should regularly store copies of your documents on a file server, floppy disks, or a backup tape. If you store copies of your documents regularly, you'll have another copy of your work if a problem occurs.

Using the Read-Only Option

The read-only option keeps you from accidentally making changes to a document that you want to preserve. No special process is required to open a read-only document, but any changes to the document are prevented until the option is removed.

Many commands aren't available in a read-only environment; they appear dimmed on the menus and toolbars. When you try to save a read-only document, the program asks if you want to override the protection.

▶ **To save a document with read-only protection**

1. From the File menu, choose Save As.

2. If the document is still untitled or you want the read-only version to have a different name, type a name for the file.

3. Check the Save as read-only box.

4. Choose Save.

▶ **To remove the read-only protection**

1. From the File menu, choose Save As.

2. Leave the file name unchanged.

3. Uncheck the Save as read-only box and choose Save.

4. When the system asks if you want to replace the file, choose Yes.

   The program opens the Overwrite Read Only File dialog box.

5. Choose the way you want to save the file:
   - To update the file and save it with read-only protection, check Read Only File.
   - To update the file and save it without read-only protection, check Read/Write File.

6. Choose OK.

Backing Up at Regular Intervals

When the quick-load backup feature is in use, all open documents that have been named are saved at regular intervals, the length of which you choose. The program saves a quick-load copy of each open document between the times you save manually (with the Save button or the Save, Save As, or Save All commands). The program writes the quick-load backup file in an internal format and saves it in a file with the same name as the document file and an extension of .aut. If you encounter a system problem or you close the program without saving an open document properly, you lose only the changes you've made to the document since the most recent quick-load backup or manual save.

If the quick-load backup feature is in use and you save your file before closing it, the program discards the .aut file. The next time you try to open the file, the program tries to open the most recent version of the document. If the most recent version is the .aut file, the program asks if you want to open it instead of the .tex version. If you choose not to open the .aut file, the program discards it.

Note   The quick-load backup feature works only with named files. When you create a new document, you must name it before the backup process can be initiated.

The program is installed with the quick-load backup feature turned off. If you want to create backup files at regular intervals, you must turn on the feature.

▶ **To create regular quick-load backups of all open documents**

1. On the Editing toolbar, click the User Setup button ⬚ or, from the Tools menu, choose User Setup.

2. Choose the Files tab.

3. In the Miscellaneous area, check the box next to Create Quick-load Backup (.aut) Files.

4. Type or use the arrows next to the box to set the frequency.

    Choose any time interval in the range from 1 to 100 minutes. The initial default is 20 minutes.

5. Choose OK.

Each time you save a file manually, the program sets the backup counter to zero. This means that if you always save manually before the end of the specified time interval, the program never creates a quick-load backup of your document and no .aut file exists.

Creating Automatic Backups

When the automatic backup feature is in use, the program makes a copy of the previously saved version of the open document each time you manually save the document (with the Save button or the Save, Save As, or Save All commands). The backup copy, which has the same name as the original document but a file extension of .bak, is the next-to-last saved version of the document. Each new backup copy for a document file replaces the previous one. Like .tex files, backup files are ASCII files.

Note   Automatic backup files work only with named documents. When you create a new document, you must save and name it before the backup process can be initiated.

The program is installed with the automatic backup feature turned on. Turn the feature off and on from the User Setup command on the Tools menu.

▶ **To make an automatic backup each time an open document is saved**

1. On the Editing toolbar, click the User Setup button [icon] or, from the Tools menu, choose User Setup.

2. Choose the Files tab.

3. In the Miscellaneous area, check Create Backup (.bak) Files and choose OK.

Restoring Documents

You may occasionally be unable to open a document because of damage resulting from a power failure or some other computer problem. However, you may be able to restore your work if the program successfully created a .dmp file of the open document when the problem occurred or if you had the automatic backup or quick-load backup features turned on the last time you worked in the file.

Each time you open a document, the program attempts to open the most recent version of the document. Normally, that version is the .tex file, but if a problem has occurred, the most recent version may have a file extension of .dmp, .aut, or even .bak, depending on which features were in effect at the time.

- If the most recent version of the document is a .dmp file, the program asks whether you want to open it instead of the .tex file. If you do, the program opens the .dmp file and discards the .aut file for the document, if any. When you save the .dmp file, the program saves it as a .tex document.

- If the most recent version of the document is an .aut file, the program asks whether you want to open it instead of the .tex file. If so, the program opens the .aut file. When you save the .aut file, it is saved as a .tex document. If you choose to open the .tex file, the program discards the .aut file.

- If neither a .dmp file nor an .aut file exists for the document, the most recent undamaged version of the document may be a .bak file, if you had automatic backups in effect when the problem occurred. The backup copy is the next-to-last saved version of the original file. If you need to use the backup file, first rename it using a file extension of .tex and then open it as you would any program document. When you save the backup file, the program saves it with a .tex extension.

Closing Documents

Close your document when you've finished the current working session.

▶ **To close a document**

1. Close the document:
   - If you want to close all views of the open document, from the File menu, choose Close.
     or

- If you want to close the active window, press CTRL+F4 or click the Close button ☒ for the document window.
  or
- If you want to close all views of all open documents, from the Window menu, choose Close All.

2. If the program prompts you to save your recent changes, choose Yes to save the changes or No to discard them.

3. If the program prompts you to name the document, choose Yes to name and save the document or No to discard the document.

Leaving the Program

▶ **To leave the program**

1. From the File menu, choose Exit.

   or

   Press ALT+F4.

   or

   At the top left corner of the title bar in the program window, double-click the program symbol, or click the symbol once and then choose Close.

   or

   At the top right corner of the program window, click the Close button ☒ .

2. If the program displays a warning asking whether you want to save your most recent changes, choose Yes to save them or No to discard them.

   or

   If the program displays a warning asking whether you want to save the unnamed document you're working in, choose Yes to name and save your document or No to discard it.

3 Creating Text

When you open a document, the insertion point appears at the top left of the document window. If you've opened a new document, you can begin entering material right away. If you've opened an existing document, you may need to move the insertion point before you add to the existing material.

Entering text is straightforward, even when special characters or alphabets are involved. Moving around your document with the mouse or the keyboard is similar to moving around in other computer applications. Special navigation tools help you move quickly through your document. Because entering text is so straightforward, you can focus on the content you want to create.

This chapter explains how to enter and edit text and special characters, and how to use tags to add emphasis and structure to text. Chapter 5 "Using Graphics and Tables" provides information about creating tables.

Understanding Text and Mathematics

Usually, the program defaults to text. That is, it assumes that it should interpret what you enter as text rather than mathematics. When you start the program, the Math/Text button on the Standard toolbar appears as $\boxed{\text{T}}$. Until you actively change to mathematics, the program assumes that whatever you type is text. When you change to mathematics, the Math/Text button appears as $\boxed{\text{M}}$.

Understanding the Differences

The program treats text and mathematics differently. When the insertion point is in text, the program

- Interprets anything you type as text.
- Displays alphabetic characters upright, not italicized.
- Inserts a space when you press the spacebar between words and sentences.

As explained in more detail in Chapter 4 "Creating Mathematics," when the insertion point is in mathematics, the program

- Interprets anything you type as mathematics.
- Italicizes alphabetic characters and displays numbers upright.
- Automatically formats expressions and inserts space around operators such as $+$ and relations such as $=$.
- Advances the insertion point to the next mathematical object when you press the spacebar.

On the screen, document shells distinguish between text and mathematics in the document window: text appears in black and mathematics in red. Chapter 8 "Formatting Documents" describes how to change the default colors.

Toggling Between Text and Mathematics

The Math/Text button on the Standard toolbar indicates whether the insertion point is in text or mathematics. You can *toggle,* or change from text to mathematics and back, several different ways.

▶ **To start or return to text**

- On the Standard toolbar, click the Math/Text button to switch to [T] .
  or
- From the Insert menu, choose Text.
  or
- Press one of these keyboard shortcuts for changing from mathematics to text: INSERT or CTRL+M or CTRL+T.

▶ **To start or return to mathematics**

- On the Standard toolbar, click the Math/Text button to switch to [M] .
  or
- From the Insert menu, choose Math.
  or
- Press one of these keyboard shortcuts for changing from text to mathematics: INSERT or CTRL+M or CTRL+T.

You can customize the toggle between text and mathematics in several other ways, as described in Chapter 12 "Customizing the Program."

Entering and Editing Text

Entering text in *SWP, SW,* and *SNB* is straightforward.

▶ **To enter text**

- Move the insertion point to where you want to begin typing, make sure the Math/Text

  toggle appears as [T] , and type the text from the keyboard.

You may need to include special text characters and symbols in your documents, especially if you work in a language other than English. You can enter special characters and symbols using the mouse or the keyboard, as explained later in this section, or with fragments, as explained on page 55. See Chapter 4 "Creating Mathematics" for information about entering mathematical symbols and characters.

Standard clipboard, drag-and-drop, and Context menu operations are available to cut, copy, paste, and delete selections. These standard editing operations and two special editing tools, the spell check feature and the find and replace feature, are described in Chapter 6 "Using Editing Techniques and Tools."

You can also edit the appearance and structure of the text by adding emphasis such as boldface or italics, by creating section headings, and by creating lists, as described later in this chapter. Chapter 8 "Formatting Documents" contains additional details about adding and deleting space, inserting page breaks, and modifying other aspects of the document format.

A third way to edit text is by changing the *properties* of individual characters. For example, you may want to add an accent to a character so that *a* becomes *ä*.

▶ **To edit the properties of a character**

1. Select the character or place the insertion point to its right.

2. Choose **Properties**:

   - On the Standard toolbar, click the Properties button [Q] .
     or
   - From the **Edit** menu, choose **Properties**.
     or
   - Press CTRL+F5.
     or

   - Click the right mouse button or press the Application key [icon] to open the **Context** menu and then choose **Properties**.

3. In the **Character Properties** dialog box, make the changes you want.

4. Choose **OK**.

Typing Special Characters

You can enter special characters and symbols from the Latin-1 and Latin Extended-A panels on the Symbol Panels toolbar, as shown on page 8. If you use certain characters frequently, you can add them to the Symbol Cache toolbar, as described on page 9. Then, you can enter them with a single click of the mouse. Also, if a character has a LaTeX name, you can enter the character from the keyboard. Entering TeX command names requires a different process; see page 369.

▶ **To enter a character or symbol from a symbol panel**

1. On the Symbol Panels toolbar,

   - Click [£ 1] to open the Latin-1 panel.
     or
   - Click [Łĕ] to open the Latin Extended-A panel.

2. Click the character or symbol you want.

▶ **To enter a character or symbol from the Symbol Cache toolbar**

- Click the symbol or character you want.

▶ **To enter a character or symbol from the keyboard**

- Press CTRL+*name*, where *name* is the LaTeX name of the character.
  As an illustration, to obtain the ® symbol, hold down the CTRL key while you type **textregistered**.

Typing ANSI Characters

If your keyboard has a numeric keypad, you can use it to enter ANSI characters. Appendix B "Keyboard Shortcuts" contains a table of ANSI characters and their associated numbers.

▶ **To enter an ANSI character**

1. Hold down the ALT key.

2. On the numeric keypad, enter **0**.

3. On the numeric keypad, enter the number for the ANSI character you want.

   For example, to enter ¥, enter **0165** on the keypad.

4. Release the ALT key.

Typing Accented Characters

Characters accented with special symbols, such as ~ or ^, are common in languages other than English. You can use the mouse to enter an accented character from the Latin-1 and Latin Extended-A Unicode panels on the Symbol Panels toolbar (page 7), or you can type a character and add an accent to it. Accents above and below the character are available:

Accents above the character

Accents below the character

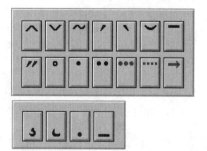

Certain accents, which appear in red in the Character Properties dialog box, force the program into mathematics:

$$\ddot{o} \qquad \dddot{o} \qquad \vec{o}$$

▶ **To enter an accented character from a symbol panel**

1. On the Symbol Panels toolbar, click [£¹] to open the Latin-1 panel or [Lě] to open the Latin Extended-A panel.

2. Click the accented character you want.

▶ **To add an accent to a typed character**

1. Select the character you want to accent or place the insertion point to its right.

2. Choose Properties.

3. Select the accent you want from the Character Properties dialog box, and choose OK.

or

Double-click the accent.

You can enter some character accents with keyboard shortcuts. See Appendix B "Keyboard Shortcuts" for a complete list.

Typing Punctuation

Besides the standard symbols that appear on your keyboard, the program recognizes several common punctuation marks and symbols. The program recognizes curled opening and closing quotation marks (" and "), inverted question marks (¿), and inverted exclamation points (¡). Similarly, in addition to the hyphen (-) used to create compound words such as *double-sided* or *sister-in-law,* the program recognizes the *en dash* (–) used for number or time ranges, as in 4–9 or March–May, and the *em dash* (—) used to mark parenthetical information or a summary phrase or clause, as shown in the next sentence. The program recognizes all three punctuation marks—the hyphen, the en dash, and the em dash.

You can enter these punctuation marks with the mouse or with special keystrokes. When you use keystrokes, you use more than one keystroke to enter a punctuation mark. For example, to enter an en dash, you press the hyphen key (-) twice. Regardless of the number of keystrokes you use to enter a punctuation mark, the program interprets each mark as a single symbol.

▶ **To enter a punctuation mark from a symbol panel**

1. On the Symbol Panels toolbar, click [£¹] to open the Latin-1 panel or [" "] to open the General Punctuation panel.

2. Click the punctuation mark you want.

▶ **To enter a punctuation mark with special keystrokes**

- Use the keystrokes in the following table:

To enter	With the keyboard
- (hyphen)	Press -
– (en dash)	Press - two times
— (em dash)	Press - three times
¿	Press ? then press the backprime mark (')
¡	Press ! then press the backprime mark (')
"	Press the backprime mark (') two times

Automatic hyphenation deserves special mention. The program automatically hyphenates the text when you typeset your document but not when you produce it without typesetting or when you use *SNB*. However, you can request *discretionary,* or conditional, hyphenation for specific words in case they occur at the end of a line. If you've inserted a discretionary hyphen in a word, the program will break the word at that point if necessary, both in print and, if Invisibles are turned on, in the document window. For more information about breaks, see Making Final Formatting Adjustments, page 192.

▶ **To enter a discretionary hyphen**

1. Place the insertion point where you want the word to break, if necessary.

2. From the Insert menu, choose Spacing.

3. Choose Break.

4. Choose Discretionary hyphen and then choose OK.

Typing Numbers Using the Numeric Keypad

When typing numbers, you may prefer to use the numeric keypad, which has keys and numbers arranged like those on a conventional adding machine. The function of the keypad depends on the NUM LOCK key:

- With NUM LOCK on, you can type numbers and mathematical symbols using the keypad.

- With NUM LOCK off, you can move the insertion point using the keypad.

The Status bar displays the current state of the NUM LOCK key. The designation NUM indicates that NUM LOCK is on.

▶ **To enter numbers from the numeric keypad**

1. Turn NUM LOCK on.

2. Type the number.

Entering Text with Fragments

In the course of your work, you may find that you need to type some text items, such as your name or address, again and again. You can store these frequently typed items as *fragments*—information saved in separate files for later recall—and import them into your documents with a minimum of commands.

The program comes with many predefined fragments. The most commonly used fragments are stored in the `Frags` directory of your program installation. The subdirectory `Constants` houses many predefined mathematics fragments, such as **Mean value theorem**, that contain common equations or theorems. Chapter 4 "Creating Mathematics" contains more information about them. Note that some fragments contain fields that appear as small gray boxes on the screen. When you typeset the document in *SWP* or *SW*, the fields are interpreted correctly.

You can create new fragments and you can import previously defined fragments into the current document. A fragment that you save while working in one document is available to all documents.

▶ **To display a list of all fragments in the Frags directory**

- Click the Fragments popup list .
  or

- From the **File** menu, choose **Import Fragment**.
  or

- Press ALT+4.
  Because the fragments in the `Frags` directory are used more often, the program lists them first, followed by those in the `Constants` subdirectory and any other subdirectories you add. Fragments in subdirectories are indented in the list so you can distinguish them easily.

Importing Fragments

When you import a fragment, its contents are pasted into your document at the insertion point.

▶ **To import a fragment**

1. Place the insertion point where you want to import the fragment.

2. Import the fragment:

   a. Click the Fragments popup list or press ALT+4.
   b. Click the name of the fragment you want, or use the arrow keys to select the fragment and press ENTER.

   or

   a. From the **File** menu, choose **Import Fragment**.
   b. Select the fragment you want and choose **Open**.

or

- Press CTRL+**name**, where **name** is the name of the fragment you want to insert. This method works only for fragments with names at least two characters long.

Note   If you use the CTRL+**name** shortcut to insert a fragment that has the same name as a TeX command, the program inserts the TeX command instead of the fragment. See Appendix B "Keyboard Shortcuts" for a list of TeX commands that the program recognizes and see Chapter 4 "Creating Mathematics" for information about using TeX commands.

Creating Fragments

A fragment can contain both text and mathematics and can carry tags. When you create a fragment, the program saves it by default with an extension of .frg. Also by default, the program saves the fragment in the Frags directory so it is displayed closer to the top of the fragments list. If you prefer, you can save your fragment in a subdirectory within the Frags directory. You can also save your fragment in any other directory; however, if you do, the fragment name won't appear on the Fragments popup list or in the Import Fragment dialog box. You can change the default directory for fragments; see Chapter 12 "Customizing the Program."

▶ **To create a fragment**

1. Select the information that you want to save as a fragment.

2. On the Fragments toolbar, click the Save Fragments button [icon] or, from the File menu, choose Save Fragment.

3. Type a file name to be used to recall the fragment.

   Avoid using the name of a TeX command for your fragment. Appendix B "Keyboard Shortcuts" contains a list of TeX commands recognized by the program.

4. Unless you want to create a new subdirectory to hold the fragment, leave the directory unchanged.

5. Choose Save.

If you have saved the fragment in the Frags directory or one of its subdirectories, the program immediately inserts its name in the fragments list.

Deleting Fragments

You can delete a fragment you no longer need. If you delete a fragment provided with the program, you can recover it by reinstalling the software.

▶ **To delete a fragment**

1. From the File menu, choose Import Fragment.

2. Select the fragment you want to delete from the Frags directory or the directory in which the fragment resides.

3. Press DELETE and choose Yes to confirm the deletion.

4. Choose Cancel to close the dialog box.

Using Tags with Text

Many document formatting tasks are accomplished by applying *tags*. Tags are collections of formatting and behavior properties that affect the appearance, structure, and content of your document. Tag properties determine the appearance of these document elements, among many others:

- Fonts.

- Paragraphs and headings.

- List items and lead-in objects.

- Plot captions.

- Mathematics.

When you apply a tag to information in your document, the program applies the properties of the tag to the information.

Several kinds of tags are available:

- *Text tags* emphasize words or phrases within a paragraph.

- *Section tags* define whole paragraphs as section headings and provide the structure of your document.

- *Body tags* define the structure to the main text of your document.

- *Item tags* define whole paragraphs as items in some kind of list, as a theorem or theorem-like statement, or as front matter.

In other words, text tags define emphasis within paragraphs; section and body tags define the structure of paragraphs within documents; and item tags define items in a series, with each item consisting of one or more paragraphs.

By using tags, you can create a consistent appearance throughout your document without having to format each element individually. Each time you tag a paragraph in your document as, say, a subsection, you'll produce a heading paragraph whose text appears in a consistent font size and typeface and with consistent indention. No further formatting is required. All paragraphs tagged as subsections will have the same appearance, both in the current document and in all documents created with the same shell.

The appearance and behavior of tagged information depends on the properties of the corresponding tag. In *SWP* and *SW*, the tag properties are *defined twice* for each shell: once in the typesetting specifications, which are used when you typeset the document, and once in the style (.cst file), which is used when you display your document in the document window or produce it without typesetting. The two property definitions for a given tag may differ significantly even though the name of the tag is the same. In *SWP* and *SW,* the way you produce your document determines which property definition is used and, consequently, how your document appears on the preview screen or in print. See Chapter 8 "Formatting Documents" for more information about how styles and typesetting specifications affect tags and tagged information, and see Chapter 7 "Previewing and Printing" about producing documents with and without typesetting.

Applying Tags

You can apply tags from the popup lists on the Tag toolbar, with the Apply command on the Tag menu, or with the function keys on the keyboard. When you apply a text tag, the program applies the tag to the current selection or, if you haven't made a selection, to the next thing you type. When you apply an item tag or a section/body tag, the program applies the tag to the paragraph containing the insertion point.

Not all tags are available in all environments. For example, you can't enter a section tag within a list. When a tag isn't available, it doesn't appear on the corresponding popup list.

▶ **To apply a tag from a popup list**

1. On the Tag toolbar, click the popup box or press the shortcut for the list containing the item tag, section/body tag, or text tag you want.

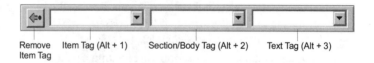

Remove   Item Tag (Alt + 1)   Section/Body Tag (Alt + 2)   Text Tag (Alt + 3)
Item Tag

2. Click the tag you want to apply.

▶ **To apply a tag using the Apply command**

1. From the Tag menu, choose Apply.

2. From the Apply Tag dialog box, select the tag you want and choose OK.

▶ **To apply a tag using the function keys**

• Press the function key assigned to the tag you want.
  By default, the function keys on your keyboard are assigned to certain tags:

Key	Tag	Key	Tag
F2	Remove Item Tag	F7	Numbered item
F3	Body Text	F8	Bullet item
F4	Normal	F9	Typewriter
F5	Bold	F11	Section head
F6	Emphasized	F12	Subsection head

However, function key assignments may change, depending on the style (.cst file) for your document. See Chapter 8 "Formatting Documents" for a discussion of styles. Also, you can change the key assignments with the Function Keys command on the Tag menu. See Chapter 12 "Customizing the Program" for more information.

Adding Emphasis with Text Tags

You can use text tags to add emphasis to text or to differentiate words or phrases within a paragraph. Although many text tags have names that indicate content, such as *Define* or *Typewriter,* others have names that indicate appearance, such as *Bold* or *Italics.* Text that doesn't carry any special emphasis is tagged as Normal. The text tags that are available and the appearance of those tags in the document window and in print depend on the document shell and its style and typesetting specifications.

Regardless of the name of the tag, you should think of text tags as adding meaning to words by emphasizing them in some way. For example, in this manual, we emphasize certain words *like this* to indicate program terminology. That is, we add to their meaning by indicating that they have special use within the context of the program. Some tags, such as Calligraphic, start mathematics automatically; see page 105. Note that the properties of other tags, such as section tags used for headings, may also produce emphasized text. In that case, when you apply the section tag to a selection, the selection will automatically appear emphasized.

▶ **To apply a text tag to a selection**

1. Select the text you want to tag.

2. Apply the tag.

   You can apply several frequently used text tags (Normal, Bold, Italic, and Emphasized) with these buttons on the Editing toolbar: **N** , **B** , *I* , and *E* .

▶ **To apply a text tag to the next information you type**

1. Apply the tag you want.

2. Type the text you want to tag.

3. Apply the Normal tag so that the next text you type isn't emphasized.

▶ **To remove a text tag**

- Select the tagged text and apply the Normal tag.

   Text tags are applied individually rather than in combination. However, if you occasionally want to create special text effects, you can apply more than one text tag to a selection by carefully nesting the tags. In the example below, the sentence and the spaces at either end of the sentence have been tagged as Typewriter. The middle of the sentence, but not the first and last words, has been tagged as Bold. The phrase *example of multiple* and the spaces at either end of the phrase have been tagged as Large. The word *multiple,* but not the spaces on either side of it, has been tagged as Italic. This is the result:

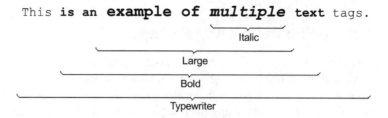

Note that if you try to apply multiple tags to selections that share the same start or end points, the program doesn't accumulate the tags. Instead, it uses the tag you applied most recently to format the selection.

Adding Structure with Section and Body Tags

Section and body tags define the structure of most *SWP, SW,* and *SNB* documents. Each paragraph automatically has an associated tag, usually Body Text. The section and body tags that are available and their appearance in the document window and in print depend on the document shell and its style.

Body tags structure individual paragraphs. The program considers all text to be body text, unless it has another body or section tag. Most shells provide body tags for centering a paragraph, setting off a quotation from the main body of the document, and creating a paragraph that automatically starts mathematics.

▶ **To apply a body tag**

1. Place the insertion point in the paragraph you want to tag. If you haven't yet typed the paragraph, place the insertion point where you want the paragraph to begin.

2. Apply a body tag.

3. Type the paragraph if it doesn't already exist.

Note   If you want to apply a body paragraph tag to several consecutive paragraphs, make a selection that starts anywhere in the first paragraph and ends anywhere in the last paragraph. Then, apply the tag. The program applies the tag to any paragraph that contains a part of the selection, even if the entire paragraph wasn't selected.

▶ **To change a tagged paragraph to body text**

1. Place the insertion point in the paragraph.

2. Apply the Body Text tag.

▶ **To center a paragraph**

1. Place the insertion point in the paragraph you want to tag. If you haven't yet typed the paragraph, place the insertion point where you want the paragraph to begin.

2. Apply a tag for centering.

3. Type the paragraph if it doesn't already exist.

Section tags define the major divisions of your document and provide the heading structure. By applying section tags to whole paragraphs in your document, you can create multiple levels of headings, such as chapters, sections, subsections, and so on. Headings can contain mathematics and graphics. Section tags aren't available in certain environments, such as lists.

The Section Headings box in the Navigate toolbar serves as an online table of contents for your document and as a navigational tool. Chapter 1 "Understanding the Workplace" contains more information about navigating from section to section.

▶ **To apply a section tag**

1. Place the insertion point in the paragraph to be tagged as a section heading. If you haven't yet typed the paragraph, place the insertion point where you want the paragraph to begin.

2. Apply a section tag.

3. Type the paragraph if it doesn't yet exist.

▶ **To remove a section tag**

1. Place the insertion point in the tagged text.

2. Apply the Body Text tag.

The program returns the paragraph to body text.

▶ **To move to a particular section in the current document**

1. On the Navigate toolbar, click the Section Heading popup list or press ALT+5.

The Section Heading box lists the headings in the document and highlights the heading of the section that contains the insertion point. See Chapter 8 "Formatting Documents" for information about displaying section headings in the Navigate toolbar.

2. In the list, click the section heading you want.

The program moves to that section and places the insertion point at the beginning of the heading.

Creating Lists with Item Tags

A list is a series of items, each consisting of one or more paragraphs and each beginning with a specific *lead-in object:* an automatically generated number, a bullet, or some customized text that you supply. You can create lists up to four layers deep and you can create *nested lists,* or lists within lists.

You create lists and enter lead-in objects with item tags. You can enter the item tag first and then create the list item, or you can apply an item tag to an existing paragraph. The item tag in effect at the insertion point is named in the Item Tag popup box. Note that list tags aren't available in certain environments, such as headings.

The available item tags depend on the document shell. Most shells have a Numbered List Item tag that produces lists similar to this one:

1. First item

2. Second item
   a. Sub-item
   b. Sub-item

3. Third item

Most shells also have a Bullet List Item tag that produces lists similar to this one:

- First item
- Second item
  - Sub-item
  - Sub-item
- Third item

The Description List Item tag available in most shells produces lists with lead-in objects that you supply, perhaps like this:

Lead-in One	First item
Lead-in Two	Second item
Sub one	Sub-item
Sub two	Sub-item
Lead-in Three	Third item

If you don't supply a lead-in object for an item in a description list, the list item appears with no lead-in object, by itself on the line, like the items in this list:

First item
Second item
   Sub-item
   Sub-item
Third item

The appearance of item tags in the document window and in print depends on the document shell and its style and typesetting specifications. See Chapter 8 "Formatting Documents" for more information about how styles and typesetting specifications affect the appearance of tagged information.

Theorems and theorem-like statements are created as list items; see Chapter 4 "Creating Mathematics" for details. Bibliographies are also created as lists, as described in Chapter 9 "Structuring Documents for Typesetting."

▶ **To enter a list**

1. Press ENTER to begin a new paragraph.

2. Apply the item tag for a numbered, bulleted, or description list.

   The program displays the lead-in object and provides the correct indention. For description lists, the program opens a **Properties** dialog box for the lead-in object:

   a. In the **Label** area, enter a lead-in object.
   b. Choose **OK**.

3. Type the list item and press ENTER.

   Each time you press ENTER to begin a new paragraph, the program assumes you're starting a new list item and automatically provides the correct lead-in object and indention.

4. If you want the new paragraph to be part of the preceding list item, create a continuation paragraph:

   a. Press BACKSPACE to delete the automatic lead-in object at the start of the continuation paragraph.
   b. Type the continuation paragraph.
   c. Press ENTER to create the next list item.

   Continuation paragraphs, such as this one, extend the ideas expressed in the first paragraph of the list item. They don't have a separate lead-in object.

5. Repeat steps 3 and 4 to enter all the list items.

6. End the list:

   a. On the Tag toolbar, click the Remove Item Tag button .
      or
   b. Press the function key for Remove Item Tag. The default assignment is F2.
      or
   c. From the **Tag** menu, choose **Apply**, select **Remove Item Tag**, and then choose **OK**.
      Note that if the last list item is nested several layers deep in the list, you must apply Remove Item Tag more than once to end the list.

▶ **To apply a list tag to an existing paragraph**

1. Place the insertion point in the paragraph.

2. Apply the tag for the type of list you want.

Creating Nested Lists

You can nest list items up to four levels deep by applying multiple list item tags to the item paragraphs. Each application of the list item tag nests the paragraph at a deeper level, as shown here:

1. This paragraph carries one list item tag.

  a. This paragraph carries two list item tags.

    i This paragraph carries three list item tags.

      (1) This paragraph carries four list item tags.

        ⋮

You can mix list types in a nested list:

1. First level item

  a. Second level item

    i Third level item

      • Fourth level item

        ⋮

The Item Tag popup box on the Tag toolbar indicates the item tag most recently applied to the paragraph containing the insertion point.

▶ **To create a nested list**

- Start a new list while the insertion point is inside an existing list.
  The program creates and displays a lead-in object for the nested list item.

  To remove nesting from a list paragraph, use the Remove Item Tag to remove the most recently applied item tag from the paragraph containing the insertion point. For example, if you remove an item tag while the insertion point is in item 1.c of this list:

        1. Software Companies
          a. Company A
          b. Company B
          c. MacKichan Software, Inc.
        2. Hardware Companies

the list will look like this:

        1. Software Companies
          a. Company A
          b. Company B
        2. MacKichan Software, Inc.
        3. Hardware Companies

with MacKichan Software, Inc. in a class by itself.

▶ **To remove the most recently applied item tag**

1. Place the insertion point in the tagged text.

2. On the Tag toolbar, click the Remove Item Tag button .

   or

   From the Tag menu, choose Apply, select (Remove Item Tag), and choose OK.

   or

   Press the function key assigned to the Remove Item Tag button. The default is F2.

▶ **To leave an inner list**

- Press ENTER to create a new list paragraph and then remove the item tag.

Restarting the Numbering of a List

You can reset the lead-in number at any point in a numbered list.

1. Open the Lead Item Properties dialog box for the item with which you want to begin renumbering:

   - Double-click the lead-in object.

     or

   - Place the insertion point immediately to the right of the lead-in object and then choose Properties.

2. Check the Reset box and choose OK.

   The program will set numbering back to 1 at the current level.

Customizing Lead-in Objects

You can customize the lead-in object for any kind of list. The contents of a lead-in object must be contained in a single paragraph, and can include text, mathematics, and special characters. You can apply tags to the contents, as in this description list:

First $\left(a^2\right)$ Item one in a description list.

Second $\left(b^2\right)$ Item two. The lead-in object is in boldface.

Third $\left(c^2\right)$ Item three. The lead-in object is in italics.

When you produce your document without typesetting it, a list with customized lead-in objects appears much as it does in the document window. When you typeset your document, the appearance of customized lead-in objects depends on the typesetting specifications for the list. For more information, see Chapter 8 "Formatting Documents."

In a description list, each item is preceded by a lead-in object containing customized text that you supply. You determine the contents of the lead-in object, and the style and the typesetting specifications for your document determine the appearance. In most document shells, the length of the lead-in object determines the left edge of the description list item itself (as in the list above), regardless of whether or not you typeset the document.

In a numbered or bulleted list, each item is preceded by a lead-in object containing an automatically generated number or bullet. You can replace the contents of the lead-in object with any text, mathematics, or special characters you want. When you produce the document without typesetting it, the list appears much as it does in the document window. However, when you typeset the document, the text of the list items usually aligns at a left margin determined by the typesetting specifications. Therefore, a customized lead-in object for a numbered or bulleted list may extend into the left margin of the page, like this:

First (a^2) Item one in a numbered list with customized lead-in objects.

Second (b^2) Item two.

Third (c^2) Item three.

▶ **To supply a customized lead-in object for an existing list item**

1. Select the lead-in object or place the insertion point immediately to its right and then choose **Properties**.

   or

   Double-click the lead-in object.

2. In the **Level** box, set the level of the lead-in object you want to customize.

3. Click **Custom**.

4. Type the text you want to appear in the lead-in object, and choose **OK**.

4   Creating Mathematics

Entering mathematics is straightforward. You can focus on content when you're entering mathematics, just as when you're entering text. You use familiar mathematical notation to enter mathematical characters, symbols, and objects into your document, and you use simple commands to create displayed or in-line mathematics. The program automatically displays your mathematics correctly in the document window.

Editing mathematics is equally straightforward. You can edit mathematics using standard clipboard and drag-and-drop operations to cut, copy, paste, and delete selections. Also, you can use the find and replace feature to locate or change mathematical information. Although the program automatically formats your mathematics according to internationally accepted standards, you may occasionally want to edit the appearance of your mathematics by changing the properties of symbols, characters, objects, and displays.

This chapter explains how the program treats mathematics and gives instructions for entering and editing mathematical information. It explains how to enter mathematical symbols and characters and how to create automatically formatted objects, such as fractions, radicals, and operators. It also explains how to create in-line and displayed mathematics, including multiline displays, and how to use tags with mathematics.

Understanding Mathematics and Text

Nearly always, the program defaults to text. When you start the program, the Math/Text button on the Standard toolbar appears as $\boxed{\text{T}}$. This means that the insertion point is in text. The program assumes that whatever you enter is text until you tell it you want to enter mathematics. Then the button appears as $\boxed{\text{M}}$.

Understanding the Differences

Mathematics and text are treated differently. When the insertion point is in mathematics, the program

- Interprets what you type as mathematics.
- Italicizes alphabetic characters.
- Displays numbers upright.
- Automatically inserts space around operators such as + and relations such as =.
- Formats mathematics according to internationally recognized standards and provides correct spacing in expressions.
- Recognizes math names and displays them according to the Math defaults established in the User Setup dialog box.

- Advances the insertion point to the next object when you press the spacebar.
- Inserts a prime character when you press the close quotation mark key (').

On the other hand, when the insertion point is in text, the program

- Interprets what you type as text.
- Displays alphabetic characters upright rather than in italics.
- Inserts a space when you press the spacebar, unless you change the defaults established in the User Setup dialog box.

On the screen, document shells use color to distinguish between mathematics and text. The default color for mathematics is red; the default color for text is black. Math names for functions, operators, and variables are shown in gray. You can change these default colors by modifying the properties of the corresponding tags, as described in Chapter 8 "Formatting Documents."

The program automatically formats your mathematics correctly when you display or print your document. You can duplicate your mathematics by pasting or exporting a graphic image of selected mathematics, formatted exactly as it appears in the document window, to documents created with other word processing or Internet applications. See Chapter 5 "Using Graphics and Tables" for more information.

Toggling Between Mathematics and Text

The Math/Text button on the Standard toolbar indicates whether the insertion point is in text or mathematics. You can change from text to mathematics and back again several different ways. Use the method you prefer.

▶ **To start or return to mathematics**

- On the Standard toolbar, click the Math/Text button to switch to $\boxed{\text{M}}$.
  or
- From the Insert menu, choose Math.
  or
- Press one of these keyboard shortcuts for changing from text to mathematics: INSERT or CTRL+M or CTRL+T.

Note   If you insert a mathematical symbol, character, or object from one of the toolbars or from the Insert menu, the program automatically changes to mathematics.

▶ **To start or return to text**

- On the Standard toolbar, click the Math/Text button to switch to $\boxed{\text{T}}$.
  or
- From the Insert menu, choose Text.
  or
- Press one of these keyboard shortcuts for changing from mathematics to text: INSERT or CTRL+M or CTRL+T.

You can customize the toggle between text and mathematics in several other ways. See Chapter 12 "Customizing the Program" for more information.

Understanding In-Line and Displayed Mathematics

In-line and *displayed* mathematics behave differently. In-line mathematics appears in a line of text. By default, any operators are sized to fit within the line, and limits are positioned to the right of operators and functions. The numerators and denominators of fractions are set in small type; for example,

$$\ldots \text{ and let } S = \sum_{n=1}^{k} \frac{a_n + b_n}{c_n}. \text{ Then } S \text{ is } \ldots$$

Displayed mathematics appears centered on a separate line and set off from the information above and below by additional space. Operators within the display are larger than in-line operators, limits are positioned above and below operators and functions, and the numerators and denominators of fractions are set in full-size type, like this:

$$\ldots \text{ and let}$$
$$S = \sum_{n=1}^{k} \frac{a_n + b_n}{c_n}$$
$$\text{Then } S \text{ is } \ldots$$

The program assumes you want to enter in-line mathematics unless you tell it otherwise. See page 98 for instructions and more information about displayed mathematics.

Entering and Editing Symbols and Characters

You can enter and edit mathematics as naturally as you enter and edit text.

Entering Symbols and Characters

The program provides many options for entering symbols and characters. With the mouse, you can enter symbols and characters directly from the symbol panels and the Symbol Cache toolbar. You can add the symbols you use most frequently to the Symbol Cache toolbar, as described on page 9. With the keyboard, you can enter Greek letters and many symbols using special key prefixes, as shown in Appendix B "Keyboard Shortcuts." If you know TEX, you can enter symbols and characters by holding down the CTRL key and typing the corresponding TEX commands. Also, you can enter text and then convert it to mathematics. The prime symbol requires special mention.

▶ **To enter symbols and characters from the toolbars**

- Click the symbol or character you want on the Symbol Cache toolbar.

or

- On the Symbol Panels toolbar, click the panel you want and then click the symbol or character.

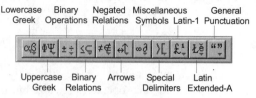

▶ To enter symbols from the keyboard

- Press CTRL+S and then press the key for the symbol you want.
  Appendix B "Keyboard Shortcuts" provides the keyboard mapping for mathematical symbols. For example, to enter $\sum$, press CTRL+S and then press S.

▶ To enter Greek characters

- On the Symbol Panels toolbar, click [αβ] or [ΦΨ] and then click the character you want.
  or

- Press CTRL+G and then press the key for the character you want.
  or

- Hold down the CTRL key and enter the TEX command for the character you want.

Appendix B "Keyboard Shortcuts" provides the keyboard mapping and TEX commands for uppercase and lowercase Greek characters.

▶ To enter symbols and characters with TEX

1. Hold down the CTRL key.

2. Omitting the initial backslash (\), type the TEX command for the symbol or character you want and then release the CTRL key.

For example, if you hold down the CTRL key and type **sigma,** the program inserts σ into your document. The program recognizes the TEX commands listed in Appendix B "Keyboard Shortcuts."

▶ To convert text to mathematics

- Select the text you want to convert to mathematics and then start mathematics.
  The program converts the selection to mathematics, removing all ordinary spaces in the selection.

The prime symbol is a large character that sits on the baseline. You can create expressions such as y' by placing the prime symbol in a superscript. The superscript raises the character and scales down its size. When the insertion point is in mathematics, you can create expressions containing primes either with the mouse or with the keyboard, but the two methods are very different. If you use the mouse to enter a prime, the program neither positions nor scales the symbol. If you use the keyboard to enter a prime, the program positions and scales the symbol automatically.

▶ **To enter a prime with the mouse**

1. On the Math Templates toolbar, click the Superscript button $\boxed{N^x}$ or, from the Insert menu, choose **Superscript**.

2. Open the Miscellaneous Symbols panel on the Symbol Panels toolbar and click the prime character $\boxed{\prime}$.

3. Press the spacebar or RIGHT ARROW to leave the superscript.

▶ **To enter a prime with the keyboard**

- With the insertion point in mathematics, press the close quotation mark key (').
  The program scales down the prime character and places it in a superscript, and then returns the insertion point to the main line.

Editing Symbol and Character Properties

In addition to editing symbols and characters with the standard clipboard and drag-and-drop operations described in Chapter 6 "Using Editing Techniques and Tools," you can edit the properties of mathematical symbols and characters.

▶ **To edit the properties of a mathematical symbol or character**

1. Select the symbol or character or place the insertion point to its right.

2. Choose **Properties**:

   - On the Standard toolbar, click the Properties button $\boxed{Q}$.
     or
   - From the Edit or Context menu, choose **Properties**.
     or
   - Press CTRL+F5.
     The program opens the **Character Properties** dialog box.

3. Make the changes you want and choose **OK**.

Adding Mathematical Accents

You can edit the properties of a symbol or character to add a mathematical accent. Symbols and characters can carry these mathematical accents, which are available from the **Character Properties** dialog box:

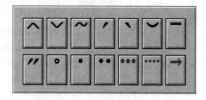

Accents above the character

Accents below the character

Certain accents, which appear in red in the dialog box, force the program into mathematics:

$$\ddot{o} \qquad \dddot{o} \qquad \vec{o}$$

▶ **To add a mathematical accent**

1. Enter the symbol or character to be accented.

   or

   Select an existing symbol or character or place the insertion point to its right.

2. Add the accent:

   a. Choose **Properties**.
   b. From the **Character Properties** dialog box,
      Select the accent you want to add and choose **OK**.
      or
      Double-click the accent.

You can enter some accents from the keyboard. See Appendix B "Keyboard Shortcuts."

▶ **To remove a mathematical accent**

1. Position the insertion point to the right of the accented symbol or character.

2. Choose **Properties**.

3. Click the selected accent to deselect it.

4. Choose **OK**.

Adding Negation

Because their typeset appearance is superior, we recommend that whenever possible you use the Negated Relations symbol panel to enter negated symbols and characters. Alternatively, you can edit the properties of symbols and characters to add or remove negation. Note that if you enter negated symbols and characters from the Negated Relations panel, you can't remove the negation by editing the properties of the symbol or character.

▶ **To negate a character or symbol**

1. Enter the symbol or character to be negated.

   or

   Select an existing symbol or character or place the insertion point to its right.

2. Edit the character or symbol properties:
   - Choose Properties, check Negate, and then choose OK.
     or
   - Type CTRL+N.

▶ **To remove negation from a symbol or character**

1. Select or position the insertion point to the right of the negated character.

2. Choose Properties.

3. In the Character Properties dialog box, uncheck Negate.

4. Choose OK.

Entering and Editing Mathematical Objects

You can enter mathematical objects—such as fractions, subscripts, and integrals—from the Math toolbars and from the Insert menu. Many of the most common objects also have keyboard shortcuts. Some mathematical objects, such as fractions and radicals, have defaults that you can customize. See Chapter 12 "Customizing the Program" for more information.

Entering Objects with Templates

When you enter a mathematical object in your document, the program inserts a *template* representing the object and places the insertion point within the template in an *input box* so you can complete the object. The input boxes appear on screen if you turn on the Input Boxes command on the View menu.

For example, when you select the Fraction command or click the Fraction button, the program inserts a fraction template that shows a horizontal bar between two small input boxes. The input boxes represent the numerator and the denominator. The insertion point appears in the numerator box, like this:

Depending on the object it represents, a template may have several small input boxes. Some input boxes are hidden. For example, depending on the default settings for your installation, when you enter a radical, the program displays this:

If you then press TAB, the insertion point moves to an input box for the root, which appears like this:

$$\sqrt[\square]{\square}$$

Templates expand as necessary. Bracket and radical templates expand both horizontally and vertically to encompass their contents; fraction bars extend as far as necessary to encompass the longest string of characters within the fraction; and matrix cells expand as needed.

Until you move the insertion point outside the template, the program includes anything you enter as part of the object. When you've completed the object, click to the right of the template with the mouse or press the spacebar or repeatedly press RIGHT ARROW until the insertion point moves outside the template.

▶ To enter a mathematical object

- On either of the Math toolbars, click the button for the object you want.
  or

- From the Insert menu, choose the object you want.
  or

- Press the keyboard shortcut for the object you want. See Appendix B "Keyboard Shortcuts" for a list of objects that you can enter quickly with shortcuts.
  The program inserts a template representing the object and places the insertion point in the template so you can complete the object.

Another way to create a mathematical object is by applying a template to a selection. You can also make a selection part of a template. Once you've created an object, you can delete its contents and retain the template or delete the object but retain the contents.

▶ To apply a template to a selection

1. Select the information to which you want to apply the template.

2. Enter the template for the mathematical object you want to create.

The program places your selection within the object. If the template has several input boxes, the program places the selection in the primary one.

▶ To make a selection part of a template

1. Enter the template for the mathematical object you want to create.

2. Select the information you want to place in the template.

3. Use drag-and-drop techniques to copy or move the selection to the template.

or

1. Make the selection.

2. Copy or cut the selection to the clipboard.

3. Enter the template.

4. Paste the selection into the template.

▶ **To delete a mathematical object**

1. Select the object.

2. Press DELETE or BACKSPACE or, from the Edit or Context menu, choose Delete.

▶ **To delete the contents of an object without deleting the template**

1. Select the contents of the input box.

2. Press DELETE or BACKSPACE or, from the Edit or Context menu, choose Delete.

▶ **To delete a template without deleting the contents**

- Place the insertion point to the left of the template and press DELETE.
  or

- Place the insertion point to the right of the template and press BACKSPACE.

Note   This process works differently when a template has more than one input box (except in the case of radicals and mathematical labels). If you've filled only the first input box, the program deletes the template without deleting the contents. If you've filled more than one input box, the program deletes the template as well as its contents.

▶ **To move from box to box within a template**

- Use the TAB key or the arrow keys.
  or

- Point to the input box you want and click.
  If you're entering the template in a dialog box, press the arrow keys, not the TAB key, to move from box to box. The TAB key moves the control to the next command.

Editing Mathematical Objects

To edit your mathematics, you can use standard clipboard and drag-and-drop operations to cut, copy, paste, and delete (see Chapter 6 "Using Editing Techniques and Tools"). Some objects have special editing features; they are discussed throughout this chapter. See also page 104 for information about using tags with mathematics. As with text, you can edit mathematical objects by changing their properties.

▶ **To edit the properties of a mathematical object**

1. Select the object or place the insertion point to its right.

2. Choose **Properties**:

   - On the Standard toolbar, click the **Properties** button $\boxed{Q}$.
   or

   - Click the right mouse button or press the Application key $\boxed{\textrm{\Epsilon}}$ to open the **Context** menu, and then choose **Properties**.
   or

   - Double-click the object.
   Be careful to double-click the object itself and not one of its fields. For example, you should double-click the bar of a fraction, not the numerator or denominator.
   or

   - From the **Edit** menu, choose **Properties**.
   or

   - Press CTRL+F5.

   The program opens a context-sensitive dialog box; that is, the dialog box that is opened depends on the selected object or, if you haven't made a selection, on the object to the left of the insertion point.

3. Make the changes you want and choose **OK**.

Entering Fractions and Binomials

Fractions and binomials are treated similarly. The program automatically extends the bar of a vertical fraction or binomial as far as necessary to encompass the entire fraction. By default, the numerator and denominator are set in a small-size font for in-line fractions, as in $\frac{a+b}{2}$, and in a full-sized font for displayed fractions, as in

$$\frac{a+b}{2}$$

For each fraction, you can override the defaults by changing the properties of the fraction. You can toggle on and off the fraction line, change the line thickness, or change the size of the numerator and denominator to achieve effects like these:

$$\frac{x}{1+\frac{x}{2}} \quad \frac{x}{1+\dfrac{x}{2}} \quad 1+\frac{x}{2}$$

You can change the defaults from the **Math** tab sheet in the **User Setup** dialog box. See Chapter 12 "Customizing the Program" for more information.

Note that you can enter a fraction of the type x/y by typing a slash to distinguish the numerator and denominator. Although you can use *SWP* or *SNB* to perform computations with them, fractions created with a slash have no automatic formatting features.

Fractions

▶ **To enter a vertical fraction**

- On the Math Templates toolbar, click the Fraction button ⊟ .
  or
- From the Insert menu, choose Fraction.
  or
- Type CTRL+F.
  See Appendix B "Keyboard Shortcuts" for other shortcuts.

▶ **To override the size defaults for a fraction**

1. Select the fraction or place the insertion point to its right.

2. Choose Properties.

3. In the Size options area of the Fraction Properties dialog box, choose Big or Small.

▶ **To return to the size defaults**

1. Select the fraction or place the insertion point to its right.

2. Choose Properties.

3. In the Size options area of the Fraction Properties dialog box, choose Auto.

   We encourage the use of the Auto default in most circumstances.

Binomials

The program treats binomials, the Legendre symbol, and Euler numbers as *generalized fractions:*

$$\text{Binomial} \qquad \binom{n}{k}$$

$$\text{Legendre symbol} \qquad \left(\frac{a}{b}\right)$$

$$\text{Euler number} \qquad \left\langle\frac{a}{b}\right\rangle$$

▶ **To enter a binomial or generalized fraction**

1. On the Math Objects toolbar, click the Binomial button (::) or, from the Insert menu, choose Binomial.

2. If you want delimiters for the binomial, select the left and right delimiters.

If you don't want delimiters, uncheck **With Delimiters**.

3. Make any necessary changes to the line and size and then choose **OK**.

4. Enter the expression.

Entering Radicals

When you enter a radical, an input box for the root appears in the template. If you don't want the input box to appear, you can change this default from the **Math** tab sheet in the **User Setup** dialog box. Radicals expand automatically to encompass the entire radicand.

▶ **To enter a radical**

- On the Math Templates toolbar, click the Radical button .
  or

- From the **Insert** menu, choose **Radical**.
  or

- Press CTRL+R.
  Additional keyboard shortcuts for entering a radical appear in Appendix B "Keyboard Shortcuts."

▶ **To add a root to a radical**

1. Select the radical or place the insertion point to its right.

2. Choose **Properties**.

   The program displays the **Radical Properties** dialog box.

3. Choose the template that shows a root.

4. Choose **OK**.

5. Enter the root.

   or

1. Place the insertion point under the radical.

2. Press TAB.

   If you're working in a dialog box, enter the radical with the template that shows a root, then press the UP ARROW key to move between the radicand and the root.

3. Enter the root.

▶ **To enclose an existing expression in a radical**

- Select the expression and enter a radical.

▶ **To remove a radical from an expression**

- Place the insertion point to the left of the radical and press DELETE.
  or

- Place the insertion point to the right of the radical and press BACKSPACE.

Entering Subscripts and Superscripts

You can enter subscripts and superscripts using the menu commands or the toolbar buttons. You can also create subscripts and superscripts by applying the templates to selections. The program automatically uses a smaller type size for text in subscripts and superscripts. See Entering Operators and Limits on page 80 for details about creating multiline subscripts and superscripts.

▶ **To enter a subscript**

- On the Math Templates toolbar, click the Subscript button N_x .
  or

- From the Insert menu, choose Subscript.
  or

- Press CTRL+L.

▶ **To enter a superscript**

- On the Math Templates toolbar, click the Superscript button N^x .
  or

- From the Insert menu, choose Superscript.
  or

- Press CTRL+H.

Appendix B "Keyboard Shortcuts" lists additional ways to enter sub- and superscripts.

If you enter a new subscript when the insertion point is outside and to the right of an existing subscript, the program doesn't insert a new subscript. Instead, it moves the insertion point into the existing subscript. Similarly, if you enter a new superscript when the insertion point is outside and to the right of an existing superscript, the program moves the insertion point into the existing superscript. On the other hand, if you enter a new subscript or superscript when the insertion point is inside an existing subscript or superscript, the program adds the new object.

▶ **To apply a subscript or superscript template to a selection**

1. Select the mathematics you want to be a subscript or a superscript.

2. Enter a subscript or superscript.

   The program places your selection in the template.

▶ **To create an expression with a simultaneous subscript and superscript**

1. Enter the expression.

2. Enter the subscript.

3. Press TAB.

4. Enter the superscript.

or

1. Enter the expression.

2. Enter the subscript.

3. Move the insertion point outside the subscript and to the right.

4. Enter the superscript.

Tip   With either method, you can enter the superscript first and then create the subscript.

Entering Operators and Limits

These operators are available from the **Operator** dialog box:

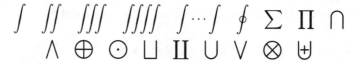

Two operators, $\sum$ and $\int$, are available from the Math Templates toolbar. Several operators—$\sum$, $\int$, $\prod$, $\oplus$, and $\otimes$—also have keyboard shortcuts. See Appendix B "Keyboard Shortcuts" for more information.

Entering Operators

▶ **To enter an operator**

1. On the Math Objects toolbar, click the Operator button ▨ .

   or

   From the **Insert** menu, choose **Operator**.

2. From the **Operator** dialog box, select the operator you want.

3. Choose OK.

Entering Limits

You add limits to operators using the Subscript and Superscript commands. By default, when an operator is in line, it is small and the limits are set to the right, like this: $\sum_{i=1}^{n} a_i$. When an operator is displayed, it is large and the limits are set above and below, like this:

$$\sum_{i=1}^{n} a_i$$

The exception is the integral operator, for which the default is that limits are always set to the right.

You can override these defaults when you enter the operator or when you edit its properties. However, we recommend that you choose the defaults (Auto for both Limit Position and Size) whenever possible.

▶ To enter limits for an operator

1. Enter the operator.

2. Enter a subscript.

3. Enter the lower limit.

4. Press TAB. (If you're entering the operator in a dialog box, use the arrow keys to move to the right of the operator, then enter a superscript.)

5. Enter the upper limit.

   Of course, you can enter the upper limit first and then enter the lower limit.

Multiline Limits

You can create multiline limits in operators:

$$\sum_{\substack{0 \leq i \leq m \\ 0 < j < n}} P(i, j)$$

You can edit multiline limits in the same way you edit column vectors. For details, see Entering Matrices and Vectors later in this chapter.

▶ To enter a multiline limit

1. Enter the operator.

2. Enter a subscript or a superscript.

3. Enter the first line of the limit.

4. With the insertion point at the end of the limit, press ENTER.

5. Enter the next line of the limit.

6. Press the spacebar or RIGHT ARROW to leave the limit.

Entering Brackets

The program has two kinds of brackets: standard brackets, which are available from the keyboard, and expanding brackets, which are available from the Insert menu and the Math toolbars. Certain bracket combinations have keyboard shortcuts; see Appendix B "Keyboard Shortcuts." You can also enclose an existing expression in expanding brackets by applying brackets to a selection.

Standard brackets, which can be entered singly, don't change in size. Expanding brackets, which are always entered in matched or unmatched pairs, are elastic: they expand or contract to match their contents. The program provides these symbols for use as left or right members of expanding bracket pairs:

$$( ) [ ] \{ \} \langle \rangle \lfloor \rfloor \lceil \rceil \mid \| / \setminus \Updownarrow \uparrow \Uparrow \downarrow \Downarrow$$

When you need a single expanding bracket, such as to contain a set of equations, you complete the pair of brackets with an *empty bracket*. Empty brackets don't appear in print. They are shown as vertical dotted lines in the Brackets dialog box and, if you've turned on Helper Lines from the View menu, in the document window, as shown at the right of this example of a case expression:

$$f(x) = \begin{cases} 0 & \text{if } x < 0 \\ 1 & \text{if } x \geq 0 \end{cases}$$

▶ **To enter expanding brackets**

1. On the Math Objects toolbar, click the Brackets button ⬚ or, from the Insert menu, choose Brackets.

   The program opens the Brackets dialog box.

2. Select the left and right brackets you want and choose OK.

▶ **To enclose an existing expression in expanding brackets**

- Select the expression and enter the brackets.

▶ **To change bracket symbols**

1. Select the bracket, including its contents.

   or

   Place the insertion point to the right of the right bracket.

2. Choose Properties to open the Brackets Properties dialog box.

3. Select the symbols you want for the left and right brackets and choose OK.

▶ **To remove expanding brackets from an expression**

- Place the insertion point to the left of either bracket and press DELETE.
  or
- Place the insertion point to the right of either bracket and press BACKSPACE.

Entering Matrices and Vectors

A matrix is a rectangular array:

$$\begin{bmatrix} a & b \\ c & d \end{bmatrix}$$

A vector is a matrix with one column or one row:

$$\begin{bmatrix} a \\ b \end{bmatrix} \qquad \begin{bmatrix} d & e \end{bmatrix}$$

In *SWP* and *SNB*, you can perform computations with matrices and vectors. Note that these computations aren't possible with tables, because tables aren't mathematical objects, even when they contain mathematical expressions.

The cells of a matrix or vector expand to encompass their contents. To work with a matrix or vector more easily, you can outline the cells on the screen with the **Helper Lines** command on the **View** menu. These outlines don't appear in print and are intended only as an editing guide.

Matrices and vectors can be displayed on a line by themselves or can appear in a line of text. You can set the baseline of an in-line matrix or vector so that the surrounding text is aligned with the top row, bottom row, or vertical center of the object:

$$\text{Baseline set on top row:} \quad \begin{matrix} 1 & 2 \\ 3 & 4 \end{matrix}$$

$$\text{Baseline set at vertical center:} \quad \begin{matrix} 1 & 2 \\ 3 & 4 \end{matrix}$$

$$\text{Baseline set on bottom row:} \quad \begin{matrix} 1 & 2 \\ 3 & 4 \end{matrix}$$

However, when matrices and vectors are enclosed in delimiters, alignment is always automatically set at the vertical center.

Entering Matrices

▶ **To enter a matrix**

1. On the Math Objects toolbar, click the Matrix button ⊞ or, from the **Insert** menu, choose **Matrix**.

2. In the **Matrix** dialog box, set the dimensions and baseline of the matrix.

3. Set the alignment of the columns within the matrix.

4. Select the delimiters to enclose the matrix.

   If you select delimiters, the baseline and column alignment for the matrix are set automatically at the center.

5. Choose OK.

   The program places the insertion point in the input box in the top left cell.

6. Enter the contents of the cell.

7. Press TAB to move to the next cell.

   If you're entering the matrix in a dialog box, use the arrow keys to move from cell to cell.

8. When the content is complete, press the spacebar or the RIGHT ARROW to leave the matrix.

▶ **To insert a column vector from the keyboard**

1. Place the insertion point inside a mathematical object that isn't a mathematics display.

   For example, place the insertion point between two brackets.

2. Type the first value in the vector and press ENTER.

   The program displays an input box under the first value.

3. Type the next value.

4. If you need another value, press ENTER.

5. Repeat steps 3 and 4 until the vector is complete.

6. Press the spacebar or press the RIGHT ARROW to leave the vector.

Editing Matrices

Options for editing matrices are more varied than for other mathematical objects. Once you've created a matrix, you can change its dimensions by adding or deleting rows and columns, and you can change the properties of the matrix by changing the alignment of its contents, the baseline, or the delimiters. In this version, you can copy and paste information in multiple cells from one matrix to another, as described in Chapter 6 "Using Editing Techniques and Tools."

Adding and Deleting Matrix Rows and Columns

You add rows and columns to a matrix with the Insert Row(s) and Insert Column(s) commands on the Edit or Context menu. Note that these commands don't appear on the menu unless the insertion point is in or to the right of a matrix.

▶ **To add rows or columns to a matrix**

1. Place the insertion point anywhere in the matrix, but not within another mathematical object.

2. From the Edit or Context menu, choose Insert Row(s) or Insert Column(s).

   Depending on your choice, the program opens the Insert Rows or the Insert Columns dialog box.

3. In the dialog box, select the number of rows or columns you want to add.

4. Enter the position of the insertion.

   The arrow on the sample matrix moves to the point you indicate.

5. Choose OK.

You can delete an entire matrix row or column or a group of rows or columns. Also, you can delete the contents of a cell, row, or column, but leave the row or column in the table.

▶ **To delete an entire row or column**

1. Select the entire row or column.

2. Press DELETE or BACKSPACE or, from the Edit or Context menu, choose Delete.

▶ **To delete the contents of a cell**

1. Select the contents of the cell.

2. Press DELETE or BACKSPACE or, from the Edit or Context menu, choose Delete.

   The program deletes the contents of the cell and replaces it with an empty input box.

Note that if you select and delete the contents of all the cells in an entire row or column in a single operation, the program will delete that row or column from the matrix. You can delete the contents of a row or column but keep the empty row or column in the matrix by deleting the contents of at least one cell in a separate operation.

▶ **To delete the contents of a row or column without deleting the row or column itself**

1. Select all but one cell of the row or column.

2. Press DELETE or BACKSPACE or, from the Edit or Context menu, choose Delete.

3. Select the contents of the remaining cell.

4. Press DELETE or BACKSPACE or, from the Edit or Context menu, choose Delete.

   The program deletes the contents of the cells in the row or column but leaves the input boxes for you to refill.

Editing Matrix Properties

From the Matrix Properties dialog box, you can change the vertical alignment of the columns. The contents of each column or row can be aligned separately. You can also change the matrix baseline and the delimiters enclosing the matrix. If you add delimiters to a matrix, the program automatically determines the column alignment and the baseline.

▶ **To align the information in matrix columns**

1. Select the cells or columns you want to align.

2. Choose Properties.

3. Choose the column alignment you want for the selection.

4. Choose OK.

▶ **To change the baseline of a matrix**

1. Select the matrix or place the insertion point to its right.

2. Choose Properties.

3. In the Baseline area, choose the baseline you want.

4. Choose OK.

▶ **To change the delimiters enclosing a matrix**

1. Select the matrix or place the insertion point to its right.

2. Choose Properties.

3. In the Built-in Delimiters area, choose the enclosure you want.

   Remember that the program automatically determines the alignment and baseline of the matrix when you add delimiters.

4. Choose OK.

Editing Vectors

Vectors respond differently from other matrices to the action of pressing ENTER, DELETE, or BACKSPACE. The differences enhance the entry and editing of vectors. In addition to adding cells to a vector from the Edit or Context menu, you can add and delete cells by splitting and combining adjacent cells. You can copy and paste information in multiple cells from one vector to another, as described in Chapter 6 "Using Editing Techniques and Tools."

▶ **To add a cell to a column vector by splitting an existing cell**

1. Place the insertion point in the cell that is to be split.

2. Press ENTER.

▶ **To combine two adjacent cells in a row vector**

- Place the insertion point to the right of the cell boundary you want to delete and press BACKSPACE.

  or

- Place the insertion point to the left of the cell boundary you want to delete and press DELETE.

Entering Case Expressions

A case expression is of this form: $f(x) = \begin{cases} 0 \text{ if } x < 0 \\ 1 \text{ if } x \geq 0 \end{cases}$.

The right side of the equation is a matrix surrounded by brackets. The right bracket is an empty bracket. The empty bracket appears on the screen as a dotted vertical line, as shown on page 82, but it doesn't print.

▶ **To enter a case expression**

1. Enter the expression to the left of the =, and then enter the =.

2. Create a matrix with no delimiters.

   In most cases, the matrix should have three columns and at least two rows.

3. Enclose the matrix in brackets with an empty right bracket.

4. Enter the case expression in the matrix.

▶ **To align a case expression**

- Edit the properties of the matrix to align the expression as you want.

Entering and Creating Math Names

A special set of multicharacter names, called *math names,* is defined for the program. The math names include many common variables, operators, and functions, such as log and sin, that have meaning for the computational engine. See the online Help and *Doing Mathematics with Scientific WorkPlace and Scientific Notebook* for detailed information. You can create your own multicharacter math names for variables, operators, or functions.

Entering a math name in your document automatically starts mathematics. Math names appear on the screen in gray upright text.

Many of the math names defined in your program installation are also defined as *automatic substitution* sequences. Although you can enter math names from Math Name dialog box, you can speed your work by entering them directly from the keyboard; the program can automatically recognize the math names as you type them. For example, the math name cos is defined as an automatic substitution sequence. When you type **cos** in mathematics, the *co* appears on the screen in italics until you type the *s*, and then the entire function name *cos* changes to an upright cos and is grayed on the screen. The function cos has been substituted for the three-letter sequence *c*, *o*, and *s*, just as if you had entered it from the Math Name dialog box. However, if automatic substitution is turned off and you type **cos** in mathematics, the letters in the sequence appear in italics as the individual variables *c*, *o*, and *s*. See Entering Mathematics with Automatic Substitution, page 96, for additional information.

Entering Math Names

You can enter a math name from the Math Name dialog box or from the keyboard.

▶ **To enter a recognized math name from the Math Name dialog box**

1. On the Math Objects toolbar, click the Math Name button or, from the Insert menu, choose Math Name.

   The program opens the Math Name dialog box so you can select the math name you want.

2. Scroll through the Name list to select the name you want, or type the name in the box at the top of the Name area.

3. If the math name you select can have limits, set the placement of the limits.

4. Choose OK.

▶ **To enter a recognized math name from the keyboard**

1. Check the Enable Automatic Substitution checkbox in the Automatic Substitution dialog box or on the Edit tab sheet of the User Setup dialog box.

2. Place the insertion point where you want the math name to appear.

3. Start mathematics.

4. Type the math name.

   The program inserts the name directly into your document.

Tip   If you want to enter $\cos h$, $\sin h$, or $\tan h$ instead of $\cosh$, $\sinh$, or $\tanh$, type the first three letters, press the spacebar, and then type **h.** Pressing the spacebar tells the program to stop searching for additional characters to add to the function name.

Adding Limits to Math Names

Some math names, such as $\max$ and $\lim$, can have limits. When a math name is in line, the program places the limits at the right:

$$f(x) = \lim_{n \to \infty} x_n$$

When the math name is displayed, the program places the limits above or below:

$$f(x) = \lim_{n \to \infty} x_n$$

You can override these defaults for all math names from the Math tab sheet in the User Setup dialog box. From the Math Name dialog box, you can override the defaults for existing math names when you enter them or edit their properties. However, we recommend that you use the Auto setting whenever possible.

▶ **To add limits to a math name**

1. Enter the math name.

2. Use the Subscript and Superscript commands to enter the limits.

Math names can have multiline limits. See Entering Operators and Limits on page 80.

Creating Math Names

You can create multicharacter variable names for use in mathematics. If you designate a math name as an operator, you can also designate the placement of its limits, if any.

With *SWP* or *SNB*, you can use math names in computations. For example, you can create the names Force, Mass, and Acceleration and assign a value to Mass and Acceleration. Then you can use the math names to write the equation

$$\text{Force} = \text{Mass} \times \text{Acceleration}$$

and compute the value of Force. However, if you start mathematics and enter the words Force, Mass, and Acceleration without having first defined them as multicharacter variable names, the program considers each letter in each word to be a variable.

The program can automatically recognize the math names you create. See Entering Mathematics with Automatic Substitution, page 96, for additional information.

▶ **To create a custom math name**

1. Start mathematics.

2. On the Math Objects toolbar, click the Math Name button [sin cos] or, from the Insert menu, choose Math Name to open the Math Name dialog box.

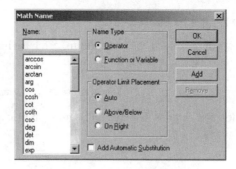

3. In the **Name** box, type the math name you want to create.

4. In the **Name Type** area, select **Operator** or **Function or Variable**.

5. If the math name is an operator, set the placement of the limits.

6. If you want to add the math name to the program's list of math names, choose **Add**.

7. If you want the program to recognize the math name as you type, check **Add Automatic Substitution** to define it as an automatic substitution sequence.

8. Choose **OK**.

Entering Labeled Expressions

You use a template to enter a label over or under an expression. Templates for labeled expressions have two parts: the expression to be labeled and the label itself. The label is set in the subscript/superscript type style. In the formula

$$\underbrace{x + \cdots + x}_{k \text{ times}}$$

the label is "k times" and the expression being labeled is $\underbrace{x + \cdots + x}$. You can apply a label to an existing expression and you can change the position of the label. Edit the label itself with standard editing techniques.

▶ **To enter a labeled expression**

1. On the Math Objects toolbar, click the Label button or, from the **Insert** menu, choose **Label**.

2. In the **Label** dialog box, choose the label position you want and choose **OK**.

3. In the larger box of the template, enter the expression to be labeled.

4. Click the smaller box or press TAB.

5. In the smaller box, enter the label.

6. Press the spacebar or the RIGHT ARROW to leave the expression.

▶ **To apply a label to an existing expression**

- Select the expression and enter the label.

▶ **To remove a label from an expression**

- Place the insertion point to the left of the entire labeled expression and press DELETE.
  or
- Place the insertion point to the right of the entire labeled expression and press BACKSPACE.

▶ **To move the label to the top or bottom**

1. Select the entire labeled expression.

2. Choose **Properties**.

3. Choose the label position you want and choose **OK**.

Entering Decorations

Collectively, wide accents and bars, arrows, and boxes above and below expressions are known as *decorations*. The program provides two special wide accents:

$$\widehat{xyz} \qquad \widetilde{xyz}$$

and these horizontal bars, braces, and arrows above or below expressions:

$$\overline{x+y} \qquad \overleftarrow{x+y} \qquad \overrightarrow{x+y} \qquad \overleftrightarrow{x+y} \qquad \overbrace{x+y}$$

$$\underline{x+y} \qquad \underleftarrow{x+y} \qquad \underrightarrow{x+y} \qquad \underleftrightarrow{x+y} \qquad \underbrace{x+y}$$

You can place a box around an expression. The box can be exactly the size of the expression or can be set off from the expression with a little extra space:

$$\boxed{x+y=z} \qquad \boxed{\,x+y=z\,}$$

▶ **To enter a decoration**

1. On the Math Objects toolbar, click the Decoration button ⬌ or, from the **Insert** menu, choose **Decoration**.

2. Select the decoration you want and choose **OK**.

3. Complete the expression.

4. Press the spacebar or the RIGHT ARROW to leave the expression.

▶ **To apply a decoration to an existing expression**

- Select the expression and enter the decoration.

▶ **To remove the decoration from an expression**

- Place the insertion point to the left of the entire expression and press DELETE.
  or

- Place the insertion point to the right of the entire expression and press BACKSPACE.

▶ **To change the decoration**

1. Select the entire expression or place the insertion point to its right, and then choose Properties.

2. From the Decoration Properties dialog box, select the decoration you want and choose OK.

Entering Horizontal Spaces in Mathematics

Because the program automatically provides appropriate spacing for mathematics, you don't need to use the spacebar to type horizontal spaces in mathematics. In fact, by default the spacebar doesn't add space if the insertion point is in mathematics. In some situations, however, the program doesn't have enough information to space your mathematics exactly as you want it and you may occasionally want to add extra space to an expression. For example, in the expression

$$\int_a^b f(x)dx$$

you can add a little extra space (a thin space) between $f(x)$ and dx to improve the appearance:

$$\int_a^b f(x)\,dx$$

You can add these horizontal spaces inside mathematical expressions:

Name	Size
Em space	width of M
2-em space	width of MM
Required	$\frac{2}{9}$ em
Nonbreaking	$\frac{2}{9}$ em
Thin space	$\frac{1}{6}$ em
Thick space	$\frac{5}{18}$ em
Zero space	0 em
Negative thin space	$-\frac{1}{6}$ em
Italic correction	Depends on character to left

In addition to these fixed amounts of horizontal space, you can enter positive and negative custom space. Also, you can indicate places in an expression where a break is appropriate, required, or prohibited. Chapter 8 "Formatting Documents" has details. Some horizontal spaces have keyboard shortcuts; see Appendix B "Keyboard Shortcuts."

▶ **To enter horizontal space in mathematics**

1. On the Editing toolbar, click the Space button [e.m] or, from the Insert menu, choose Spacing, and then choose Horizontal Space.

2. In the Horizontal Space dialog box, select the button for the space you want and choose OK.

The zero space, which translates to the TEX empty group, is used with prescripts such as the 2 in this expression:

$$_2Z_3$$

To enter the expression $_2Z_3$, enter a zero space, enter 2 as a subscript, then complete the expression. Since subscripts and superscripts adjust to the size of the objects to their left, placing them after a zero space ensures that they appear at a fixed position.

Entering Units of Measure

In *SWP* and *SNB,* you can add units of measure for physical quantities—including units from the System of International Units, or SI units—to mathematical values. You can convert the values from one unit of measure to another and you can perform computations on equations containing values that have units of measure. You can also enter compound unit names, such as $\frac{\text{ft}}{\text{s}}$ or ft lb by writing them as fractions or products. By default, unit names appear in green on your screen so you can distinguish them.

You can enter a unit of measure from the Unit Name dialog box or with a keyboard shortcut. The shortcuts, derived from the common abbreviation of the unit, begin with **u,** as in **uA** for Ampere (A), **udeg** for degree (°), or **ucel** for Celsius (°C). The shortcuts shown in the following table are exceptions.

For		Type
h	hour symbol	uhr
m	meter symbol and its derivatives	ume
Å	angstrom symbol	uan
C	Coulomb symbol	uCo
T	Tesla symbol	uTe
l	Liter symbol	uli
Ω	symbols for ohm and its derivatives	uohm
°C	degrees Celsius	ucel
°F	degrees Fahrenheit	ufahr
°	degree symbol (plane angle)	udeg
′	(degree) minute	udmn
″	(degree) second	uds
lbf	pound-force	ulbf
lb	pound-mass	ulbm

The shortcuts are case-sensitive and often contain uppercase letters. Appendix B "Keyboard Shortcuts" lists the shortcuts for the available units of measure.

Note   You can also enter units of measure by typing them as text or by using symbols or characters available from the symbol panels, but units of measure entered in these ways have no computational value.

▶ **To enter a unit of measure**

1. Start mathematics and enter a value.

2. Enter the unit:
   - Type **u** followed by the symbol for the unit you want.
     For example, type **ukW** for kilowatts (kW) and **ugal** for gallons (gal). Remember to type uppercase where necessary. See Appendix B "Keyboard Shortcuts" for a list of available shortcuts.

   or

   a. On the Math Objects toolbar, click the Unit Name button ⌗�⌗ or, from the Insert menu, choose Unit Name.
   b. From the **Physical Quantity** list in the **Unit Name** dialog box, select a measurement category.
   c. From the **Unit Name** list, select the unit name you want.
   d. Choose **Insert**.
      The **Unit Name** dialog box remains open so you can enter other units. To close it, click ☒ in the upper right corner of the box.

Entering Mathematics with Fragments

You can store frequently typed mathematics as fragments, or information saved for later recall, just as you can store text (see page 55). Fragments can be imported into your documents quickly.

The program is installed with many predefined fragments. The most commonly used fragments are stored in the `Frags` directory of your program installation. The `Constants` subdirectory houses many predefined mathematical constants, expressions, and theorems, many of which carry a unit of measure.

You can create any new fragments that you need. Each fragment can include both text and mathematics. When you create a fragment, the program saves it by default with an extension of `.frg`. Also by default, the program saves the fragment in the `Frags` directory. If you prefer, you can save your mathematical fragments in the `Constants` subdirectory or in some other subdirectory within the `Frags` directory.

You can also save your fragments in a different directory; however, if you do, the fragment name won't appear on the Fragments popup list or in the Import Fragment dialog box. See Chapter 12 "Customizing the Program" to change the default directory. A fragment that you save in one document is available to all documents.

You don't have to start mathematics to import a fragment containing mathematics. When you import a fragment, the program pastes its contents into your document at the insertion point, automatically toggling between text and mathematics as necessary.

▶ **To see a list of all fragments in the Frags directory**

- Click the Fragments popup list .
  or

- From the File menu, choose Import Fragment.
  or

- Press ALT+4.

You can import a fragment with the mouse or the keyboard. If the fragment name contains at least two characters, you can import the fragment with a shortcut.

▶ **To import a fragment**

1. Place the insertion point where you want to import the fragment.

2. Click the Fragments popup list or press ALT+4 and then select the name of the fragment you want.

   or

   From the File menu, choose Import Fragment, select the fragment you want, and choose Open.

   or

   If the fragment name is at least two characters long, press CTRL+*name*, where *name* is the name of the fragment you want to insert.

Note   If you use CTRL+*name* to insert a fragment that has the same name as a TeX command, the program inserts the TeX command instead of the fragment. For a list of recognized TeX commands, see Appendix B "Keyboard Shortcuts."

▶ **To create a fragment containing mathematics**

1. Create the information that you want to save as a fragment, changing from text to mathematics as necessary.

2. Select the information.

3. On the Fragments toolbar, click the Save Fragment button or, from the File menu, choose Save Fragment.

4. Type a file name to be used to recall the fragment.

   Avoid using the name of a TeX command for your fragment.

5. Unless you want to create a new subdirectory to hold the fragment, leave the directory unchanged.

6. Choose OK.

If you have saved the fragment in the Frags directory or one of its subdirectories, the program immediately inserts its name in the fragments list.

Entering Mathematics with Automatic Substitution

You can enter mathematics quickly using *automatic substitution*. When automatic substitution is turned on and the insertion point is in mathematics, the program replaces special sequences of letters or numbers that you enter with predefined mathematical expressions.

You can define and edit your own substitution sequences and expressions. For example, if you frequently use the expression $\sum_{n=1}^{10}$ in your work, you can define an automatic substitution sequence called *sum10* so that you can enter the expression quickly. If you type **sum10** when the insertion point is in mathematics, the letters *sum* appear in italics and the *1* appears in red until you complete the name of the sequence by typing the *0*. Then, the entire sequence is replaced with $\sum_{n=1}^{10}$.

You can enable or disable the automatic substitution of sequences at any time. If you disable automatic substitution, the program doesn't substitute mathematical expressions when you type the corresponding sequences of letters or numbers. That is, if you disable automatic substitution and type **sum10** when the insertion point is in mathematics, the program displays $sum10$ instead of substituting the expression $\sum_{n=1}^{10}$.

The math names for many common functions, operators, and variables have been defined as substitution sequences in your program installation. If a math name has been defined as an automatic substitution sequence, the program can automatically recognize the math name as you type it, providing the insertion point is in mathematics and automatic substitution is turned on. As an example, the math name cos has been defined as an automatic substitution sequence. If you type **cos** when the insertion point is in mathematics, the *co* appears on the screen in italics until you type the *s*, and then the entire function name *cos* changes to an upright cos and is grayed. The function cos has been substituted for the three-letter sequence *c*, *o*, and *s*.

Entering frequently used mathematical expressions with automatic substitution sequences differs slightly from entering them with fragments. You can enter a fragment when the insertion point is in text or mathematics; the program toggles between the two as necessary. You can enter an automatic substitution sequence only in mathematics and only when automatic substitution is turned on. However, automatic substitution sequences are usually faster to enter from the keyboard than fragments.

▶ **To turn automatic substitution on or off**

1. On the Editing toolbar, click the User Setup button ![icon] or, from the Tools menu, choose User Setup.

2. Choose the Edit tab.

3. Check the Enable Automatic Substitution box to turn the option on, or uncheck the box to turn the option off.

   or

1. From the Tools menu, choose Automatic Substitution.

2. Check the Enable Automatic Substitution box to turn the option on or uncheck the box to turn the option off.

▶ **To enter mathematics using an automatic substitution sequence**

1. Make sure that Enable Automatic Substitution is checked in the Automatic Substitution dialog box or on the Edit tab sheet of the User Setup dialog box.

2. Place the insertion point where you want the mathematics to appear.

3. Start mathematics and type the automatic substitution sequence.

   The program replaces the sequence with the corresponding mathematical expression.

▶ **To delete an automatic substitution sequence and replacement expression**

1. From the Tools menu, choose Automatic Substitution.

2. Select the substitution sequence for the expression you want to remove.

3. Choose Remove and then choose OK.

▶ **To define a new automatic substitution sequence**

1. From the Tools menu, choose Automatic Substitution.

   The program opens the Automatic Substitution dialog box:

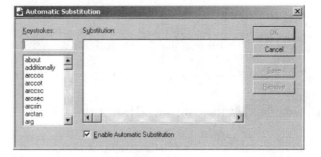

2. In the Keystrokes box, type the automatic substitution sequence.

   Sequences must consist of alphabetic and numeric characters only; they are case-sensitive.

3. Place the insertion point in the Substitution box and enter the replacement expression:
   - Type the mathematics you want to replace the sequence.
     The replacement expression can be any valid mathematics expression. You can use the menu commands and toolbar buttons to enter the expression, or you can paste a mathematical expression from the clipboard to the Substitution box.
     or

- If the substitution sequence is a custom math name,

  i On the Math Objects toolbar, click the Math Name button or, from the Insert menu, choose **Math Name**.

  ii Select the math name you want to use and choose **OK**.

4. Choose **Save**.

5. Repeat steps 2–4 to enter and save any additional substitution sequences and their corresponding replacement expressions.

6. Choose **OK**.

▶ To edit a replacement expression

1. From the **Tools** menu, choose **Automatic Substitution**.

2. In the **Keystrokes** box, select the substitution sequence for the expression you want to edit.

3. In the **Substitution** box, edit the expression.

   You can use the menu commands and the toolbar buttons to edit the expression.

4. Choose **Save**.

5. Repeat steps 2–4 to edit and save any other expressions.

6. Choose **OK**.

Creating and Editing Mathematical Displays

As noted on page 69, you must indicate when you want to create a mathematical display. You can create a new display and change in-line mathematics to displayed mathematics or vice versa. You can number, label, and assign a key to mathematical displays.

Several commands on the **View** menu help you work with displayed mathematics. If you check **Helper Lines**, a box outlining the display appears on the screen. If you check **Input Boxes**, outlines for the input boxes inside the display also appear. These outlines don't appear in print when you typeset and, depending on the print options (see page 163), may or may not appear in print when you don't typeset.

▶ To create a mathematics display

- On the Math Objects toolbar, click the Display button .
  or

- From the **Insert** menu, choose **Display**.
  or

- Press CTRL+D.

The program inserts a centered display on a new line and places the insertion point inside the display in an input box so you can enter your mathematics.

▶ **To display in-line mathematics**

1. Select the mathematics to be displayed.

2. Create a display.

   The program places your selection in the display, formatting the size and position of mathematical elements appropriately.

▶ **To change a single-line display to in-line mathematics**

- Place the insertion point to the left of and outside the display and press DELETE.
  or

- Place the insertion point to the right of and outside the display and press BACKSPACE.

   If you need to display and align several equations, we suggest you use a multiline display instead of a series of single-line displays. For example, here are two separate displays:

$$x = a + \cos\theta - b$$
$$y = b + \sin\theta$$

These two equations look much better if they are aligned on the $=$ signs using a multiline display:

$$
\begin{aligned}
x &= a + \cos\theta - b \\
y &= b + \sin\theta
\end{aligned}
$$

▶ **To create a multiline display**

1. Enter a display.

2. Type the first line and press ENTER to start the next line.

3. Type the next line.

   The program automatically aligns the lines on the first binary relation ($=$, $<$, etc.) in each line.

4. When all the lines have been entered, press the RIGHT ARROW key to leave the display.

   Although the program correctly formats displayed mathematics, you may want to edit the properties of a display to add custom equation numbers or custom labels. You may also want to override the automatic alignment in a multiline display or add vertical space to each line. And you may want to add a *key,* or unique name, for displays so that you can create automatic cross-references or hypertext links to the displays from elsewhere in your document. See Adjusting Breaks in Mathematical Expressions on page 196 for information about breaking large mathematical expressions that you don't want to display.

If you have *SWP* or *SW,* you can edit the display to add automatic or custom equation numbers and you can add vertical space to each line of the display. If a display has a key, you can create automatic cross-references to the display when you typeset your document.

Adding Automatic Equation Numbers

SWP and *SW* can automatically number the displayed equations in your document. By default, the program doesn't number displayed equations, but you can change the default. Also, you can turn automatic numbering on and off for individual displayed equations. Automatic numbering isn't available in *SNB.*

In the document window, automatically numbered displays are shown with a # symbol in a small box to the side, as in the following display:

$$a^2 + b^2 = c^2$$

In print, the number appears differently depending on whether or not you produce your document by typesetting it, as described in Chapter 7 "Previewing and Printing." When you print the document by typesetting it, the program replaces the # symbol with the number of the displayed equation and formats the number according to the typesetting specifications for the document. Some specifications, such as those that include $\mathcal{AMS}$ packages, require the number to be typeset in parentheses or otherwise annotated. When you print the document without typesetting it, the program doesn't replace the symbol with a number and no special formatting occurs.

▶ **To turn on automatic numbering of displayed mathematics**

1. From the Tools menu in *SWP* or *SW,* choose User Setup.

2. Choose the Math tab sheet.

3. Check the box labeled Automatically Number New Equations and choose OK.

▶ **To turn on automatic numbering for an individual display**

1. Uncheck Automatically Number New Equations in the User Setup dialog box.

2. Place the insertion point in the display and press TAB.

   The program inserts a small box containing a # symbol to the right of the equation.

   or

1. Uncheck Automatically Number New Equations in the User Setup dialog box.

2. Select the display to be numbered and choose Properties.

3. In the Number area of the Display Properties dialog box, check Auto.

   If the display is a multiline display, choose the Line Number and check Auto for each line you want to number.

4. Choose OK.

▶ **To remove a number from a display**

1. Select the display and choose **Properties**.

2. In the **Number** area of the **Display Properties** dialog box, check **None**.

   If the display is a multiline display, choose the **Line Number** and check **None** for each line you don't want to number.

3. Choose **OK**.

Adding Custom Equation Numbers and Labels

Instead of numbering a display automatically, you can give the display a custom number or use text to label it. If automatic numbering is turned on in *SWP* or *SW*, the custom numbers and labels you enter replace the automatically generated numbers.

In the document window, displays with custom numbers are shown with the custom number or label in a small box to the side of the display, like this:

$$a^2 + b^2 = c^2$$

Pythagoras

In print, the number appears differently depending on whether or not you produce your document by typesetting it. When you print the document by typesetting it, the program places the custom number or label to the side of the display. When you print the document without typesetting it, the custom number or label appears according to the print options you've set. See Chapter 7 "Previewing and Printing."

▶ **To add a custom number or label to a display**

1. Select the display and choose **Properties**.

2. If the display is a multiline display, select the line you want to number.

3. In the **Number** area of the **Display Properties** dialog box, check **Custom**.

4. In the entry box, type the custom number or label.

5. If you're using *SWP* or *SW* and you don't want $\mathcal{A}_{\mathcal{M}}\mathcal{S}$ formatting, check **Suppress Annotation**.

6. If the display is a multiline display, repeat steps 2–5 for each line for which you want a custom number or label.

7. Choose **OK**.

Using Letters in Line Numbers of a Multiline Display

When you typeset your document in *SWP* or *SW*, you have an alternative to numbering each line of a multiline display separately: you can use a single number for the entire display and add a letter to each line to indicate its sequence within the display. The sequence can continue to subsequent lines in the display, even if the lines are separated from one another by text. You can also create subequation numbering using TEX fields; see the online Help for additional information. This feature isn't available in *SNB*.

In the document window, the small box to the side of the display contains a # symbol. In print, the number appears differently depending on whether or not you produce your document by typesetting it. When you print the document by typesetting it, the program places the number to the right of the display. The number appears as the sequential number of the display followed by a letter. For example, the lines in a 3-line display might be numbered 4a, 4b, and 4c. When you print the document without typesetting it, the program doesn't replace the symbol with a number and no special formatting occurs.

▶ **To enable lettering for a multiline display**

1. Select the display and choose Properties.

2. Choose Advanced.

3. Check the box labeled Enable Subequation Numbering.

4. If you want to continue the lettering sequence from the previous display, check the box labeled Subequation Continuation.

5. For each line of the display that you want to letter, check Auto.

6. Choose OK.

Aligning a Multiline Display

Creating a series of displayed equations as a multiline display instead of several single-line displays yields a better printed appearance for your mathematics. The program automatically aligns each line of a multiline display on the first binary relation in the line, according to the standard rules of LaTeX. If you prefer, you can change the alignment of a display line by selecting those characters on which you want to align the expression. You can center each line of the display or specify that the contents of the display be aligned as a single equation on multiple lines.

Although the program automatically determines how multiline displays appear in print, in *SWP* and *SW* you can add additional space between the lines. The space is included when you typeset your document, but not when you display it in the document window or when you produce it without typesetting.

▶ **To set the alignment of a line**

1. Place the insertion point to the left of the character you want to align with other lines.

2. From the Edit or Context menu, choose Set Alignment.

▶ **To center each line of a multiline display**

1. Select the display and choose Properties.

2. Choose Advanced.

3. Check Enable Alignment.

4. Select Each Line Centered.

5. Choose OK.

▶ **To align a multiline display as a single equation on multiple lines**

1. Select the display and choose Properties.

2. Choose Advanced.

3. Check Enable Alignment.

4. Select Single Equation on Multiple Lines.

5. Choose OK.

▶ **To add additional space between the lines of a multiline display**

1. Select the display and choose Properties.

2. In the Line Number box, select the line after which you want to add space.

3. In the Units box, select the unit of measure for the space.

4. In the box labeled Space After this Line, enter the amount of additional space you want between the lines.

5. Choose OK.

   Remember   This option isn't available in *SNB*.

Adding Keys to Displayed Mathematics

If you want to create hypertext links to a display or, in *SWP* and *SW*, cross-references to a display from elsewhere in your document, you must add a key to the display. A multiline display can have a key for each line and for the display as a whole. Displays with custom numbering can't have keys.

When Markers is checked on the View menu, the key appears in the document window in parentheses in the small box containing the display number. The key doesn't appear when you typeset the document in *SWP* or *SW*, but it does appear when you print the document without typesetting. More information about creating cross-references and keys appears in Chapter 9 "Structuring Documents for Typesetting."

▶ **To add a key to a display line**

1. Select the display and choose Properties.

2. Select the line number for which you want a key.

3. In the box labeled Key for this Line, enter the key and then choose OK.

▶ **To add a key for a whole multiline display**

1. Select the display.

2. Choose **Properties**.

3. Choose **Advanced**.

4. Check **Enable Subequation Numbering**.

5. In the box labeled **Key for Whole Display**, enter the key and choose **OK**.

Using Tags with Mathematics

As explained in Chapter 3 "Creating Text," many document formatting tasks are accomplished by applying *tags*. Tags are collections of formatting and behavior properties that affect the appearance, structure, and content of your document. Tag properties determine the appearance of many elements in your document, including in-line and displayed mathematics, matrices, formulas, and plots. When you apply a tag to mathematics in your document, the program applies the properties of the tag to the mathematics.

You can apply text tags, section/body tags, and item tags to mathematics. By using tags, you can create a consistent appearance throughout your document without having to format each element individually. For example, each time you tag information in your document as a theorem you'll produce a paragraph whose text appears in a consistent font size and typeface and with consistent indention. No further formatting is required. All paragraphs tagged as theorems will have the same appearance, both in the current document and in all documents created with the same shell.

Important   The appearance and behavior of tagged information depends on the properties of the corresponding tag. In *SWP* and *SW,* the tag properties are *defined twice* for each shell: once in the typesetting specifications, which are used when you typeset the document with LaTeX or PDFLaTeX, and once in the style (.cst file), which is used when you display your document in the document window or produce it without typesetting. The two property definitions for a given tag may differ significantly even though the name of the tag is the same. See Chapter 8 "Formatting Documents" for more information about how styles and typesetting specifications affect tags and tagged information.

In *SWP* and *SW,* the way you produce your document determines which property definition is used and, consequently, how your document appears on the preview screen or in print. See Chapter 7 "Previewing and Printing" about producing documents with and without typesetting.

You can apply tags from the popup lists on the Tag toolbar, with the **Apply** command on the Tag menu, or with the function keys on the keyboard. When you apply a text tag, the program applies the tag to the current selection or, if you haven't made a selection, to the next thing you type. When you apply a section/body tag or an item tag, the program applies the tag to the paragraph containing the insertion point.

▶ **To apply a tag**

- On the Tag toolbar, click the popup box containing the tag you want and then click the tag you want to apply.

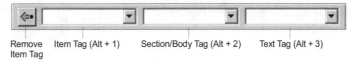

Remove   Item Tag (Alt + 1)   Section/Body Tag (Alt + 2)   Text Tag (Alt + 3)
Item Tag

or

- From the Tag menu, choose Apply and then select the tag you want.
  or

- From the Context menu, choose Apply Tag and then select the tag you want.
  or

- Press the function key assigned to the tag you want.
  You can change the key assignments with the Function Keys command on the Tag menu. See Chapter 12 "Customizing the Program" for more information.

Adding Emphasis with Text Tags

In mathematics, calligraphic text denotes sets or integral transforms; blackboard bold denotes the set of real numbers or natural numbers; and boldface text often indicates vectors and matrices. You can use these conventions in your document by applying text tags to your content.

The Blackboard Bold, Calligraphic, Fraktur, and Bold Symbol tags automatically start mathematics. If you apply one of these tags to a selection, the selection is changed to mathematics even if it was originally text. If you apply one of these tags without having made a selection, the next thing you type will be mathematics and will have the tag you applied. Note that Calligraphic and Blackboard Bold are valid only for uppercase letters. Applying these tags to lowercase letters yields strange symbols.

The Bold tag and the Bold Symbol tag have similar names but different behaviors. The Bold tag doesn't automatically start mathematics. If you apply the Bold tag to a selection in mathematics, the program bolds any variables in the selection and changes them from an italic to an upright font. This may not be the effect you want.

The Bold Symbol tag automatically starts mathematics. If you apply the Bold Symbol tag to a selection in mathematics, the program bolds the selection. It changes any variables, math names, and symbols in the selection but otherwise doesn't change the font. These examples show the differences in the effect of the two tags in mathematics.

$$\begin{array}{ll}\text{Original expression in mathematics} & x = r\cos\theta \\ \text{Expression with Bold tag} & \mathbf{x} = \mathbf{r}\cos\theta \\ \text{Expression with Bold Symbol tag} & \boldsymbol{x} = \boldsymbol{r}\cos\theta\end{array}$$

The text tags that are available and their appearance on the screen and in print depend on the shell you used to create your document. You can apply the Normal and Bold text tags with the $\boxed{\text{N}}$ and $\boxed{\textbf{B}}$ buttons on the Editing toolbar. See Chapter 8 "Formatting

Documents" for more information about how styles and typesetting specifications affect the appearance of tagged information.

▶ **To apply a text tag to mathematics**

- Select the mathematics you want to tag and then apply the tag.
  or
- Apply the tag you want, type the mathematics you want to tag, and then apply the Normal tag to remove the emphasis from the next thing you type.

▶ **To remove a text tag**

- Select the tagged information and then apply the Normal tag.

Adding Structure with the Body Math Tag

A special body tag called Body Math defines paragraphs that automatically start mathematics. The Body Math tag speeds the entry of a series of mathematical expressions. Each time you press ENTER with the insertion point in a Body Math paragraph, the program starts a new paragraph and automatically switches to mathematics.

The body tags that are available depend on the shell you used to create your document. See Chapter 8 "Formatting Documents" for more information about how styles and typesetting specifications affect the appearance of tagged information.

▶ **To create a Body Math paragraph**

1. Place the insertion point in the paragraph you want to tag. If you haven't yet typed the paragraph, place the insertion point where you want the paragraph to begin.

2. Apply the Body Math tag.

3. Type the paragraph if it doesn't already exist.

Note   If you want to apply a body paragraph tag to several consecutive paragraphs, make a selection that starts anywhere in the first paragraph and ends anywhere in the last paragraph. Then, apply the tag. The program applies the tag to any paragraph that contains a part of the selection, even if the entire paragraph wasn't selected.

Adding Theorem Statements with Item Tags

You create theorems, corollaries, lemmas, axioms, and other theorem-like statements with the theorem tags on the Item Tag popup list. Theorem tags aren't available in all shells. If you need to include theorem statements in your document, make sure the shell you use includes the tags you need.

If you have *SWP* or *SW,* you can number theorem statements automatically. When you typeset your document, LaTeX automatically formats and numbers any theorems and, if you've created keys for the theorems, creates any cross-references to them. Most typesetting specifications number theorems sequentially throughout a document. Cross-references appear as the number of the theorem. See Chapter 8 "Formatting Documents" for more information about how styles and typesetting specifications affect the appearance of tagged information. See Chapter 9 "Structuring Documents for Typesetting" for information about numbering theorems and creating markers and cross-references in *SWP* and *SW*.

Note   To generate automatic theorem numbers, you must typeset the document; that is, you must use the **Compile**, **Preview**, or **Print** commands on the **Typeset** menu. If you use the **Preview** or **Print** commands on the **File** menu, the program doesn't use LaTeX to produce the document. Thus, neither the theorem numbers nor the cross-references are generated.

Most shells with theorem tags automatically italicize the body of the theorem statement, like this:

Theorem 1   *Let S be a sheaf of germs of holomorphic functions....*

Once you've created a theorem, you can add an explanatory label for it; for example,

Theorem 2 (Hunter)   *Let S be a sheaf of germs of holomorphic functions....*

▶ **To enter a theorem statement**

1. Place the insertion point at the end of the paragraph that is to precede the theorem.

2. Press ENTER.

3. Apply the theorem tag you want.

   The program indicates the tag by placing an appropriate word (such as *Theorem* or *Corollary*) in a lead-in object at the beginning of the new paragraph.

4. Type the statement of the theorem and press ENTER.

5. If you want to create an additional paragraph within the theorem statement, press BACKSPACE, type the paragraph, and then press ENTER.

6. When all paragraphs have been entered, end the theorem statement:

   - On the Tag toolbar, click the Remove Item Tag button ⬚ .
     or
   - From the **Tag** menu, choose **Apply**, select **Remove Item Tag**, and then choose **OK**.
     or
   - Press the function key associated with Remove Item Tag. The default assignment is F2.

▶ **To convert one or more existing paragraphs to a theorem statement**

1. Select the paragraphs.

2. Apply the theorem tag you want.

3. If your selection included more than one paragraph, delete the lead-in object at the start of each continuation paragraph that you don't want to be a separate theorem statement:

   a. Place the insertion point at the start of each continuation paragraph.
   b. Press BACKSPACE to delete the lead-in object.

▶ **To add a theorem label**

1. Double-click the theorem lead-in object, or select the lead-in object and then choose Properties.

2. Choose Custom.

3. Enter the label in the Custom box.

4. Choose OK.

5 Using Graphics and Tables

Visual elements such as pictures, drawings, and tables enhance documents by illustrating concepts and presenting complex information in an easy-to-read format. This chapter explains how to create tables and how to include illustrations created in popular graphics formats. It also explains how to create pictures of text and mathematics for use in other applications, in effect copying the information exactly as it appears in your document.

Working with Graphics

You can include a picture or illustration in your document either by importing a graphics file created with another software application or by pasting an image from the clipboard into your document. When you import or paste a graphic, the program automatically encloses the image in a container called a *frame*. The program manages imported and pasted graphics differently.

You can also create a picture of information in your document, formatted as it appears in the document window, for use in another application. You can either paste a picture of the information to the clipboard as a Windows Enhanced Metafile (.emf) graphic or export it to a graphics file in a different format.

Importing Graphics

The program uses *graphics filters* to import and display graphics created in a variety of vector and raster formats, so you can use graphics created with other applications in your document. When you import a graphic, the program creates a pointer to the graphics file and displays the image in your document. The graphic remains as a separate file in its original location on your system. If you use the Save As command to save your document under another name or in a new location, the program maintains the pointer to the graphic from the new file and location. If you delete the graphic from your document, the graphics file remains in its original location.

▶ **To import an entire graphics file**

1. Place the insertion point where you want the graphic.

2. On the Editing toolbar, click the Import Picture button or, from the File menu, choose Import Picture.

3. In the Import Picture dialog box, select the drive, directory, and file type of the graphics file you want to import.

4. In the File Name box, type or select the name of the file you want and choose OK.

The program creates the link to the graphics file and displays the image in the document.

Pasting Graphics

When you paste a graphic from the clipboard into your document, the program places the graphic in a new file in the same directory as the document, creates a pointer to the file, and displays the image in your document. The graphic is associated specifically with your document but remains as a separate file in the same directory.

The program stores the pasted graphic in a Windows metafile (.wmf) or a bitmap (.bmp) file, depending on the source of the graphic, and automatically generates a unique string of characters as a file name. You may want to change the generated name to a name that describes the graphic and provides a better reference for the file. You can change the name from within the program just one time.

If you use the Save As command to save your document under another name or in a new location, the program makes a copy of the graphics file and creates a pointer from the new document to the copy of the graphics file. It associates the copy with the newly saved document file, placing the copy of the graphic in the same directory. However, if you have renamed the graphics file, the program doesn't make a copy of it. Instead, it leaves the renamed graphics file in the original directory and modifies the pointer in the new document so that it points to the renamed graphics file. If you delete a pasted graphic from your document, the program deletes the graphics file, unless you have renamed it.

▶ **To paste a graphic from another application into a document**

1. Open the graphic from within the application.

2. Select the graphic or the portion of the graphic that you want to paste.

3. Copy the selection to the clipboard.

4. Return to your *SWP, SW,* or *SNB* document.

5. Place the insertion point where you want the graphic to appear.

6. On the Standard toolbar, click the Paste button ▣ or, from the Edit or Context menu, choose Paste.

▶ **To change the file name of a pasted graphic**

1. Select the graphics frame, choose Properties, and choose the Picture Properties tab.

2. Replace the name in the File Name box with a name you choose for the graphic. Leave the file extension unchanged.

   You can use a complete path name to choose a directory for the graphics file or use only the file name to save the graphic in the same directory as your document. If your document hasn't yet been named and saved, the program saves the graphic in a temporary directory.

3. Choose OK.

Working with Frames

Many frame properties, such as the placement on the page, size, and appearance of the frame in the document window and in print, are set by default. You can change the defaults from the Graphics tab sheet in the User Setup dialog box. Chapter 12 "Customizing the Program" contains more information.

Understanding Frame Placement

Frames and the images they contain can appear in line, like this: , or they can be displayed on a line by themselves, like this:

In-line and displayed frames appear where you place them, regardless of how you produce your document.

Additionally, in *SWP* and *SW* frames can *float;* that is, they can remain unanchored to a specific location until you typeset your document. When you typeset, LATEX or PDFLATEX places the frame in the best possible place. Several options for floating placement are available:

Option	Position of the floating frame
Here	As close as possible to the entry point in the text
Top	At the top of a page
Bottom	At the bottom of a page
On a Page of Floats	On a separate page containing only floating frames

By default, the formatter first tries to position a floating frame at the top of the page, then at the bottom, and then on a page with other floating frames. However, you can specify as many placement options as you want and you can combine options to achieve the best possible placement of the floating frame when you typeset your document. You can change the floating placement defaults from the User Setup dialog box; see Chapter 12 "Customizing the Program" for more information. If you print your document without typesetting it, a floating frame appears in print on a line by itself at the place where it was entered in the document, as if it were a displayed frame. Floating frames aren't available in *SNB*.

Plots created in *SWP* or *SNB* have the same placement properties as graphics frames. For more information about creating plots, see the online Help and *Doing Mathematics with Scientific WorkPlace and Scientific Notebook.*

Understanding Automatic Frame Features

The availability and use of automatic frame features depend on the frame placement and the way you produce your document.

Feature	Floating frame		In-line frame	Displayed frame
	With typesetting	Without typesetting		
Automatic numbering	yes	no	no	no
Keys for cross-references	yes	no	no	no
Keys for hypertext links	yes	yes	yes	yes
Captions	yes	yes	yes	yes
Caption (short form)	yes	no	no	no

As the table above indicates, the most powerful frame features are available for floating frames in typeset documents. When you typeset an *SWP* or *SW* document containing a floating frame, the formatter automatically numbers the frame. If you assign a key to a floating frame, you can use the key in cross-references from elsewhere in the typeset document, as described on page 248. In online documents, you can use the key for hypertext links.

In addition, floating frames can have captions above or below the frame. If the typesetting specifications for the document include a list of figures, the formatter uses the automatic frame number and the caption to create the list of figures when the document is typeset. If the caption is long, you can specify a special short form of the caption for inclusion in the list of figures.

The features available for floating frames are reduced if you produce your document without typesetting. When you produce the document without typesetting it, the program doesn't use LaTeX or PDFLaTeX and thus doesn't number floating frames automatically. Therefore, if you have assigned a key to a floating frame, the program ignores any cross-references to it. However, you can use the key for hypertext links if the document is online. Note that depending on the length of the caption and the width of the frame, the entire caption may not appear in print. The program doesn't generate a list of figures and short-form captions aren't used.

The features of in-line and displayed frames operate differently from the features of floating frames. Regardless of the way you produce the document, the program doesn't automatically number in-line and displayed frames. Therefore, although you can assign a key to in-line and displayed frames, the keys can't be used for cross-references. The keys can be used for hypertext links in online documents.

In-line and displayed frames can have captions underneath, but the program doesn't include the captions in a list of figures. As with floating frames, when you typeset your document, the formatter prints the entire caption with the in-line or displayed frame, just as it does for floating frames. When you display the document in the document window or produce it without typesetting, however, the width of the frame determines how much of the caption appears, as shown on page 116.

Editing the Frame Properties

You can edit the properties of a frame to modify the placement on the page, the appearance, and the size of the frame. You can print only the frame or iconify the frame so that it appears as a small gray box when you display your document in the document window or print without typesetting. Also, you can add a caption and provide a key for cross-references and hypertext links to the frame. Edit the frame properties using the tab sheets in the **Graphic Properties** dialog box.

   Although you can modify the frame, you can't modify the image contained in the frame except to move, resize, or crop it in relation to the frame, as described in Resizing, Cropping, and Moving Graphics on page 118. If you want to modify the image in any other way, you must use the software application with which the graphics file was created.

▶ **To edit the properties of a graphics frame**

1. Click the frame so that eight black handles appear around it.

   or

   Select the frame.

   or

   Place the insertion point to the right of the frame.

2. On the Standard toolbar, click the Properties button or, from the **Edit** or **Context** menu, choose **Properties**.

   or

   In the graphics frame, click the Graphic Properties button [🔲] .

   or

   Press CTRL+F5.

3. Choose the tab you want:
   - The **Layout** tab sheet controls the size and placement of the frame in your document and also controls some aspects of how the frame appears in the document window and in print.
   - The **Labeling** tab sheet controls the key, caption, and icon name for the frame.
   - The **Picture Properties** tab sheet controls the size and placement of the image within the frame.

4. Edit the properties as necessary.

5. Choose **OK**.

Remember   When you choose **OK** or **Cancel** in a tabbed dialog box, you accept or discard the changes made on all tab sheets, not just the tab sheet in front.

Placing a Frame

Graphics can appear in displayed or in-line frames. In *SWP* and *SW*, graphics can also appear in floating frames. When you first import or paste a graphic, its frame is placed according to the graphics defaults set for your installation. You can override the default placement for an individual frame by editing its properties.

▶ **To edit the placement of a frame in the document**

1. Select the frame, choose Properties, and choose the Layout tab to display the Layout tab sheet.

2. In the Placement area, choose the placement you want.

   The tab sheet changes depending on your choice.

   - If you choose In Line, you can set the amount you want the frame to be offset from the baseline of the surrounding text. An offset of 0 aligns the bottom of the frame with the text baseline. A positive offset lowers the frame; a negative offset raises it.

   - If you choose Displayed, the program centers the frame on its own line. No options are available.
   - If you choose Floating, you can choose the floating placement options you want: Here, Top of Page, Bottom of Page, or On a Page of Floats.

3. Choose OK.

Setting the Frame Appearance

The graphics defaults determine whether the framed image initially appears on the screen and in print with or without the frame outline, whether the frame and its image are iconified, or whether the frame outline appears but its image doesn't. You can override the defaults to set the screen appearance of each frame. Independently, you can set the way the frame appears when you print your document without typesetting it. For example, you may want to show the outline of the frame around the image in the document window but have the image appear without an outline in print. When you typeset your document, the typesetting specifications may override these settings.

Large graphics are often slow to display and print. You can save time while you work by displaying frames as icons or without their corresponding images. If you don't typeset your document, you can use iconified or empty frames to speed the production of document drafts. If you typeset, these print options aren't available. When you use either option, remember to change them before you print the final version of your document.

▶ **To edit the appearance of a frame in the document window and in print**

1. Select the frame, choose Properties, and choose the Layout tab to display the Layout tab sheet.

2. In the Screen Display Attributes area, select the way you want the frame to appear on the screen:

Option	Effect
Use Model Screen Attributes	Display the frame according to the screen attributes set in the User Setup dialog box
Picture in Frame	Display the image with a frame outline
Picture Only	Display the image without a frame outline
Frame Only	Display the frame outline without the image
Iconified	Display a small gray box representing the graphic

3. In the Print Attributes area, select the way you want the frame to appear in print:

Option	Effect
Picture in Frame	Print the image with a frame outline
Picture Only	Print the image without a frame outline
Frame Only*	Print the frame outline without the image
Iconified*	Print a small gray box representing the graphic

*Not available with typesetting in *SWP* and *SW*

4. If you choose to iconify the frame, either in print on in the document window, enter a name to identify it on the frame icon:

a. Choose the Labeling tab.

b. In the Name box, enter the name that you want to appear on the frame icon.

If you don't enter a name, the program uses the name of the graphics file.

Note   The program also uses the name to create ALT text for the graphic when you export the document as an HTML file.

5. Choose OK.

Sizing a Frame

When you import or paste a graphic, the size of its frame depends on the graphics default settings in the User Setup dialog box (see page 326). If the settings specify that all frames must fit a specified default size, the program creates a frame of that size and sizes the image accordingly. If the Fit to Default Size option is turned off, the program imports or pastes the image in its natural size and fits the frame around it. The frame is slightly larger than the image it contains.

Ordinarily, the automatic frame size is adequate. However, if you produce your document without typesetting it, the size of the frame determines the length of the caption that can be printed with it, as shown on page 116. You may want to change the size of the frame if you expect to use a long caption or if you want an unusual amount of white space around the image. Note, however, that the size specifications for the frame and the image are somewhat interdependent. Changing the size of the frame may affect the size of the image it contains. If you change the size of the frame you may need to change the size of the image as well; see page 118.

▶ **To edit the size of a frame**

1. Select the frame, choose **Properties**, and choose the **Layout** tab to display the **Layout** tab sheet.

2. In the **Size** area, change the dimensions of the frame by entering new values for width and height as necessary.

3. Use the **Units** box to change the measurement unit for the dimensions, if necessary.

    Changing the unit adjusts the values for the width and height of the frame.

4. If you want to leave the size of the image inside the frame unchanged,

    a. Choose the **Picture Properties** tab.
    b. In the **Sizing** area, check **Custom**.
    c. Check **Maintain Aspect Ratio**.
    d. In the **Scaling (percent)** area, enter **100** for the **Horizontal** or the **Vertical** value.

5. Choose **OK**.

Labeling a Frame

A frame can have a key, a caption, and a name. If you produce your document without typesetting it, the key can be used in hypertext links. If you typeset your document in *SWP* or *SW,* the key for a floating frame can be used in cross-references to the frame from elsewhere in the document and, in PDF files, in hypertext links.

The typesetting specifications and the style determine the appearance of captions, which can contain text and mathematics. The captions you create appear under in-line and displayed frames and either over or under floating frames, according to your specifications. If you produce your document without typesetting it, approximately as much of the caption as can fit in the width of the frame will appear in print.

This is a small

If the frame is small or the caption is long, you may want to increase the width of the frame. If you typeset your document, the captions appear in their entirety, like this:

This is a small butterfly.

Additionally, if the typesetting specifications for your document call for a list of figures, the caption for a floating frame, or a special short form of the caption, can be used to generate the list. See Chapter 9 "Structuring Documents for Typesetting" for information about creating a list of figures.

By default, the name of the frame for an imported graphic is the name of the graphics file it contains. The name of the frame for a pasted graphic is *Figure*. If you iconify the frame, the program uses the name to identify the icon. It also uses the name (with its full path, for imported graphics) to create ALT text for the graphic when you export your document to HTML. You can change the name easily.

▶ **To add a key and caption for a frame**

1. Select the frame, choose **Properties**, and choose the **Labeling** tab.

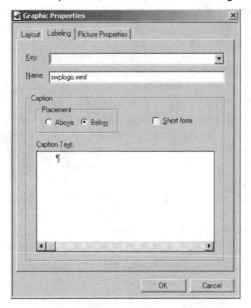

2. In the **Key** box, enter a unique key for the frame.

   Click the arrow next to the **Key** box to see a list of keys already defined for the document.

3. In the **Placement** area, check **Above** or **Below** to specify the location of the caption.

   Captions for in-line and displayed frames can appear only below the frame.

4. In the **Caption Text** box, enter the caption for the frame, tagged the way you want.

5. If you want to add a short caption for a floating graphic, check the **Short form** box.

   Note that this checkbox appears only if the selected frame is a floating frame. The program opens a second **Caption Text** box so you can enter the short caption. If you typeset your document, the short caption will appear in the list of figures and the long caption will appear with the frame.

6. In the **Name** area, enter the name you want to appear on the icon if you iconify the frame.

   Remember that the program also uses the name to create ALT text for the graphic if you export the document as an HTML file.

7. Choose **OK**.

Resizing, Cropping, and Moving Graphics

In addition to changing the size of a frame, you can resize, crop, or move an image in relation to its frame.

Remember   To change the image itself, you must use the application program with which the image was created.

You can use the mouse to quickly resize, crop, or move an image, or you can use the Picture Properties tab sheet in the Graphic Properties dialog box to work with more precision. Any sizing or cropping changes that you make with the mouse are reflected in the Graphic Properties dialog box.

Using the Mouse to Work with Graphics

You can use the mouse to modify graphics by resizing them or by *panning* and *zooming* in and out to crop them. When you *pan* a graphic, you move the image in relation to its frame, without changing its size; only the part of the image remaining in the frame appears on the screen or in print. When you *zoom in* on a graphic, the portion of the image that you select fills the entire frame. When you *zoom out,* the entire image fits in the portion of the frame that you select. The size and location of the frame are unchanged.

Before you can use the mouse to modify a graphic, you must first select the graphic by clicking the mouse in the frame:

- If you click once in the frame to select the graphic, eight small black handles appear around the frame, and a small Properties icon appears in the lower right-hand corner of the frame. If you click the icon, the program opens the Graphic Properties dialog box.

- If you double-click in the frame to modify a graphic, eight small gray handles appear around the frame. The mouse pointer changes to ⏚, and several other icons appear:

Pan

Zoom In

Zoom Out

Graphic Properties

▶ **To raise or lower an in-line graphic with the mouse**

- Click the graphic, then click inside the frame and drag it up or down to the baseline location you want.

▶ **To resize a graphic with the mouse**

1. Click the graphic.

2. Click and drag one of the handles on the frame to expand or contract the graphic.

As you drag the handle, the program draws a rectangle, which represents the size of the graphic you will see when you release the mouse button.

- If you click and drag a corner handle, the program maintains the proportion between the current height and width of the graphic.

- If you click and drag a side or top handle, the program won't maintain the proportion and the Maintain Aspect Ratio attribute will be turned off.

3. Release the mouse button.

▶ To pan a graphic using the mouse

1. Double-click the graphic.

The mouse pointer changes to 🖐️ .

2. Click and drag the graphic to produce a dotted rectangle that encloses part of the image and then release the mouse button.

The dotted rectangle can extend beyond the frame. When you release the mouse button, the part of the image that shows in the dotted rectangle will appear in the frame. For example, if you pan this graphic:

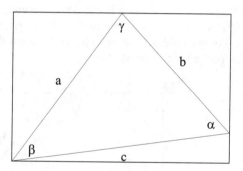

to drag the dotted rectangle to this position:

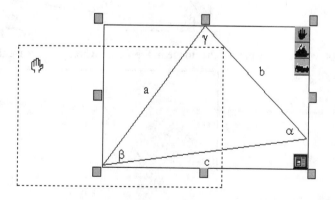

you will see this part of the image in the frame when you release the mouse button:

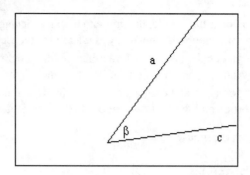

▶ To zoom in

1. Double-click the graphic.

2. Click the Zoom In icon 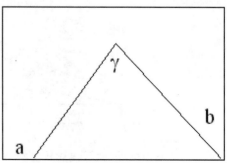 .

The pointer appears as cross hairs ╪ when the mouse is over the graphic.

3. Click and drag to produce a dotted rectangle and then release the mouse button.

The rectangle can extend beyond the frame. When you release the mouse button, the part of the image that appears in the dotted rectangle will expand to fill the entire frame. If Maintain Aspect Ratio is checked, the rectangle maintains its proportions as you drag it. For example, if you zoom in on the original triangle shown above so that you produce a dotted rectangle like this:

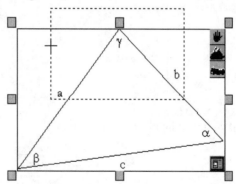

you will see this part of the image in the frame when you release the mouse button:

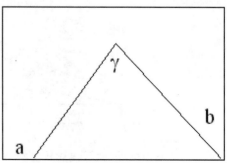

▶ **To zoom out**

1. Double-click the graphic.

2. Click the Zoom Out icon 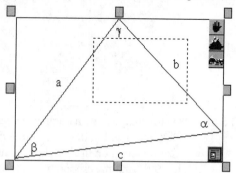 .

The pointer appears as cross hairs ✛ when the mouse is over the graphic.

3. Click and drag to produce a dotted rectangle and then release the mouse button.

When you release the mouse button, the part of the image that shows inside the frame will contract to fit inside the dotted rectangle. If Maintain Aspect Ratio is checked, the rectangle maintains its proportions as you drag it. For example, if you zoom out on the original triangle in our example to produce a dotted rectangle like this:

you will see the image contracted to fit inside the rectangle when you release the mouse button:

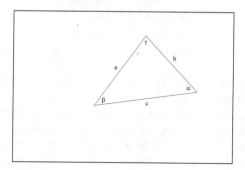

Using the Picture Properties to Work with Graphics

If you use the dialog box to resize, crop, or move graphics, understanding how the various Picture Properties affect one another is important. The options in the Sizing area can override other size settings, including the frame size setting on the Layout tab sheet. The size specifications for a frame and its corresponding image can affect one another.

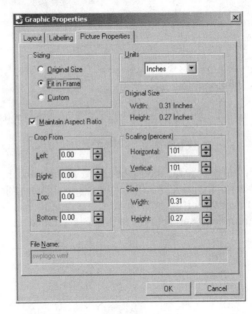

Option	Effect
Original Size	Use the image in its natural size (specified in the Original Size area) and fit the frame around it, regardless of the frame size specified on the Layout tab sheet; reset the scaling values to 100% and the cropping values to 0
Fit in Frame	Fit the image inside a frame that is the size specified on the Layout tab sheet. If Maintain Aspect Ratio is checked, maintain the proportions of the image; adjust the scaling and cropping values as necessary
Custom	Size the image according to the specifications for scaling percentage, size, cropping, or adding white space

As you crop or add space, the program changes the Size dimensions of the image. If the scaling value is 100, the width and height measurements always equal the natural width and height of the image, as recorded in the Original Size area. Also, the values in the Crop From, Scaling, and Size areas can affect one another. If the scaling factor is other than 100, the sum of the width values set in the Crop From and Size areas always equal the natural width of the image multiplied by the scaling factor. The height values behave similarly. Note that cropping the image and adding space around the image affect the size of the frame.

▶ **To resize or crop a graphic**

1. Select the graphic and choose Properties.

2. Choose the Picture Properties tab to open the Picture Properties tab sheet.

3. In the Sizing area, select Custom.

4. If you want to change the unit of measure, click the arrow in the Units area to select a new unit.

The Units box shows the unit in effect.

5. Check Maintain Aspect Ratio to keep the image in proportion as its size changes.

6. Use the boxes in the Crop From area to enter the amount of the image you want to remove from or the amount of white space you want to add to each side of the image in its current size.
   - To crop from the image, enter positive numbers.
   - To add white space to the image, enter negative numbers.

7. Set the size of the image.
   - If you want to scale the image to a percentage of its original size, enter the horizontal and vertical percentages in the Scaling (percent) area.
   - If you want to set the exact size of the image, enter the width and height measurements in the Size area.

If you checked the Maintain Aspect Ratio box, entering one value for size or scaling causes the other value to change proportionately. If you didn't check the box, you must enter both values. Note too that the values in the Scaling and Size areas correspond; a change in one causes a change in the other. Scaling and size changes also affect the cropping specifications.

8. Choose OK.

▶ **To move an image within the frame**

1. Select the graphic and choose Properties.

2. Choose the Picture Properties tab and in the Sizing area, select Custom.

3. If necessary, change the unit of measure.

4. Check Maintain Aspect Ratio to keep the image in proportion as it moves.

5. In the Crop From area, enter a positive measurement in the box for the direction in which you want to move the image within the frame.

The program crops the specified amount from the specified edge, effectively moving the image in that direction.

6. Enter an equal but negative measurement in the opposite direction.

The program adds white space to maintain the frame size.

7. Choose OK.

Exporting Pictures

You can create a picture of your text and mathematics and then paste or export that picture to another document, even if the target document has been created with a different application. The picture you paste or export reflects the careful formatting you see in the document window. This feature is particularly useful if you need to create properly formatted mathematics in *SWP*, *SW*, or *SNB* and then duplicate the mathematics elsewhere, such as in other word processing applications.

You create a picture from information you select in the active document window. Your selection can extend beyond a single paragraph and can contain text and mathematics occurring in displays, matrices, tables, lists, or ordinary paragraphs. You can paste the selection to the clipboard as a Windows Enhanced Metafile (.emf) graphic and then copy it into any application that accepts Enhanced Metafile objects. Alternatively, you can export the picture of the information to a graphics file, selecting the type of graphic most appropriate for your needs from among the available formats.

The width of the picture depends on the width of the document window when you make the selection. The height of the picture expands to accommodate the selection; if the selection is lengthy and extends beyond a page, the picture expands vertically to include as much of the selection as possible. (Note that extremely large selections may cause error messages. In these cases, make several smaller selections and create a series of smaller pictures.) You may also be able to change the size of the pasted or exported picture, depending on the capabilities of the target application.

Unless you change the default options, all lines and text are shown in black and paragraph and page backgrounds are transparent, as are gray boxes. Also by default, the export process ignores all the settings on the View menu except for the zoom factor; therefore, invisibles, helper lines, input boxes, index entries, and markers don't appear in the exported picture. However, you can change the options so that the picture you create reflects any or all of the current View settings.

If you want the picture to appear in different colors; to show invisibles, lines, and boxes; or to reflect a certain view percentage, you must set the export options accordingly and perhaps also customize the View settings before you create the picture. See Chapter 12 "Customizing the Program" for additional information.

▶ **To specify export settings for a picture**

1. From the Tools menu, choose Export Settings.

2. Choose the Export as Picture Options tab shown on the next page.

3. Select the settings you want.

4. Choose OK.

   Note that you can set the zoom factor for the export independently of the display in the document window.

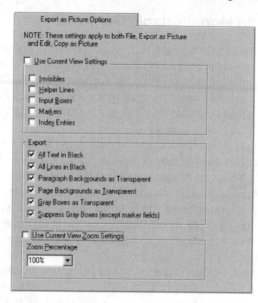

► **To create and use a picture of selected information**

1. Customize the appearance of the information in the document window so that it appears the way you want.

   or

   Customize the Export as Picture options so that information is copied or exported the way you want.

2. Select the information from which you want to create the picture.

3. If you expect to use the picture only once and the graphics format of the image is of no consequence, copy the selection to the clipboard:

   a. From the Edit or Context menu, choose Copy Picture.
   b. Open the target document and paste the contents of the clipboard where you want it to appear.

4. If you expect to use the picture frequently or you need to use a particular graphics format, export the picture to a graphics file:

   a. From the File or Context menu, choose Export as Picture.
   b. Enter a name and location for the graphics file.
   c. In the Save as type area, select the graphics format you want to use.
   d. Choose Save.
   e. Open the target document and import the file containing the picture.

Creating More Portable Graphics

If you expect to open your *SWP* or *SW* document on another platform or LATEX installation, you can take steps to improve the portability of the graphics in your document.

First, make sure you save your document with the Portable LATEX filter. Portable LATEX documents include the *graphicx* package, which allows typesetting to work with the print drivers on other installations. See Using LATEX Packages on page 226 for more information about packages.

Second, choose the formats for your graphics carefully. When you create graphics for documents that you expect to open outside *SWP* or *SW*, use formats that are appropriate for the target platform or installation. Encapsulated PostScript (.eps) graphics are perhaps the most portable from platform to platform.

Third, if you're using *SWP*, create graphics from your plots. When you create a plot, the program can automatically generate a plot snapshot. Ordinarily, the program creates Windows Metafiles (.wmf files), which aren't portable to UNIX installations. If you need to generate a plot in an *SWP* document and you expect to open the document later on a different platform or installation, save your document as a Portable LATEX file, exporting the plot as an .eps file, as described on page 33. For extensive information about generating plots, see the online Help and *Doing Mathematics with Scientific WorkPlace and Scientific Notebook*.

▶ **To create .eps graphics of plot files for portable LATEX files**

1. From the Tools menu, choose Computation Setup and choose the Plot Behavior tab.

2. Check Generate Plot Snapshots Automatically and choose OK.

3. From the Typeset menu, choose General Settings and then choose Portable La-TeX Graphics Settings.

4. In the Export Plots as Graphics area, check Export plots as graphics.

5. In the Graphics type for plot export box, select *.eps (Encapsulated Postscript).

   If *.eps (Encapsulated Postscript) is not listed, you must install and configure a special WMF2eps print driver that is used in the conversion process. See the online Help for instructions.

6. Choose OK to close the dialog boxes.

7. Generate the plot.

8. Save your document as a Portable LATEX file.

Finally, when you want to copy or send a document that contains graphics, use the Document Manager so that any graphics files associated with your document are included correctly. For more information, see Chapter 11 "Managing Documents."

Creating Tables

	Head	Head	Head	
A table can appear in line with text, like this

Head	Head	Head
item	item	item
item	item	item

, or it can be set off from the text in a paragraph and centered on its own line, like this:

Head	Head	Head
item	item	item
item	item	item

If a table is in line, you can set its baseline so the surrounding text is aligned with the top row, bottom row, or vertical center of the table.

SWP and *SW* also have a special construct that allows the creation of tables that can float unanchored to a specific place until you typeset your document. Tables created with this special construct can have keys for use in cross-references and hypertext links. These tables, which can be automatically numbered by LATEX or PDFLATEX when you typeset, can also have captions. If the typesetting specifications for the document include a list of tables, the formatter uses the caption and the table number to create the list of tables when you typeset the document. However, if you print your document without typesetting, tables that float appear at the point of entry. No number is assigned to the table, cross-references and lists of tables aren't generated, and the caption doesn't appear in print. Tables that float aren't available in *SNB*.

Although the program treats a table as if it were a single text character, a table consists of rows and columns of boxes called *cells*. You can add, delete, merge, and split cells; add lines to define cells; and align the information in the table columns the way you want.

You enter information into a table by typing it as you would any other information in your document. You can also paste information from multiple cells into other cells in the same or different tables. See Chapter 6 "Using Editing Techniques and Tools."

The cells in a table can contain text, graphics, and mathematics, on which you can perform computations if you use *SWP* or *SNB*. However, because the table itself isn't a mathematical object, you can't perform mathematical computations on the table as a whole as you can on a matrix. If you want to be able to perform matrix operations, be sure you create a matrix, not a table. See Chapter 4 "Creating Mathematics" for information about creating matrices.

Creating In-Line Tables

Creating an in-line table involves entering a table with a specified number of rows and columns, setting the initial column and baseline alignment, and then filling the table with information. You can center an in-line table in a paragraph on a line by itself.

When you enter an in-line table, the program creates an empty table according to the dimensions you specify. Each cell in the table contains an empty input box and the insertion point appears in the input box in the top left cell. To make working with tables easier, you can display an outline of the table cells on the screen by choosing **Helper Lines** from the **View** menu. The outlines serve only as an editing guide; they don't print when you typeset your document and, depending on the print option settings, may or may not print when you produce the document without typesetting.

▶ **To enter an in-line table**

1. On the Standard toolbar, click the Table button 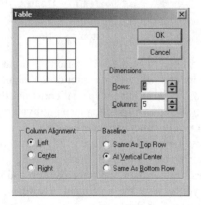 or, from the Insert menu, choose Table to open the Table dialog box.

2. In the Dimensions area, specify the number of rows and columns you want in the table.

3. In the Baseline area, specify the alignment of the table baseline.

4. In the Column Alignment area, specify the table column alignment and then choose OK.

   The program creates an empty table in the specified dimensions, as in this example:

   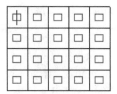

   Each cell in the table contains an empty input box. The insertion point appears in the input box in the top left cell so that you can begin entering information.

▶ **To center a table in a paragraph on its own line**

1. Start a new paragraph.

2. Create an in-line table.

3. Place the insertion point in the new paragraph.

4. From the Section/Body Tag popup list, choose the Centered tag.

Creating Tables That Can Float

Creating a table that floats in *SWP* or *SW* involves importing a fragment containing a table of predefined size, four rows and three columns. The table is surrounded by several TEX fields containing commands that provide a way to enter a key and a caption for the table and a way to determine placement of the table and the caption on the page. The formatter automatically numbers tables that float, but you can suppress the number.

Once you've entered the fragment, you fill the table with information, just as you do with an in-line table. You can edit the table properties and the TEX fields as necessary, but caution is in order if you're unfamiliar with TEX and LATEX. See Chapter 9 "Structuring Documents for Typesetting" for more information about TEX fields and keys.

When you typeset your document, LATEX positions tables that float according to the way you set the four placement options for the table frame:

Option	Position of the table
Here	As close as possible to the entry point in the text
Top	At the top of a page
Bottom	At the bottom of a page
On a Page of Floats	On a separate page containing only floating objects

Remember that tables created with this fragment float to a location only when you typeset your document. If you produce your document without typesetting it, the tables appear where you entered them and the captions don't appear in print.

▶ **To create a table that can float**

1. Place the insertion point where you want to enter the table.

2. From the Fragment popup list, select **Table - (4x3, floating)**.

   or

   a. From the **File** menu, choose **Import Fragment**.
   b. Choose the fragment named **Table - (4x3, floating).frg** and then choose **OK**.

   The program inserts a table with four rows and three columns. On the screen you see this:

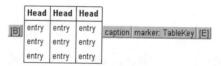

   The gray boxes include TEX fields that contain typesetting commands and a marker for the table. The insertion point appears to the right of the fragment.

3. Edit the number of rows and columns in the table as described in Editing Table Dimensions, on page 131, so that the table has the dimensions you want.

4. Replace the predefined contents of each cell with the information you want.

To change the placement options for a table created with the fragment, you must open and edit one of the TeX fields imported with the fragment.

Caution   When you work inside the TeX fields, you enter LaTeX code directly. Be extremely careful, especially if you're not very familiar with TeX and LaTeX.

▶ **To change the floating placement option for a table**

1. In the table fragment, double-click the [B] box or place the insertion point to its right and choose **Properties**.

   The program opens the field represented by the gray box, which contains this string of TeX commands:

   $$\verb|\begin{table}[tbp] \centering|$$

   The square brackets near the middle of the string contain the placement options in order of preference: t (top of page), b (bottom of page), and p (on a page of floats).

2. Edit the placement options as necessary and then choose **OK**.

   You can add or remove options, including the option h (here), and you can rearrange the options within the brackets.

   To add a caption to a table created with the fragment, you must open and edit another TeX field in the fragment. Because the field contains a LaTeX command, you must be careful not to enter in the caption any characters that have meaning for TeX or LaTeX, such as %, unless you precede them with a backslash.

   If you add a caption, the program automatically creates the table number when you typeset your document, unless you suppress the number. If you suppress the table number, cross-references to the table can't occur. For more information on cross-references, see Chapter 9 "Structuring Documents for Typesetting."

▶ **To specify numbering, a caption, and a key for a table that can float**

1. Double-click the caption box or place the insertion point to its right and choose **Properties**.

   The program opens the field represented by the gray box, which contains this string of TeX commands:

   $$\verb|\caption{Table Caption}|$$

2. If you don't want LaTeX to number the table, insert an asterisk (*) immediately after the word *caption*.

   Remember that if the table has no number, you can't create cross-references to it.

3. If you want to add a caption, select the words *Table Caption* and replace them by typing the caption you want for the table.

4. Choose **OK**.

5. If you want to add a key for the table, double-click the `marker: TableKey` box or place the insertion point to its right and choose **Properties** to open the **Marker Properties** dialog box.

   A key is required to create cross-references to the table.

6. Select the contents of the **Key** box and replace it with the key you want for the table.

7. Choose **OK**.

   The location of the `caption` box in the fragment determines the placement of the caption when the document is typeset. If the gray box follows the table, the formatter places the caption under the table. If the gray box precedes the table, the formatter places the caption over the table. Use cut and paste techniques to move the gray box as necessary.

Moving Around in Tables

You can use the mouse or the keyboard to move the insertion point from cell to cell.

▶ **To place the insertion point in a cell using the mouse**

- Click the mouse in the cell.

▶ **To move from cell to cell using the keyboard**

- Press the TAB key or the arrow keys.

Editing Table Dimensions

Once you've created a table, you can change its dimensions by adding or deleting rows and columns and by merging or splitting cells.

Adding and Deleting Rows and Columns
You can add a row or column anywhere in a table.

▶ **To add a row or column to a table**

1. Place the insertion point in the table or immediately to its right.

   or

   Select the entire table or any group of cells in the table.

2. From the **Edit** or **Context** menu, choose **Insert Row(s)** or **Insert Column(s)**.

   The program displays the **Insert Rows** or **Insert Columns** dialog box.

3. Specify the number of rows or columns you want to insert.

   If you selected a group of cells before you opened the dialog box, the number of rows or columns to add is set to the number of rows or columns you selected.

4. Specify the position of the insertion.

If you selected a group of cells before you opened the dialog box, the insertion arrow is shown to the left of or below the selection. Note that the table illustration shown in the dialog box changes according to your specifications.

5. Choose OK.

You can delete an entire row or column or a group of rows or columns. Also, you can delete the contents of a cell, row, or column, but leave the row or column in the table.

▶ **To delete an entire row or column**

1. Select the entire row or column.

2. Press DELETE or BACKSPACE or, from the Edit or Context menu, choose Delete.

▶ **To delete several columns**

1. Select at least one cell in each column you want to delete.

2. From the Edit or Context menu, choose Delete Columns.

▶ **To delete the contents of a cell**

1. Select the contents of the cell.

2. Press either DELETE or BACKSPACE or, from the Edit or Context menu, choose Delete.

If you select and delete the contents of the cells in an entire row or column in a single operation, the program will delete that row or column from the table. You can delete the contents of a row or column but keep the empty row or column in the table by deleting the contents of at least one cell in a separate operation.

▶ **To delete the contents of a row or column without deleting the row or column itself**

1. Select all but one cell of the row or column.

2. Press DELETE or BACKSPACE or, from the Edit or Context menu, choose Delete.

3. Select the contents of the remaining cell.

4. Press either DELETE or BACKSPACE or, from the Edit or Context menu, choose Delete.

The program deletes the contents of the cells in the row or column but leaves the input boxes for you to refill.

Merging and Splitting Cells

The program can merge cells horizontally and can split cells that have been merged.

▶ **To merge cells horizontally**

1. Select the cells you want to merge.

2. From the Edit or Context menu, choose Merge Cells.

   If your selection includes more than one row, cells in each row of your selection are merged horizontally but not vertically. The rows remain distinct.

▶ **To split previously merged cells**

1. Select the cell or cells.

   Your selection can cover multiple rows. If you want to split a single empty cell, place the insertion point in it.

2. From the Edit or Context menu, choose Split Cells.

   The program splits the cell or cells and leaves the contents in the leftmost cell. The rows remain distinct.

Editing Table Properties

You can edit the properties of a table to define the cells with lines, as these examples show:

Heading One	Heading Two	Heading Three
item	item	item
item	item	item

Heading One	Heading Two	Heading Three
item	item	item
item	item	item

Heading One	Heading Two	Heading Three
item	item	item
item	item	item

Heading One	Heading Two	Heading Three
item	item	item
item	item	item

You can align the contents of the table columns and of individual cells. Also, if a table is in line, you can set its baseline so the surrounding text is aligned with the top row, bottom row, or vertical center of the table:

Baseline at bottom:
1	2
3	4
Baseline at center:
1	2
3	4
Baseline at top:
1	2
3	4

In *SWP* and *SW*, you can specify the width of table columns. The program uses the specified widths when you typeset your document, but it ignores specified widths when you don't typeset. You make all these changes from the tab sheets in the **Table Properties** dialog box.

▶ **To edit the properties of a table**

1. Select the table or place the insertion point immediately to its right.

   or

   Select the cell or cells whose properties you want to edit.

2. On the Standard toolbar, click the Properties button 🔍 or, from the **Edit** or **Context** menu, choose **Properties**.

3. Choose the tab sheet you want and edit the table properties as necessary.

4. Choose **OK**.

▶ **To add or remove lines around table cells**

1. Select the cells for which you want to add or remove lines.
   - If you want to modify the lines around a single cell, select the cell's contents.
   - If the cell is empty, move the insertion point into it.

2. Choose **Properties** and then choose the **Lines** tab to display the **Lines** tab sheet.

3. In the **Line Style** area, check the type of line you want.

4. In the **Line Position** area, check the positions of the lines you want to add, uncheck the positions of lines you want to remove, and then choose **OK**.

▶ **To change the alignment of columns or cells**

1. Select the columns or cells you want to align.

2. Choose Properties and then choose the Alignment tab.

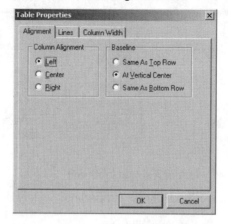

3. In the Column Alignment area, set the alignment you want for the selected columns or cells.

4. Choose OK.

▶ **To change the baseline alignment of an in-line table**

1. Select the table or place the insertion point to its right.

2. Choose Properties and choose the Alignment tab.

3. In the Baseline area, select the alignment you want and choose OK.

▶ **To specify the width of a table column for typesetting**

1. Select the column or columns whose width you want to set.

2. If the table has only one row, select the entire contents of the cell.

3. Choose Properties.

4. Choose the Column Width tab shown on the next page.

5. If you want the program to set the column width to accommodate the widest entry in the column, check Use Automatic Width, which is the default.

6. If you have *SWP* or *SW* and want to set the column width yourself,

   a. Uncheck Use Automatic Width.
   b. Enter a value and a unit of measure for the width.

7. Choose OK.

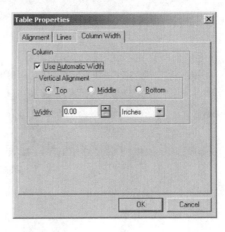

▶ **To specify the width of a single table cell**

1. Select the cell and choose Properties.

2. Choose the Column Width tab.

3. Uncheck Use Automatic Width.

4. Enter a value and a unit of measure for the width and choose OK.

When you specify the width of a cell, the program displays in the cell a gray box containing a width measurement, like this: 1.25in . The contents of the cells aren't visible. When you produce your *SWP* or *SW* document by typesetting it, the program uses LaTeX or PDFLaTeX to lay out the table according to the column widths you specify. The contents appear correctly, wrapping within the cell as necessary to fit the specified width. When you produce your document without typesetting it, the program prints the table as it appears on the screen, with the gray boxes showing and their contents hidden. You can examine and edit the contents of a cell represented by a gray box.

▶ **To examine and edit the contents of a cell represented by a gray box**

- Place the insertion point at the right edge of the cell and choose Properties.

Working with Imported Tables

If you use *SWP* or *SW* to open a LaTeX document containing a floating table, the typeset appearance and the screen appearance of the table will be dramatically different. For example, an imported floating table that looks like this when you typeset print:

Heading One	Heading Two	Heading Three
item a	item b	item c
item d	item e	item f

1. This is the caption

will look like this in the document window:

When the program imports the LaTeX file, it places the table in a text frame object that behaves somewhat like a graphic. In the document window, the frame object is iconified so that it appears as a gray box. If you typeset the document, the table appears correctly. If you don't typeset the document, the table appears as a gray box. If you want to edit the imported table, you must edit the properties of the frame object.

Note   Don't use *SNB* to open a LaTeX document containing a floating table.

▶ **To edit the properties of a text frame object**

1. Click the frame so that eight black handles appear on the frame.

   or

   Select the frame.

   or

   Place the insertion point to the right of the frame.

2. On the Standard toolbar, click the Properties button or, from the Edit or Context menu, choose **Properties**.

   or

   In the frame, click the Graphic Properties button ▣ .

   or

   Press CTRL+F5.

3. Choose the tab you want:
   - The **Layout** tab sheet controls the floating placement of the frame in your document.
   - The **Labeling** tab sheet controls the key, caption, and icon name for the frame.
   - The **Contents** tab sheet contains the table itself.

   Note that not all options on the tab sheets are active.

4. Edit the frame properties as necessary and choose **OK**.

   Remember that when you choose **OK** or **Cancel** in a tabbed dialog box, you accept or discard the changes made on all tab sheets, not just the tab sheet in front.

▶ **To edit the properties or contents of the imported table**

1. Select the frame, choose **Properties**, and choose the **Contents** tab.

   The program displays the imported table in the **Edit Contents** area of the **Contents** tab sheet, as in this example:

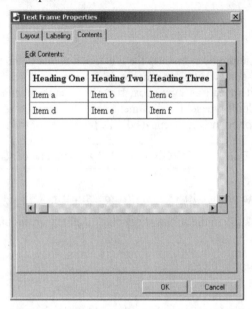

2. If you want to edit the properties of the table:

   a. Select the table or the table cells you want to edit and choose **Properties**.
   b. From the **Table Properties** dialog box, choose the tab sheet you want.
   c. Edit the table properties as necessary.
      As with any other table, you can add, delete, merge, and split cells; add lines to define cells; and align the information in the table columns the way you want. The cells in the table can contain text, graphics, and mathematics.

3. If you want to edit the contents of the table, use standard editing techniques to change the information in the cells.

4. Choose **OK**.

   Remember that when you choose **OK** or **Cancel** in a tabbed dialog box, you accept or discard the changes made on all tab sheets, not just the tab sheet in front.

6 Using Editing Techniques and Tools

In *SWP, SW,* and *SNB,* you edit the content of your document much as you would in any other word processing application: by adding, deleting, changing, copying, or moving information. In addition to using the **Properties** command to modify characters, symbols, and mathematical objects, you can take advantage of standard editorial operations and techniques. Copying capabilities extend beyond documents. You can copy information to the clipboard using a format that renders the best possible representation of information created with the program when you paste it to another application.

Editing is simplified with two tools, Find and Replace and Spell Check. With Find and Replace, you can quickly locate and change information throughout your document. With Spell Check, you can check the spelling in all or part of your document using a language dictionary and a user dictionary whose contents you determine.

Chapter 8 "Formatting Documents" explains how to edit the appearance of your document.

Editing Operations and Techniques

Chapter 3 "Creating Text" and Chapter 4 "Creating Mathematics" explain how to use the **Properties** command to modify characters, symbols, and mathematical objects. In addition, you can edit the content of your document with standard cut, copy, and paste operations; standard drag-and-drop mouse techniques; and **Context** menu commands. You can also use the BACKSPACE or DELETE key to correct your typing mistakes as you work and to remove information permanently from your document. Further, you can undo your most recent deletion or operation if you haven't typed anything in the meantime.

Deleting and Reinserting Information

You can delete information permanently from your document. If you change your mind, you can undo the most recent deletion, but only if you've made no other editing changes since that deletion and if the **Undo** command on the **Edit** or **Context** menu is active. Otherwise, you can't reinsert the deleted information unless you retype it.

When you delete information, the program remembers the mathematics state and the item, section, body, and text tags in effect for the first object in the deletion. (Chapter 8 "Formatting Documents" explains tags and how to use them to format your document.) If you don't move the insertion point before you enter new information, the program applies the mathematics state and remembered tags to the new information. On the other hand, if you move the insertion point before you enter new information, the program discards the remembered information.

▶ **To delete information permanently**

- Place the insertion point to the right of the information to be deleted and press BACKSPACE.

  or

- Place the insertion point to the left of the information to be deleted and press DELETE.

  or

- Select the information to be deleted and then press BACKSPACE or DELETE or, from the Edit or Context menu, choose Delete.

▶ **To undo the most recent deletion**

- On the Standard toolbar, click the Undo button .

  or

- From the Edit or Context menu, choose Undo Deletion.

  or

- Press CTRL+Z.

  or

- Press ALT+BACKSPACE.

Using Cut, Copy, and Paste Operations

Using commands on the Edit menu, buttons on the Standard toolbar, or the corresponding keyboard shortcuts, you can cut or copy a selection to the clipboard and paste it to a new location or to a different application. Your selection remains on the clipboard until it is overwritten by the next clipboard operation.

Two copy commands on the Edit menu are similar, Copy and Copy as Internal Format. When you use Copy, the program places selected information on the clipboard in two formats, the program's internal format (which is unchanged from earlier versions of the program) and a filtered Unicode format. The Unicode format, which is the best possible representation of the selected material, has been designed to be more compatible with other applications. When you use Copy as Internal Format, the program places the information on the clipboard in the internal format only; that is, it behaves as did the Copy command in earlier versions of the program. See Chapter 5 "Using Graphics and Tables" for information about the third copy command, Copy Picture.

When you paste clipboard information copied from the program into an *SWP, SW,* or *SNB* document, the results are the same regardless of the copy command you use, because the program always uses its own internal format. However, when you paste to a different application, the results may differ markedly. If you place information on the clipboard using the Copy as Internal Format command, the only information on the clipboard is in the internal format. Most applications simply paste the contents of the clipboard without attempting to interpret the format. The result may not be particularly useful. On the other hand, if you use the Copy command, the application can take advantage of the more widely interpretable Unicode format, and the information that appears in the new application is quite similar to that in your *SWP, SW,* or *SNB* document. Note that when you paste the clipboard contents into the target application, the font in use can affect the results.

When you	The program
Cut a selection to the clipboard	Moves the selection to the clipboard; deletes it from your document
Copy a selection to the clipboard	Copies the selection to the clipboard in two formats; leaves it in your document
Copy a selection to the clipboard as internal format	Copies the selection to the clipboard in internal format; leaves it in your document
Paste a selection from the clipboard	Pastes the contents of the clipboard into your document; leaves in on the clipboard

If you place text on the clipboard from another application, it is pasted into your document as unformatted text. If the clipboard contains a graphic with a file extension of .wmf or .bmp, the graphic is pasted into your document in that same format.

▶ To cut a selection to the clipboard

- On the Standard toolbar, click the Cut button [icon].
  or
- From the Edit or Context menu, choose Cut.
  or
- Press CTRL+X. The selection is cut when you release the CTRL key.

▶ To copy a selection to the clipboard in multiple formats

- On the Standard toolbar, click the Copy button [icon].
  or
- From the Edit or Context menu, choose Copy.
  or
- Press CTRL+C. The selection is copied when you release the CTRL key.

▶ To copy a selection to the clipboard in internal format only

- From the Edit menu, choose Copy as Internal Format.

▶ To paste the contents of the clipboard at the insertion point

- On the Standard toolbar, click the Paste button [icon].
  or
- From the Edit or Context menu, choose Paste.
  or
- Press CTRL+V. The selection is pasted when you release the CTRL key.

You can use standard copy and paste techniques to copy the contents of table and matrix cells to cells in other tables and matrices.

▶ **To copy and paste information in tables, matrices, and vectors**

1. In the source table, matrix, or vector, select the cells containing the information you want.

2. Choose **Copy**.

3. In the destination table, matrix, or vector, select the cells to which you want to copy the information.

4. Choose **Paste**.

The program compares the dimensions of the copied cells to those of the destination cells. If the dimensions match, the program pastes the information into the destination table or matrix. If the dimensions match in one direction only and that one is a full row or column, the program replaces the selection in the destination table, matrix, or vector, removing or adding columns or rows as necessary. If the dimensions don't match in either direction, the program erases the contents of the selected destination cells and then pastes the copied cells in the top left cell.

Using Paste Special

With the **Paste Special** command, you can specify the format in which text on the clipboard is pasted into your document. You can specify that the text is to be pasted as Internal Format, in which case the program attempts to interpret it, or as Unformatted Text, in which case the program doesn't attempt to interpret it.

For example, if you're working in *SWP, SW,* or *SNB* and you copy the Greek letter α to the clipboard and then use **Paste Special** to paste it into your document in Internal Format, the program inserts α at the insertion point. However, if you paste the α into your document as Unformatted Text, the program inserts this at the insertion point:

$$\$\backslash alpha\$$$

Similarly, you can copy unformatted text from another application and have the program interpret it in the internal format. If you're working in another application and place the unformatted text **$\backslash$alpha$** on the clipboard and then use Paste Special to paste the clipboard contents to your document as Text in Internal Format, the program inserts α.

Note that incorrectly formed expressions pasted to the clipboard can create problems when the program tries to interpret those expressions as internal format. Note also that although the internal format agrees with TEX and LATEX for many symbols, it doesn't necessarily agree for other elements, including matrices and tables.

The **Paste Special** command is useful for inserting information copied from a line editor so that it appears in your document with the line breaks as they appear in the line editor. Font specifications made in other applications aren't preserved.

Tip   The program filters and treats clipboard text in much the same way as the ASCII and ANSI document filters. If you want to preserve line ends and spacing from the clipboard, paste into a paragraph that you've tagged as Body Verbatim.

These paste options are available:

Format	Effect
Internal Format	
Paste as Unformatted Text	Information placed on the clipboard from *SWP*, *SW*, or *SNB* is pasted into the document without being interpreted as internal format
Paste as Internal Format	Information placed on the clipboard from *SWP*, *SW*, or *SNB* is pasted into the document after being interpreted as internal format
Text	
Paste as Unformatted Text	Information on the clipboard is pasted into the document exactly as it appears on the clipboard; the program doesn't attempt to interpret it
Paste as Internal Format	Information on the clipboard is pasted into the document after being interpreted as internal format
Picture	Graphic information on the clipboard is pasted into the document as a Windows Metafile (.wmf) or bitmap (.bmp)
Unicode Text	Information on the clipboard information is pasted into the document as Unicode characters

▶ **To paste information from the clipboard in a specific format**

1. Place the insertion point where you want to insert the information.

2. From the Edit or Context menu, choose Paste Special.

3. Select the format you want and choose OK.

   The program pastes the contents of the clipboard into your document using the specified format. The selection remains on the clipboard until you cut or copy again.

Using Drag-and-Drop Techniques

You can use drag-and-drop techniques to delete, copy, and move selections with the mouse. When you use drag-and-drop techniques to delete information, the information is deleted permanently. You can reinsert it immediately with the Undo command, but if you make any other editing choices before you try to reinsert the deleted information, you must retype it.

   Some drag-and-drop techniques are assigned to the mouse buttons by default, but others are not. You can enable all drag-and-drop techniques on the Edit tab sheet in the User Setup dialog box. See Chapter 12 "Customizing the Program" for more information. If the Context menu is enabled (see Using the Context Menu, later in this chapter), you can use it in all drag-and-drop operations. The instructions for using drag-and-drop techniques for deleting and moving a selection assume the defaults are enabled.

▶ **To delete a selection**

1. Select the information you want to delete.

2. Without pressing any mouse buttons, move the mouse pointer within your selection.

3. Press and hold down the left mouse button.

   The mouse pointer changes to the scissors pointer ✂, indicating that your selection will be cut from its current position.

4. While holding down the mouse button, drag the mouse pointer to the side of the window, outside the text region. The most convenient place is the scroll bar.

5. Release the mouse button to remove the selection permanently from your document.

▶ **To move a selection**

1. Select the information you want to move.

2. Without pressing any mouse buttons, move the mouse pointer within your selection.

3. Press and hold down the left mouse button.

   The mouse pointer changes to the scissors pointer ✂, indicating that your selection will be cut from its current position.

4. While holding down the mouse button, drag the mouse pointer to the place where you want the selection to appear.

   The insertion point follows the mouse pointer as you do this, showing you accurately where your selection will appear.

5. Release the mouse button.

   The program moves your selection from its former position to the place where you released the mouse button.

You can copy a selection using drag-and-drop techniques if the Right Button Always Copies box is checked in the User Setup.

▶ **To copy a selection**

1. From the Tools menu, choose User Setup and choose the Edit tab sheet.

2. In the Mouse Dragging Behavior area, check Right Button Always Copies, and choose OK.

3. Select the information you want to copy.

4. Without pressing any mouse buttons, move the mouse pointer within your selection.

5. Press and hold down the right mouse button.

The mouse pointer changes to the copy pointer , indicating that the selection will be copied.

6. While holding down the mouse button, drag the mouse pointer to the place where you want the selection to be copied.

The insertion point follows the mouse pointer as you do this, providing an accurate guide to where your selection will appear.

7. Release the mouse button.

The program copies your selection to the place where you released the mouse button.

▶ **To cancel a drag-and-drop operation while it is in progress**

1. Keep holding down the mouse button and return the insertion point to within the selection.

2. Release the mouse button.

▶ **To undo a drag-and-drop operation**

- On the Standard toolbar, click the Undo button or, from the Edit or Context menu, choose Undo.

▶ **To disable drag-and-drop operations**

1. From the Tools menu, choose User Setup.

2. Choose the Edit tab sheet.

3. In the Mouse Dragging Behavior area, uncheck Left Button Moves and Right Button Always Copies, and choose OK.

Using the Context Menu

As in most Windows applications, you can edit quickly using the Context menu, a context-sensitive menu that lists those operations that are available for the current selection or the item under the mouse pointer. The Context menu isn't listed by name on the Menu bar.

▶ **To toggle the Context menu off and on**

1. From the Tools menu, choose User Setup.

2. Choose the Edit tab sheet.

3. In the Mouse Dragging Behavior area, check or uncheck Right Button Menu to turn the Context on or off.

4. Choose OK.

▶ **To use the Context menu**

1. Select or place the mouse pointer over the information you want to edit.

2. Click the right mouse button or press the Application key on your keyboard to display the menu.

The program displays the Context menu for the selection or the item under the mouse pointer.

▶ **To use the Context menu for drag-and-drop operations**

1. Select the information you want to delete, move, or copy.

2. Without pressing any mouse buttons, move the mouse pointer within your selection.

3. Press and hold down the right mouse button as you drag the insertion point to a new location.

The mouse pointer changes to ⬚.

4. Release the mouse button to display the Context menu of available drag-and-drop operations.

5. Select the operation you want.

Using Find and Replace

With the Find and Replace commands on the Edit menu, you can quickly locate or change text or mathematics in your document. You can

- Search for all occurrences of a specified word, phrase, or sequence of characters.
- Search for all occurrences of a mathematical expression or a combination of mathematics and text.
- Search for text or mathematics with a specific tag, such as Emphasize or Section.
- Search for text with a specific pattern of capitalization.

And you can

- Replace each occurrence of the specified text or mathematics with different text or mathematics.
- Replace the tags applied to each occurrence of the specified text or mathematics.

We suggest you save your document before you use Replace. If you don't like the results, you can close the document without saving the changes.

Specifying Search and Replacement Patterns

When you choose the Find or Replace command, the program opens a dialog box in which you can specify the search and replacement patterns. The program retains the search and replacement patterns and any tags applied to them until you change them, even if you close the program, unless you specify that they shouldn't be retained from one work session to the next. To specify new search and replacement patterns, first delete the old patterns and remove the tags, then enter the new patterns.

▶ **To discard search and replacement patterns when you close a session**

1. From the Tools menu, choose User Setup.

2. On the General tab sheet, uncheck Save Find/Replace Text and choose OK.

The menu commands, toolbars, and popup lists are active when the Find and Replace dialog boxes are open, so you can type text and mathematics just as you do when you enter information in a document. The ALT key combinations are not active, however; use the mouse to select menu items. You can also copy information from your document and paste it in the dialog boxes.

Searching for Text Patterns

If your search pattern is in text, the program searches both the text and mathematics in the search area for occurrences of the pattern. Ordinarily, a text search locates the characters you specify anywhere they occur, whether they stand alone or appear as part of a word. For example, if you search for the text characters *on,* the program will find *on, tone,* and *Ontario.* Two search options help you define a text search more precisely:

- The Whole Words Only option locates specified text characters only when they appear as a separate word and not when they are part of another word. For example, if you want to locate the text characters *on* and specify Whole Words Only, the program will locate only the word *on.*

- The Exact Case option locates specified text characters only when they match a particular pattern of capitalization. For example, by entering *Brown* and specifying Exact Case, the program will locate the name *Brown* but bypass uncapitalized references to the color *brown.*

Searching for Mathematics Patterns

If your search pattern is in mathematics, the program searches within the mathematics in the search area for occurrences of the pattern. That is, if your search pattern is an x in mathematics, the program searches only the mathematics in the search area, ignoring the text and thus finding x in $x = a + b$ but bypassing words such as *exit* and *hexadecimal.*

If you specify an empty mathematical template as the search pattern, the program finds all occurrences of that template in the search area. For example, if you enter an empty fraction, the program finds all fractions in the search area. You can enter an empty matrix of any shape to search for all matrices, regardless of their shape.

The program uses a search method that finds matches on the initial part of a word. Because *SWP, SW,* and *SNB* treat mathematical objects as words, you may find that a search for a mathematical expression yields unexpected results. For example, the expression x^2 consists of two words, the variable and the superscript. If you specify x^2 as the search pattern, the program will find x^{2y}, x_n^2, and x^2. The **Whole Words Only** option can help you define a mathematics search more precisely. Use the **Whole Words Only** option to locate an exact match of a mathematics search pattern.

If you specify a replacement pattern for all occurrences of a mathematics search pattern and the mathematical objects found in the search don't match the search pattern exactly, the program asks you to confirm each replacement.

Searching for Tagged Patterns

All search and replacement patterns carry tags. Unless you specify otherwise, the program applies the default paragraph tag for the document, which is defined in the .cst file for the document.

▶ **To determine the default paragraph tag for your document**

1. From the Tag menu, choose Appearance.

2. Select Modify Style Defaults.

3. In the Tag Properties box, select Global Properties and choose Modify.

   The program displays the default paragraph tag in the Tag for Starting Paragraphs box.

4. Choose Cancel to close the dialogs.

Note, however, that the previous search can affect application of the default paragraph tag. By default, the program remembers the previous search and replacement patterns and the tags that are applied to them. When you try to search a document after previously searching another document that has a different set of tags, the program displays in the Find dialog box the previous pattern and its tags, even if those tags are not defined for the current document. If you change the pattern but not the tag, the program will find all occurrences of the pattern if the tag used previously happens to be the default paragraph tag defined in the .cst file for the current document. Otherwise, the program will not find any occurrences of the search pattern in the current document unless they have been specifically tagged the same way.

To find all occurrences of the search pattern, regardless of the tag, apply the default paragraph tag for the current document to the search pattern.

You can modify the search by applying other tags to the search and replacement patterns. For example, you can replace every occurrence of the emphasized phrase

for all real Γ

with the phrase

for every real Λ

or you can change all occurrences of C to $\mathcal{C}$.

If you apply a tag to the search pattern, the program locates only those occurrences that carry the same tag. Thus, if you specify the word *step* with the subsection tag, the program locates the word *step* every time it appears in a subsection heading but ignores the word anywhere else in the document.

If you apply a tag to an empty search pattern—that is, choose a tag but enter no information in the search pattern—the program will find all occurrences of the tag in the search area. For example, you can search for all paragraphs in the document that are tagged as section heads. Similarly, you can replace all occurrences of a certain tag with another tag of the same type, such as replacing one kind of text tag with another. You might replace all bold text tags with italic text tags, all subsubsection heads with subsection heads, or all bulleted list items with numbered list items.

Specifying the Search Area

Unless you first specify a search area by selecting a part of your document or opening a dialog box, the program searches and replaces throughout the main part of the document. If you want to search a part of your document that appears in a dialog box—such as a footnote—you must open the dialog box before you initiate the search. Searching begins at the insertion point.

You can search your document in either direction. Ordinarily, the program searches forward from the insertion point to the end of the document. If you specify the Search Backward option, the program searches backward, locating only those occurrences of the search pattern that appear between the insertion point and the beginning of the document. The Search Backward option isn't available when you search a selection.

If you begin the search from the middle of your document, the program searches from the insertion point to the end or, if you choose Search Backward, from the insertion point to the beginning. The program then asks whether you want to continue the search in the rest of the file or stop.

Finding and Replacing

▶ **To find text or mathematics**

1. If you don't want to search the entire document, select the part you want to search.

2. On the Editing toolbar, click the Find button or, from the Edit menu, choose Find or press CTRL+Q.

3. In the Search for area of the Find dialog box, enter the text or mathematics you want to find, replacing former search patterns if necessary.

4. Select any options you need to control the search.

5. Choose Find Next to begin searching.

   The program scrolls to the first occurrence of the search pattern and shows it at the top of the screen.

6. If you want to find the next occurrence of the search pattern, choose **Find Next**.

or

If you want to make a change to the found occurrence,

a. Choose **Cancel** to return to the document window and edit the information.

b. If you want to resume the search, on the Editing toolbar, click the Find button 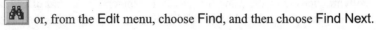 or, from the **Edit** menu, choose **Find**, and then choose **Find Next**.

7. When the program reaches the end of the selection or the document and asks if you want to continue the search, choose **Yes** to search the remainder of the document or **No** to stop the search.

▶ **To replace text or mathematics**

1. Save your document.

   If you don't like the results of the Replace operation, you can discard the changes by closing the document without saving it.

2. If you don't want to make replacements in the entire document, select the part in which you want to search and replace.

3. On the Editing toolbar, click the Replace button or, from the **Edit** menu, choose **Replace** or press CTRL+W.

4. Enter the text or mathematics you want to find in the **Search for** box, replacing former search patterns if necessary.

5. Enter the replacement text or mathematics in the **Replace with** box, replacing former replacement patterns if necessary.

6. Select any options you need to control the search.

7. To begin searching:
   - Choose **Replace All** if you want to replace all occurrences of the search pattern without confirming each replacement.
     or

   a. Choose **Find Next** if you want to confirm each replacement of the search text.
   b. When the program finds an occurrence of the search text,
      - Choose **Replace** to make the change.
        or
      - Choose **Find Next** to leave the occurrence unchanged and continue the search.

8. When the program reaches the end of the selection or the document and asks if you want to continue the search and replacement, choose **Yes** to search the remainder of the document or **No** to stop the search.

Using Spell Check

With the Spell Check tool, you can check the spelling of

- A single word.

- The words in a selection.

- The words in a text box within a dialog box.

- The words between the insertion point and the end of the document.

- The words in the entire document.

You can also use the Spell Check feature to count the words in a selection or a document.

The program checks spelling using a language dictionary and a supplementary user dictionary whose contents you determine. Each system is shipped with the American English dictionary. The program CD also contains additional dictionaries for the following languages: British English, Catalan, Danish, Dutch, Finnish, French, French Canadian, German, Italian, Norwegian (Bokmal and Nynorsk), Polish, Portuguese (Brazilian and Continental), Russian, Spanish, Swedish, and Swiss German. You can install additional dictionaries, but each one requires its own serial number. Contact MacKichan Software, Inc. to purchase a serial number for an additional dictionary.

Unless you've made a selection, you can start the spell check at the beginning of your document, regardless of the position of the insertion point. The options you select guide the operation. The program doesn't check spelling in mathematics, nor does it check words embedded within mathematics. It doesn't check words in dialog boxes, such as those for front matter and footnotes, unless you start the spell check in the dialog box.

Using the Spell Check Options

In the Spell Check dialog box, you establish the kind of spell check you want by choosing where the operation will start, what language will be used, and what options will be applied to the operation.

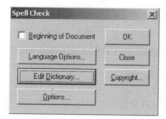

- Check the **Beginning of Document** box to begin the current spell check at the beginning of the document.

- Choose the **Language Options** button to set the language to be used in the spell check for all documents or for the current document only. (This option is relevant only if you have installed more than one language; see page 154.)

- Choose the **Edit Dictionary** button to modify the user dictionary by adding or removing words. See Modifying the User Dictionary on page 155.

- Choose the **Options** button to establish checks for repeated words, words containing numbers, and words with initial capitals.

Each time you open the program, you must set the Beginning of Document choice. Until you change them, the other option choices are retained as defaults for all spell checks in all documents.

▶ **To set the spell check options**

1. Make sure you haven't made a selection and can see the blinking insertion point.

2. On the Standard toolbar, click the Spelling button [ABC✓] or, from the Tools menu, choose Spelling.

3. Specify the options you want.

4. Choose OK to start a spell check immediately or Cancel to return to your document.

Starting Spell Check

We suggest you save your document before you check the spelling. If you don't like the results, you can close the document without saving the changes.

▶ **To check the spelling of the entire document**

1. Save your document.

2. On the Standard toolbar, click the Spelling button [ABC✓] or, from the Tools menu, choose Spelling.

3. In the Spell Check dialog box, check Beginning of Document.

4. Change the spell check options as necessary.

5. Choose OK to begin the spell check.

▶ **To check the spelling from the insertion point to the end of the document**

1. Save your document.

2. Place the insertion point in the document where you want the spell check to begin.

3. On the Standard toolbar, click the Spelling button [ABC✓] or, from the Tools menu, choose Spelling.

4. Uncheck the Beginning of Document box, then change the spell check options as necessary.

5. Choose OK to begin the spell check.

▶ **To check the spelling in a selection**

1. Save your document.

2. Select the part of the document you want to check.

3. On the Standard toolbar, click the Spelling button or, from the Tools menu, choose Spelling.

   The spell check begins immediately using the options currently set.

▶ **To check the spelling in a footnote or other dialog box**

- Open the dialog box and then start a spell check.

When the Spell Check flags a word, the program opens a dialog box that indicates the word and lists spelling alternatives. You have several options:

- Correct the misspelled word once or each time it is encountered.
- Add the word to the user dictionary.
- Skip the misspelled word once or every time it is encountered.
- Delete or skip a repeated word (if the Check for Repeated Words option is checked).
- Stop the spell check.

▶ **To correct a misspelled word**

1. Scroll the Alternatives list to find the replacement word you want.

2. If the Alternatives list contains the correct form of the word,
   - Double-click the word to replace the current occurrence.
     or
   - Select the word and choose Replace All to replace all occurrences.

3. If the Alternatives list doesn't contain the correct form of the word,

   a. Enter the correct spelling in the Replace with box.
   b. Choose Replace to change only the current occurrence of the misspelling.
      or
      Choose Replace All to replace all occurrences of the misspelling.
      If you choose Replace All, the replacement is valid only during the current spell check operation.

▶ **To add a questioned word to the user dictionary**

- Choose Add to Dictionary.
  The program places the word in the user dictionary where it remains until you remove it. See Modifying the User Dictionary, on page 155.

► **To skip a questioned word**

- Choose Skip to leave the occurrence as it is.
  or

- Choose Skip All to skip all further occurrences of the word.
  If you choose Skip All, the program skips the word only until the current spell check operation is complete.

► **To remove or skip a repeated word**

- Press DELETE to delete the word from the dialog box and then choose Replace.
  or
  Choose Skip to leave the repeated word unchanged.

► **To stop the spell check**

- Choose Cancel.

Specifying a Spell Check Language

If you have dictionaries for more than one language installed on your system, you can specify the dictionary you want to use to check the spelling of all new documents and the current document.

► **To specify a spell check language dictionary**

1. Open the Spell Check dialog box.

2. Choose Language Options.

   The system opens the Spell Check Language Options dialog box.

3. In the Default Language for New Documents box, select the language dictionary you want to use as the default for checking the spelling of all new documents.

4. In the Language for Current Document box, select the language dictionary you want to use for checking the spelling of the current document.

5. Choose OK.

6. Choose OK to start a spell check immediately or Cancel to return to your document.

   The program reflects your choice in the Language box on the General tab sheet of the Document Info dialog box.

Installing a Language Dictionary

The program must be installed before you can add additional language dictionaries. The installation program for additional dictionaries is a Windows program.

▶ **To install an additional language dictionary on your hard drive**

1. From the Help menu, choose Register.

2. Select your registration method and choose Next.

3. In the Registration Information dialog box, enter the serial number for the additional dictionary in the space provided.

   Be careful not to replace the program serial number you have already entered.

4. Complete the registration process and restart the program.

5. Insert your program CD in the CD-ROM drive.

6. From the Help menu, choose System Features.

7. Scroll the features list to find the new dictionary.

   The dictionary should be listed as "Licensed (not installed)" and the Install Dictionary button should be enabled.

8. Choose Install Dictionary.

9. When the message box appears, choose OK to close it.

10. When the program displays the Open dialog box, browse the \dict50 directory on the CD to select and run the program called InstallD.exe.

    The program installs the new dictionary.

11. At the prompt, restart the program.

Modifying the User Dictionary

You can modify the contents of your user dictionary by adding or deleting words. This feature is useful for including unusual spellings of certain words.

Tip   You may need to remove the unusual spellings from the User Dictionary when you're ready to work in another document.

▶ **To modify your user dictionary**

1. Open the Spell Check dialog box and choose Edit Dictionary.

2. If you want to add a word to the user dictionary, type the word in the Entry box and then choose Add.

3. If you want to remove a word, type the word in the Entry box or select it from the list in the bottom box, and then choose Remove.

4. When you've finished modifying the dictionary, choose OK.

5. Choose OK again to start a spell check.

or

Choose Cancel to return to the program window.

▶ **To modify the user dictionary during a spell check**

1. Start a spell check.

2. If the spell check flags a word you want to add to the dictionary, from the Spell Check dialog box, choose Add to Dictionary.

The system accepts the spelling of the word and adds it to the user dictionary. The program continues the spell check, accepting all other occurrences of the word you added.

Counting the Words in a Selection or Document

You can count the words in part or all of your document. The word count doesn't include mathematics or words in mathematics.

▶ **To count the words in a selection or document**

1. If you want to count the words in a part of the document, select the part.

or

If you want to count the words in the entire document, place the insertion point at the beginning of the document.

2. Start a spell check.

3. When the program has completed the spell check, find the number of words counted.
   - If you checked the spelling of 20 words or fewer, the number of words checked appears in the Status bar at the bottom of the program window.
   - If you checked the spelling of more than 20 words, the program displays a message that gives the number of words checked.

7 Previewing and Printing

SWP, SW, and *SNB* offer different ways to produce beautiful printed documents. If you have *SWP* or *SW,* you can typeset with LaTeX to create finely formatted documents with automatically generated cross-references, citations, numbered elements, tables of contents, and other document elements. With Version 5 of *SWP* and *SW,* you can also create typeset Portable Document Format (PDF) files with PDFTeX, which processes documents through PDFLaTeX to provide all the beauty and features of LaTeX typesetting in PDF form. The PDF files you create can be viewed on any platform using a PDF viewer such as Adobe Acrobat, so you can distribute your *SWP* and *SW* documents even more widely than with previous versions of the software. If you have *SNB* or you're using *SWP* or *SW* to produce documents that don't require typesetting, you can produce attractive documents without typesetting.

To distinguish the methods, we refer to the processes that don't involve typesetting as *preview* and *print.* We refer to the processes that involve LaTeX typesetting as *typeset compile, typeset preview,* and *typeset print,* and to those that involve PDFLaTeX typesetting as *typeset compile PDF, typeset preview PDF,* and *typeset print PDF.* (The LaTeX and PDFLaTeX processes are similar; general statements about *typesetting* refer to both.)

Producing your document with typesetting yields results that are noticeably different from producing it without typesetting. Understanding the differences between the two methods of document production and the tools associated with each method is essential to using the program effectively. This chapter explains the differences and provides detailed information about producing your documents with and without typesetting. This chapter also includes information about typesetting international documents. Chapter 8 "Formatting Documents" explains how to format documents for both types of production and Chapter 9 "Structuring Documents for Typesetting" explains how to create structural document elements, such as bibliographies and indexes, when you typeset.

Understanding Document Production

Each time you preview or print in *SWP* or *SW,* you can choose whether or not to typeset your document. Understanding the differences between producing a document with and without typesetting will help you decide when to use each method.

Differences in Document Production Methods

In *SWP, SW,* and *SNB,* you can preview or print without typesetting from the File menu commands or the buttons on the Standard toolbar:

Menu	Command	Button
File	Preview	
File	Print	

When you produce your document without typesetting, the appearance of your document depends on three sets of specifications, which are set initially by the shell you use to create your document:

- The *style*—a collection of specifications that govern the appearance of each tag in the document window. The style is stored in a .cst file.

- The *page setup specifications*—specifications that govern page margins, headers, footers, and page numbers.

- The *print options*—specifications that govern whether certain elements, such as gray boxes and helper lines, appear in print.

Note These specifications have no effect on your document if you typeset it.

You can modify the specifications as needed. You can set the page setup specifications and the print options in the document window. Chapter 8 "Formatting Documents" discusses the details of formatting a document for production without LATEX typesetting.

When you produce your document without typesetting it, the program sends the document to a non-LATEX previewer or to the printer using many of the same routines with which it displays the document in the document window. That means that what you see in the preview window or on paper is similar to what you see as you work on your document in the document window. Note that the document window doesn't reflect the page setup specifications or the print options, so you don't see margins, headers, footers, or page numbers on the screen.

If you have *SWP* or *SW*, you can typeset from the Typeset menu or the buttons on the Typeset toolbar:

Menu	Command	Button	Menu	Command	Button
Typeset	Compile		Typeset	Compile PDF	
Typeset	Preview		Typeset	Preview PDF	
Typeset	Print		Typeset	Print PDF	

When you typeset, the appearance of your document depends on these specifications, which are set initially by the document shell:

- The *typesetting specifications*—a collection of instructions related to typesetting many document elements, including those represented by the tags on the Tag toolbar in the program window; stored in files with extensions of .cls and .sty.

- Any LATEX *packages* or *document class options*—instructions specified for the document or the shell that modify the typesetting specifications in some way; stored in files with a .sty or .clo extensions.

- Any additional TEX or LATEX *commands*—instructions that you've entered in the body or preamble of the document or via input files (such as \input{tcilatex}) that further modify the typesetting instructions.

- The BIBTEX style specified for the document, if any.

Note These specifications have no effect on your document if you don't typeset it.

Some modifications to the typesetting specifications are possible from within the program, but we advise against attempts at extensive modification of the specifications, unless you are extremely familiar with TEX and LATEX. Chapter 8 "Formatting Documents" discusses formatting a document for typesetting. See also *Typesetting Documents in Scientific WorkPlace and Scientific Word,* which accompanies *SWP* and *SW.*

When you typeset your document, the program compiles it with LATEX or PDFLATEX, according to the command you choose. The compilation process automatically provides hyphenation, kerning, ligatures, sophisticated paragraph and line breaking, sophisticated mathematics layout, and other formatting features. It also provides automatic generation of document elements including tables of contents, lists of figures and tables, cross-references, footnotes and margin notes, automatically numbered sections and equations, indexes, and bibliographies. The typeset document usually has a different appearance from what you see as you work in the document window.

The typesetting process is similar for LATEX and PDFLATEX and the two processes produce typeset files that are nearly identical.

- When you typeset with LATEX, the compilation yields a *device independent file,* or DVI file, which is a finely typeset version of your document. The program then sends the DVI file to the typeset previewer or to the printer, depending on the command you choose.

- When you typeset with PDFLATEX, the compilation yields a PDF file that contains your typeset document embedded with all necessary fonts and, if you have set the options for PDF output as described on page 165, with graphics that have been converted to formats acceptable to PDFLATEX. The program then opens the PDF viewer on your system to preview or print the typeset PDF file, according to the command you choose.

More information about using other previewers and print drivers is available in the online Help and later in this chapter.

Differences in the Final Product

We emphasize that producing your document with and without typesetting yields noticeably different results. If you don't typeset, the program produces your document using many of the same routines it uses to display the document in the document window. The resulting appearance in similar to what you see when you open your document in a document window. If you typeset, the program uses LATEX or PDFLATEX to compile your document and generate any specified automatic document elements. Because of these added features and the sophisticated LATEX formatting in use, the appearance of your typeset document may be quite different from its appearance in the document window. This table summarizes the differences:

Production without typesetting	Production with typesetting
Similar appearance to display	Different appearance from display
No DVI or PDF file	DVI file compiled by LATEX or PDF file compiled by PDFLATEX
No automatically generated elements	Automatically generated elements
Format based on style, page setup, print options	Format based on typesetting specifications, options, packages, and commands

The same document may look different produced with and without typesetting. To illustrate, we've reproduced here the first page of this chapter as it would appear if printed without typesetting. Compare it to the first page of this typeset chapter. Note the differences in the numbering and spacing for the chapter heading, the placement and spacing around headings, the appearance of the two cross-references in the third paragraph, and the spacing and amount of the information on the page.

Previewing and Printing

SWP, *SW*, and *SNB* offer different ways to produce beautiful printed documents. If you have *SWP* or *SW*, you can typeset with to create finely formatted documents with automatically generated cross-references, citations, numbered elements, tables of contents, and other document elements. With Version 5 of *SWP* and *SW*, you can also create typeset Portable Document Format (PDF) files with PDF, which processes documents through PDF to provide all the beauty and features of typesetting in PDF form. The PDF files you create can be viewed on any platform using a PDF viewer such as Adobe Acrobat, so you can distribute your *SWP* and *SW* documents even more widely than with previous versions of the software. If you have *SNB* or you're using *SWP* or *SW* to produce documents that don't require typesetting you can produce attractive documents without typesetting

To distinguish the methods, we refer to the processes that don't involve typesetting as preview and print. We refer to the processes that involve typesetting as typeset compile, typeset preview, and typeset print, and to those that involve PDF typesetting as typeset compile PDF, typeset preview PDF, and typeset print PDF. (The and PDF processes are similar; general statements about typesetting refer to both.)

Producing your document with typesetting yields results that are noticeably different from producing it without typesetting Understanding the differences between the two methods of document production and the tools associated with each method is essential to using the program effectively. This chapter explains the differences and provides detailed information about producing your documents with and without typesetting This chapter also includes information about typesetting international documents. Chapter ref: format "Formatting Documents" explains how to format documents for both types of production and Chapter ref: typeset "Structuring Documents for Typesetting" explains how to create structural document elements, such as bibliographies and indexes, when you typeset

Understanding Document Production

Each time you preview or print in *SWP* or *SW*, you can choose whether or not to typeset your document. Understanding the differences between producing a document with and without typesetting will help you decide when to use each method.

Differences in Document Production Methods

In *SWP*, *SW*, and *SNB*, you can preview or print without typesetting from the File menu commands or the buttons on the Standard toolbar:

Menu	Command	Button
File	Preview	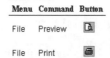
File	Print	

When you produce your document without typesetting the appearance of your document depends on three sets of specifications, which are set initially by the shell you use to create your document:
- The style—a collection of specifications that govern the appearance of each tag in the document window. The style is stored in a .cst file.
- The page setup specifications—specifications that govern page margins, headers, footers, and page numbers.
- The print options—specifications that govern whether certain elements, such as gray boxes and helper lines, appear in print.

Note   Note   These specifications have no effect on your document if you typeset it. You can modify the specifications as needed. You can set the page setup specifications and the print

If you have *SWP* or *SW*, we suggest that you follow these general guidelines to choose how to produce your document:
- When a finely typeset document appearance is a high priority, typeset preview or typeset print the document with the commands on the Typeset menu.

- When you need a finely typeset PDF document for viewing on multiple platforms, typeset the document with the PDF commands on the Typeset menu.

- When a finely typeset document appearance and automatically generated document elements aren't a priority or you need output quickly, preview or print the document with the commands on the File menu.

Producing Documents without Typesetting

Previewing and printing without typesetting is available in *SWP*, *SW*, and *SNB*. The result is a previewed or printed image that is similar to what you see in the document window. When you need output quickly and when fine typesetting isn't a priority, you can preview your document, print it on the printer, or print it to a file without using LaTeX or PDFLaTeX.

Previewing Documents without Typesetting

You can preview the way your document will look without actually sending it to the printer. When you preview a document without typesetting it, the program opens a preview window inside the program window, and displays your document in it. If your document requires no further changes, you can print it from the preview window. (Note that the program uses a different, independent preview screen when you typeset preview your document.)

▶ **To preview a document without typesetting**

- On the Standard toolbar, click the Preview button or, from the File menu, choose Preview.
  The program opens a preview window inside the program window and displays your document according to the style, print options, and page setup specifications in effect for the document, and the page orientation and paper size specifications in effect for the default printer.

▶ **To change the display of previewed pages**

- From the Menu bar in the preview window, choose Two Page or One Page.

▶ **To move to a different previewed page**

- Press PAGE UP or PAGE DOWN or, from the Menu bar in the preview window, choose Next Page or Prev Page.

▶ **To change the magnification of the display**

- Click the left mouse button or, from the Menu bar in the preview window, choose Zoom in or Zoom out.

▶ **To leave the preview window**

- From the Menu bar in the preview window, choose Close.

Printing Documents without Typesetting

You can print without typesetting from the preview window or from the program window. Also, you can print to a file.

▶ **To print a document from the preview screen without typesetting**

1. On the Standard toolbar, click the Preview button or, from the File menu, choose Preview.

2. From the Menu bar of the preview window, choose Print.

3. In the Print dialog box, make any necessary selections:
   - Select the printer you want to use.
     The program prints to any Windows print device, including facsimile devices. If you need to install a print device, refer to your Windows documentation for instructions.
   - Select the range of pages you want to print. The default is All.
   - Select the number of copies you want to print. The default is 1.
   - Check Collate if you want the copies collated.
   - If you want to send the document to a file instead of a printer, check Print to file. The availability of some of these options depends on the selected print driver.

4. Choose OK.

▶ **To print a document from the program window without typesetting**

1. On the Standard toolbar, click the Print button ; from the File menu, choose Print; or press CTRL+P.

2. In the Print dialog box, make any necessary selections:
   - Select the printer you want to use.
   - Select the range of pages you want to print. The default is All.
   - Select the number of copies you want to print. The default is 1.
   - Check Collate if you want the copies collated.
   - If you want to send the document to a file instead of a printer, check Print to file. The availability of some of these options depends on the selected print driver.

3. Choose OK.

▶ **To print a document to a file without typesetting**

1. Print the document from the preview screen or the program window.

2. In the Print dialog box, check Print to file and choose OK.

3. When the Print to File dialog box opens, specify a name and directory for the file, and then choose Save.

Setting Print Options

When you preview or print your document without typesetting it, you can set print options to turn printing on or off for certain document elements, such as helper lines and invisibles. Also, you can print using the zoom factor in effect for the document window or you can set a different zoom factor, which can be particularly useful for creating presentation materials. If you have a color printer, you can use the print options to enable color printing of lines, text, and backgrounds. See Chapter 8 "Formatting Documents" for information about setting colors for document elements.

The print options listed below are available from the Print Options tab sheet in the Document Info dialog box. Remember that these options have no effect when you typeset preview or typeset print your document.

Option*	Effect on previewed and printed document
Use Default Print Options	Use the built-in print defaults
Use Current View Settings	Show invisibles, helper lines, input boxes, index entries, and markers only if they are turned on in the View menu
Invisibles	Show invisibles despite View setting
Helper Lines	Show helper lines despite View setting
Input Boxes	Show input boxes despite View setting
Markers	Show markers despite View setting
Index Entries	Show index entries despite View setting
Print	
All Text in Black	Show tagged text in black despite color specified for the tag
All Lines in Black	Show lines in black despite color specified
Background as Transparent	Show no background color for paragraphs
Gray Boxes as Transparent	Show no background color for gray boxes
Suppress Gray Boxes (except markers)	Show no gray boxes except index entries and markers (index entries and markers can be turned on and off in the View Settings area)
Use Current View Zoom Settings	Use the zoom factor in effect for the window
Zoom Percentage	Set the zoom factor used for printing

* Some of the options are mutually exclusive, such as the Zoom settings

▶ **To set print options**

1. From the File menu, choose Document Info.

2. On the Print Options tab sheet, check the options you want.

3. If you want the current settings to be the defaults for all your documents, choose Make Default.

4. Choose OK.

Producing Documents with Typesetting

Your *SWP* or *SW* installation includes extensive typesetting support. *SWP* and *SW* are supplied with TrueTEX, which includes a TEX formatter, a TEX screen previewer, scalable TrueType fonts, and support for PDFTEX. This manual assumes you're using TrueTEX. However, you can use other preview and print drivers; see Changing the Preview and Print Driver Settings on page 177. No other software is necessary to generate PDF files, but you must have a PDF viewer (such as Adobe Acrobat, which you can download) to preview and print PDF files.

You can access the TEX formatter and screen previewer from within *SWP* and *SW* or from the program submenu on the Windows **Programs** menu; PDFLATEX is available from within *SWP* and *SW*.

When you install *SWP* or *SW*, you install LATEX support that includes these elements:

- The TEX Computer Modern (cm) fonts.

- The TEX DC fonts, text-only fonts that contain characters to support many non-English languages. The DC fonts keep the same characters as the Computer Modern fonts and extend the typesetting capabilities of TEX to many languages other than English.

- `latex_ml.fmt` and `pdflatex_ml.fmt`, the default LATEX format files. The files are precompiled for the DC fonts and contains a non-English hyphenation pattern set for German, French, and Dutch.

  LATEX *format files* are special binary files that contain a precompiled and rapid-loading version of the commands in the LATEX macro set. Format files also contain hyphenation patterns and information for preloaded fonts. The format files transform the TEX formatter into a LATEX or PDFLATEX formatter when you typeset your document. If you are familiar with TEX and LATEX, you can create a new format file to include the hyphenation patterns for other languages; see online Help for more information.

- `latex.fmt` and `pdflatex.fmt`, additional format files. The files are precompiled for the cm fonts and contain an English hyphenation pattern set only.

In some circumstances, working with TEX and LATEX requires information that is beyond the scope of this manual. You can find more information about TEX in *The TEXbook* by Donald E. Knuth. You can find more information about LATEX in *LATEX: A Document Preparation System* by Leslie Lamport; *The LATEX Companion* by Michel Goossens, Frank Mittelbach, and Alexander Samarin; and *A Guide to LATEX: Document Preparation for Beginners and Advanced Users* by Helmut Lopka and Patrick W. Daly.

In *SWP* or *SW*, you can typeset your document with LATEX or PDFLATEX. With a few exceptions, the processes are the same, and they produce typeset documents with essentially identical appearances but different file types. DVI and PDF files differ in the type of graphics they can use. Also, typeset PDF files can support some features that typeset DVI files can't. In particular, in PDF files you create from your *SWP* and *SW* documents, you can take advantage of LATEX packages such as *rotating* that aren't supported by the TrueTEX Previewer. If you add the *hyperref* package to your document, the PDF compilation process changes any cross-references to hypertext links and creates a table of contents linked to the body of the document. See page 288 for more information about the *hyperref* package.

Before you typeset your document, you can choose an output option to indicate whether you want DVI or PDF output. The program uses the option to prepare the file and any mathematics, plots, and graphics it contains for DVI or PDF output. The default is DVI output. Regardless of the setting, however, the system produces successful DVI or PDF files when you typeset your document. If you're creating a PDF file and you change the default to PDF output, the program creates the PDF file and preserves any temporary files created during the typesetting process. If you don't change the default to PDF output, the program still creates a PDF file, but it doesn't preserve the temporary files. For most users, this isn't a consideration.

▶ **To select options for typesetting**

1. From the Typeset menu, choose Output Choice.

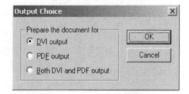

2. Click the option you want.

   DVI output is the default.

3. Choose OK.

The program also has default settings for typesetting PDF files containing plots and graphics. The defaults are adequate for nearly all documents, and most users won't need to change them.

However, you can specify different settings if necessary using the process described in detail in Chapter 2 "Creating Documents." You can leave plots and graphics in the original format, choose not to export them, or export them in the default format (PDF) or the format you designate. You can specify different formats for different types of graphics, such as raster or vector graphics, or for types of graphics that you group together in sets. A graphics file type can appear in more than one set. The program applies the selected export formats to the sets in the order in which the sets are listed in the PDF Graphics Export Options dialog; you can change the order. If you choose to export plots as graphics, the program applies a single format to all plots. In addition to choosing the export formats, you can choose a naming scheme for exported graphics. The program uses the scheme to name the exported graphics and plots before they are embedded in the PDF file. The program usually exports graphics and plots to a subdirectory of the directory containing the document file, but you can designate a different subdirectory if you prefer. See page 272 for information about creating PDF files from master and subdocuments.

▶ **To specify settings for PDF output**

1. From the Typeset menu, choose General Settings.

2. If your document contains hypertext links to files with a .tex extension and you want those links converted in the typeset PDF file to links to files with a .pdf extension, click Convert .tex link targets to .pdf.

3. If you want to change the graphics export settings for PDF typesetting, choose **PDF Graphics Settings** and change the settings as described beginning on page 34, specifying graphics directories, formats, and naming schemes, as necessary.

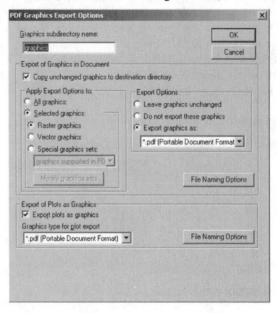

4. Choose **OK** to close the **General Typesetting Settings** dialog box.

When you typeset, using the commands on the **Typeset** menu and Typeset toolbar, the program compiles your document with LaTeX or PDFLaTeX and then previews or prints as you choose. Remember that you can save a considerable amount of time and paper if you save your document before you preview it and if you preview carefully before you print.

Typeset Compiling Documents

When you typeset, the program compiles your document with LaTeX or PDFLaTeX to interpret any TeX commands, create automatic numbering, resolve all internal cross-references, and generate any automatic document elements that you've specified or that are specified by the typesetting specifications for the document. Automatically generated document elements include tables of contents, lists of figures and tables, bibliographies, and indexes, among others.

Depending on the complexity of your document, the program may pass it through LaTeX or PDFLaTeX more than once. For example, if your document contains cross-references, two passes are necessary. If your document has a table of contents, three passes are required. The program sets the number of passes automatically, but you can change it. As part of the compilation process, special auxiliary files are created for recording the location of headings, cross-references, and markers; these auxiliary files, which have a file extension of .aux, are used in the creation of tables of contents and cross-references. The program also creates a record of the compilation, which is stored in a .log file. While the compilation is in progress, the program is suspended.

- When you typeset with LaTeX, a button appears on the Windows task bar, and a **LaTeX** dialog box appears in the program window to indicate the status of the compilation process. You can view the process in detail by opening the LaTeX window to view the information in the .log file; see Working with LaTeX and PDFLaTeX later in this chapter for more information.

- When you typeset with PDFLaTeX, a **pdfLaTeX** dialog box opens to indicate the compilation status. The TrueTeX preview screen opens a PDFLaTeX window that displays the details of the LaTeX compilation and the creation of the PDF file.

The compilation process typesets your document according to its typesetting specifications and produces either a DVI file that contains your typeset document in a form independent of any output device or a PDF file that contains your typeset document in a form that can be read on any platform with a PDF viewer, such as Adobe Acrobat. You can then preview or print the DVI or PDF file.

When you typeset preview or typeset print your document, the program automatically compiles the document if it doesn't find a current DVI or PDF file. However, with the **Compile** and **Compile PDF** commands on the **Typeset** menu, you can compile your document independently and then preview or print the typeset document at a later time. The **Compile** and **Compile PDF** commands are active only when you've saved the document and made no further changes.

▶ **To compile a document without previewing or printing**

1. If you're creating a typeset PDF file, select the PDF options you want, as described on page 165.

2. Save the document.

3. On the Typeset toolbar, click the Typeset DVI Compile button or, from the **Typeset** menu, choose **Compile**.

   or

   On the Typeset toolbar, click the Typeset PDF Compile button or, from the **Typeset** menu, choose **Compile PDF**.

4. From the **Compile** or **Compile PDF** dialog box, select the options you want:
   - If your document contains a BIBTeX bibliography field and you want to create the bibliography, check **Generate a Bibliography**.
   - If your document contains index entries and you want to create the index, check **Generate an Index**.

   Chapter 9 "Structuring Documents for Typesetting" contains more information about creating bibliographies and indexes.

5. Note the name and location of the typeset file to be created and choose **OK**.

The program displays the LaTeX or pdfLaTeX dialog box to indicate the number of times your document will be passed through LaTeX and the number of the pass in progress.

- If you want to change the number of passes, set a new number in the Pass box.
- If you want to stop a pass, choose Cancel in the LaTeX dialog box.

The program displays the compilation details in the LaTeX window or in the PDFLaTeX window inside the TrueTeX preview screen. When the DVI or PDF file has been created, the program returns to the document window.

The compilation process is often lengthy. Errors can occur during the processing if the compiler encounters incorrect LaTeX syntax. See Working with LaTeX and PDFLaTeX on page 172 for more information.

You can save time by saving your document before you typeset it. If you save a document immediately before you typeset, the program creates a DVI or PDF file during the typeset process and retains the file afterwards. If you don't make any changes to the document before you typeset preview or typeset print again, the program skips the compilation step and sends the DVI or PDF file directly to the previewer or the print driver. On the other hand, if you don't save the document immediately before you typeset preview or typeset print it, the program works with temporary files and discards them after the typeset process has been completed. Even if you haven't made any changes to the document, it must be recompiled the next time you typeset preview or typeset print.

Similarly, if you save the auxiliary files when you compile, the program uses those files the next time you typeset preview or typeset print, if you haven't saved your document in the meantime. If you save the .aux files, the program will be able to typeset preview or typeset print after a single LaTeX or PDFLaTeX pass, rather than two or three.

▶ **To save the auxiliary files for your document**

1. From the Typeset menu, choose General Settings.

2. Check the box labeled Use old .aux files if possible and then choose OK.

Typeset Previewing Documents

You can preview your typeset document to see how it will appear in print without actually sending the document to the printer. Previewing also gives you an opportunity to check for any changes you need to make. Remember that you can save time by saving your document before you preview it.

If a valid DVI or PDF file for your document isn't already present when you preview, the program compiles your document with LaTeX or PDFLaTeX, as described on page 166. After the compilation, the program opens either the TrueTeX Previewer or your PDF viewer and displays the typeset file on the screen exactly as it will appear in print. Note that the TrueTeX preview screen and PDF viewer are independent of *SWP* and *SW* and different from the preview window used when you preview without typesetting.

▶ **To typeset preview a document**

1. Change the output settings, if necessary (see page 165).

   In most cases, the default settings are adequate.

2. Save the document.

   If you don't save the document, the program works with temporary files.

3. On the Typeset toolbar, click the Typeset DVI Preview button 🔲 or, from the Typeset menu, choose Preview.

   or

   On the Typeset toolbar, click the Typeset PDF Preview button 🔲 or, from the Typeset menu, choose Preview PDF.

   • If the program finds a file valid DVI or PDF file for your document, it displays it in the TrueTEX preview screen or in the window of your PDF viewer.

   • If it doesn't find a file, the program compiles your document.

   If an error occurs during compilation, the LATEX or PDFLATEX window displays an error message. See Working with LATEX and PDFLATEX , later in this chapter.

   When the compilation is complete, the program displays the document in the TrueTEX preview screen or the PDF viewer as it will appear in print.

4. Examine your document carefully and note any necessary changes.

The TrueTEX preview screen provided with the program has scroll bars at the bottom and the right and a menu bar across the top with which you can move around in your document and customize the way the previewed document appears on the preview screen. Use the scroll bars, arrow keys, and commands on the View menu to move around a displayed page. Use the PAGE UP and PAGE DOWN keys to move to adjacent pages and the Go to Page command on the Edit menu to move to a specific page. Use the Zoom in command on the View menu or drag the mouse to describe a box around a portion of the text when you want to magnify. Use the commands on the Options menu to customize the preview screen display. Instructions for using other TrueTEX options appear online; choose Help from the menu bar in the TrueTEX Previewer.

Typeset Printing Documents

You can typeset print a document from the program window or, when you have previewed a document, from the TrueTEX preview screen or the PDF viewer.

Typeset Printing from the Program Window

Whether you typeset print with LATEX or with PDFLATEX, the process is straightforward. When you typeset print your document, the program compiles the document if a valid DVI or PDF file for the document isn't already present (see page 166) and then sends the typeset file to the printer.

▶ **To typeset print from the program window**

1. Change the output settings you want, if necessary (see page 165).

   In most cases, the default settings are adequate.

2. Save the document.

   If you don't save the document, the program works with temporary files.

3. On the Typeset toolbar, click the Typeset DVI Print button or, from the **Type-set** menu, choose **Print**.

   or

   On the Typeset toolbar, click the Typeset PDF Print button ![PDF] or, from the **Type-set** menu, choose **Print PDF**.

4. Make these selections in the **Print** dialog box:

   a. If you want to specify a different printer, choose **Setup** to change the printer specifications and then choose **OK**.
      The program prints to any Windows print device, including facsimile devices. If you need to install a print device, refer to your Windows documentation for instructions.

   b. Select the number of copies you want to print. The default is **1**.

   c. Select the pages you want to print. The default is **All**.
      This option is available for DVI files only. If you want to print selected pages of a PDF file, you must first preview the document as described on page 171.

   d. Set a step factor to print pages at a specified interval. The default is **1**, or every page.
      To print all odd pages, select **1** as the first page and step by **2**. To print all even pages, select **2** as the first page and step by **2**.

   e. If you want to print to a file, check **Print to File**.
      This options is available for DVI files only. If you want to print a PDF file to a file, you must first preview the document as described on page 171.

   f. If you want to print from back to front, check **Print in Reverse Order**.

5. When all the settings are correct, choose **OK**.

   • If you are printing to a file, enter the name of the output file when the program prompts you and then choose **OK**.
     The program places the output file in the same directory as your document.

   • If a valid DVI or PDF file is present for your document, the program bypasses the compilation and prints the file.

   • If a valid DVI or PDF file isn't present, the program compiles your document and then sends it to the printer.
     If a compilation error occurs, the LATEX window opens to display an error message. See Working with LATEX and PDFLATEX on page 172 for more information about correcting errors.

Typeset Printing from a Preview Screen

If your document needs no further changes when you typeset preview it, you can send it directly from the TrueTEX preview screen to a printer or to a file. You may need to set up a printer before you print.

▶ **To set up a printer from a preview screen**

1. From the File menu in the TrueTEX Previewer, choose Print Setup.

   or

   From the File menu in your PDF viewer, choose Print.

2. In the Name box, select the printer you want to use and change the properties of the printer as necessary.

   Note that depending on your print driver, some items in the Properties dialog box, such as page size, page orientation, and paper source, may or may not work correctly from the previewer. For more information on print drivers, see Changing the Preview and Print Driver Settings, later in this chapter.

3. In the Size box, enter the size of the paper in the printer.

4. In the Source box, enter the paper feed source for the printer.

5. If you need to change the paper orientation, click the button corresponding to the orientation you want.

6. Make any other settings required by the print driver.

7. Choose OK.

▶ **To typeset print the document from a preview screen**

1. Typeset preview your document.

2. From the File menu in the TrueTEX Previewer or your PDF viewer, choose Print.

3. Select the printer you want.

4. Make these and any other necessary selections in the Print dialog box:
   - Set the orientation, size, or source of the paper, if necessary.
   - Set the range of pages to be printed. The default is All.
   - Set the number of copies to be printed. The default is 1.
     Note that depending on your print driver, other items in the Properties dialog box, such as page size, page orientation, and paper source, may or may not work correctly from the previewer. For more information on output drivers, see Changing the Preview and Print Driver Settings, later in this chapter.
   - If you want to print the document to a file, check Print to file.

5. When all the settings are correct, choose Print.

The previewer displays a print status bar at the top of the document image as it sends your document to the printer. The bar indicates which page is being sent.

▶ **To cancel printing from a preview screen**

- Click the print status bar at the top of the document image on the TrueTEX preview screen.
  or
- Click the Cancel button on the print status dialog box.

Working with LATEX and PDFLATEX

The information in this section is specific to the version of TrueTEX provided with *SWP* and *SW*. These comments may not apply if you have customized your installation to use a different version of TEX, as described later in the chapter.

When you typeset, you can watch the details of the compilation, which are displayed in the LATEX window or the PDFLATEX window. If errors occur during the compilation, you may be able to determine how to resolve them using the information.

Although you must create typeset PDF files from inside *SWP* or *SW*, you can typeset with LATEX from outside the program. Also, if your computer is connected to a network server, you may be able to use external LATEX processing.

Using the LATEX and PDFLATEX Windows

You can monitor the progress as the program compiles you document. When you typeset a PDF file, the PDFLATEX window opens automatically in the TrueTEX preview screen. You can open the LATEX window during a compilation. Note that if LATEX is unable to complete the compilation, the window opens automatically to display an error message.

▶ **To open the LATEX window**

- Click the LATEX button ![INITEX - swp0000] when it appears on the Windows task bar during compilation.

▶ **To close the LATEX window and leave the compilation in progress**

- In the upper-right corner of the LATEX window, click the Minimize button ![_].

▶ **To stop the current LATEX pass**

- From the File menu in the LATEX window, choose Exit.
  or
- Double-click the Control box in the upper-left corner of the LATEX window.
  or
- If the LATEX window is open, press ALT+F4.

Correcting Compilation Errors

Occasionally, LATEX and PDFLATEX may be unable to compile a document. The most common cause of problems is the entry in a document of incorrect, mistyped, or incomplete TEX or LATEX commands. If a compilation error occurs, an error message is displayed in the LATEX or PDFLATEX window, and recorded in the .log file. Processing waits for user input. If all activity ceases when you try to typeset compile, preview, or print your document, look in the window for an error message, which will help you identify and correct the error.

A knowledge of TEX and LATEX will help you correct compilation errors. For more information, see *Typesetting Documents in Scientific WorkPlace and Scientific Word.*

▶ **To identify a compilation error**

1. Find the error message in the LATEX or PDFLATEX window.

2. Look for the corresponding line number, which indicates where the error has occurred. It usually refers to a line in your document, but it can also refer to a line in one of the included typesetting specification files.

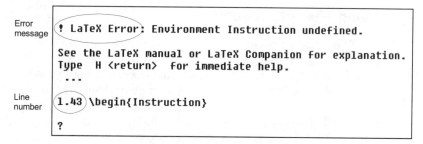

The error messages contain much helpful information. The exclamation point signals the error and the information on that line describes the nature of the problem. The line number (here, 43) indicates approximately where the error has occurred, either in your document or in a related typesetting specifications file. The question mark indicates that LATEX is waiting for you to tell it what to do. These commands are the most useful responses:

Type	To
S	Scroll without stopping, even if other errors occur
H	Obtain help
X	Quit

3. Close the window and attempt to correct the error.

Since lines in a document don't correspond to lines in the .tex file, you may need to use an ASCII editor to locate the error.

A complete transcript of the compilation process, including error messages, appears in the .log file, which has the same name as your document. If you saved your document before printing or previewing, the program places the .log file in the same directory as the .tex file. If you didn't save your document before printing or previewing or if your document is located on a remote or read-only drive, the program copies your document to your local temp directory, along with the .log file.

The .log file records precisely what happens during the typesetting process. Among other information, it includes

- The document class and any class option files used by the document.
- The names of any LaTeX packages used by the document.
- The names of any files read and closed.
- The numbers of all pages processed.
- The size of the typeset file.
- Any warnings and messages related to compilation problems, such as unresolved cross-references, improperly matched delimiters, misspelled commands, missing command arguments, or overfull or underfull boxes.

We suggest that you maintain the .log file until you've resolved the error. The file may be required if you request technical support.

When you typeset a PDF file, PDFLaTeX may compile the document successfully but encounter difficulties as the typeset file is converted to PDF. In particular, missing fonts can cause problems. The error messages can help you identify and correct the problem.

Using TrueTeX Directly

If your document has correct LaTeX syntax, you can use TrueTeX to typeset compile, preview, and print your document without opening *SWP* or *SW*. If your document is a subdocument (see Chapter 9 "Structuring Documents for Typesetting") or if you are creating a typeset PDF file, you must typeset from within *SWP* or *SW*.

Note   The TrueTeX Formatter is a complete implementation of TeX. You can use it to compile Plain TeX files and perform other operations, such as creating custom format files and installing LaTeX packages from the normal .dtx package distribution file. These operations are beyond the scope of this manual.

▶ **To typeset compile from outside the program**

1. From the Windows **Start** menu, choose **Programs** and then choose the *SWP* or *SW* menu item.

2. On the program submenu, choose the TrueTeX Formatter.

   The TrueTeX Formatter window opens and within it, the **Open TeX File** dialog box.

3. Select the document file and directory, and click **Open**.

   LaTeX creates the DVI file and places it in the same directory as the document file. The two files will have the same file name but different file extensions.

▶ **To typeset preview or typeset print from outside the program**

1. From the Windows **Start** menu, choose **Programs** and then choose the *SWP* or *SW* menu item.

2. On the program submenu, choose the TrueTeX Previewer.

3. From the File menu in the TrueT_EX preview screen, choose Open.

The program opens the Open DVI File dialog box, which lists all DVI files in the current directory.

4. Select the DVI file for the document you want to preview and choose Open.

The previewer displays the DVI file in the TrueT_EX preview screen.

5. If you want to print the file,

a. Choose Print from the File menu.
b. Make the selections you want in the Print dialog box and choose OK.

Using External Processing

If your computer is connected to a network server that can run L^AT_EX, you may be able to set up your installation so that document files can be sent directly to this server for L^AT_EX compiling and printing. If you can use the server, you can avoid waiting for L^AT_EX to compile your file.

Changing the T_EX Formatter Settings

When you typeset your document, the T_EX formatter compiles your document and creates the DVI or PDF file. The standard T_EX formatter provided with *SWP* and *SW* is TrueT_EX, which includes support for PDFT_EX. However, many T_EX systems are available and you may have access to one or more of them. If so, you can use a different T_EX system to compile your documents. With *SWP* and *SW*, you can use T_EX systems such as

- **PCT_EX**, which uses PCT_EX32 from Personal T_EX, Inc.
- **Y&Y**, which uses the Y&Y T_EX system.
- **MiKT_EX**, a public domain T_EX system for 32-bit Windows.
- **emT_EX**, a public domain T_EX system for 16-bit Windows.

The program uses the formatter that is selected in the Expert Settings dialog box. You can change to a different formatter. However, the formatter you use must be compatible with the output drivers being used on your system; that is, for your document to preview or print correctly, the formatter must output a DVI or PDF file that the drivers can understand and interpret correctly.

If you want to use a different formatter, you may need to add or modify the command line settings with which the program invokes the formatter. When you typeset your document, the program substitutes values for the specified settings and calls the selected formatter. However, it doesn't attempt to determine whether the syntax you enter will work correctly. The settings are recorded in the system registry. If they are incorrect, your document won't be typeset and your system might not operate properly.

The settings and command line syntax vary for each formatter. The syntax must be what the selected formatter expects. A precise description of the settings for other T_EX formatters is beyond the scope of this manual. For information about command line settings, refer to the documentation accompanying the formatter you want to use. You should not attempt to change the command line settings unless you know TEX and LATEX well.

Caution   Don't attempt to modify the settings unless you know TEX, LATEX, and the formatter very well.

▶ **To modify the TEX formatter settings**

1. From the Typeset menu, choose Expert Settings.

2. In the Typeset Options dialog box, choose the tab for the formatter you want to change, either the DVI Format Settings tab or the PDF Format Settings tab.

3. From the tab sheet,

   - If you want to modify the settings for the current formatter, choose Add/Modify.
   - If you want to use a different formatter, click the arrow next to the Select a formatter box, select the formatter you want from the list, and then choose Add/Modify.

   The program opens the dialog box for the formatter you want to change. This example shows the TeX to DVI Formatter dialog box; the TeX to PDF Formatter dialog box is identical and works the same way.

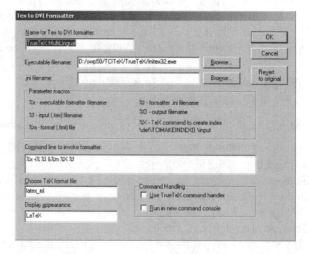

4. In the Executable filename box, enter the path name of the executable (.exe) file for the formatter.

5. In the .ini filename box, enter the path name of the .ini file for the formatter.

6. In the box labeled Command line to invoke formatter, enter the command line parameters required to run the formatter.

   The command lines vary depending on the formatter you select. Use the syntax and commands in the Parameter macros area as a guide to the command syntax and refer to the documentation for the formatter. Make sure the syntax is correct.

7. In the Choose TeX format file box, enter a name for the format file.

The default value for the LaTeX format file is `latex_ml`. The default value for the PDFLaTeX format file is `pdflatex_ml`. Note that `pdflatex_ml` isn't listed in the TeX to PDF Formatter dialog box because the TrueTeX command handler is active. The command handler provides the name of the format file to the program.

8. If you want to change the name of the formatter as it appears in compilation messages, enter the new name in the Display appearance box.

9. If the formatter requires the TrueTeX command handler, check Use TrueTeX command handler.

Note that the settings are correct for preinstalled formatters. See the TrueTeX documentation for more information.

10. If you select a TeX formatter that is driven by a batch file, check Run in new command console to ensure that the TeX environment is set up correctly.

11. If you make an error, choose Revert to original and enter the settings again.

12. Choose OK.

Changing the Preview and Print Driver Settings

TrueTeX provides output drivers for previewing and printing your typeset document. If you wish, you can modify the settings for the drivers or use different drivers altogether. The output drivers you use must be compatible with the TeX formatter being used on your system. In other words, you must use output drivers that can understand and correctly interpret the DVI or PDF file created by the formatter.

If you want to use different output drivers, you may need to add or modify the command line settings with which the program invokes the previewer and the printer. When you typeset preview or print your document, the program substitutes values for the specified settings and calls the driver you select, but the program doesn't attempt to determine whether the syntax will work correctly. The settings are recorded in the system registry. If they are incorrect, your document won't be typeset and your system might not operate properly.

The settings and the command line syntax vary for each driver. The syntax on the command line must be what the selected preview or print driver expects. A precise description of the settings for other output drivers is beyond the scope of this manual. For information about command line settings, refer to the documentation accompanying the preview or print driver you want to use. You should not attempt to change the command line settings unless you know TeX and LaTeX well.

Caution   Don't attempt to modify the settings unless you know TeX, LaTeX, and the preview and print drivers well.

▶ **To modify the settings for the typeset preview driver**

1. From the Typeset menu, choose Expert Settings and then choose the tab for the output driver settings you want to change, either the DVI Preview Settings tab or the PDF Preview Settings tab.

2. If you want to modify the current preview driver settings, choose Add/Modify.

   or

   If you want to use a different previewer, click the arrow next to the box labeled Select a previewer, select the driver you want from the list of available drivers, and then choose Add/Modify.

   The program opens the dialog box for the previewer, as shown on the next page. This example uses the DVI Preview Driver dialog box; the PDF Preview Driver dialog box is identical and works the same way.

3. In the Executable filename box, enter the path name of the executable (.exe) file for the preview driver.

4. In the .ini filename box, enter the path name of the .ini file for the preview driver.

5. In the box labeled Command line to invoke preview driver, enter the command line parameters required to run the preview driver.

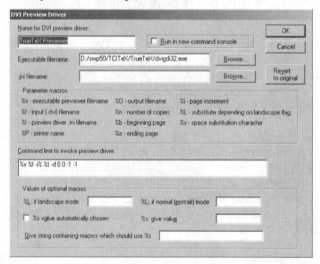

The command lines vary depending on the output driver you select. Use the syntax and commands in the Parameter macros area as a guide to the command syntax and refer to the documentation for the preview driver. Make sure the syntax is correct.

6. In the Values of optional macros area, enter new values of any optional macros you want.

   The optional macros are strings that must be substituted in the command line. Use the syntax and commands in the area as a guide to the command syntax and refer to the documentation for the preview driver. Make sure the syntax is correct.

7. If you make an error, choose **Revert to original** and enter the settings again.

8. Choose **OK**.

▶ **To modify the settings for the typeset print driver**

1. From the **Typeset** menu, choose **Expert Settings** and then choose the tab for the output driver settings you want to change, either the **DVI Print Driver Settings** tab or the **PDF Print Driver Settings** tab.

2. If you want to modify the current print driver settings, choose **Add/Modify**.

   or

   If you want to use a different print driver, click the arrow next to the **Select a print driver** box, select the driver you want from the list of available drivers and then choose **Add/Modify**.

   The illustration below shows the **DVI Print Driver** dialog box; the **PDF Print Driver** dialog box is identical and works the same way.

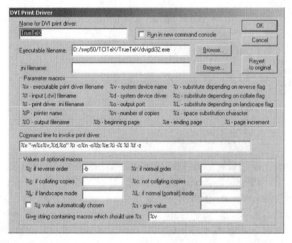

3. In the **Executable filename** box, enter the path name of the executable (.exe) file for the print driver.

4. In the **.ini filename** box, enter the path name of the .ini file for the print driver.

5. In the **Command line to invoke print driver** box, enter the parameters required to run the print driver.

   The command lines vary depending on the output driver you select. Use the syntax and commands in the **Parameter macros** area as a guide to the command syntax and refer to the documentation for the preview driver. Make sure the syntax is correct.

6. In the **Values of optional macros** area, modify the values of any optional macros you want.

   The optional macros are strings that must be substituted in the command line, depending on the settings you choose when you print. Make sure the syntax is correct.

Use the syntax and commands in the area as a guide to the command syntax and refer to the documentation for the print driver.

7. If you make an error, choose **Revert to original** and enter the settings again.

8. Choose **OK**.

To illustrate this process, suppose a DVI print driver used the syntax −C*n* to indicate *n collated copies* and the syntax −c*n* to indicate *n uncollated copies*. To set the optional macros for this driver, you would make these entries:

1. In the box labeled %c: if not collating copies, enter the string **-c%n.** When you print, the number of copies you choose in the Print dialog box replaces the value of %n.

2. In the box labeled %c: if collating copies, enter the string **-C%n.** When you print, the number of copies you choose in the Print dialog box replaces the value of %n.

3. At an appropriate position in the command line, enter **%c.** When you print, the value of −C%n or −c%n replaces the value of %c in the command line.

So, if you choose to print seven uncollated copies, %c will be replaced by the string *-c7* in the command line when the program sends the file to the printer. Similarly, if you choose to print four collated copies, %c will be replaced by the string *-C4*.

Caution   Don't attempt to modify the macro commands if you're not very familiar with TEX, LATEX, and the print driver.

Typesetting International Documents

Version 5 of *SWP* and *SW*, in combination with TrueTEX, supports international typesetting with the Lambda system. You can use this powerful combination to produce typeset documents in languages that use non-Roman character sets. See page 230 for information about typesetting documents in other non-English languages.

This version of the program includes shells for producing documents in Russian, Greek, Japanese, Korean, and Traditional and Simplified Chinese. You can follow the general process outlined below to typeset documents in other languages as well, if you're working on a Windows 2000 or Windows XP system. The information that follows assumes you are familiar with LATEX packages, TEX font handling, and the Omega system.

To typeset with Lambda, you must change the TEX formatter settings. If you're using a shell that wasn't provided with the program and you need to implement a new language, you must also take these steps:

1. Obtain the non-Roman fonts you need.

2. Create font metrics files (.ovp, .ofm, and .ovf files).

3. Create a font description file that tells LATEX how and when to use the font.

4. Create a LATEX package to load the font into your document.

5. Add the required LATEX packages to your document.

▶ **To change the TₑX formatter settings**

1. From the Typeset menu in *SWP* or *SW*, choose Expert Settings and then choose the DVI Format Settings tab.

2. Select the TeX Live Lambda formatter and choose OK.

We followed these steps to create the international shells provided with the program. If you use one of the shells, you don't need to follow this process.

▶ **To obtain non-Roman fonts**

1. From the Windows 2000 or XP Start menu, choose Settings and then choose Control Panel.

2. Choose Regional Options.

3. In the Language settings area, check the language in which you want to typeset and choose OK.

▶ **To create font metrics files**

1. Create an .ovp file:

   a. From the Typeset menu in *SWP* or *SW*, choose Preview.
   b. From the TrueTₑX Previewer File menu, choose Export Metrics.
   c. Select the TrueType font you want.
   d. Select the style, size, and script you prefer and choose OK.
   e. Choose OK to accept the default TₑXexternal font name, or enter a new name and then choose OK.
   f. Choose a directory for the font. We suggest using a temporary directory.
   g. When the system asks you about having the TₑX virtual font be a re-encoded version of the original font, choose No.

2. Create an .ovf and an .ohm file:

   a. From a command prompt, run `ovp2ovf.exe` on the .ovp file to create the two new files.
   The .exe file is located in the `TCITeX\TrueTeX` directory of your program installation.
   b. Copy the .ovf file to the `TCITeX\fonts\vf` directory of your program installation.
   c. Copy the .ofm file to the `TCITeX\fonts\tfm` directory of your program installation.
   d. If the name of the font file you chose from the Export Metrics list contained any spaces, make a copy of the .ofm file and rename the copy so that the original name is preserved, including any spaces.

▶ **To create a font description file**

1. Make a copy of the `UT1omlgc.fd` file in the `TCITeX\Omega\Lambda\base` directory of your program installation.

2. Change the file name from `UT1omlgc.fd` to **UT1*fontname*.fd** where *fontname* is a reasonable name for the font description file.

   Be sure to keep the `UT1` prefix; it is the Unicode encoding for Omega.

3. Change the file as necessary to substitute your font.

4. Save the file in the `TCITeX\TeX\LaTeX\SWomega` directory of your program installation.

▶ **To create a LaTeX font package**

1. Make a copy of one of the `.sty` files in the `TCITeX\TeX\LaTeX\SWomega` directory of your program installation.

2. Find the command **\renewcommand{\familydefault}{*name*}**.

3. Replace the name with the fontname you used to create the font description file.

4. Choose a name for the `.sty` file and save it to the `TCITeX\TeX\LaTeX\SWomega` directory.

▶ **To add the required LaTeX packages to your document.**

1. Open a new document in *SWP* or *SW*.

2. Click ▦ or, from the Typeset menu, choose Options and Packages.

3. Choose Go Native.

4. Add the font package you created, the *fontenc* package, and the *sw2unicode* package.

5. Choose OK to close the dialog boxes and return to your document.

   See *Typesetting Documents with Scientific WorkPlace and Scientific Word* for more information about LaTeX packages.

6. Create and typeset your document.

8   Formatting Documents

The tasks involved in formatting your document depend on the way you want to produce it. If you want to display your document in the document window or preview or print it without typesetting (in *SWP, SW,* and *SNB*), formatting involves working with the document style, page setup, and print options. If you want to typeset your document (in *SWP* and *SW* only), formatting involves working with the typesetting specifications, class and package options, and TEX commands used to tell LATEX and PDFLATEX how to typeset your document.

The formatting specifications are defined by the shell you use to create your document. You can use the specifications exactly as they are defined or you can modify them to create different formatting effects.

This chapter discusses how the appearance of your document changes when you typeset and when you don't. It notes the program approach to basic formatting tasks and explains how to use and modify the formatting specifications to produce a document with a pleasing appearance whether or not you typeset.

Understanding the Appearance of Documents

The appearance of your document depends on how you produce it. As explained in Chapter 7 "Previewing and Printing," when you produce a document in *SNB* or without typesetting it in *SWP* or *SW,* the program ignores the typesetting specifications and uses the screen display routines to format the document according to

- The *style (.cst file),* a collection of settings that governs the appearance of each tag in the shell.

- The *page setup specifications,* which govern page margins, headers, footers, and page numbers.

- The *print options,* which govern whether certain elements, such as gray boxes and helper lines, appear in print.

When you display the document in the document window, the program uses the style and the current View settings to format what you see. When you preview or print the document without typesetting it, the program uses the style, page setup specifications, and print options to format the document in the preview window and on paper. The way your document appears in the document window and the way it appears when you preview or print it without typesetting are similar.

However, the appearance of your document when you typeset it in *SWP* or *SW* may be noticeably different. When you typeset, the program ignores the style, page setup specifications, and print options. It processes the document through LATEX or PDFLATEX, automatically formatting the document according to these specifications:

- The *typesetting specifications,* which govern the typeset appearance of each tag in the shell as well as all other aspects of the typeset appearance of the document.

- The LaTeX *document class options,* which modify the typesetting specifications in some way.

- Any specified LaTeX *packages,* which further modify the typesetting specifications. If a LaTeX package contains formatting instructions that differ from the typesetting specifications, the instructions in the package may take precedence.

- Any LaTeX *commands* entered in the document preamble or inserted into the body of the document in TeX fields.

- The BibTeX style specified for the document, if any.

Important　*The two sets of specifications have no effect on each other.* They are completely separate. Changes to the typesetting specifications aren't reflected in the document window, and changes to the style, which are reflected in the document window, aren't reflected in your typeset document.

The way you produce your document determines which set of specifications is used:

When the document is	The program formats according to
Displayed in the document window	Style, Current **View** settings
Produced without typesetting (From **File** menu)	Style, Page setup specifications, Print options
Produced with typesetting (From **Typeset** menu)	Typesetting specifications, LaTeX options and packages, LaTeX commands

The way tag properties work provides a good illustration of the independent nature of the two sets of formatting specifications. In *SWP* and *SW,* the properties of each tag are defined twice for each document shell, once in the style and once in the typesetting specifications. When you display the document in the document window or produce the document without typesetting it, the program uses the tag properties defined in the style to format tagged information. When you typeset the document, the program uses the tag properties defined in the typesetting specifications. The results may be different, even though the names of the tags are the same.

Suppose the style for a given shell defines the font properties for the Bold tag as Times New Roman, 12-point, bold type, but the typesetting specifications for the shell define the properties for the same tag as Arial, 14-point, bold type. When you display your document in the document window or you produce it without typesetting, any information that you've tagged as Bold looks **like this.** However, when you typeset your document, the same information looks **like this.**

Similarly, suppose the style defines an indention of half an inch for paragraphs in bulleted lists, but the typesetting specifications place the list paragraphs flush with the left margin. When you display your document in the document window or you produce it without typesetting, bulleted lists look something like this:

- Item one.
- Item two.
- Item three.

When you typeset the document, bulleted lists look like this:

- Item one.
- Item two.
- Item three.

Understanding Formatting Tasks

Regardless of how you produce your document, the program handles many formatting tasks automatically. When you produce your document, the program chooses the page orientation, creates the margins, selects the fonts, and makes many other formatting decisions, all according to the style or the typesetting specifications in effect for your document. The formatting that falls to you involves tasks such as adding emphasis to text, creating headings, or placing occasional page breaks where you want them. The document window reflects only those formatting elements defined in the style (.cst) file. Preview or typeset preview your document to see the full effect of any formatting changes you make.

If you like the appearance of documents created with the shell, you don't need to modify any of the formatting specifications. On the other hand, you may want to modify either the typeset or the non-typeset appearance of your document. Changing the appearance of the document when you display it in the document window and when you preview or print it without typesetting involves modifying the style, page setup specifications, or print options. See Formatting Documents for Production without Typesetting on page 199.

Changing the appearance of the document when you typeset it is more complex. It can involve modifying the LaTeX class options, adding and modifying LaTeX packages, and adding TeX commands to the preamble or body of your document, as described in Formatting Documents for Production with Typesetting on page 222 and, in more detail, in *Typesetting Documents in Scientific WorkPlace and Scientific Word.* We discourage any attempts to modify the typesetting specifications if you aren't extremely familiar with TeX and LaTeX. If the typeset appearance of your document doesn't meet your requirements, we suggest you create a new document using a more appropriate shell. Other than saving the file for PDF production, as described on page 165, no special formatting modifications are necessary to create a typeset PDF file.

Important   If the typesetting specifications for your document were developed with the Style Editor, you can modify them with the Style Editor. Otherwise, we don't advise attempting to change the typesetting specifications to modify the typeset appearance of tagged information unless you are extremely familiar with TeX and LaTeX.

You can accomplish most, but not all, formatting tasks in familiar ways. Sometimes, however, the processes differ depending on whether or not you want to typeset your document. This section briefly notes how to accomplish many basic formatting tasks and refers you to additional information in our manuals.

Boldface

You can create bold text or mathematics with the Bold and Bold Symbol tags. The Bold Symbol tag automatically starts mathematics. Note that some shells use content-oriented tag names such as Define instead of appearance-oriented names such as Bold. The properties of other tags, such as some section heading tags, may also specify boldface text. In that case, when you apply the tag to a selection, the selection automatically appears in boldface even though you didn't specifically tag it as Bold.

- To create boldface, see Adding Emphasis with Text Tags, page 59, and Using Tags with Mathematics, page 104.

Centering

The procedure for centering information depends on what you want to center:

- To center text, see Adding Structure with Section and Body Tags, page 60 and Adjusting Horizontal Space, page 193.

- To center mathematics, see Understanding In-Line and Displayed Mathematics, page 69.

- To center graphics, see Editing the Frame Properties, page 112.

Also, some tags, especially heading tags, automatically produce centered information.

Color

Although TEX was not designed to support color, you can use color in your typeset documents if your output drivers and your printer support color. With the *color* package, you can specify the background color of an environment, a page, or a box. See *Typesetting Documents in Scientific WorkPlace and Scientific Word* for more information.

Columns

Multiple columns are available if you typeset your document. The number of columns on a page depends on the typesetting specifications. Columns don't appear in the document window, but you can see them if you typeset preview your document.

- To modify the number of columns produced when you typeset, see Modifying the Class Options, page 224, or Using LaTeX Packages, page 226.

Double-Sided Printing

Double-sided printing means offsetting the printing differently for odd-numbered and even-numbered pages. The offset allows for the space required when you bind the document. Double-sided printing is available for most shells, especially book shells, regardless of how you produce your document. *Duplex printing*—whether the printer actually prints on both sides of the paper—depends on the printer itself.

- To specify double-sided printing when you typeset, see Line Spacing later in this section and Modifying the Class Options on page 224.

- To specify double-sided printing when you don't typeset, see Modifying the Page Margins, page 219.

Double Spacing

Double spacing is available with or without typesetting. Documents appear double-spaced in the document window only if the style specifies double spacing. You can see the typeset appearance of double-spaced text if you typeset preview your document.

- To create double spacing when you typeset, see Using LaTeX Packages, page 226. If the document shell was created with the Style Editor, use the Style Editor to change the line spacing instead.

- To create double-spaced documents when you don't typeset, see Modifying the Paragraph Properties of a Tag, page 206.

Fonts

Fonts are determined by the typesetting specifications and the style. We don't recommend attempting to change the fonts called for by the typesetting specifications. However, if you expect to open your document on another platform or in another installation, you can improve the portability of the document by choosing font packages carefully, as described on page 231.

- To specify the fonts used when you don't typeset, see Modifying the Font Properties of a Tag, page 205.

Headers and Footers

The typesetting specifications and the page setup determine the presence, layout, and content of headers and footers. Headers and footers are shown when you preview your document but not in the document window.

- To modify the headers and footers used when you typeset, see Using LaTeX Packages, page 226.

- To modify the headers and footers used when you don't typeset, see Modifying the Headers and Footers, page 220.

Headings

To create section headings, apply one of the section tags to selected or new information (see Adding Structure with Section and Body Tags, page 60). The style and the typesetting specifications determine the appearance of headings.

- To modify the headings used when you typeset, see Using LaTeX Packages, page 226.

- To modify the headings used when you don't typeset, see Modifying the Current Style, page 202.

Hyphenation

Automatic hyphenation is available when you typeset your document. However, you can request *discretionary,* or conditional, hyphenation for specific words in case they occur at the end of a line. If you've inserted a discretionary hyphen in a word, the program will break the word at that point if necessary, both in print and, if Invisibles are turned on in the View menu, in the document window.

- To modify automatic hyphenation when you typeset your document, see Using the Babel Package, page 230.

- To insert discretionary hyphenation, see Typing Punctuation, page 53.

Indention

The indention of paragraphs, headings, and lists is determined by the tag properties set in the style and the typesetting specifications. When you apply a tag to a selection, the selection is indented according to the paragraph properties specified for the tag. The way you produce the document determines which set of tag properties is used.

- To suppress indention at the beginning of a paragraph, see Adjusting Horizontal Space, page 193.

- To modify the indention used when you typeset, refer to *Typesetting Documents in Scientific WorkPlace and Scientific Word*.

- To modify the indention used when you don't typeset, see Modifying the Current Style, page 202.

Italics

To create italics, apply the Italics tag to selected or new information (see page 58). Note that some shells use content-oriented tag names such as *Emphasized* instead of appearance-oriented names such as *Italics*. The properties of other tags and other typesetting specifications may use italics to format certain document elements, such as the title of a paper. In that case, when you apply the tag to a selection, the selection automatically appears in italics even though you didn't specifically tag it as Italics.

- To create italics, see Adding Emphasis with Text Tags, page 59.

Justification

The program shows justification in the document window according to the tag properties set in the style. To see how paragraph justification will appear when you typeset, typeset preview your document.

- To modify the justification used when you typeset, refer to *Typesetting Documents in Scientific WorkPlace and Scientific Word*.

- To modify the justification used when you don't typeset, see Modifying the Paragraph Properties of a Tag, page 206.

Kerning

Kerning is the amount of horizontal space between letters and characters. When you typeset your document, the program automatically adjusts the kerning, but it isn't adjusted if you produce your document without typesetting it. Kerning isn't shown in the document window. Whether or not you typeset, you may occasionally want to add horizontal space to your mathematics or text.

- To add horizontal space, see Adjusting Horizontal Space, page 193.

Leading

Leading is the amount of space between printed lines of text or mathematics. When you typeset your document, the program automatically adjusts the leading according to the typesetting specifications to produce a well-spaced page. When you don't typeset your document, the program doesn't adjust the leading and the line spacing is determined by the paragraph properties set in the style (see Line Spacing, below). Leading isn't shown in the document window. Whether or not you typeset, you may occasionally want to add additional vertical space between lines in your document.

- To add vertical space, see Adjusting Vertical Space, page 195.

Ligatures

Ligatures are typeset characters that, in certain fonts, combine two or more letters, such as the *fi* in *Scientific*. When you typeset your document, LaTeX automatically provides ligatures; ligatures aren't available without typesetting.

Line Breaks

The program breaks lines automatically in the previewer and in print, according to the style or the typesetting specifications. When you display your document, the program breaks lines according to the width of the document window. Occasionally, you may want to override the automatic line breaks and force a line break in the middle of a paragraph. You can also force a line break in a heading. Because forced breaks in headings can cause difficulties with typesetting, you must use a special structure to break a heading in a document that you want to typeset.

- To force a line break in a paragraph, see Adjusting Line and Page Breaks, page 197.

- To force a line break in a heading, see Creating Section Headings, page 245.

Line Spacing

The program spaces lines automatically according to the style or the typesetting specifications. Some shells create double-spaced documents. The *setspace* package provides line spacing options for typesetting in *SWP* and *SW*. Whether or not you typeset your document, you may want to make occasional adjustments to the line spacing.

- To add space between two lines, see Adjusting Vertical Space, page 195.

- To modify the line spacing used when you typeset, refer to *Typesetting Documents in Scientific WorkPlace and Scientific Word*.

- To modify the line spacing used when you don't typeset, see Modifying the Paragraph Properties of a Tag, page 206.

Lines and Boxes

You can add simple boxes and solid and dotted lines to your document. If you typeset your document, you can box larger portions of text.

- To add simple boxes and lines, see Entering Decorations, page 91.

- To add solid and dotted lines, see Adding Lines, page 198.

- To box large portions of text when you typeset, see Using LaTeX Packages, page 226.

Lists

Lists are created with item tags. The appearance of lists depends on the properties of the item tags as set in the style and in the typesetting specifications.

- To create lists, see Creating Lists with Item Tags, page 62.

- To modify lists produced when you typeset, see Using LaTeX Packages, page 226.

- To modify lists produced when you don't typeset, see Modifying the Behavior Property of a Tag, page 214.

Margins

Print margins aren't reflected in the document window, because the text is fitted to the size of the window, but you can see how the margins will look in print if you preview the document. You can specify on-screen margins that have no effect on the printed document; see page 217.

- To modify the margins used when you typeset, see Using LaTeX Packages, page 226.

- To modify the margins used when you don't typeset, see Modifying the Page Margins, page 219.

Page Breaks

The program creates page breaks automatically in the previewer and in print, according to the page setup specifications or the typesetting specifications. When you display your document, the program doesn't show automatic page breaks, because text is fitted to the size of the window. Occasionally, you may want to override the automatic page breaks and force a break.

- To force a page break, see Adjusting Line and Page Breaks, page 197.

Page Format

The page format of your document is governed by the typesetting specifications and by the style and page setup specifications of the document shell. The way you produce your document determines which specifications the program uses. Certain page format elements, such as margins, automatic page breaks, and headers and footers, appear only when you preview or print your document, and not in the document window. Whether the page format is offset for odd-numbered and even-numbered pages depends on the shell you choose. Remember that the page format must be appropriate for the paper size in your printer. In *SWP* and *SW*, you can use the *layout* package to create a diagram of the page format determined by the typesetting specifications for your document.

- To create a diagram of the typeset layout of your document, see Using LaTeX Packages, page 226.

- To modify the page format used when you don't typeset, see Modifying the Page Setup, page 219.

Page Numbering

Whether the pages of your document are numbered and where those numbers appear on the page are functions of the page setup specifications and the typesetting specifications.

- To modify the page numbering when you typeset, see Using LaTeX Packages, page 226.

- To modify the page numbering when you don't typeset, see Modifying the Page Numbering, page 221.

Page Orientation

Portrait and landscape page orientations are determined by the printer setup, the typesetting specifications, and the capabilities of your printer.

- To change the printer orientation, see Chapter 7 "Previewing and Printing."

- To change the page orientation for typesetting, see Modifying the Class Options, page 224.

Page Size

Page size is the size of the printed area on a piece of paper. The page size depends on the page setup specifications and on the typesetting specifications. The page size isn't reflected in the document window, where text is broken to fit the window.

- To modify the page size used when you typeset, see Using LaTeX Packages, page 226.

- To modify the page size used when you don't typeset, see Modifying the Page Margins, page 219.

Paper Size

The printer setup determines the size of the paper on which you print your document. Be sure the page format is appropriate for the size of the paper you want to use. The program doesn't reflect the size of the paper in the document window, where text is broken to fit the window size, but you can see it when you preview. You can modify the page setup and the typesetting specifications to accommodate different sizes of paper. If you use paper of a different size, remember to change the margins for your document and, if you typeset preview your document, change the options for the TrueTeX preview screen to accommodate the new paper size.

- To modify the paper size for which the document is typeset, see Modifying the Class Options, page 224.

- To modify the paper size used when you don't typeset, see Chapter 7 "Previewing and Printing."

Tabs

The TAB key has a different effect depending on the location of the insertion point.

Location	Effect
Text	Insert horizontal space according the default
Matrix or table	Move the insertion point to the next cell
Template	Move the insertion point to the next input box
Dialog box	Move the attention to the next command

By default, if you press TAB when the insertion point is in text, the program enters a 2-em space. You can change the default to ignore the key stroke or to enter a horizontal space of the width you specify.

- To modify the TAB default, see Chapter 12 "Customizing the Program."

Typeface

The typefaces used in your document—such as Arial or Times New Roman—depend on the tag properties set in the style and in the typesetting specifications. The fonts you see in the document window are defined in the style; they may be very different from those defined by the typesetting specifications. We don't recommend attempting to change the typeface called for by the typesetting specifications.

- To specify the typeface used when you don't typeset, see Modifying the Font Properties of a Tag, page 205.

Type Size

The size of the type used for body text in your document depends on the tag properties set in the style and in the typesetting specifications. The size of type used for other elements, such as headings and footnotes, changes in proportion to the size of type used for body text. You can modify the type sizes specified in the style, and you may be able to modify the size of body text specified in the typesetting specifications.

- To modify the type sizes used when you typeset, see Modifying the Class Options, page 224.

- To modify the type sizes used when you don't typeset, see Modifying the Font Properties of a Tag, page 205.

Underlining

The program has no underlining command in the usual sense. On rare occasions you may want to emphasize a word with underlining instead of with one of the text tags. In those cases you can use the decoration for Bar Under , available from the **Decoration** dialog box. If you typeset your document in *SWP* or *SW*, you can add the *ulem* package to create underlines.

- To underline a word, see Entering Decorations, page 91.

- To add underlining when you typeset, see Using LATEX Packages, page 226.

Making Final Formatting Adjustments

Text and mathematics spacing, line breaks, and page breaks are automatic. As you enter information, the program automatically adds the appropriate amount of space after punctuation and between text and mathematical elements. The program also creates line and page breaks wherever necessary to fit the material onto the printed page according to the style or the typesetting specifications for the document.

In the document window, the program breaks each line wherever necessary to fit the information inside the document window. If you change the size of the window, the program automatically adjusts the on-screen line breaks. The size of the printed page and the size of the document window aren't the same, so the line breaks you see on the screen aren't those that will appear in print, regardless of how you produce your document. You can examine how line and page breaks will occur in print if you preview or typeset preview your document.

The automatic features of the program ensure that your printed document will have a beautiful appearance. Usually, you won't need to provide final adjustments to correct line breaks, page breaks, or breaks in mathematics. Occasionally, though, you may want to specify spacing changes, especially in larger articles and books. In some places, you may also want to add vertical or horizontal space or insert lines, called *rules,* such as those that surround the note below.

Note   We encourage you to focus on creating and refining the content of your document instead of its appearance. Experiment with various shells to discover those that best suit your needs.

► **To prepare a large document for final printing**

1. Complete all work on the content of the document.

2. Preview or typeset preview the document and check carefully for any cramped horizontal or vertical spacing, mathematics too large to break properly, or bad line or page breaks.

   Remember   The spacing in your document will differ depending on whether or not you typeset it.

3. Starting from each forced page break in your document (such as at the beginning of each chapter), make spacing adjustments.

4. After each series of adjustments, save and preview or typeset preview the document.

5. When the spacing is satisfactory, print or typeset print the document.

Adjusting Horizontal Space

As you enter text and mathematics, the program automatically adds the appropriate amount of horizontal space between items. However, you may occasionally want to increase or reduce the horizontal space between words or elements on a line. Similarly, you may want to require or prevent a break at a certain point, or remove the indention for a paragraph. You can alter the horizontal space between text or mathematical characters using the Spacing command on the Insert menu. These spacing options are available:

Space	Size
Em Space	Width of the letter M
2-Em Space	Width of the letters MM
Normal Space	$\frac{2}{9}$ em
Required Space	$\frac{2}{9}$ em
Non-breaking Space	$\frac{2}{9}$ em
Thin Space	$\frac{1}{6}$ em
Thick Space	$\frac{5}{18}$ em
Zero Space	0 em
Italic Correction	Depends on the character to the left
Negative Thin Space	$-\frac{1}{6}$ em
Custom	As specified
No Indent	0 em (removes paragraph indention)

Certain of these spaces have specialized uses. For example, a zero space is useful when you create prescripts, as described in Chapter 4 "Creating Mathematics." The program automatically adds space at the end of italicized words so that they don't appear to lean into upright words, but you can add additional correction.

Additionally, you can specify custom horizontal space. In *SWP* or *SW*, you can specify whether custom horizontal space should be discarded if it falls at the end of a typeset line or included regardless of where it falls on the page.

Custom horizontal space can have a fixed length or it can stretch. If you specify fixed space, the program will insert exactly that amount of space when you produce your document. As an illustration, we've added $\frac{1}{2}$ inch of fixed horizontal space at this point   before the rest of the sentence. If you specify stretchy space, the program will determine the amount of space that is inserted based on the *stretch factor* you supply and the location of the space on the line. A stretch factor of 1 fills the current line. If you set the stretch factor to 1, you can fill the space with dots or with a line. At the end of this sentence, for example, we've added space with a stretch factor of 1 and specified that the space be filled with dots. . . . .
Stretchy space can be useful for justifying or centering an isolated line of text, such as a header or footer in a document produced without typesetting:

- You can left-justify the information on a line by placing stretchy space with a stretch factor of 1 after the information. If the paragraph properties specify indention, insert a horizontal space of No Indent before the text.

- You can right-justify the information on a line by placing stretchy space with a stretch factor of 1 before the information.

- You can center the information on a line by placing stretchy space with a stretch factor of 1 both before and after the information. If the paragraph properties specify indention, insert a horizontal space of No Indent before the first stretchy space.

▶ **To insert horizontal space on a line**

1. Place the insertion point where you want additional space.

2. On the Editing toolbar, click the Space button **e..m** or, from the Insert menu, choose Spacing and then choose Horizontal Space.

3. Choose the type of space you want.

4. If you want to insert an exact amount of custom space, choose Custom and then choose Fixed.

   a. In the Width box, specify the amount of space you want inserted.
   b. In the Units box, specify the unit of measure.

5. If you want the program to determine the amount of space to be inserted, choose Custom and then choose Stretchy.

   a. In the Factor box, specify the stretch factor.
   b. If the stretch factor is 1, specify the fill in the Fill With box.

6. If you're using *SWP* or *SW* and you want the space to be included regardless of where it falls on the typeset line, check Always.

   or

If you want the space to be discarded if it falls at the end of a typeset line, check Discard at Line End.

If you don't typeset your document, the program always includes the custom space.

7. Choose OK.

If Invisibles are turned on from the View menu, horizontal spaces appear in the document window as small horizontal lines. The lines help you see and edit the spaces. The lines don't appear when you typeset your document, but they may appear when you produce the document without typesetting, depending on the print options for your document and the settings on the View menu.

Adjusting Vertical Space

The style and the typesetting specifications automatically determine the spacing between paragraphs and between lines and other elements. Occasionally, you may want to add vertical space to your document. A *strut* forces the maximum line space required by the font. The space increases the consistency of line spacing in situations where the spacing depends on the letters in the text, such as in table cells. Similarly, a *math strut* increases the consistency of vertical spacing within mathematics where spacing varies because of the characters in the mathematics. In *SWP* and *SW*, custom space can be discarded if it falls at the end of a typeset page or required regardless of where it falls on the page.

You can add vertical space with the Spacing command on the Insert menu:

Space	Size
Small Skip	About $\frac{5}{16}$ inch between lines in a 12-point font
Medium Skip	About $\frac{3}{8}$ inch between lines in a 12-point font
Big Skip	About $\frac{7}{16}$ inch between lines in a 12-point font
Strut	About $\frac{3}{16}$ inch between lines in a 12-point font
Math Strut	About $\frac{7}{32}$ inch between lines in a 12-point font
Custom	As specified

If you plan to typeset your document in *SWP* or *SW*, you can also add vertical space with several fragments. The Vertical Fill (TeX Field) fragment adds as much vertical space as can fit on the page, but removes the space if it falls at the end of a typeset page. The Vertical Fill–always (TeX Field) fragment adds as much vertical space as can fit on the page, regardless of where it falls when you typeset. In the document window the fragments appear as small gray boxes containing the word *rvfill* or *vfill* surrounded by square brackets. When you typeset your document, LATEX adds the space. We suggest you place fragments that generate additional vertical space in paragraphs by themselves. See Chapter 3 "Creating Text" for information about using fragments.

▶ **To insert vertical space**

1. Move the insertion point to the line after which you want to add space.

2. From the Insert menu, choose Spacing, and then choose Vertical Space.

3. From the Vertical Space dialog box, select the vertical space you want to insert.

4. If you want to insert custom space, choose Custom.

    a. In the Depth box, specify the amount of space you want inserted.

    b. In the Units box, specify the unit of measure.

    c. If you're using *SWP* or *SW* and you want the space to be included anywhere it falls on the typeset page, check Always.

      or

      If you want the space to be discarded at the end of a typeset page, check Discard at Page Boundary.

If you don't typeset your document, the program always includes the custom space.

5. Choose OK.

You can delete vertical spaces only when Invisibles are turned on from the View menu. When Invisibles are turned on, vertical spaces appear in the document window as vertical lines proportional to the specified length. The lines help you see and revise vertical spaces. The lines don't appear when you typeset your document, but they may appear when you produce the document without typesetting, depending on the print options for your document and the settings on the View menu. See Setting Print Options in Chapter 7 "Previewing and Printing."

Adjusting Breaks in Mathematical Expressions

If a mathematical expression extends into the margin because it is too large to break properly, we suggest you display it. If you don't want to display the expression, you can indicate places where a break is appropriate, required, or not allowed. In general, it is preferable to suggest a break rather than to force one. If a break is suggested rather than forced, it may not occur if later changes move the expression to a position where a break is no longer necessary.

▶ **To adjust a break**

1. Place the insertion point in the expression where you want to suggest, force, or prevent a break.

2. From the Insert menu, choose Spacing and then choose Break.

3. Choose the break option you want:

- If you want to suggest a break, choose Allowbreak.
- If you want to force a break, choose Newline.
- If you want to prevent a break, choose No break.

4. Choose OK.

If Invisibles are turned on from the View menu, breaks in mathematics appear in the document window as small marks in the expression. The marks don't appear when you typeset your document, but they may appear when you produce the document without typesetting, depending on the print options for your document and the settings on the View menu.

Breaking a mathematical expression across several lines is more difficult when the expression is enclosed in parentheses. Simply breaking the line at an opportune place may cause the parentheses to expand to encompass both lines. You can avoid the difficulty in two ways. First, you can break the expression manually, maintain the appearance of the parentheses by using empty brackets to enclose one end of each resulting line and then correct the spacing with zero-width rules (see Adding Lines on page 198). Second, if you're using *SWP* or *SW* and you know TEX, you can surround the expression with large TEX brackets instead of expanding brackets used by the program. Like any other character, TEX brackets exist as independent objects; they behave just like large versions of the brackets that you obtain by pressing the bracket keys on your keyboard. If you surround an expression with TEX brackets, the program doesn't consider your expression to be a single unit as it does when you use expanding brackets, and TEX breaks the expression automatically when you typeset your document.

Adjusting Line and Page Breaks

The program breaks the lines and pages in your document based on the settings in the page setup specifications and the typesetting specifications. The way you produce your document determines how the breaks occur. Remember that automatic line and page breaks are ignored in the document window, where the program breaks the information to fit the size of the window.

Although the page setup specifications and the typesetting specifications determine how many characters fit on a given line and how many lines of text and mathematics fit on a given page, you can force a line or page break at any point in your document. These breaks are available:

Break	Effect
Newline	Starts a new line at the break
Linebreak	Starts a new line at the break and fully justifies the text on the line
Custom newline	Starts a new line at the break after a specified amount of vertical space
Newpage	Starts a new page and a new paragraph at the break
Pagebreak	Starts a new page after the current line

See related information on page 53 about requesting discretionary hyphenation when words fall at the end of a line.

Note   Creating breaks in typeset headings requires a special procedure. See Section Headings on page 245.

▶ **To start a new paragraph**

- Press ENTER.
  The program ends the current paragraph and moves the insertion point to the leftmost position in the first line of the new paragraph.

▶ **To force a line or page break**

1. Place the insertion point where you want the line break to occur.

2. From the Insert menu, choose Spacing and then choose Break.

3. Choose the type of break you want.

4. If you want to specify the amount of space to skip before beginning the new line,

   a. Choose Custom newline.
   b. In the Depth box, specify the amount of space to be added.
   c. In the Units box, specify the unit of measure.
   d. If you want the break to occur regardless of where it falls on the typeset page, check Always.
      or
      If you want the break to be discarded at the end of a typeset page, check Discard at Page Boundary.

   If you don't typeset your document, the program always includes custom space.

5. Choose OK.

   If Invisibles are turned on from the View menu, page breaks appear in the document window as ▮ and line breaks appear as ↵ . When you specify a custom newline, the line break mark is extended by a vertical line proportional to the space you specify. The marks don't appear when you typeset your document, but they may appear when you produce the document without typesetting, depending on the print options for your document and the settings on the View menu.

▶ **To delete a page break**

- From the View menu, turn on Invisibles to display the breaks, then select the break and press BACKSPACE or DELETE.

Adding Lines

Although the style you choose determines where lines appear in your document, you may want to add solid lines to set off certain portions of the document. You can specify the thickness and length of the line as well as the *lift,* or where the line falls in relation to the baseline of the surrounding text. For example, if you specify a rule with a lift of 0.0 inch, a width of 1.0 inch, and a height of 0.02 inch, you produce a line like this ——————————— right on the baseline. Similarly, if you specify a rule with a lift of 0.02 inch, a width of 2.5 inches, and a height of 0.05 inch, you produce a line like this ▬▬▬▬▬▬▬▬▬▬▬▬▬▬ that sits slightly above the baseline. Also, by specifying a rule with a lift of -.20 inch, a width of 0.02 inch, and a height of .3 inch, you can produce a vertical line that extends below the baseline, like this: | .

You can add lines and dotted lines with stretchy horizontal space. See Adjusting Horizontal Space earlier in this chapter.

► **To add a line**

1. Place the insertion point where you want the line to begin.

2. From the Insert menu, choose Spacing.

3. Choose Rule to open the Rule dialog box:

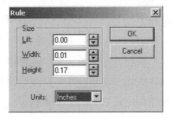

4. In the Lift box, specify the elevation of the line above the baseline.

5. In the Width box, specify the length of the line.

6. In the Height box, specify the height of the line.

7. In the Units box, specify the unit of measure for the specifications.

8. Choose OK.

Formatting Documents for Production without Typesetting

When you preview or print your document without typesetting (that is, from the File menu), the program processes the document using the same routines with which it displays it in the document window. The appearance of your document depends on the style, page setup specifications, and print options.

Understanding the Style (.cst) File

The shell you use to create your document determines its style. The style, which has a file name extension of .cst, is a collection of settings that determine the properties—that is, the appearance and behavior—of each tag defined for the shell. The program uses the style file when you display a document in the document window or produce it without typesetting.

If the style produces a document format that doesn't fit your requirements, you can modify the current style, and you can add new body and text tags to the style as necessary. You can create a new style and subsequently use it to create documents or apply it to existing documents with a similar structure. If necessary, you can change to a different style. Please be aware, however, that dramatic style changes can have unpredictable results.

Important   Changing the style (.cst) file has no effect on the typeset appearance of your document.

Understanding Tag Properties

The .cst file sets the properties for specific tags as well as default properties that affect the whole document. The settings determine these and many other properties (not all tags have the same properties):

- Face, size, slant, weight, and color of type.
- Justification, indention, line spacing, and background color of paragraphs.
- Color, width, alignment, and type characteristics of lead-in objects and list items.
- Spacing, color, and relative size of mathematical objects and operators.
- Tag for the following paragraph and presence of the tag in the popup list.
- Spacing and background color for graphics, plots, and plot captions.

Understanding how tag properties interact will help you modify them when necessary.

- **Basic properties**. Tag properties define the basic appearance of tagged text in terms of the properties noted in the list above. Tag properties also define the appearance of special objects (such as citations, lead-in objects, tables, and mathematical displays) when they occur within tagged text. Basic tag properties behave in a straightforward manner.

  For example, assume a given style defines Body Text as 12-point, Times New Roman type. It defines hypertext links that occur in Body Text as 12-point, Arial type. The style also defines the text of Numbered List Items as black, 12-point, Times New Roman type, but it specifies that hypertext links that occur in numbered lists should appear in 10-point, Arial type. Thus, hypertext links appear in the same typeface in both Body Text and Numbered List Items, but they are smaller when they occur in Numbered Lists:

This body text paragraph contains a hypertext link and introduces a numbered list.

1. This item contains a hypertext link.

2. This item doesn't.

- **Nested properties**. Tags can be nested and so can their properties. The style determines the properties it uses beginning with the innermost tag.

  To illustrate, suppose a given style specifies that hypertext links that occur in Body Text appear in 12-point, bold, Arial type. It also specifies that hypertext links that occur in text tagged as Small appear in 8-point, bold, Arial type. If a hypertext link occurs inside text tagged as Small, and that text occurs within Body Text, the style uses the hypertext link properties defined for the Small tag:

> The first sentence of this body text paragraph contains a **hypertext link**. This sentence, which contains a **hypertext link**, is tagged as small. This is the remainder of the body text paragraph.

- **Inherited properties**. Rather than specifying a value for a tag property, the style can specify that the property be *inherited*. The style uses the corresponding value from the text to the left and right.

  For example, the style might specify that text tagged as Body Text appear as black, 12-point, Times New Roman type and that hypertext links that occur in Body Text appear in bold type but otherwise inherit their font properties from the surrounding text. When hypertext links occur in Body Text, the style produces them in bold type that is the same size and typeface as the surrounding text.

> The first sentence of this body text paragraph contains a **hypertext link**. This is the remainder of the body text paragraph.

- **Unspecified properties**. Although .cst files can specify all possible properties for all tags, most styles contain a limited set of specifications. If the style doesn't define a specific or inherited value for a particular tag property, the style uses the corresponding property value for the surrounding tag.

  Suppose a style specifies that Body Text appear as 12-point, Times New Roman type, and that hypertext links that occur within Body Text appear as 12-point, Arial type. Suppose the style also specifies that text tagged as Small appear as 10-point, Times New Roman type. The style makes no specifications for hypertext links that occur within text tagged as Small. Because no properties are specified for hypertext links in Small text, the style uses the hypertext link properties specified for the surrounding text. Thus, hypertext links in Small text appear just as they do in the surrounding Body Text: in 12-point, Arial type:

> The first sentence of this body text paragraph contains a hypertext link. This sentence, which contains a hypertext link, is tagged as small. This is the remainder of the body text paragraph.

Now suppose the style specifies that Body Text appear as 12-point, Times New Roman type and that hypertext links that occur within Body Text appear in bold Times New Roman type but inherit their size. The style also specifies that text tagged as Small appear as 10-point, Times New Roman type, but it makes no specifications for hypertext links that occur within text tagged as Small. Because no properties are specified for hypertext links in Small text, the style uses the hypertext properties for the surrounding tag, Body Text. Those properties specify that hypertext links appear as bold, Times New Roman type but inherit the size property of the text to their left and right, which in this case is Small. Thus, hypertext links in Small text appear as bold 10-point, Times New Roman type:

> The first sentence of this body text paragraph contains a **hypertext link**. This sentence, which contains a **hypertext link**, is tagged as small. This is the remainder of the body text paragraph.

- **Default properties**. Styles include a collection of default properties that are used when no other properties apply in a given context.

  For example, a style defines Heading 1 as bold, 18-point, Arial type and Heading 2 as bold, 14-point, Arial type. It defines no typeface values for Headings 3–5, but includes default Font properties of regular, 12-point, Times New Roman type. The style distinguishes between the fonts used for Heading 1 and Heading 2, but Headings 3–5 appear in an identical font:

> # Heading 1
> ## Heading 2
> Heading 3
> Heading 4
> Heading 5

Modifying the Current Style (.cst) File

If the non-typeset appearance of tagged information in your document doesn't quite meet your formatting needs, you can modify it by changing the tag properties defined in the style (.cst) file. You can modify all possible tag properties, including the properties of front matter tags, from within the program.

When you make modifications to the tag properties, the program applies the changes to the current document. You can discard the changes you make after the current editing session or you can save them permanently. Permanent changes affect the appearance of the current document and that of all documents created with the same style.

Remember Modifying the style doesn't affect the typeset appearance of your document.

The style file contains two kinds of settings: those that are *specific to a given tag*, such as using green for mathematics if the mathematics occurs in a centered paragraph, and those *default settings* that apply to every tag in the style, such as using red for mathematics regardless of where the mathematics occurs. If the two conflict, as in this example, the settings specified for the tag override the defaults for the document as a whole.

You can modify both the tag-specific and the default settings. The process involves selecting the tag whose properties you want to modify, selecting the property itself, making the changes, and finally saving them. Although the process is generally the same for all tags, the specific choices available differ according to the tag and the property you select. Below, we outline the general process and then describe specific differences.

Important   These settings don't affect the way fonts appear when you typeset the document.

▶ **To modify the properties of a tag defined in the style file**

1. On the Editing toolbar, click the Tag button 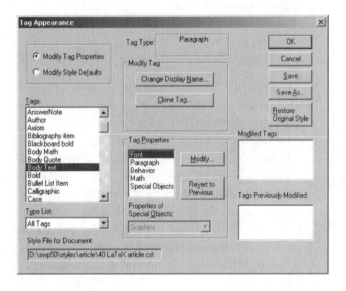 or, from the **Tag** menu, choose **Appearance**.

   The program opens the **Tag Appearance** dialog box.

2. Change the properties:

   a. In the **Type List**, select the type of tag you want to modify.
   b. In the **Tags** list, select the specific tag whose properties you want to modify.
      The list may include tags that don't appear in the popup lists for the current style.
   c. In the **Tag Properties** area, select the property type you want to change. If you select **Special Objects**, select a property type from the list marked **Properties of Special Objects**.
   d. Choose **Modify**.
      The **Style Properties** dialog box opens and indicates with a check mark in the **Properties Specified** list those properties for which specifications appear in the .cst file. Unchecked properties use the corresponding settings for the surrounding text or, in their absence, the default settings for the style.

e. If you don't want to use a default specification for a given property, check the property and then use the corresponding controls to change the settings.

f. If you want to change a specification for a property, use the corresponding controls to set the settings you want.

g. If you want any font properties for the tag to be inherited from the current environment, check the property in the Properties Specified list and the corresponding property box in the Inherit area.

Checking a box in the Inherit area disables the corresponding property control.

h. When all the properties have been specified, choose OK.

The program changes the tag properties and enters the tag name in the Modified Tags list. If you have modified other tags during the current editing session, the names of those tags appear in the Tags Previously Modified list.

i. Repeat steps a–h for all the tags you want to modify.

j. If you decide you don't want the changes for a particular tag property,

i Select the tag.

ii Select the property in the Tag Properties area.

iii Choose Revert to Previous.

k. If you decide you don't want any of the tag property modifications, choose Restore Original Style to return to the settings saved in the style file.

3. Choose the way you want to save your changes to the style file:

- If you want to change the tag appearance for the current document and for all other documents created with the style,

  i Choose Save to modify the current style.

  ii Choose OK twice to return to your document.

  The program modifies the .cst file and applies the changes to the current document and to all other documents created with the style.

- If you want to change the tag appearance for the current document but leave it unchanged for all other documents created with the current style,

  i Choose Save As to create a new style.

  ii Specify a file name for the new style file, and choose Save and then choose OK.

  The program creates a new .cst file and applies it to the current document. By default, the program saves the new style in the same directory as the current style. If you specify a different style directory, the name of the new style won't appear when you display the styles available for documents of this type.

- If you don't want to save the changes permanently, choose OK twice to return to your document.

  The program applies the changes to the current document but discards them when you close the document. Saving the document doesn't preserve the changes.

If you've modified more than one tag, choosing OK accepts the changes for all modified tags according to the save option you specified. Choosing Cancel discards the changes for all modified tags.

4. If you created a new style or added a tag to the existing style, save your document to apply the new style file.

Modifying the Font Properties of a Tag

You can modify these font properties for most tags:

- Face – The name of the type design, such as Arial or Times New Roman.

- Slant – The angle of the type, such as italic or upright.

- Weight – The emphasis of the type, such as bold.

- Size – The height of the type, usually measured in points. One point is $\frac{1}{72}$ inch.

- Color – The color in which the type appears on your screen. This property also affects the color in which the type appears in print, depending on your printer, print commands, and print options.

▶ **To change the font properties of a tag**

1. On the Editing toolbar, click the Tag button 🅰 or, from the Tag menu, choose Appearance and then select the tag whose font properties you want to modify.

2. In the **Tag Properties** area, double-click Font, or select Font and then choose **Modify**.

   The program opens the Font dialog box.

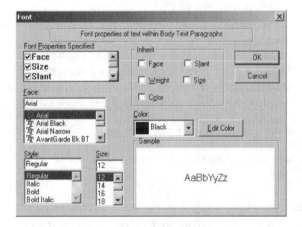

3. If you want to change a specification, check the corresponding property in the **Font Properties Specified** list.

4. If you want any font properties for the tag to be inherited from the current environment, check the corresponding property box in the Inherit area.

   Checking a box for an inherited property disables the corresponding property list.

5. Change the face, style, and size of the font as necessary.

6. If you want to change the color of the font, click the arrow at the side of the Color list or choose Edit Color.

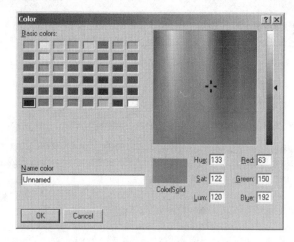

a. Select the color you want:
  - From the Basic colors boxes, click the color you want.
    or
  - Set the Hue, Saturation, and Luminosity or Red, Green, and Blue values.
    or
  - Click the color you want on the spectrum and then select the brightness on the scale at the right.

b. If you want to assign a name to the color, type the name in the Name color box and choose OK.

Remember   Color changes affect the way the font appears on the screen and, if you have a color printer, on paper when you print without typesetting. If you typeset your document, these color settings are ignored.

7. When your changes are complete, choose OK.

8. Save the changes to the style file and choose OK.

Modifying the Paragraph Properties of a Tag

You can change these paragraph properties for most section, body, and item tags:

- Alignment (justification) – The way the paragraph is aligned with the right or left margin, with both margins, or with the center of the page.

- Background color – The color over which the paragraph text appears on your screen and, depending on your printer and print options, on paper.

- Indention – The amount of space all lines of the paragraph should be indented from the margin on the left and right sides, and the additional amount of space to be added to the indention on the first line and on other lines.

- Line spacing – The amount of space between lines of the paragraph.

- Paragraph spacing – The amount of space before and after paragraphs of this type. This space is cumulative. That is, if you have two consecutive paragraphs of the same type, the program inserts space both after the first paragraph and before the second paragraph.

► **To change the paragraph properties of a tag**

1. On the Editing toolbar, click the Tag button 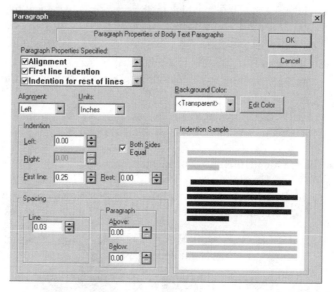 or, from the **Tag** menu, choose **Appearance** and then select the tag whose paragraph properties you want to modify.

2. In the **Tag Properties** area, double-click **Paragraph**, or select **Paragraph** and then choose **Modify** to open the **Paragraph** dialog box.

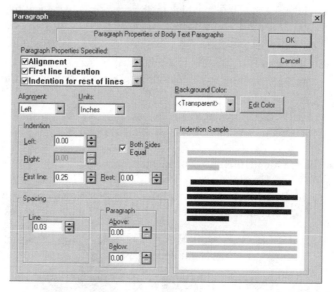

3. If you want to change a specification, check the corresponding property in the **Paragraph Properties Specified** list.

4. In the **Alignment** box, set the paragraph justification you want for the tag.

5. Use the **Left** and **Right** scroll boxes to set the amount that all lines are indented from the margins, changing the unit of measure if necessary. If you want equal indention on both sides, check **Both Sides Equal**.

6. Use the **First line** and **Rest** scroll boxes to set the amount of additional indention for the first line in a paragraph and for all other lines.

   The **Sample** area shows the effect of the alignment and indention changes you make. The example above shows that a paragraph created with the specified tag will be left-justified. All lines will be indented .25 inch from the left and right margins, with the first line indented an additional .25 inch on the left.

7. If you want to change the background color of the paragraph, click the arrow at the side of the **Background Color** list to open the list of available colors. If the color you want isn't listed, you can edit the list as described on page 205.

8. Change the line and paragraph spacing as necessary.

9. When your changes are complete, choose OK.

10. Save the changes to the style file and choose OK.

Modifying the Mathematics Properties of a Tag

When mathematics occur in tagged content, the tag properties determine these aspects of the appearance of mathematics:

- Color – The colors in which mathematics, mathematical functions, and unit symbols appear in the document window and, depending on your printer and the print options, on paper.

- Object size – The size in which scripts, scripts within scripts, operators, and big operators are presented, measured as a percent of the text font size specified for the tag.

- Font – The type font in which mathematics, mathematical functions, and unit symbols are presented.

▶ **To change the mathematics properties of a tag**

1. On the Editing toolbar, click the Tag button 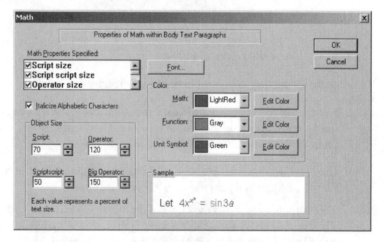 or, from the Tag menu, choose Appearance and then select the tag whose math properties you want to modify.

2. In the Tag Properties area, double-click Math, or select Math and then choose Modify to open the Math dialog box.

3. If you want to change a specification, check the corresponding property in the Math Properties Specified list.

4. If you want to italicize alphabetic characters that occur in mathematics (except those occurring in math names or unit names), check Italicize Alphabetic Characters.

5. Change the size of mathematical objects as necessary.

6. If you want change the font used for mathematics, choose Font and modify the font properties as described on page 205 and then choose OK.

7. If you want to change the color of mathematics, functions, or unit symbols, click the arrow at the side of each Color list to open the list of available colors. If the color you want isn't listed, you can edit the list.

8. When your changes are complete, choose OK.

9. Save the changes to the style file and choose OK.

Modifying the Properties of Special Objects

Most tags are associated with several special objects, each of which has a set of properties that determines its appearance inside the tagged environment:

- Lead-in objects.
- Graphics and plots.
- Tables, matrices, and mathematical displays.
- Other objects including citations, cross-references, formulas, input buttons, hypertext links, and hypertext targets.

Modifying the Lead-in Properties of a Tag

Lists and other item tags such as theorems have lead-in objects, as described on page 62. The program formats the lead-in objects separately from the items themselves. You can change these lead-in properties for the item tags in the style:

- Color – The colors in which the background and any mathematics or mathematical functions used in the lead-in object appear on the screen and, depending on your printer and print options, on paper.
- Font – The face, style, size, and color of the type used for text and mathematics in the lead-in object.
- Alignment – The horizontal alignment of the contents of the lead-in object.
- Minimum label width – The minimum width of the lead-in object.
- Label separation – The amount of space separating the lead-in object from the list item.

You can change the style of the numbers or bullets in the lead-in object by changing the global properties of the style, as described on page 216. You can change the properties for the list item itself by changing the font or paragraph properties of the item tag.

▶ **To modify the lead-in properties of a tag**

1. On the Editing toolbar, click the Tag button 🄰 or, from the Tag menu, choose Appearance and then select the tag whose lead-in properties you want to modify.

2. In the Tag Properties area, click Special Objects.

3. From the **Properties of Special Objects** list, select **Lead-in** and then choose **Modify** to open the **Lead-in Settings** dialog box shown on the next page.

4. If you want to change a specification, check the corresponding property in the **Lead-in Properties Specified** list.

5. If you want any mathematics properties for the lead-in object to be inherited from the current environment, check the property in the **Properties Specified** list and the corresponding property box in the **Inherit** area.

Checking a box for an inherited property disables the corresponding property list.

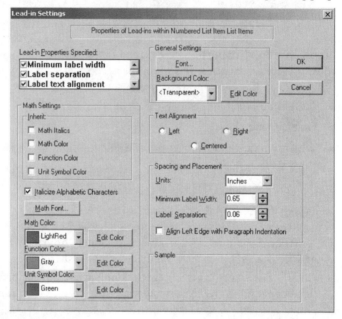

6. If you want to change the background color of the lead-in object or of mathematics within the lead-in, click the arrow at the side of the corresponding **Color** list or choose the corresponding **Edit Color** button and make the changes, as described on page 205.

7. If you want to set the font used for text or mathematics in the lead-in object, choose **Font** or **Math Font** and make changes, as described on page 205.

8. Set the horizontal alignment of text in the lead-in object, the minimum width of the lead-in object, and the amount of space separating the lead-in object from the text of the list item. Change the unit of measure as necessary.

9. If you want the left edge of the lead-in object to be indented exactly like the current paragraph, check **Align Left Edge with Paragraph Indention**.

10. When your selections are complete, choose **OK**.

11. Save the changes to the style file and choose **OK**.

Modifying the Tag Properties of Graphics and Plots

When plots and graphics occur in tagged text, the tag properties determine the space surrounding them and the background color used for their captions. The tag properties also determine the font used for plot labels. You can change these graphics and plot properties for many section, body, and item tags:

- Spacing – The space surrounding graphics or plots.

- Color – The color in which the background of any captions appears on the screen and, depending on your printer and print options, on paper.

- Font – The face, style, size, and color of the type used for text and mathematics in captions and plot components.

You can change the label for the graphic or plot or the plot components, axes, and view by selecting the graphic or plot and choosing Properties.

▶ **To modify the graphics and plot properties of a tag**

1. On the Editing toolbar, click the Tag button 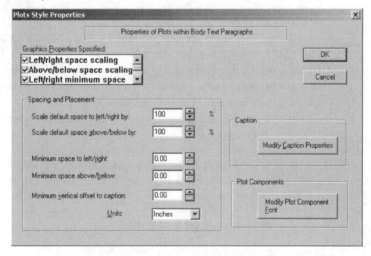 or, from the Tag menu, choose Appearance and then select the tag whose graphics or plot properties you want to modify.

2. In the Tag Properties area, click Special Objects.

3. From the Properties of Special Objects list, select Graphics or Plots and then choose Modify.

The Graphics Style Properties dialog box has no Plot Components area but is otherwise identical.

4. If you want to change a specification, check the corresponding property in the Properties Specified list.

5. If you want to change the spacing around graphics or plots, use the scroll boxes at the side of each property list to choose a scale factor or a minimum space, changing the unit in which to measure the space as necessary.

6. If you want to modify the appearance of graphics or plot captions, choose Modify Caption Properties to open the Captions Style Properties dialog box:

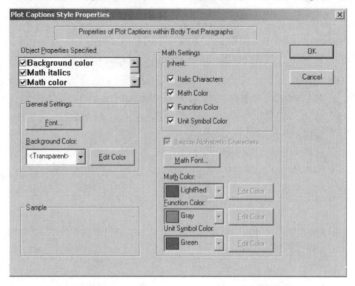

a. In the Properties list, check each property you want change.

b. If you want to change the background color of the graphics caption or of mathematics within the caption, click the arrow at the side of the corresponding Color list or choose the corresponding Edit Color button to select the color you want, as described on page 205.

c. If you want to change the caption font for text or mathematics, choose Font or Math Font to select the font you want, as described on page 205.

d. If you want the properties of any mathematics in the caption to be inherited from the current environment, check the property in the Properties list and the corresponding property box in the Inherit area.

   Checking a box for an inherited property disables the corresponding property list.

e. When your selections are complete, choose OK.

7. If you want to modify the font used for plot components, choose Modify Plot Component Font to open the Plots Font dialog box, change the settings as described on page 205, and then choose OK.

8. When your selections are complete, choose OK.

9. Save the changes to the style file and choose OK.

Modifying the Tag Properties of Tables, Matrices, and Displays

When tables, matrices, and mathematical displays occur in tagged text, the tag properties determine the space surrounding them, the space between rows, and, for tables and matrices, the space between columns. Text tags don't have table, matrix, or display properties, but many section, body, and item tags do.

► **To modify the table, matrix, or display properties of a tag**

1. On the Editing toolbar, click the Tag button 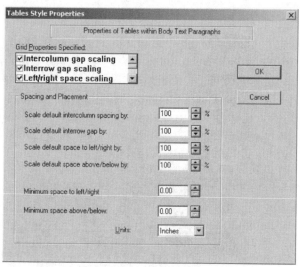 or, from the Tag menu, choose Appearance and then select the tag whose table, matrix, or display properties you want to modify.

2. In the Tag Properties area, click Special Objects.

3. From the Properties of Special Objects list, select Table, Matrix, or Displays and then choose Modify.

   The Matrix dialog box is identical. The Display dialog box doesn't contain a control for intercolumn spacing.

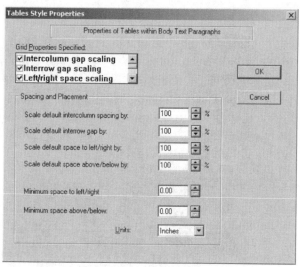

4. If you want to change a specification, check the corresponding property in the Grid Properties Specified list.

   The scaling percent is based on default values determined by the current font size.

5. When your selections are complete, choose OK.

6. Save the changes to the style file and choose OK.

Modifying the Tag Properties of Other Text Objects

You can modify the appearance of mathematics, the font, and the background color used for citations, cross-references, hypertext links and targets, input buttons, and formulas when they occur in tagged text.

► **To modify the tag properties of other text objects**

1. On the Editing toolbar, click the Tag button 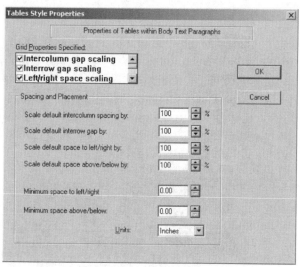 or, from the Tag menu, choose Appearance and then select the tag whose properties you want to modify.

2. In the Tag Properties area, click Special Objects.

3. From the **Properties of Special Objects** list, select the object whose properties you want to change and then choose **Modify** to display the **Style Properties** dialog box shown on the next page.

   The dialog boxes for cross-references, hypertext links, hypertext markers, input buttons, and formulas are identical.

4. If you want to change a specification, check the corresponding property in the **Object Properties Specified** list.

5. If you want any mathematics properties for the object to be inherited from the current environment, check the property in the **Properties Specified** list and the corresponding property box in the **Inherit** area.

   Checking a box for an inherited property disables the corresponding property list.

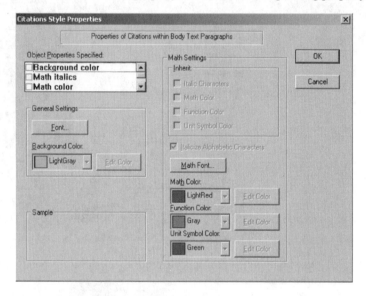

6. If you want to modify the font used for text or mathematics, choose **Font** or **Math Font** and make changes as described on page 205.

7. If you want to change the background color of the object or the color of mathematics within the object, click the arrow at the side of the corresponding **Color** list or choose **Edit Color** to select the color you want, as described on page 205.

8. When your selections are complete, choose **OK**.

9. Save the changes to the style file and choose **OK**.

Modifying the Behavior Property of a Tag

For each section and body tag, the behavior property determines the tag to be applied automatically to the subsequent paragraph. For example, you might set the behavior of the Chapter tag to specify that the paragraph that follows a chapter heading be tagged automatically as Body Text. Similarly, you might set the behavior of the Body Quote tag so that the paragraph that follows each Body Quote paragraph is also tagged as Body Quote. The behavior property also determines whether the tag name appears in the Tag toolbar popup list.

If the selected tag is a section, the behavior property determines its level in the hierarchy of section tags. The level determines how tagged text appears in the Section Heading list on the Navigate toolbar; see page 15.

If the selected tag is a numbered or bulleted list, the dialog box differs: the Tag for Following Paragraph setting is disabled and the behavior properties include the designation of the style of the numbers or bullets in the lead-in object.

▶ To modify the tag behavior property set in the style

1. On the Editing toolbar, click the Tag button 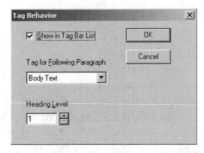 or, from the Tag menu, choose Appearance and then select the tag whose behavior properties you want to modify.

2. In the Tag Properties area, double-click Behavior, or select Behavior and then choose Modify.

3. If you want the tag name to appear in the popup lists on the Tag toolbar, check the box labeled Show in Tag Bar List.

4. Use the scroll box at the side of the Tag for Following Paragraph area to select the tag to be automatically applied to the next paragraph.

5. If the tag is a section tag, set the heading level you want.

6. When your changes are complete, choose OK.

7. Save the changes to the style file and choose OK.

▶ To change the style of list numbering or bulleting

1. On the Editing toolbar, click the Tag button 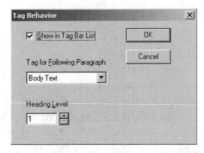 or, from the Tag menu, choose Appearance.

2. In the Tags list, select the Numbered List Item or Bullet List Item.

3. In the Tag Properties area, double-click Behavior, or select Behavior and then choose Modify to open the Tag Behavior dialog box.

The dialog box for numbered items lists numbering styles.

4. Check Specify bulleting or Specify numbering.

5. Use the scroll boxes at the side of each property list to select the nesting level and then the bullet or number style you want.

   You can choose a different bullet or number style for each nesting level in the list.

6. Choose OK.

7. Save the changes to the style file and choose OK.

Modifying the Style Defaults

The *style default* settings aren't assigned to a particular tag. Instead, they apply to every tag in the style *if no other property setting is in effect.* That is, if a given tag property and the corresponding properties of any surrounding tags have neither specific nor inherited values, the style uses the default settings for the property.

For example, suppose you set the style default so that tables have at least $\frac{1}{4}$ in. of space on all sides. If you also specify that tables contained in a Body Quote paragraph have $\frac{1}{3}$ in. of space on all sides, the program will ignore the default and place $\frac{1}{3}$ in. of space around any tables that occur in Body Quote paragraphs. However, suppose neither you nor the style file specifies the spacing around tables in Body Quote paragraphs. Then, the program uses the default and separates the table from the text by $\frac{1}{4}$ in. on all sides.

You can set style defaults for the nontypeset appearance of these tag properties: fonts; paragraphs; input buttons; hyperlinks and hypertext targets; references and citations; mathematics; tables, matrices, and displays; graphics and plots; and lead-in objects.

▶ To modify a property setting

1. On the Editing toolbar, click the Tag button [icon] or, from the Tag menu, choose Appearance and then select Modify Style Defaults.

2. In the Tag Properties area, select the property whose default values you want to set.

3. Follow the instructions in the preceding sections to set the defaults.

4. When your changes are complete, save the changes to the style file and choose OK.

Modifying the Global Properties

Several additional properties, called *global properties,* affect the style at large rather than specific tags and deserve special mention. You can set these global properties:

- The default tag for the starting paragraph of any new documents created with shells that use the style file. (Most shells already have a tag applied to the starting paragraph.)

- The number of heading levels displayed in the Navigate toolbar.

- The margins used when you display the document on the screen. These settings don't affect the printed appearance of your document in any way.

- The lead-in style for numbered and bulleted lists.

▶ **To modify the global properties for the style**

1. On the Editing toolbar, click the Tag button 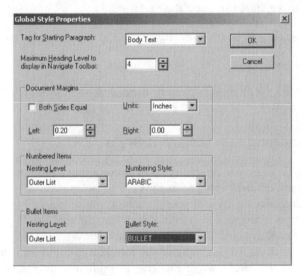 or, from the Tag menu, choose Appearance and then select Modify Style Defaults.

2. In the Tag Properties area, select Global Properties and choose Modify.

3. Modify the settings as necessary.

4. When your changes are complete, choose OK.

Adding Body and Text Tags

Occasionally you may find you need more body and text tags than are available with the style. In that case, you can create a new tag by *cloning,* or copying, an existing tag and then modifying the new tag as necessary.

▶ **To clone a body or text tag**

1. On the Editing toolbar, click the Tag button 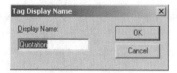 or, from the Tag menu, choose Appearance.

2. In the Tags list, select the body or text tag you want to clone.

3. Choose Clone Tag.

4. Enter a name for the new tag and choose OK.

    The program displays the name in the Tags list and in the corresponding tag popup list in the program window.

5. In the Tags list, select the new tag.

6. Select and modify the tag properties as necessary.

7. Choose OK.

8. Save the changes to the style file and choose OK.

Changing to a Different Style

In most cases you can change your document to a different style (.cst file). However, because dramatic changes in style can cause unpredictable results, we urge that if you must change the style of your document, you change to a style with a similar structure.

If your document was created with a special shell or a Style Editor shell, changing the style can have unpredictable results. In other words, if the .cst file for your document resides in the [Special] or the sebase directory of your program installation, be particularly careful about changing to a different style. Changing the style may cause the document to load incorrectly or not at all. Changing the style of a document that wasn't created with the program isn't recommended.

▶ **To change a document to a different style**

1. From the File menu, choose Style.

2. Select the style you want from the list.

3. If you want to choose a style in the current document directory, choose Advanced and select the style you want from the list.

4. Choose OK.

Modifying the Page Setup

When you produce your document without typesetting it, the page setup specifications determine these aspects of the document appearance:

- Page margins.
- Headers.
- Footers.
- Page numbers.

The shell you use to create your document may contain default specifications for the page setup, but you can change them according to your needs. If you're using *SWP* or *SW,* remember that the specifications for margins, headers, footers, and page numbers may differ noticeably for typeset and nontypeset document production. Refer to Understanding the Appearance of Documents on page 183 for more information.

Important   The page setup specifications have no effect on the typeset appearance of your document.

▶ **To modify the page setup specifications**

1. From the File menu, choose Page Setup.

2. Choose the tab you need:
   - Choose the Margins tab to specify left, right, top, and bottom margins.
   - Choose the Headers/Footers tab to specify headers, footers, and page numbers.
   - Choose the Counters tab to specify the starting page number and the page numbering style.

3. Change the specifications as necessary and choose OK.

Modifying the Page Margins

The page margins used when you preview or print without typesetting are set initially by the shell you use to create your document, but you can modify them. Remember that the program ignores page margins when it displays your document in the document window, where the text is broken to fit the size of the document window. (However, if you have specified on-screen margins in the global defaults for the style, as described on page 217, the program applies them when you display the document.)

▶ **To modify the page margins set in Page Setup**

1. From the File menu, choose Page Setup and then choose the Margins tab, shown on the next page.

2. Specify the unit of measure for the margins and the left, right, top, and bottom margins for your document.

3. If you want to mirror the margins on even- and odd-numbered pages, check Mirror Margins.

4. Choose OK.

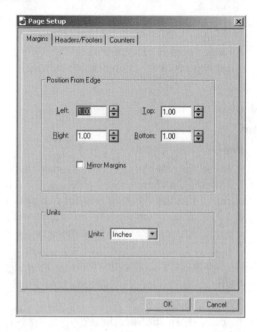

Modifying the Headers and Footers

The shell for your document may specify headers and footers, which can contain both text and mathematics. If the shell doesn't specify headers and footers, you can add them from the Page Setup dialog box. The headers and footers specified in the Page Setup dialog box don't appear when you typeset your document or when you display it in the document window.

▶ **To modify the headers and footers set in Page Setup**

1. From the File menu, choose Page Setup and choose the Headers/Footers tab shown on the next page.

2. In the Page Options section, specify whether the headers and footers should appear the same or differently on the even- and odd-numbered pages and on the first page of your document.

3. In the list box labeled Apply To, select the pages on which the header or footer you specify should appear: even, odd, all, or first.

4. Place the insertion point in the Header or Footer input box and type the information.

   You can enter both text and mathematics, and you can use the toolbar buttons, tags, and menu commands to format the content you enter.

5. If you want to insert an automatic page number, filename, time, or date in the header or footer, place the insertion point where you want the item to appear and click the corresponding button.

   Use stretchy space, as described on page 194, to right-justify, left-justify, or center these elements.

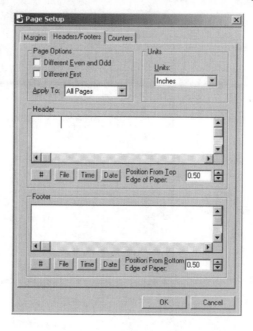

6. Specify the distance from the item to the top or bottom edge of the paper and the unit in which the distance is measured.

7. Repeat steps 3-6 until you've specified all headers and footers for all types of pages.

8. Choose OK.

Modifying the Page Numbering

Page numbers appear in headers or footers. If page numbering is specified for your document, the numbering occurs automatically when you preview or print. The program ignores page numbering when it displays your document in the document window. You can change the page numbering from the Page Setup dialog box.

► **To modify the page numbering set in Page Setup**

1. From the File menu, choose Page Setup and choose the Headers/Footers tab.

2. In the Page Options area, specify whether the headers and footers should appear the same or differently on the even- and odd-numbered pages and on the first page of your document.

3. Place the insertion point in the Header or Footer area where you want the page number to appear and click the page number button [#].

4. Format the page number:

   a. Choose the Counters tab shown on the next page.
   b. Select the page number format you want.
   c. Set the counter to the starting page number.

5. Choose OK.

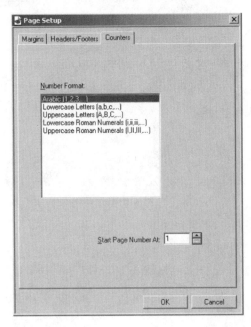

Modifying the Print Options

When you preview or print your document in *SNB* or without typesetting it in *SWP* or *SW,* you can use the Print Options tab sheet in the Document Info dialog box to turn printing on or off for certain document elements, such as helper lines and invisibles, and to set the zoom factor to be used when you print. If you have a color printer, you can use the print options to enable color printing of lines, text, and backgrounds. Remember that these options have no effect when you typeset your document. See Setting Print Options on page 163 for detailed information.

▶ **To set print options**

1. From the File menu, choose Document Info and choose the Print Options tab sheet.

2. Choose the options you want.

3. If you want the current settings to be the default for all your documents, choose Make Default.

4. Choose OK.

Formatting Documents for Production with Typesetting

As noted in Chapter 7 "Previewing and Printing," when you compile, preview, or print your document from the Typeset menu in *SWP* or *SW,* the program processes your document through LaTeX or PDFLaTeX to generate a DVI or PDF file. The DVI and PDF files are finely typeset versions of your document that may contain automatically generated document elements such as cross-references, tables of contents, and numbers for equations. When you typeset, the program ignores the style file, the page setup specifications, and the print options. Consequently, the typeset document usually has a different appearance from what you see in the document window. Typesetting isn't available in *SNB*.

The typeset appearance of the document depends on the typesetting specifications for the shell you used to create the document. Additionally, each shell has a *document class* that defines the fundamental structure of the shell as a book, article, or other document type, and defines the constructs and elements that the shell may contain. In some cases, you can modify the typeset appearance of a document from within the program by changing the class options, adding and modifying LaTeX packages, and adding LaTeX commands in the preamble or the body of the document.

Some typesetting considerations can affect more than document appearance. Remember that when you produce a typeset PDF file, you can set the output options as described on page 165. Also note that you can use LaTeX font packages to improve the portability of your document when you send it to a different platform or LaTeX installation. If you want to typeset a document designed for online use, some modifications may be necessary. See Chapter 10 "Creating Documents for Online Use."

If the typesetting specifications for a document were developed with the Style Editor, you can modify them with the Style Editor. Otherwise, attempting to change the typesetting specifications to modify the typeset appearance of tagged information isn't advisable, unless you are extremely familiar with TeX and LaTeX.

See the companion manual *Typesetting Documents in Scientific WorkPlace and Scientific Word,* which contains detailed information about formatting documents and tailoring their typeset appearance to your needs. For additional information on TeX and LaTeX, you may want to refer to *The TeXbook* by Donald E. Knuth; *LaTeX, A Document Preparation System* by Leslie Lamport; *The LaTeX Companion* by Michel Goossens, Frank Mittelbach, and Alexander Samarin; and *A Guide to LaTeX: Document Preparation for Beginners and Advanced Users* by Helmut Kopka and Patrick W. Daly.

Understanding the Typesetting Specifications

The typesetting specifications govern all aspects of the typeset appearance of your document: type face, type size, margins, page size, line spacing, location and appearance of headers and footers, paragraph layout and indention, section headings, page breaks, and countless other typographic details. The specifications are contained in files with extensions of `.sty`, `.clo`, and `.cls`.

The typesetting specifications are set initially by the shell used to create your document. You can modify the shell somewhat by adding options to the document class and by adding packages to the shell, but we strongly advise against attempts at extensive modification of the typesetting specifications, especially if you aren't extremely familiar with TeX and LaTeX. If the shell doesn't produce the typeset results you want, you may be able to modify it from within the program. Otherwise, start a new document with a shell that better meets your requirements. Chapter 2 "Creating Documents" has more information about shells. Chapter 7 "Previewing and Printing" discusses the details of typesetting a document.

Important   The changes made in the Tag Appearance dialog box have no effect on the typesetting specifications or the typeset appearance of your document.

Modifying the Class Options

The document class for the shell defines the LaTeX constructs and elements available for the shell and for all documents associated with it. Most document classes have *class options* that define typesetting specifications in some detail. Each option has a default setting; these defaults differ from shell to shell. For documents created with most shells, you can modify the typesetting specifications somewhat by changing the document class options. Document class options control these and other typesetting details:

- Body text font size.
- Paper size.
- Page orientation.
- Print side.
- Quality of printed output.
- Presence of a title page.
- Column use.
- Equation numbering.
- Typesetting language.

The options available for your document are listed on the Class Options tab sheet of the Options and Packages dialog box, available from the Typeset menu.

Important   The document class options don't affect the appearance of your document when you display it in the document window or preview or print it without typesetting.

If you're extremely familiar with LaTeX, you can *go native;* that is, you can force the program to use class options that aren't available with your program installation. When you select from the list of available options, the program creates the correct command syntax for your selection. However, when you go native, the program passes the typesetting options directly to LaTeX or PDFLaTeX without checking for correct syntax.

▶ **To determine the document class of a document**

1. On the Typeset toolbar, click the Options and Packages button [image] or, from the Typeset menu, choose Options and Packages.

2. Choose the Class Options tab.

3. Note the class name in the first line of information and choose OK.

▶ **To modify a document class option**

1. On the Typeset toolbar, click the Options and Packages button [image] or, from the Typeset menu, choose Options and Packages.

2. Choose the Class Options tab.

3. Choose **Modify** to open the **Options for documentclass** dialog box shown on the next page.

4. Scroll the **Category** list to select the option you want to modify.

   The available categories change for each shell, and the options change depending on the category selected.

5. In the **Options** column, select the setting you want.

   The settings you select appear in the box labeled **Currently Selected Options**.

6. Choose **OK** to close the dialog boxes and return to your document.

7. Remember that in a tabbed dialog box, choosing **OK** accepts the changes made on all tab sheets in the dialog box and choosing **Cancel** discards the changes made on all tab sheets in the dialog box.

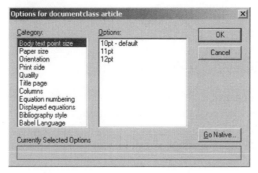

▶ **To use a class option not included with your program installation**

Caution   The program passes the typesetting options directly to LATEX or PDFLATEX for processing when you typeset your document. We strongly advise against attempts at extensive modification of the specifications unless you are extremely familiar with TEX and LATEX.

---

1. Place the option (`.clo`) file in the same directory as the document class (`.cls`) file.

   If you are unable to locate the document class, then copy the option file to the `TCITeX\TeX\LaTeX` subdirectory in the program directory.

2. Open the document.

3. On the Typeset toolbar, click the Options and Packages button 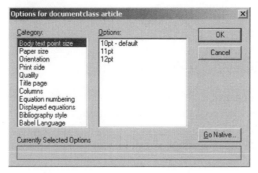 or, from the **Typeset** menu, choose **Options and Packages**.

4. Choose the **Class Options** tab.

5. Choose **Modify**.

6. If a dialog box appears stating the no options are listed for the style, choose **OK**.

7. Choose **Go Native** to open the **Native LaTeX Options** dialog box:

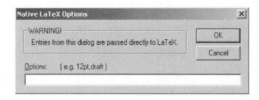

8. Enter the option you want to apply to your document and then choose **OK**.

   The program passes your entries directly to LaTeX or PDFLaTeX. Make sure you use correct syntax.

9. Choose **OK** to close the dialog boxes and return to your document.

Using LaTeX Packages

LaTeX packages enable the program to customize typesetting in some way, such as by modifying headers and footers, specifying a new page layout, using a different language for section heading names, or creating a bibliography or an index. Some packages have their own options, which you can modify. The packages are set initially by the shell you use to create your document, but you can modify, add, or remove them as needed. Many LaTeX packages available with the program installation are described and documented in the file `OptionsPackagesLatex.tex` in the `SWSamples` directory. The order in which you specify packages can affect typesetting behavior.

If you're extremely familiar with LaTeX, you can go native to force the program to use LaTeX packages that aren't available with your program installation. Note that when you select from the list of available packages, the program creates the correct command syntax for your selection. However, when you go native, the program passes the package information directly to LaTeX or PDFLaTeX without checking for correct syntax.

By default, the program automatically manages LaTeX packages, adding certain packages such as *amsmath* to most *SWP* and *SW* documents. In Version 5, you can manage packages yourself and prevent the program from adding packages automatically.

Adding and Removing LaTeX Packages

▶ **To add a package to the document**

1. On the Typeset toolbar, click the Options and Packages button ▦ or, from the Typeset menu, choose **Options and Packages**.

2. Choose the **Package Options** tab:

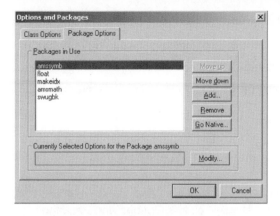

3. If the package you want isn't listed, choose **Add**.

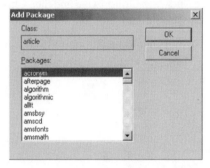

4. Scroll the **Packages** list to select the package you want and then choose **OK**.

5. Select the package options:

    a. Choose **Modify** to open the **Options for Package** dialog box.

    b. Select the option settings you want and then choose **OK**.
       Note that the selected options are listed on the **Package Options** tab sheet.

6. Use the **Move up** and **Move down** controls to order the package correctly in the list.

7. Choose **OK** to return to your document.

Remember that in a tabbed dialog box, choosing **OK** accepts the changes made on all tab sheets in the dialog box and choosing **Cancel** discards the changes made on all tab sheets in the dialog box.

▶ **To remove a package from the document**

1. On the Typeset toolbar, click the Options and Packages button ⊞ or, from the **Typeset** menu, choose **Options and Packages**.

2. Choose the **Package Options** tab.

3. Select the package you want to remove.

4. Choose **Remove** and then choose **OK**.

▶ **To add a package not included with your program installation**

1. Create a new subdirectory in the `TCITeX\TeX\LaTeX` subdirectory of your program installation.

2. Copy the package to the new subdirectory and perform any other steps required to install the package.

   For example, if you have `.dtx` and `.ins` files, you must run LaTeX on the `.ins` file.

3. Open the document to which you want to add a package.

4. On the Typeset toolbar, click the Options and Packages button 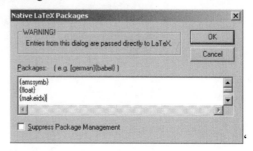 or, from the Typeset menu, choose Options and Packages.

5. Choose the Package Options tab and then Choose Go Native to display the Native LaTeX Packages dialog box.

6. Enter the name of the package you want enclosed in curly braces and include any package options you want to apply, using correct syntax according to the package documentation.

7. Choose OK to close the dialog boxes and return to your document.

▶ **To suppress program management of LaTeX packages**

1. On the Typeset toolbar, click the Options and Packages button or, from the Typeset menu, choose Options and Packages.

2. Choose the Package Options tab and choose Go Native.

3. Check Suppress Package Management and choose OK.

Modifying LaTeX Package Options

You can specify settings for package options. Generally, if a package has options available, the program lists them on the Package Options tab. If an option is marked as *default,* it is already in effect if no other option is selected in the current group. Defaults usually don't appear in the Currently Selected Options box. Selecting a default option has no effect other than to display its name in the box.

When you select a listed option setting, the program creates the correct command syntax for the selection. You can also go native to specify package option settings. However, if you go native, the program passes your commands directly to LATEX or PDFLATEX without checking for correct syntax. Be sure to enter the commands correctly.

▶ **To modify package options**

1. On the Typeset toolbar, click the Options and Packages button 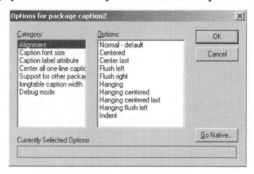 or, from the Typeset menu, choose **Options and Packages** and then choose the **Package Options** tab.

2. Select the package you want to modify and choose **Modify**.

3. If the **Options** dialog box lists options for the package,

   a. In the **Category** box, select the option you want.
   b. In the **Options** box, select the setting you want.
   The selected options appear in the **Currently Selected Options** area.
   c. Repeat steps a and b for each option you want to modify.
   d. Choose **OK** to return to the **Package Options** tab sheet.
   Note that the tab sheet reflects the options you have selected.

   or

   If the **Options** dialog box lists no options for the package,

   a. Choose **Go Native**.

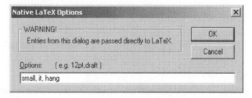

   b. In the **Native LaTeX Options** dialog box, enter the commands for any package options you want to apply.
   The documentation for each package outlines the syntax and arguments of the commands for the available options. Additional information is available in the online Help and in *Typesetting Documents in Scientific WorkPlace and Scientific*

Word. Remember that incorrect syntax can prevent typesetting and can damage your document.

c. Choose OK to return to the Package Options tab sheet.

Note that it reflects the options you have selected.

4. Choose OK to return to your document.

Using Special LaTeX Packages

Several LaTeX packages deserve special mention. The *babel* package helps TeX work more reliably for non-English languages. The *times* and *mathtime* packages provide greater portability if you expect to open your document on another installation.

Using the Babel Package

The *babel* package addresses hyphenation, punctuation, and other language-specific issues so that TeX, which was intended to be used with English, works more reliably for languages other than English. The *babel* package also corrects problems that occur with embedded English strings. TeX uses embedded strings to place certain words, such as *Chapter* or *Section,* into your documents. If you're working in a language other than English, the process needs correction. When *babel* is running with a specific language, it uses strings appropriate for that language in place of the embedded English strings.

If you're working with a non-English document created with a Style Editor style, you may need to modify the style so that *babel* substitutes the correct strings for automatic division headings. The online Help contains instructions.

Theorem objects must be treated separately. Typically, the words that are typeset in the lead-in objects of theorem statements are set in the \newtheorem statements in the document preamble. To use different words, modify the statements in the preamble. See Modifying the Preamble, page 232.

If you've changed the default LaTeX formatter, you must ensure that the Multilingual LaTeX formatter is selected.

Caution   Don't attempt to modify the TeX formatter settings unless you know TeX and LaTeX very well.

▶ **To check the format selection**

1. From the Typeset menu, choose Expert Settings and then choose the DVI Format Settings tab.

2. From the Select a formatter list, choose TrueTeX MultiLingual.

3. Choose Add/Modify.

4. In the Choose TeX format file box, check the name of the format file.

To use the package, you must add it to your system, possibly with a language option. The availability of certain languages depends on the languages you build into your LaTeX format. The *babel* package is not compatible with the Lambda system. More information about format files and *babel* appears in the online Help and in *Typesetting Documents in Scientific WorkPlace and Scientific Word.*

Choosing Font Packages for Greater Portability

If you expect to open the DVI file for your document on another platform or another LaTeX installation, you can improve the portability of your typeset document by choosing font packages carefully. First, use Computer Modern fonts. The most portable files are those you create with Computer Modern (cm) fonts, without adding the multilingual extensions (DC fonts). In other words, using a Standard LaTeX Article shell with no modifications to the font packages produces the most portable files. Generally, PostScript and LaTeX symbol fonts are also portable.

Second, if Times fonts are required for your document, you can increase the portability of the document by using either the *times* or *mathtime* package. Both packages use the widely accepted PostScript New Font Selection Scheme (PSNFSS) for LaTeX and can be used on different platforms.

In addition to yielding greater portability, the packages yield ligatures and improved kerning in Times text when you typeset your document. If you use the *times* package, the text in your document is set in Times and the mathematics is set in a Computer Modern font, like this:

By the triangle inequality for integrals and the above inequalities, for $n \geq N$;

$$\left| \int_c \left[f(z) - \sum_{k=0}^{n} a_k z^k \right] dz \right| \leq \epsilon \cdot (\text{length of } C)$$

Since ϵ is arbitrary, the limit is zero.

If you use the *mathtime* font package, you can avoid combining font families because both text and mathematics are set in Times, like this:

By the triangle inequality for integrals and the above inequalities, for $n \geq N$,

$$\left| \int_c \left[f(z) - \sum_{k=0}^{n} a_k z^k \right] dz \right| \leq \epsilon \cdot (\text{length of } C)$$

Since ϵ is arbitrary, the limit is zero.

In the two examples above, notice the differences in the summation signs, Greek letters, and other mathematical symbols.

▶ **To check the types of fonts used in your typeset document**

1. On the Typeset toolbar, click the Typeset DVI Preview button or, from the Typeset menu, choose **Preview**.

2. From the **Text** menu in the TrueTeX Previewer, choose **Table of Fonts Used in Document**.

3. Scan the entries in the TeX Name column.

If DC fonts are listed, change the format settings for typesetting as described on page 175 to select a formatter that doesn't use multilingual extensions.

▶ **To choose a different font package**

1. On the Typeset toolbar, click the Options and Packages button ▦ or, from the Typeset menu, choose Options and Packages.

2. Choose the Package Options tab.

3. Select the font package currently in use and choose Remove.

4. Choose Add.

5. Scroll the list of available font packages and select the package you want.

6. Choose OK.

7. If you select the Mathtime package, select the No TS1 option:

    a. Choose Modify.
    b. In the Options list, select No TS1.
    c. Choose OK.

8. Choose OK.

Modifying the Preamble

The *preamble* of any .tex document is a collection of commands that specify processing instructions for the document. Automatically, the program enters any necessary commands in the preamble of your document.   If you're extremely familiar with TeX and LaTeX, you can modify your document by adding raw LaTeX code into the preamble. However, if you enter incorrect commands in the preamble, you may damage your document irreparably. The program places any preamble commands before the \begin{document} statement in the .tex file for your document. The preamble must not contain any commands that generate typeset output, but it can contain definitions such as \def, \newtheorem, \newcommand, \renewcommand, and \renewenvironment.

Caution   We strongly urge you to make a backup copy of your document before you make any modifications to the preamble. Don't attempt to modify the preamble of your document unless you know TeX and LaTeX very well.

▶ **To enter a command in the preamble**

1. From the Typeset menu, choose Preamble to open the LaTeX Preamble dialog box.

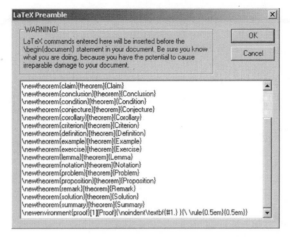

2. Place the insertion point where you want the command to appear.

3. Enter the TEX command you want and then choose OK.

Using the Style Editor

The Style Editor (a separate application program with its own icon in the program sub-menu) creates LATEX typesetting specifications. With the Style Editor, you can modify any existing set of Style Editor typesetting specifications or create new typesetting spec-ifications. The online Help contains instructions for using the Style Editor.

▶ **To open the Style Editor**

• From the Tools menu, choose Style Editor.
  or

• From the Windows Start menu, choose the Style Editor from the program submenu.

▶ **To determine whether a document has a Style Editor shell**

1. From the File menu, choose Document Info.

2. Choose the General tab sheet.

   The Document Shell section indicates where the shell is a Style Editor shell.

9 Structuring Documents for Typesetting

Note   The information in this chapter pertains only to *SWP* and *SW*. Typesetting isn't available with *SNB*.

At its highest level, the structure of a document consists of *front matter, body,* and *back matter.* The front matter is the information that appears at the beginning of your document. It often includes a title area, a table of contents, an abstract, a list of figures, and a list of tables. The body of the document often includes information structured into chapters, sections, subsections, and smaller divisions, as well as lists and theorems. The body can also include notes, cross-references to other parts of the document, and bibliography citations. The back matter, which follows the body, often includes a series of appendixes, a bibliography, and an index. Typesetting with LaTeX and PDFLaTeX simplifies the generation of the structural elements in the front matter, body, and back matter of your document.

In *SWP* and *SW,* many structural elements, such as lists, theorems, and headings, are created by applying item, section, and body tags to information in the document. Others are generated automatically when you typeset the document according to the typesetting specifications for the document shell. These elements are created from fields that are predefined for the shell or that you enter with tags or TeX fields. They include

- Title area or title page.
- Table of contents.
- List of figures.
- List of tables.
- Abstract.
- Cross-references to other parts of the document.
- Bibliography citations.
- Bibliography lists.
- Indexes.

The available elements depend on the typesetting specifications for the document shell.

When you typeset your document, the LaTeX or PDFLaTeX formatter generates the structural elements, building them from fields that contain TeX commands and, occasionally, predefined information. If you don't typeset your document, the fields are ignored; the elements aren't generated and don't appear. For example, if the typesetting specifications for the document shell provide for a table of contents, LaTeX or PDFLaTeX will generate it automatically when you typeset your document. If you don't typeset, the table of contents won't be generated. (If you don't want to typeset your document but you still want a table of contents, you can create it manually. Note, however, that if you subsequently typeset your document, you'll have two tables of contents, one that you've created manually and one that has been generated automatically.)

In *SWP* and *SW,* the way you produce your document governs the appearance of the structural elements it contains. See Chapter 8 "Formatting Documents" for more information.

- If you typeset your document, the program processes your document through the formatter to generate and format the document according to the typesetting specifications for the document shell. The results of LaTeX and PDFLaTeX typesetting don't appear in the document window, but you can examine the way your typeset document will look in print if you preview it from the TrueTeX Previewer or your PDF viewer.

- If you don't typeset your document, the program formats your document according to the style, page setup, and print options for the document shell. No structural elements are generated. The results are similar to what you see in the document window.

Different typesetting specifications create different document structures. The results you get when you create a document with a given shell may differ substantially from those you get when you use a different shell. For more information about shells, refer to *A Gallery of Document Shells for Scientific WorkPlace and Scientific Word* on your program CD in PDF form. For more information about typesetting, refer to *Typesetting Documents in Scientific WorkPlace and Scientific Word.*

This chapter explains how to create structural elements in the front matter, body, and back matter when you typeset your document in *SWP* or *SW.* It also explains how you can use LaTeX and PDFLaTeX typesetting features to structure and manage large documents.

Note   The generated elements described in this chapter aren't available if you don't typeset your document.

Understanding Predefined Fields

The typesetting specifications for most shells have some predefined fields in the front matter or the body of the document. The fields might specify the date of publication, the closing for a business letter, or the abstract for an article. To guide you as you create your document, the fields occasionally contain predefined information, which you replace with your own content. Most predefined fields are created with item tags.

Remember   If you don't typeset your document, it isn't processed through LaTeX and the information in predefined fields is ignored.

In the document window or in a dialog box, a predefined field appears as a small, often shaded box that contains the name of the field, followed by its contents. For example, depending on the shell, the **Front Matter** dialog box might contain fields and predetermined information for several items, like this:

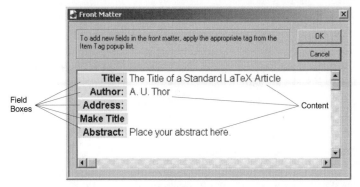

Similarly, the shell document for a letter or memo might display fields in the document window for the address, date, closing, and other elements:

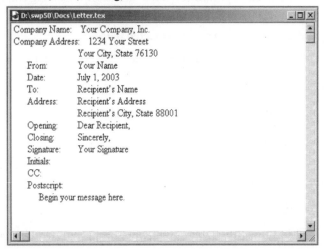

You can add structure to your document by creating, deleting, or editing fields and the predefined information they contain. When you typeset the document, the formatter generates and formats the predefined fields using the information you provide.

▶ To complete or edit a predefined field

- If the field contains predefined information, select the information and replace it with the information you want.

  or

- If the field is empty, enter the information you want.

When a field appears in a dialog box, you can use all the editing and entry features that are available in the program window. A field can contain both text and mathematics.

▶ To create a continuation paragraph in a predefined field

- Place the insertion point at the end of the field and press ENTER.

  The program automatically creates continuation paragraphs when you press ENTER at the end of a field paragraph.

▶ **To delete a field**

1. Select the entire field.

   Click at the right of the end of the preceding field or paragraph and drag down to the end of the last paragraph of the field you want to delete.

2. Press DELETE.

   or

1. Delete the contents of the field.

2. On the Tag toolbar, click the Remove Item tag button ⬒ to remove the field.

3. Press DELETE or BACKSPACE to delete the remaining empty paragraph.

▶ **To add a new field or restore a deleted field**

1. Place the insertion point at the end of the paragraph that is to precede the new field.

2. Press ENTER.

3. Apply the item tag for the field you want.

4. To the right of the field box, type the text of the field.

▶ **To create two consecutive fields of the same type**

1. Create the first field.

2. Place the insertion point at the end of the first field and press ENTER.

3. On the Tag toolbar, click the Remove Item tag button ⬒ to remove the item tag from the new paragraph and end the first field.

4. Apply the item tag for the field you want.

   You now have two consecutive field boxes with the same label.

5. Type the information for the second field.

▶ **To change a field to a different type**

1. Place the insertion point in the field you want to change.

2. Apply the item tag for the field you want.

   The program reflects the change in the label on the field box.

Creating and Editing the Front Matter

The front matter items generated when you typeset your document depend on the document type (such as book, article, or letter) and on the typesetting specifications for the document shell. The available items differ from shell to shell. Commonly available front matter items include a title area or title page, table of contents, list of figures, list of tables, and abstract. Some shells, particularly thesis shells, contain many other often unique front matter items.

For most shells, the defined front matter items are contained in fields in the Front Matter dialog box. Style Editor shells differ: the front matter fields are often in the body of the document. Usually, you create the front matter content by entering information into the fields. All text in the Front Matter dialog box must be entered in an appropriate field. The program discards any text not in a field when you save your document.

When you typeset, the formatter generates and formats the front matter information according to the typesetting specifications. Occasionally, the order in which the front matter items are printed depends on the order in which the corresponding fields appear in the Front Matter dialog box. In those cases, you can change the order in which front matter items appear in print by changing the order in which the corresponding fields appear in the Front Matter dialog box.

Important   You must typeset your document to generate the information in the front matter. If you produce your document without typesetting it, the program doesn't process the document with LaTeX or PDFLaTeX and the front matter isn't generated.

▶ **To create or edit the front matter in your document**

1. On the Typeset toolbar, click the Front Matter button ⊞ or, from the Typeset menu, choose Front Matter.

   The program opens the Front Matter dialog box, which usually contains predefined fields for common front matter items. The start of each field is indicated by a shaded box labeled with the name of the field.

2. Enter the front matter information into the various fields.

   You can use all the editing and entry features available in the program window.

3. Edit or delete existing fields or add new fields according to the instructions in Understanding Predefined Fields earlier in this chapter.

Creating a Title Area or Title Page

Depending on the typesetting specifications for the shell, the title area or title page usually contains fields for the document title, the author's name, and additional information such as the publication date. Your particular document shell may use items with different names. All available items are shown in the Apply Tag dialog box.

Small documents such as articles are usually typeset with the title information in a special title area. Larger documents such as books, theses, and some reports are printed with that information on a separate title page. The typesetting specifications determine whether the document has a title area or a title page and how the information in the front matter fields is formatted. For some shells, you can toggle between a title area and a title page by modifying the document class options. See Chapter 8 "Formatting Documents" for more information.

▶ **To create the title information**

1. On the Typeset toolbar, click the Front Matter button ⊞ or, from the **Typeset** menu, choose **Front Matter**.

2. If fields for the title, author, and date are already present, complete each one with the corresponding information.

   or

   If the fields you need aren't present, add them with the corresponding item tags and complete the corresponding information.

   Note If you remove the Date field from the front matter, the formatter prints the current date as part of the title information. If you leave the Date field blank, the program suppresses the printing of a publication date.

3. Place the insertion point at the end of the last field in the title information and press ENTER.

4. Apply the Make Title tag.

   The **Make Title** field must appear after all the items used to build the title information. The field triggers a command that tells the program to create the title area. If this field isn't present, no title area is created in the printed document. You can use this feature to turn off the title area or title page temporarily while retaining the information needed to generate it. The **Make Title** field should contain no text. The program ignores any text you type in this field.

   The order of the **Make Title** field relative to certain other front matter fields (such as the **abstract** or **Make TOC** fields) is also important. In some shells, you can change the order of front matter information by changing the order in which the corresponding fields appear in the **Front Matter** dialog box.

5. Choose **OK**.

Entering information for multiple authors requires a slightly different procedure.

▶ **To enter information for multiple authors**

1. In an author field, enter the name of the first author, press ENTER, and apply the Remove Item Tag.

2. If the shell requires author's address, apply an address tag and enter the address, pressing ENTER as often as necessary to enter all lines of the address.

3. Repeat steps 1 and 2 for each additional author.

Note Because the typeset appearance of the title information is dictated by the typesetting specifications, adding new fields to the front matter may not necessarily change the way the title information appears in print. If the shell doesn't yield title information formatted according to your requirements, choose a different shell.

Creating a Table of Contents

You can create an automatic table of contents based on the section tags in your document. The typesetting specifications for the document govern how many heading levels appear in the table of contents. When you typeset the document, the formatter automatically generates the table of contents and other front matter. The table of contents appears when you typeset preview but not in the document window.

The process of creating an automatic table of contents differs if the document was created with a Style Editor shell. The General tab sheet in the Document Info dialog box indicates whether the shell is a Style Editor shell. See Chapter 11 "Managing Documents" for more information about the Document Info.

If you add the *hyperref* package to your document and then typeset with PDFLATEX, the formatter links the table of contents entries to the document with hypertext links. (This technique doesn't work for documents created with Style Editor shells.) See page 288 for more information about the *hyperref* package.

▶ **To create a table of contents**

1. On the Typeset toolbar, click the Front Matter button ▦ or, from the Typeset menu, choose Front Matter.

2. Place the insertion point at the end of the field that immediately precedes the table of contents.

   The order in which the table of contents, list of figures, and list of tables appear in print depends on the order in which their corresponding fields appear in the Front Matter dialog box.

3. Press ENTER.

4. Apply the Make TOC tag.

   The Make TOC field, which should contain no text, triggers a command that tells the program to create the table of contents. The program ignores any text in the field.

5. Choose OK.

▶ **To create a table of contents for a Style Editor document**

1. At the beginning of the body of the document, apply the Contents tag.

2. Type the title you want for the table of contents.

3. Press ENTER.

4. On the Typeset Object toolbar, click the TEX button ▦ or, from the Insert menu, choose Typeset Object and then choose TeX Field.

5. In the entry area, type **TableOfContents** and then choose OK.

Remember   LATEX and PDFLATEX require at least three passes to generate a table of contents.

Creating a List of Figures

If the shell for your document contains a list of figures as part of the front matter, the formatter can create a list of figures based on the captions of the floating graphics frames in your document. See Chapter 5 "Using Graphics and Tables" for more information about creating captions for graphics in floating frames.

When you typeset the document, the formatter automatically generates the list of figures along with any other front matter. The list of figures doesn't appear in the document window, but you can see it when you typeset preview. The typesetting specifications determine the appearance of the list of figures. If the captions for your graphics are long, you can create shortened captions for use in the list of figures. See Chapter 5 "Using Graphics and Tables" for details.

The process of creating an automatic list of figures differs depending on whether the typesetting specifications for the shell were created with the Style Editor. The General tab sheet in the Document Info dialog box indicates whether the document was created with a Style Editor shell. See Chapter 11 "Managing Documents" for more information about the Document Info.

▶ **To create a list of figures**

1. On the Typeset toolbar, click the Front Matter button [image] or, from the Typeset menu, choose Front Matter.

2. Place the insertion point at the end of the field that should immediately precede the list of figures.

3. Press ENTER.

4. Apply the Make LOF tag and then choose OK.

   The Make LOF field triggers a command that tells the formatter to create the list of figures. The field should contain no text. The program ignores any text you type in this field.

▶ **To create a list of figures for a Style Editor document**

1. In the body of the document, place the insertion point at the end of the Contents section and then press ENTER.

2. From the Section/Body Tag list, apply the ListOfFiguresSection tag if it is available for the document shell.

3. Type the title for the list of figures and then press ENTER.

4. On the Typeset Object toolbar, click the TEX button [image] or, from the Insert menu, choose Typeset Object and then choose TeX Field.

5. In the edit field of the TeX dialog box, type **ListOfFigures** and then choose OK.

Remember   LATEX and PDFLATEX require at least three passes to generate a list of figures.

Creating a List of Tables

If the front matter for the document shell contains a list of tables, the formatter can create a list of tables based on the captions of the floating tables in your document. See Chapter 5 "Using Graphics and Tables" for more information about creating captions for tables that can float.

When you typeset the document, the formatter automatically generates the list of tables along with any other front matter. The list of tables doesn't appear in the document window, but you can see it when you typeset preview. The typesetting specifications determine the appearance of the list of tables.

The process of creating an automatic list of tables differs if the typesetting specifications for the shell were created with the Style Editor. The General tab sheet in the Document Info dialog box indicates whether the document was created with a Style Editor shell. See Chapter 11 "Managing Documents" for more information about the Document Info.

▶ **To create a list of tables**

1. On the Typeset toolbar, click the Front Matter button 🗐 or, from the Typeset menu, choose Front Matter.

2. Place the insertion point at the end of the field that should immediately precede the list of tables.

3. Press ENTER.

4. Apply the Make LOT tag.

   The Make LOT field triggers a command that tells the formatter to create the list of tables. The field should contain no text. The program ignores any text you type in this field.

5. Choose OK.

▶ **To create a list of tables for a Style Editor document**

1. In the body of the document, place the insertion point at the end of the Contents section and then press ENTER.

2. From the Section/Body Tag list, apply the ListOfTablesSection tag if it is available for the document shell.

3. Type the title for the list of tables and then press ENTER.

4. On the Typeset Object toolbar, click the TₑX button 🗐 or, from the Insert menu, choose Typeset Object and then choose TeX Field.

5. In the edit field of the TeX dialog box, type **ListOfTables** and then choose OK.

Remember   LaTeX and PDFLaTeX require at least three passes to generate a list of tables.

Creating an Abstract

The shells for many articles include an abstract as part of the front matter. You enter the abstract, which can contain both text and mathematics, in a field in the Front Matter dialog box. When you typeset the article, the formatter automatically generates the abstract along with any other front matter. The abstract doesn't appear in the document window, but you can see it when you typeset preview. The typesetting specifications determine its appearance.

▶ **To create an abstract**

1. On the Typeset toolbar, click the Front Matter button or, from the Typeset menu, choose Front Matter.

2. If an abstract field is already present, place the insertion point immediately to its right.

   or

   If an abstract field isn't present, create one:

   a. Place the insertion point at the end of the field that should immediately precede the abstract and press ENTER.
   b. From the Item Tag list, apply the Abstract tag.
   c. Place the insertion point immediately to the right of the field.

3. Type the text of the abstract.

   If the Abstract field contains predefined information, select that information and re-place it with the text of your abstract. All buttons and commands are available for entering text and mathematics in the abstract.

Structuring the Body of the Document

The structure of the body of most documents is defined by section and body paragraph tags. Each paragraph automatically has an associated tag. For most shells, the default is the Body Text tag. You structure the body of your document by applying section tags that define chapter, section, and subsection headings, and body paragraph tags that center text elements or set off quotations from the main part of a paragraph. You can provide additional structure by applying item tags to body text paragraphs to create lists and to indicate statements of theorems, propositions, lemmas, and other theorem-like statements. See Chapter 3 "Creating Text" and Chapter 4 "Creating Mathematics" for more information about using tags.

The appearance of information tagged with section and body paragraph tags depends on the way you produce your document. If you typeset, the appearance is defined in the typesetting specifications. If you don't typeset, the appearance is defined in the style. If you typeset a document designed primarily for online use, modifications of any hypertext links may be required. See Chapter 10 "Creating Documents for Online Use."

The structure of the body of the document can also be defined by objects for creating references to other parts or pages in the document, for creating notes such as margin notes and footnotes, and for inserting TeX commands. Certain shells base their structure on predefined fields in the body of the document.

Important   Remember that you must process your document with LaTeX or PDFLaTeX to generate typeset objects. If you produce your document without typesetting it, the objects aren't generated.

Creating Section Headings

Depending on the shell, your documents can contain tags for chapter, part, and section headings and for four levels of subheadings. The tags are listed in the Section/Body Tag popup list in the Tag toolbar. When you typeset your document, the program creates the section headings, numbering them automatically, if called for in the typesetting specifications. The typesetting specifications determine how the section headings appear in print, which heading levels are numbered, which numbering scheme is used, and which headings appear in the table of contents. You can remove the section numbers easily if you don't want them. Section headings can contain mathematics and graphics.

In the document window, the program displays section headings according to the style. They often appear larger than body text and in a different color, and they may be indented or centered to help you see the structure of your document clearly.

▶ **To apply a section tag**

1. Place the insertion point within the paragraph to be tagged. If you haven't yet typed the paragraph, place the insertion point where you want the section heading paragraph to begin.

2. On the Tag toolbar, click the Section/Body Tag popup box or press ALT+2 and then click the tag you want to apply.

   or

   From the Tag menu, choose Apply, select the tag you want, and then choose OK.

   or

   Press the function key assigned to the tag you want. See page 58 for the default function key assignments.

3. Type the paragraph if it doesn't yet exist.

▶ **To remove a section tag from a paragraph**

- Apply the Body Text tag to the paragraph.

▶ **To remove the number from a section heading**

1. Place the insertion point at the first of the heading.

2. Choose Properties.

3. In the Section Properties dialog box, check Unnumbered.

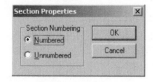

4. Choose OK.

The formatter ignores unnumbered sections when creating page headers. Thus, if you create an unnumbered appendix, the page headers on the appendix pages reflect the name of the previous section heading rather than the appendix.

If a section heading is so long that it breaks awkwardly on the page, you can force it to break at an appropriate place. When you typeset your document, the program uses the unbroken text to generate the table of contents and the headers, if they are specified by the typesetting specifications for your document. It uses the broken text to create the heading in the body of the document. Because forced line breaks in headings can cause typesetting difficulties, be sure to use the following special procedure to insert a break in a heading. You can also create a short form of a long heading for use in the headers and the table of contents; see the online Help or *Typesetting Documents in Scientific WorkPlace and Scientific Word for instructions*.

▶ **To force a line break in a heading**

1. Type the heading and apply the section tag you want.

2. Duplicate the heading at the start of the line.

3. Enclose the duplicate heading at the start of the line in square brackets.

4. Insert the line break in the unbracketed heading.

Creating Theorem and Theorem-Like Statements

In *SWP* and *SW,* you use item tags to identify theorem and theorem-like statements such as propositions, lemmas, and corollaries. Theorem tags are available only in certain shells. If you want to include theorems and theorem-like statements in your document, make sure the shell you choose includes the elements you need. For more information about specific shells, refer to *A Gallery of Document Shells for Scientific WorkPlace and Scientific Word* on the program CD. Chapter 4 "Creating Mathematics" contains additional information about entering theorem-like statements.

The typeset appearance of these statements depends on the typesetting specifications for the shell you choose. Many typesetting specifications use italics for the body of a theorem statement, like this:

Theorem 1   *Let S be a sheaf of germs of holomorphic functions....*

▶ **To enter the statement of a theorem**

1. Place the insertion point at the end of the paragraph that is to precede the theorem.

2. Press ENTER.

3. From the Item Tag list, apply the theorem tag you want.

4. Type the statement of the theorem.

5. Press ENTER.

6. For each additional paragraph within the theorem statement, press BACKSPACE, type the paragraph, and then press ENTER.

7. When all paragraphs have been entered, press ENTER, apply the Remove Item Tag to end the theorem statement.

▶ To remove a theorem tag from a paragraph

- Place the insertion point in the paragraph and apply the Remove Item Tag.

When you typeset your document, LATEX or PDFLATEX automatically formats and numbers any theorems and, if you've created markers for the theorems, creates any cross-references to them. The cross-references appear as the number of the theorem.

Note   To generate theorem numbers, you must typeset the document with LATEX. If you don't typeset, neither the theorem numbers nor the cross-references are generated.

Most typesetting specifications use a common numbering sequence throughout a document for theorems and theorem-like statements, resulting in numbers like these: Theorem 1, Corollary 2, Lemma 3, Theorem 4, and so on. Usually, the sequence is determined by the \newtheorem statements that appear in the document preamble. See Chapter 8 "Formatting Documents" for more information about the document preamble.

If you are familiar with TEX and LATEX, you can change the numbering sequence for your document by changing the \newtheorem statements in the preamble. The statements looks like this:

$$\newtheorem\{\textit{counter}\}\ [\textit{counter\_basis}]\ \{\textit{Counter\_title}\}$$

The *counter* names the environment to be counted; the *counter_basis* is the source of the count; and the *Counter_title* is the label for the environment. For example, the statement

```
\newtheorem{corollary}[theorem]{Corollary}
```

applies the label *Corollary* to statements tagged with the corollary tag and numbers the statements using the numbering sequence used for theorems.

If you want to provide independent instead of common numbering for a theorem-like environment, you must remove the counter_basis entry from the corresponding \newtheorem statement. In the example above, you can provide independent numbering for corollary statements by changing the \newtheorem statement so that it looks like this:

```
\newtheorem{corollary}{Corollary}
```

Typesetting Documents in Scientific WorkPlace and Scientific Word has more information about numbering theorems, including information about numbering theorems within chapters or sections.

Caution We strongly urge you to make a backup copy of your document before you make any modifications to the preamble. Don't attempt to modify the preamble of your document unless you know TEX and LATEX very well. If you enter incorrect commands in the preamble, you may damage your document irreparably.

▶ **To change the theorem numbering sequence**

1. From the Typeset menu, choose Preamble.

2. Modify the `\newtheorem` statements as necessary and then choose OK.

Creating Cross-References

Paragraphs can contain cross-references to other numbered parts of your document, such as equations, graphics, mathematical displays, theorems, tables, sections, and bibliography items, and to the pages on which those items appear. Cross-references have two parts: an item *marker,* which contains a unique key, and the *reference* to the item, which uses the key to create the cross-reference. The marker links the key to the automatically generated number of the marked item (such as the section number or table number). When you typeset your document, the program automatically replaces the key with the item number to which it refers.

For example, if you mark section 5.3.3 of your document with the key *main idea,* you can create an automatic cross-reference to that section of the document. In the document window, the reference appears as a gray box containing the key, like this:

$$\ldots \text{refer to section } \boxed{\text{ref main idea}} \text{ for} \ldots$$

When you typeset your document, the program processes it through the formatter twice to resolve the cross-references and replaces the key with the number of the item. In print, the reference appears as

$$\ldots \text{refer to section 5.3.3 for} \ldots$$

Similarly, you can create an automatic cross-reference to the page on which section 5.3.3 appears. In the document window, the page reference appears like this:

$$\ldots \text{refer to page } \boxed{\text{pageref main idea}} \text{ for} \ldots$$

When you typeset your document, the program replaces the key with the page number on which the marked item appears. In print, you might see something like this:

$$\ldots \text{refer to page 157 for} \ldots$$

If you want to create a typeset PDF file, you can add the *hyperref* package to your document to extend the options for ordinary cross-references. With the package, you can place an automatic identifier, such as *section, page,* or *chapter,* before the cross-reference. When you create a PDF file from your document, PDFLATEX changes the cross-references to hypertext links. However, you can prevent the change. If your document includes the *hyperref* package, the process of creating cross-references varies slightly. The appearance of cross-references in the document window may vary as well, depending on the type of cross-reference you select. Chapter 10 "Creating Documents for Online Use" contains information about creating hypertext links with the *hyperref* package.

Note   You must typeset your document to create automatic cross-references. If you don't typeset the document, the cross-reference fields and markers appear in print according to the print options.

You can use the cross-references to numbered parts of your document to speed navigation. Once you've created the reference, you can use it to move quickly to the paragraph containing the referenced marker. Page references can't be used for navigation.

Creating Markers

To be able to create cross-references to a numbered item in your document, you must mark the item with a unique key. You can define the reference before you define the key. Each of these types of items has a special process for creating an associated marker:

- Graphics (see Chapter 5 "Using Graphics and Tables").

- Numbered equations (see Chapter 4 "Creating Mathematics").

- Items in a manually created bibliography (see Manual Bibliographies, page 258).

To create markers for all other numbered items, use the process described here.

▶ **To create a marker**

1. Place the insertion point in the item you want to mark.

2. On the Field toolbar, click the Marker button  or, from the Insert menu, choose Marker.

   The program opens the Marker dialog box.

3. Enter a unique key for the item.

   Use only letters, spaces, numbers, and the following characters in the keys:

$$? \ ! \ : \ ; \ [\ ] \ , \ . \ (\ ) \ " \ / \ *$$

4. If you want to see the keys already defined for the document, click the arrow next to the Key box.

5. Choose OK.

   If markers are turned on in the View menu, the program displays the marker in the document window in a small gray box containing the word *marker* and the key you entered, like this: marker: main idea . Markers don't appear when you typeset your document. When you print your document without typesetting it, however, the appearance of markers is governed by the print options and the settings in the View menu. If you copy a selection containing a marker, the program renames the marker to avoid creating two markers with the same name. The program indicates the new marker as a copy, like this: marker: main idea copy(1) . If you no longer need a marker, you can delete it just as you would delete anything else in your document.

▶ **To toggle the display of markers on and off**

- From the View menu, choose Markers.

Creating References

You can create a reference to any numbered item that has a marker or to the page on which the item appears. You can create the reference before you create the marker. References to bibliography items are called citations; see Bibliographies, later in this chapter, for information about creating citations.

▶ **To create a cross-reference**

1. Place the insertion point where you want the reference to appear.

   In your text, you may want to insert an appropriate identifier, such as "section," "page," or "chapter," before the reference.

2. On the Typeset Object toolbar, click the Cross Reference button 📄 or, from the Insert menu, choose Typeset Object, and then choose Cross Reference.

   The program opens the Cross Reference dialog box.

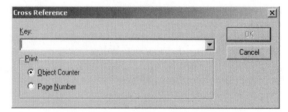

If you've added the *hyperref* package to your document, the box is expanded:

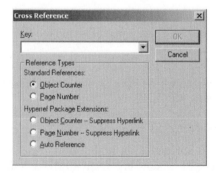

3. Enter the key of the marked item.

- If you want to create a reference to an item that already has a key, type the key in the Key box.

  or

  Click the arrow next to the Key box to display the list of keys defined for the document and scroll the list to select the key you want.

  If the key you want has been defined in a different document or subdocument, you must type the key.

- If you want to create a reference to an item that doesn't yet have a key, type the key in the Key box.

  Remember that you must define the key to complete the cross-reference.

4. Select the type of reference you want to create:

- If you want a reference to the numbered item in which the key occurs, check Object Counter.

- If you want a reference to the page on which the marked item appears, check Page Number.

- If you want to suppress hypertext links in PDF files, check Object Counter – Suppress Hyperlink or Page Number – Suppress Hyperlink.

- If you want to expand the link with an automatic identifier, such as *section, page,* or *chapter,* before the reference, check Auto Reference.

Refer to the *hyperref* package documentation for option information. If you choose the Auto Reference option, remember to check the document carefully to make sure the automatically generated information is appropriate.

5. Choose OK.

The program displays the reference on the screen in a gray box containing the word *ref* and the key you entered. If you entered a page reference, the box contains the word *pageref* and the key you entered. If you chose to suppress hypertext links in PDF files, the box contains the words *ref** or *pageref** and the key you entered. If you chose Auto Reference, the box contains the word *autoref* and the key.

When you typeset the document, the program creates the correct reference by substituting the number of the keyed item or the page on which the marker appears in place of the key.

Resolving Unmatched Cross-references

Unmatched cross-references result from missing or misreferenced markers. They appear in the typeset file as question marks, like this **??**. You can determine whether all cross-references in your document have been matched to a marker by looking at the .log file for the compiled document. If unresolved cross-references exist, a message like this appears near the end of the log file:

```
LaTeX Warning: There were undefined references.
```

Warnings elsewhere in the .log file indicate missing markers.

Navigating with Cross-References

Once you've created a cross-reference, you can use it to speed navigation through your document by *jumping,* or moving the insertion point, to the specified marker. Page references can't be used for navigation.

If you've added the *hyperref* package to your document and you haven't suppressed hypertext links for cross-references, the formatter changes cross-references to hypertext links when you create the typeset PDF file. If you create cross-references with the Auto Reference option, the identifier automatically inserted before the reference by the *hyperref* package becomes part of the link. See Jumping with Hypertext Links on page 281 for information about navigating with links.

▶ **To move to a marker specified in a cross-reference**

- Select the cross-reference and then, from the Tools or Context menu, choose Action.
  or

- If the document has been saved as read-only, click in the cross-reference.
  or

- If the document hasn't been saved as read-only, hold down the CTRL key and click in the cross-reference.
  The insertion point moves to the marker.

▶ **To return to the cross-reference**

- On the Navigate toolbar or the History toolbar, click the History Back button .
  or

- From the Go menu, choose History Back.
  The insertion point moves to the beginning of the paragraph containing the source of the most recent jump.

Creating Notes

Paragraphs can contain references to supplementary notes, such as footnotes and margin notes, that appear elsewhere in your document. Also, your documents can contain popup notes that contain supplementary information for use online. The notes aren't displayed on the screen until you activate them. See Chapter 10 "Creating Documents for Online Use" for details. Notes can contain text, graphics, and mathematics.

When you typeset your document, the program generates cross-references to each footnote. It places the number of the footnote in the text and the contents of the note at the bottom of the page. Margin notes appear in the margin of the page without a corresponding number in the text. Popup notes are typeset in the margin.

If you don't typeset your document, footnotes and margin notes appear in print according to the print options; see page 222. Popup notes appear in print as they do in the document window, according to your specifications.

Creating Footnotes

In *SWP* and *SW*, you can create sequentially numbered footnotes like this[1] if you typeset your document. You also have the option to create nonstandard footnotes, such as multiple references to the same footnote and unnumbered footnotes that have no corresponding numbers in the text. In the document window, footnotes appear as small gray boxes containing the word *footnote,* like this: footnote . When you typeset the document, the program generates a cross-reference to the footnote, placing the footnote number in the text and the note itself at the bottom of the page. Most typesetting specifications automatically number footnotes sequentially throughout your document unless you override the numbering.

See the online Help and *Typesetting Documents in Scientific WorkPlace and Scientific Word* for information about changing footnotes into endnotes using the *endnotes* package.

▶ To enter a footnote

1. Place the insertion point where you want the footnote reference to appear.

2. On the Field toolbar, click the Note button 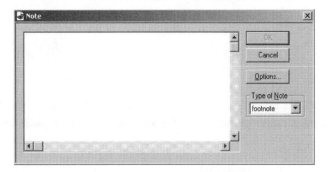 or, from the Insert menu, choose Note. The program opens the Note dialog box.

3. In the Type of Note box, select footnote.

4. Enter the text of the footnote and choose OK.

   You can enter mathematics, text, and graphics, and you can apply tags, as in the document window. You can also use cut and paste techniques to copy information from the main part of your document to a footnote.

   You can enter multiple references to the same footnote in two ways. We prefer the first method described below, because the program creates the references automatically. In the second method, you create the references manually. If you subsequently add or remove footnotes earlier in your document, you must renumber the manually created references.

---

[1]   Because much of the information in footnotes is overlooked by the reader, we suggest you use footnotes sparingly.

► To enter multiple references to the same footnote

1. Enter the footnote at the first reference point:

   a. On the Field toolbar, click the Note button or, from the Insert menu, choose Note.
   b. In the Type of Note box, select footnote.
   c. Enter the text of the footnote and then enter a marker for the footnote, as described on page 249.
   d. Choose OK.

2. At each subsequent reference point to the footnote,

   a. Enter a superscript and toggle to text.
   b. Insert a cross-reference to the marker in the footnote.
   c. Leave the superscript template.
   When you typeset your document, the program will replace the marker with the number of the footnote.

or

1. Enter the footnote at the first reference point.

2. At each subsequent reference point to the footnote:

   a. On the Field toolbar, click the Note button or, from the Insert menu, choose Note.
   b. In the Type of Note box, select footnote.
   c. Choose Options and check Override Automatic Number.
   d. Enter the number of the footnote you want to refer to in the Footnote Number box.
   You may need to typeset preview the document to determine the correct number.
   e. Check Mark Only.
   When you check Mark Only, the program places the footnote number in the text but doesn't print the footnote at the bottom of the page.
   f. Choose OK to leave the Footnote Options dialog box.
   g. Choose OK to return to the document.

► To add a footnote without a number or an in-text reference

1. On the Field toolbar, click the Note button or, from the Insert menu, choose Note.

2. In the Type of Note box, select footnote.

3. Enter the text of the note.

4. Choose Options and check Text Only.

   When you check Text Only, the program prints the note at the bottom of the page, but doesn't place a footnote number in the text.

5. Choose OK to leave the Footnote Options dialog box.

6. Choose OK to return to your document.

In some environments, including mathematics and tables, LaTeX doesn't allow footnotes. In those circumstances, you can create a footnote by placing a footnote marker in the place where the footnote is disallowed and placing the text of the footnote in the next possible location in which footnotes are allowed.

▶ **To add a footnote in an environment where footnotes aren't allowed**

1. Place the insertion point where you want the reference to occur.

2. Create the footnote marker:

   a. On the Field toolbar, click the Note button or, from the Insert menu, choose Note.
   b. In the Type of Note box, check footnote.
   c. Choose Options, select Mark Only, and choose OK.
   d. Choose OK to return to your document.

3. Place the insertion point at the next possible location in which footnotes are allowed.

4. Create the text of the footnote:

   a. On the Field toolbar, click the Note button or, from the Insert menu, choose Note.
   b. In the Type of Note box, check footnote.
   c. Enter the text of the footnote.
   d. Choose Options, select Text Only, and choose OK.
   e. Choose OK to return to your document.

Creating Margin Notes

This is the text of a margin note.

Paragraphs can contain references to margin notes like the one that appears on this page. Margin notes, which can contain both text and mathematics, aren't numbered. In the document window, margin notes appear as small gray boxes containing the words *Margin note,* like this: Margin note . When you typeset the document, the program places the note in the margin at a point determined by the typesetting specifications.

▶ **To enter a margin note**

1. Place the insertion point approximately where you want the margin note to begin.

   The typesetting specifications determine the exact line on which the note begins. If you want a margin note to appear close to a section heading, place the insertion point on the line following the heading.

2. On the Field toolbar, click the Note button or, from the Insert menu, choose Note.

3. In the Type of Note box, select Margin note.

4. Enter the text of the note and then choose OK.

You can enter mathematics, text, and graphics, and you can apply tags, just as in the document window. You can also use cut and paste techniques to copy information from the main part of your document to a margin note.

Creating TeX Fields

If you are very familiar with TeX and know the TeX command for an object or operation not available in *SWP* or *SW,* you can enter it in your document in a TeX field. In the document window, the command appears as a small gray box containing the words *TeX field,* like this: TeX field . When you save your document, the program interprets the command if possible and inserts it into your document, eliminating the corresponding field box.

You can *encapsulate* and name the TeX field to prevent the program from rendering the TeX command when you open the file. When you save the document, the program stores the command and name exactly as you enter them. In the document window, the encapsulated field appears as a gray field box containing the name you entered in square brackets, like this: [create object] . When you typeset your document, LaTeX or PDFLaTeX interprets the command and inserts it into the DVI or PDF file. Otherwise, the program ignores the field.

Important   Incorrect TeX code in an encapsulated field won't cause the program to fail when you open the document, because the code remains hidden. However, it will prevent LaTeX and PDFLaTeX from typesetting your document.

▶ **To enter a TeX command**

1. On the Typeset Object toolbar, click the TeX button ⊞ or, from the Insert menu, choose Typeset Object and then choose TeX Field.

2. In the TeX Field dialog box, type the TeX command preceded by a backslash ($\backslash$).

3. If you want to encapsulate the field, check Encapsulated and enter a field name.

4. Choose OK.

Creating Other Fields in the Body of the Document

The shell documents provided for certain document types, especially those for letters, memos, and fax messages, often have a number of predefined fields for creating information such as the date and the address. In these documents, the on-screen order of the fields above the Opening field doesn't matter, because the typesetting specifications determine the order in which the fields are typeset. If you don't typeset your document, the fields appear according to the style and the print options.

▶ To create a letter, memo, or fax message

1. On the Standard toolbar, click the New button 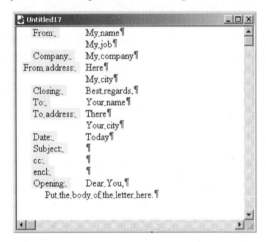 or, from the File menu, choose New.

2. In the Shell Directories list, select Other Documents and then from the Shell Files list, select a letter, memo, or fax shell and choose OK.

   The document on your screen might look something like this:

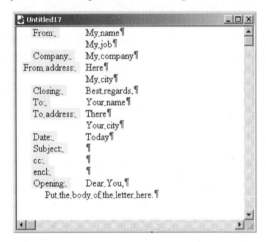

3. Edit or delete fields, or replace the predefined text with information, as necessary.

Important   If a letter or memo shell has an Opening field, you must not delete it—the program uses it as a signal to create the letter or document when you typeset.

Creating the Back Matter

Your document may contain supplementary material such as appendixes, a bibliography, or an index. Unlike the front matter, which the program creates for you from information you supply in the front matter fields, you create the back matter of your document in the document window. The typesetting specifications for the shell you use determine the typeset appearance of back matter and any cross-references to it. When you typeset your document, the formatter generates the back matter, numbering elements automatically as necessary and creating any required cross-references.

Important   You must typeset your document to generate the back matter. If you produce your document without typesetting it, the program doesn't process the document with LATEX or PDFLATEX and the back matter isn't generated.

Bibliographies, or reference lists, deserve special mention. Bibliographies appear at the end of a document or chapter. The body of the document can contain *citations,* which are cross-references to the individual items in the bibliography list. When you typeset your document in *SWP* or *SW,* the formatter automatically generates the cross-references between the citations and the bibliography item to which they refer. The appearance of the bibliography and the citations depends on the typesetting specifications for the shell. If the shell for your document supports bibliographies, you can create a bibliography manually or automatically. This section describes how to create both kinds of bibliography lists and the citations that refer to them.

Creating Appendixes

Although an appendix is part of the back matter, you enter the content of an appendix exactly as you enter the content of a chapter or section in the body of your document. When you typeset the document, the program numbers any appendixes automatically, just as it does chapters and sections in the body of the document. The numbering scheme depends on the typesetting specifications. Typically, appendixes are numbered sequentially as A, B, C, etc., and appendix subheadings are numbered sequentially beginning with the letter of the appendix, as in A.1, A.2, A.3, B.1, B.2, B.3, etc. Some shells use non-standard appendixes; details appear in the shell documents. The appendix numbers don't appear in the document window.

▶ **To create automatically numbered appendixes in standard shells**

1. Move the insertion point to the end of the paragraph immediately before the first appendix and press ENTER.

2. With the insertion point in body text, insert the **appendix** fragment.

   This fragment is a TEX field containing the command \appendix. Insert the fragment before the first appendix only.

3. Press ENTER.

4. Type the title of the appendix.

5. If the shell has an Appendix section tag, apply it to the title. Otherwise,
   - If you're using a book or report shell, apply a chapter heading tag to the title.
   - If you're using an article shell, apply a section heading tag to the title.

6. Create the content of the appendix.

Creating Manual Bibliographies

A manual bibliography, which works just like a series of cross-references, is convenient when the list of references is short and you don't plan to use those references in other articles or books. You must format entries yourself, a disadvantage if you later decide to change the style of the bibliography to suit a different requirement. For example, if you format the bibliography of an article for a journal that requires book titles in italics, then later decide to submit the article to a different journal that requires those same titles in boldface, you must make the format changes manually.

Creating a Manual Bibliography

Creating a manual bibliography involves three steps:

- Specifying a manual bibliography.

- Creating a list of bibliography items, generally at the end of your document.

- Creating a series of citations, or references, to those items in the body of the document.

When you typeset the document, the formatter generates the bibliography and automatically creates the cross-references for the citations in the body of the document, formatting them according to the typesetting specifications. Many specifications automatically number each item in the bibliography list, but you can replace a number with a label that appears in print, both in the bibliography list and everywhere you place a citation for the labeled bibliography item. You can use labels for items in the bibliography list to create author/date citations. Make sure you choose a document shell that includes the Bibliography Item tag.

▶ **To specify a manual bibliography**

1. From the Typeset menu, choose Bibliography Choice.

2. Select Manual Entry and choose OK.

▶ **To create a list of bibliography items**

1. Move the insertion point to the end of the line that is to precede the bibliography and press ENTER.

2. With the insertion point in body text, click the Item Tag popup list or press ALT+1, and then select Bibliography Item from the Item Tag popup list.

   or

   From the Tag menu, choose Apply, select Bibliography Item, and choose OK.

   The program displays a dialog box so that you can assign a key and an optional label to the item.

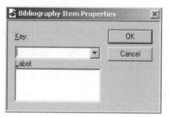

3. Enter a unique key for the item.

   You use this name when you create a citation for the bibliography item. Click the arrow next to the Key box to display a list of keys already in use in your document, or press DOWN ARROW to scroll through the list. The keys don't appear when you typeset your document.

4. If you want the item to appear in the list with a label instead of the number automatically generated for the item, enter the label in the **Label** box.

   The label can include mathematics. If you include a label for a list item, the program continues sequential numbering with the next list item. The label can also be used to create author/date citations, as explained on page 261.

5. Choose **OK**.

   In the document window, the key for the item appears in the lead-in box.

6. Type the bibliographic information for the item, using text tags to format the information correctly.

   In the document window, the information appears next to the lead-in box.

7. If you want to create another bibliographic item, press ENTER and repeat steps 3–7.

8. At the end of the bibliography, press ENTER to complete the last item.

9. Choose **Cancel** and then apply the Remove Item Tag to complete the list.

Creating Citations for Manual Bibliographies

▶ **To create a citation for a manually created bibliography item**

1. Place the insertion point where you want the citation to appear.

2. On the Typeset Object toolbar, click the Citation button 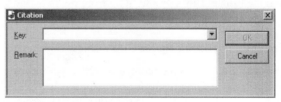 or, from the **Insert** menu, choose **Typeset Object** and then choose **Citation** to display the **Citation** dialog box.

3. Enter the key for the bibliographic item you want to cite.

   Click the arrow next to the **Key** box to display a list of all keys defined for the document.

4. If you want to add a comment to the citation, enter it in the **Remark** box.

   Comments, which can contain both text and mathematics, appear only when you typeset preview or print your document. They don't appear in the document window.

5. Choose **OK**.

The citation is displayed on the screen in a small box containing the word *cite* and the key you entered, like this:

. . . as noted in an earlier article cite: example .

When you typeset the document, the formatter creates the correct reference by replacing the key with the number of the keyed bibliography item:

. . . as noted in an earlier article [12].

If you also entered a comment, it appears after the number:

. . . as noted in an earlier article [12, based on Fermat's principle].

The typesetting specifications for the shell determine the citation appearance in print.

Once you've created a citation for a manually created bibliography item, you can use it to jump to the beginning of the bibliography item containing the referenced key.

▶ **To move to a marker specified in a citation**

- Select the citation and then, from the Tools menu, choose Action.
  or

- Hold down the CTRL key and click the citation.
  or

- If the document has been saved as read-only, click the citation.

▶ **To return to the citation**

- On the Navigate toolbar or the History toolbar, click the History Back button ⬆ .
  or

- From the Go menu, choose History Back.
  The insertion point moves to the beginning of the paragraph containing the source of the most recent jump.

Creating Author/Date Citations for Manual Bibliographies

You can create author/date citations by giving each bibliography item a label containing the author/date information you want to appear in the citation. In the document window, the program displays the citation as a small box containing the item key. When you typeset your document, the formatter ignores the number of the bibliography item and instead uses the item label containing the author/date information in the citation. You may want to change the bibliography item so that information in the label isn't repeated in the item. For example, if you want an author/date citation for an article listed in your bibliography as:

Hunter, R., Richman, F., and Walker, E. Subgroups of bounded abelian groups, Abelian Groups and Modules, CISM Courses and Lectures 287(1984), 17-36, Springer-Verlag, Vienna and New York.

you might give the item the key *Subgroups* and create a label for the item, such as:

Hunter, Richman, and Walker 1984

and then remove the authors' names from the bibliography item so that it appears as:

[Hunter, Richman, and Walker 1984] Subgroups of bounded abelian groups, Abelian Groups and Modules, CISM Courses and Lectures 287(1984), 17-36, Springer-Verlag, Vienna and New York.

In the document window, the citation appears like this:

. . . as noted in an earlier article `cite: Subgroups` .

When you typeset your document, the citation appears this way:

. . . as noted in an earlier article [Hunter, Richman, and Walker 1984].

Creating BibTeX Bibliographies

You can create an automatic bibliography with BibTeX, a public domain program created by Oren Patashnik. A BibTeX bibliography is convenient if you have a long list of references that you plan to use in other articles or books, because you don't have to create the bibliography list yourself. BibTeX generates the list automatically by extracting references from a database using the citations you insert into your document. BibTeX bibliographies, which are ASCII files that you create and edit with a standard text editor, can be used as often as you like in other documents. Also, you can change the appearance of a BibTeX bibliography automatically by specifying a different bibliography style. Creating a BibTeX bibliography involves these steps:

- Creating or obtaining a BibTeX database.

- Specifying a BibTeX bibliography and bibliography style, and inserting an instruction to include the bibliography.

- Creating a series of citations in the body of your document.

- Generating the bibliography.

When you typeset compile your document to generate a BibTeX bibliography, the program passes the document through BibTeX, which generates the bibliography by extracting the cited references from the database and placing them in a file with the same name as your document but with a .bbl extension. The file is formatted according to the specified bibliography style. The next time you typeset the document, the formatter includes the .bbl file in the document, formatting the citations according to the typesetting specifications.

Creating a BibTeX Database

Before you can create a BibTeX bibliography for your document, you must first create or obtain a database of bibliographic items in BibTeX form. The program provides several sample databases. The databases have a .bib file extension and are located by default in your program installation in the `TCITeX\bibtex\bib` subdirectory or one of its subdirectories. Each record in a BibTeX database contains the information necessary to create a bibliographic entry in a document. The records are stored in a logical format with no visual (formatting) information.

Formatting information is stored in the BibTeX style files, which have the extension .bst and are located by default in the `TCITeX\bibtex\bst` subdirectory or one of its subdirectories. You can specify a different directory for .bib and .bst files if you prefer. However, changing the directory affects your program installation as a whole. We recommend that the directory locations remain unchanged.

The details of the process of creating and editing BIBTEX databases are outside the scope of this manual, but you can find information about the process in the documents in the `WinBibDB` subdirectory of your program installation and in many LATEX books. More information is available if you typeset preview the `btxdoc.dvi` and `btxhak.dvi` files in the `TCITeX\doc\bibtex` subdirectory.

Specifying and Inserting a BibTEX Bibliography

Once you've established one or more BIBTEX databases containing the references you want, you can specify a BIBTEX bibliography and insert a command to include the bibliography in your document.

▶ **To specify a BibTEX bibliography**

1. From the Typeset menu, choose Bibliography Choice.

2. Select BibTeX and choose OK.

▶ **To insert an instruction to include the bibliography**

1. Move the insertion point to the end of the line that is to precede the bibliography and press ENTER.

2. On the Typeset Object toolbar, click the Bibliography button 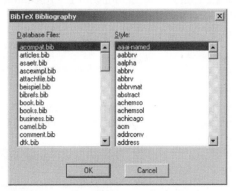 or, from the Insert menu, choose Typeset Object, and then choose Bibliography to open the BibTeX Bibliography dialog box.

3. Select the BIBTEX database files containing your references.

   You can select more than one database.

4. Select a BIBTEX style for formatting the references.

   Typeset preview the `btxdoc.dvi` file in the `TCITeX\doc\bibtex` subdirectory and see the `BibTeXBibliographyStyles.tex` file in the `SWSamples` directory for more information.

5. Choose OK.

   The program inserts into your document a gray box like this: [BIBTEX] .

▶ **To change the directories used for BibTEX databases and styles**

1. From the Typeset menu, choose General Settings.

2. In the BibTeX database directory box, enter the name of the directory you want to use for BibTEX databases.

3. In the BibTeX style directory box, enter the name of the directory you want to use for BibTEX bibliography styles.

4. Choose OK.

Note   Changing the BibTEX directories isn't recommended.

Creating Citations for a BibTEX Bibliography

Creating a citation for a BibTEX reference ensures that it will be included in the bibliography list when you generate the bibliography. You can also use the citation process to include a reference in the bibliography without citing it in the body of your document.

Specifying a BibTEX bibliography changes the Citation dialog box so that you can select citations from a BibTEX database. If your database of bibliography entries is very large, finding the reference you want to cite can be time-consuming. You can narrow your search by specifying search criteria, or *key filters,* for the database items, then choosing the reference you want from among those that fit the filters.

If you add the *authordate1-4, chicago,* or *harvard* package to your document, you can create author/date citations for BibTEX bibliographies. See the online Help or *Typesetting Documents in Scientific WorkPlace and Scientific Word* for instructions.

▶ **To create a citation for an item in a BibTEX database**

1. Place the insertion point in your document where you want the citation to appear.

2. On the Typeset Object toolbar, click the Citation button ▐▐ or, from the Insert menu, choose Typeset Object, and then choose Citation to open the BibTeX Citation dialog box.

3. If you know the key for the database item you want to cite, enter it in the **Key** box.

Otherwise, select the key for the item directly from a BIBTEX database:

a. Scroll the **Database File** list to select one of the databases listed and then choose **View Keys** to display a **Keys** dialog box shown on the next page. The box lists the keys for those items in the selected database that satisfy the current search criteria.

b. Scroll the list to select the item you want.
   If the item doesn't appear on the list, change the search criteria.

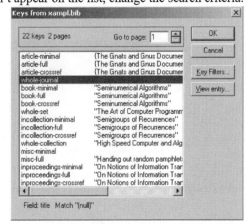

c. If you want to view the full text of the item, choose **View entry**.
   The program displays the item in a **BibTeX Database Entry** dialog box, like this:

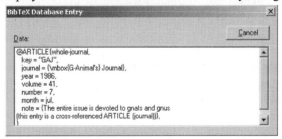

d. Choose **Cancel** to return to the list of keys.

4. When you have selected the item you want, choose **OK** to return to the **BibTeX Citation** dialog box.

5. If you want to add a text comment to the citation, enter it in the **Remark** box.

Comments appear only when you typeset, not in the document window.

6. If you want the reference to be uncited—that is, you want it to appear in the bibliography without a corresponding citation in your document—check the box labeled **Bibliography Entry Only - No Citation**.

7. Choose **OK** to return to your document.

The program inserts a citation for the item whose key you selected. The citation appears in a shaded box, like this: cite: Lamport or nocite: Lamport .

▶ **To change the search criteria for the database**

1. On the Typeset Object toolbar, click the Citation button 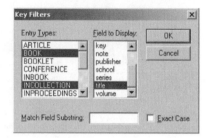 or, from the Insert menu, choose Typeset Object and then choose Citation.

2. From the Citation dialog box, select one of the databases listed.

3. Choose View Keys.

4. Choose Key Filters to open the Key Filters dialog box.

5. From the Entry Types list, select the types of items you want to cite.

   If you want to cite documents from every type of entry, select all the items in the list and make sure the Match Field Substring box is empty.

6. From the Field to Display list, choose the bibliography entry fields that you want to display in the Keys dialog box and then choose OK.

Generating a BibTeX Bibliography

Once you've inserted the instruction to include the bibliography file and created the citations, you must compile your document to generate the bibliography. During the generation, the program processes your document first through LaTeX or PDFLaTeX and then through BibTeX. The BibTeX stage automatically extracts and formats references from the database using the citations in the body of your document. The references are placed in a .bbl file. When you next typeset your document, the .bbl file is automatically included at the point where you inserted the instruction to include the bibliography. Remember that whenever you add or delete citations in the body of your document, you must regenerate the bibliography.

▶ **To generate a BibTeX bibliography**

1. Save the document.

2. On the Typeset toolbar, click the Compile button 🔲 or the Compile PDF button 🔲 or, from the Typeset menu, choose Compile or Compile PDF.

3. Check Generate a Bibliography and choose OK.

You can also run BIBTEX from the Tools command on the Typeset menu, but you must first process your document through LATEX or PDFLATEX to generate a complete and correct bibliography.

Changing the BibTEX Bibliography Style

BIBTEX formats the items in the list and the citations that refer to them with the aid of a BIBTEX bibliography style file that contains instructions on how to format the entry for a particular journal or book. You can change the format of your citations and bibliographic entries simply by changing to a different BIBTEX bibliography style file. Among the BIBTEX bibliography style files included with the program are these:

BIBTEX Style File	Format
plain.bst	Entries are labeled with numbers and sorted alphabetically
unsrt.bst	Entries are labeled with numbers and appear in the order of citation
alpha.bst	Entries are labeled using an abbreviation of the author's name and the date of publication
abbrv.bst	Entries are labeled with numbers and sorted alphabetically, with first names, months, and journal names abbreviated

Other BIBTEX bibliography style files are available. Some are appropriate only for certain databases.

▶ **To change the BibTEX bibliography style**

1. Select the BIBTEX gray box.

2. Choose Properties to open the BibTeX Bibliography Properties dialog box.

3. Scroll through the Style list to select the style you want, and choose OK.

Creating Indexes

Certain classes of documents, such as books, can contain automatically generated indexes to help readers find information. The index can have primary, secondary, and tertiary entries that cross-reference the body of the document and other index entries. When you typeset the document, the formatter automatically generates the index and the cross-references to the body of the document.

The typesetting specifications for the shell determine the appearance of the index and the index entries. Generated information doesn't appear in the document window, but you can see it when you typeset preview your document.

Generating an index involves several steps:

- Creating an index entry for each item to be indexed.

- Inserting a command to include the index.

- Generating the index itself.

Creating Index Entries

Each time you want a reference to information to appear in the index, you must create an index entry. The index entry indicates the primary entry under which you want the item to appear in the index and the secondary and tertiary entries, if any. You can index an item under as many entries as you want. For example, in the sentence

> You can add emphasis to text selections by applying tags such
> as bold, italics, or small caps.

you might index *bold* as a primary entry and also as a secondary entry under the primary entries of *emphasis, text appearance,* and *text tags,* yielding these entries in the index:

⋮

bold, 7

⋮

emphasis
    bold, 7

⋮

text appearance
    bold, 7

⋮

text tags
    bold, 7

⋮

Within the index, references appear alphabetically, with symbols preceding words. Symbols can appear in correct alphabetical order in the index if you use the symbol name as the index entry and specify a special appearance—the symbol itself—for the entry. Suppose you want to create an entry for the symbol $\int$. You might use the word *integral* as the index entry and specify a special appearance $\int$. When you typeset your document, the index might contain a sequence like this, with the $\int$ in correct alphabetical order:

⋮

implicit plots, 45
indeterminate forms, 77
$\int$, 32
integration, 33

⋮

You can specify a special appearance for a primary, secondary, or tertiary index entry.

By default, index entries point to page numbers in the body of the document. However, cross-references that point to other entries in the index can also help readers find information. For example, if all entries pertaining to *Scientific Word* are indexed under *SW*, you can help the reader find the entries by creating a cross-reference to *SW*. Your index would then have an entry like this (the word *see* is supplied automatically):

⋮

Scientific Word, *see* SW

⋮

You can include both page numbers entries and cross-reference entries in the index.

▶ **To create an index entry**

1. Place the insertion point to the right of the item you want to index.

2. On the Typeset Object toolbar, click the Index Entry button 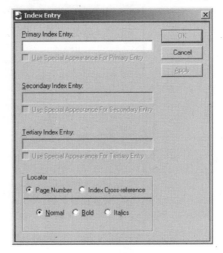 or, from the Insert menu, choose Typeset Object and then choose Index Entry.

3. In the Index Entry dialog box, type the index entry:
   - If the entry is a primary entry, type the entry in the Primary Index Entry box.
   - If the entry is a secondary entry, type the primary entry and then type the secondary entry in the Secondary Index Entry box.
   - If the entry is a tertiary entry, type the primary and secondary entries and then type the tertiary entry in the Tertiary Index Entry box.

4. If you want to substitute a special appearance or symbol for the entry, check the Use Special Appearance box under the entry and in the box that opens, type the formatted entry exactly as you want it to appear, as in the example below. Note that the Locator area defaults to a page number entry.

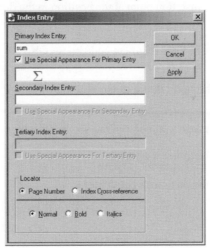

5. If you want to change the appearance of the page number in the index entry, click **Bold** or **Italics**.

6. If you want to enter a cross-reference to other index entries, click **Index Cross-reference** in the **Locator** area, and enter the index entries in the **Cross-reference(s)** box.

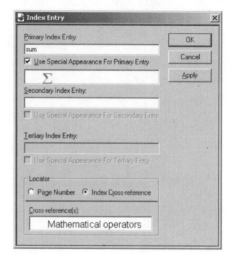

When you typeset your document, the program supplies the word *see*.

7. Choose **OK**.

Including the Index in Your Document

Your document must contain a command to include the index file in your document. The command is available as a fragment. If you expect to save your document as a Portable LaTeX file (see Chapter 2 "Creating Documents") or you expect to typeset a PDF file, you must follow a special process to include the index.

▶ **To include the index in your document**

1. Place the insertion point at the position in the document where you want the index to appear.

2. Import the index fragment and choose **OK**.

▶ **To include the index for a document saved as a Portable LaTeX file or for a typeset PDF file**

1. Place the insertion point in the document where you want the index to appear.

2. Import the index fragment.

3. Modify the document preamble:

a. From the Typeset menu, choose Preamble.

b. On a new line in the input area, type **makeindex** and then choose OK.

4. Add the makeidx package:

Important   Skip this step if your document has an $\mathcal{A}_{\mathcal{M}}\mathcal{S}$-LATEX document class.

a. On the Typeset toolbar, click the Options and Packages button ▦ or, from the Typeset menu, choose Options and Packages.

b. Choose the Package Options tab and choose Add.

c. Scroll through the list of available packages to select makeidx and choose OK.

d. Choose OK to return to the document.

Creating a LATEX Index File

The program uses the MakeIndex program to build your index from the index entries in your document. MakeIndex creates the index as a sorted LATEX file with the same name as your document and an .ind extension.

▶ **To create an index file**

1. Save the document.

2. Generate the index file:

- On the Typeset toolbar, click one of the Compile buttons (▦ or ▦) or, from the Typeset menu, choose a Compile command; check Generate an Index; and choose OK.
  or
- From the Typeset menu, choose Tools and choose Run MakeIndex.

The program automatically sets the correct number of LATEX or PDFLATEX passes so that index cross-references can be resolved.

You can also run MakeIndex from the Tools command on the Typeset menu, but you must first process your document through LATEX or PDFLATEX to generate a complete and correct index.

Managing Large Documents

Creating and managing the typesetting of large documents (such as books with front matter, a series of chapters, and back matter) can be unwieldy. You can simplify working with large documents in *SWP* and *SW* by breaking them into smaller, more manageable pieces called *subdocuments* and then including all the subdocuments in a *master document*. However, if you need to create a large document for online use, we suggest you use a single quick-load file (see Chapter 11 "Managing Documents") or a series of related documents (see Chapter 10 "Creating Documents for Online Use").

Subdocuments don't contain their own document information. Instead, they use the typesetting specifications, document information, and front matter defined for the master document. The subdocument can contain internal cross-references and cross-references to the other subdocuments associated with the master document; see page 248. When you typeset a subdocument by itself, the program resolves only those cross-references that are internal to the subdocument. Subdocuments can be used in any number of master documents. They must reside in the same directory as the master document or in a subdirectory within that directory.

Note   We recommend that the master document and all subdocuments be placed in the same directory.

For easier management of any graphics files, place the files in a subdirectory of the directory containing the documents. If the subdocuments contain many graphics, you may want to create a separate subdirectory to hold the graphics for each subdocument.

A master document stores the typesetting specifications, document information, front matter, and output options defined for the entire large document. It also contains an object for including each subdocument. Otherwise, it is the same as any other document. Any changes you make to the typesetting specifications, document information, front matter, and output options of the master document affect all the subdocuments in exactly the same way.

When you compile and preview a master document, the program resolves the cross-references and citations in all unsuppressed subdocuments and generates any specified front and back matter for the whole document.

Creating a large document involves three steps:

- Creating the master document.

- Creating the subdocuments from within the master document.

- Opening each subdocument and typing your text.

Creating Master Documents

Just as you create any document with the program, you can build a master document from a new document or a copy of any other document created with the program. Ordinarily quite small, master documents often consist of little more than a list of the objects that include subdocuments. You can edit the master document at any time to specify the front or back matter, include additional subdocuments, or enter information you want as part of the master document.

The program all document information of the master document to all the subdocuments. With the exception of selecting output options for PDF files, any changes you make to the document information of the master document affect all the subdocuments. If you plan to typeset the entire large document with PDFLATEX, you must set the PDF output options for the master document and for each subdocument, as described on page 165. If the subdocuments are open when you make changes to the master document, you must save and reopen them. If the master document is a quick-load file, you must save and reopen it before the subdocuments will be affected.

When you create a large document, we suggest you set up a separate directory to hold it. Any subdocuments must reside in the same directory as the master document or in subdirectories within that directory.

▶ **To create a master document**

1. Create a new document.

   The shell file you select for the master document applies to all subdocuments.

2. On the Typeset toolbar, click the Front Matter button ⬚ or, from the Typeset menu, choose Front Matter and then choose OK.

3. Enter any text you want as part of the master document.

4. If you plan to create a PDF file from the master document and its subdocuments, choose General Settings from the Typeset menu, select the options you want, and choose OK.

5. On the Standard toolbar, click the Save button ⬚ or, from the File menu, choose Save to name and save the master document.

   Be sure to save the document in the directory that you want to contain the master document, all the subdocuments, and any subdocument directories.

6. Create the empty subdocuments; see Creating Subdocuments, below, for details.

   Note that it is this step alone that makes a master document different from a standard document.

7. From the Typeset menu, choose Output Choice, click the option you want, and choose OK.

8. On the Standard toolbar, click the Save button ⬚ or, from the File menu, choose Save to save the master document again.

Creating Subdocuments

Each subdocument is a separate document that you can edit independently of the master document. You create a subdocument by inserting an empty subdocument in the master document, and then opening the subdocument and typing its content. You can use the Import Contents command to make an existing document into a subdocument, in which case both the original document and the subdocument share any associated graphics. You can use a subdocument in several master documents; however, the subdocument must reside in the same directory as the master document, or in a subdirectory within that subdirectory. Whenever you open a subdocument, the program uses the document information, front matter, and typesetting specifications of its most recent master document.

Note   Subdocuments are different from standard documents because they don't have their own typesetting specifications and they don't contain any of their own document information. Also, unlike standard documents, subdocuments can't be typeset previewed from outside the program.

► **To insert a subdocument into a master document**

1. In the master document, place the insertion point where you want to include the subdocument.

2. On the Typeset Object toolbar, click the Subdocument button ▢ or, from the Insert menu, choose **Typeset Object** and then choose **Subdocument**.

   If the **Subdocument** menu is dimmed or the **Subdocument** dialog box doesn't open, you must name and save the master document before you can proceed.

3. If you want to save the subdocument in a subdirectory of the master document directory, click the box next to the **Subdocument Directory** area, scroll the list to select the directory you want, and choose **OK**.

   Remember that the subdocument must reside in the same directory as the master document or in a subdirectory within that directory.

4. In the **Subdocument** area, enter a name for the subdocument.

   You can enter the name of an existing subdocument or one you haven't yet created. Click the arrow next to the entry box to display a list of all existing subdocuments in the subdocument directory you selected. The program lists only subdocuments.

5. Choose **OK**.

   The program inserts a field in the master document that includes the subdocument. In the document window, the field looks something like this: [Include SubdocumentOne] . If the subdocument you named isn't an existing document, the program creates it. If the subdocument has been included previously in another master document, the program displays a message asking you to confirm the inclusion of the subdocument in the current master document.
   - Choose **Yes** to include the subdocument.
   - Choose **No** to specify a different subdocument in the **Subdocument** dialog box.

6. Repeat steps 2–5 for each subdocument you want to include.

   You can place any text you want before, between, or after the subdocument fields.

7. On the Standard toolbar, click the Save button ▣ or, from the **File** menu, choose **Save** to save the master document.

Note   You can use the same steps to create a subdocument of a subdocument. We recommend this only in the case of very long documents.

▶ **To make an existing document a subdocument**

1. Open the master document.

2. Insert an empty subdocument using a name different from that of the existing document and choose OK.

3. Save the master document.

4. Open the new subdocument.

5. From the File menu, choose Import Contents.

6. Select the existing document and choose OK to copy the contents of the existing document into the new subdocument.

7. Save the subdocument. The original file is unchanged.

▶ **To enter or edit the content of a subdocument**

1. Open the subdocument.

   The title bar shows the names of the master document and the subdocument.

2. Enter or edit the content in the subdocument as you would for any other document.

   If you're creating a chapter, make sure the chapter heading is in the subdocument instead of the master document. That way, the chapter heading will appear when you typeset the subdocument by itself.

3. From the Typeset menu, choose Output Choice, click the option you want, and choose OK.

4. On the Standard toolbar, click the Save button 💾 or, from the File menu, choose Save.

Previewing and Printing Master Documents and Subdocuments

When you typeset subdocuments individually, the program resolves any cross-references that are internal to the subdocument but not cross-references to other subdocuments or to the master document. To resolve all cross-references in the large document and to generate all front and back matter, you must typeset print the master document. If you typeset with PDFLATEX, you must set the PDF output options for the master document as described on page 273 and save the master document. Then, close, open, and save each subdocument.

When you typeset a master document, you can work with all subdocuments or you can suppress the printing of individual subdocuments. However, the formatter doesn't resolve cross-references to suppressed subdocuments.

Note   If you produce a master document without typesetting it, the program doesn't process the document through LATEX or PDFLATEX. Thus, the large document isn't generated in its entirety. The master document is printed as if it were as isolated document, without subdocuments and without any LATEX formatting.

▶ **To preview or print a subdocument**

1. Open the subdocument.

2. If you need to change the output settings, choose Output Choice from the Typeset menu, click the option you want, and choose OK.

3. From the Typeset menu, choose a Preview or Print command.

   The program displays the Counters dialog box.

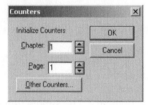

4. If you want to change the initialization point of the chapter or page number, click the corresponding arrow to change the value.

5. If you want to change the initialization point of any other counter, such as equation, section, or table numbers, choose Other Counters to display the Other Counters dialog box.

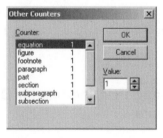

   a. In the Counter box, select the counter.
   b. In the Value box, set the initialization point you want.
   c. Repeat steps a and b for each counter you want to reinitialize.
   d. Choose OK.

6. Choose OK to leave the Counters dialog box.

   The program creates a temporary document that consists of the typesetting specifications; the preamble and the front matter from the master document; and the body of the subdocument. It then processes the temporary document and then previews or prints it, according to your instructions. See Chapter 7 "Previewing and Printing" for more information about the typesetting process.

▶ **To typeset an entire large document**

1. Open the master document.

2. If you need to change the output settings, choose Output Choice from the Typeset menu, click the option you want, and choose OK.

3. From the Typeset menu, choose a Compile, Preview, or Print command.

   The program compiles the entire large document, resolving all cross-references and citations and generating any required document elements.

▶ **To suppress the typesetting of a subdocument in a master document**

1. Open the master document.

2. Select the object that includes the subdocument you want to suppress and then choose Properties.

   or

   Double-click the object.

3. Check the Suppress Print and Preview box.

4. Choose OK.

   The object for the subdocument now includes the word *Exclude* and the name of the subdocument, perhaps like this: [Exclude SubdocumentOne] .

5. Repeat steps 2–4 for each subdocument you want to suppress.

6. From the Typeset menu, choose a Preview or Print command.

   The program compiles the large document, excluding any suppressed subdocuments. It doesn't resolve cross-references to suppressed subdocuments and previews or prints only that part of the large document that you didn't suppress.

Note   If you save the master document with subdocuments suppressed, they remain suppressed until you uncheck the Suppress Print and Preview box for each one.

Making a Subdocument into a Document

You can copy a subdocument into a separate stand-alone document that has all the characteristics and document information of the master document. Once the subdocument has been copied, you can delete it with the Document Manager command if it is no longer used by the master document.

▶ **To make an existing subdocument into a separate stand-alone document**

1. Open the master document.

2. From the File menu, choose Save As.

3. Enter a name for the new document.

4. Choose OK.

   The new document is saved with all the document characteristics defined for the original master document. The typesetting specifications, document information, and front matter sections are copied exactly.

5. Delete the contents of the body of the new document.

   The document now has a defined environment but no content.

6. From the File menu, choose Import Contents.

7. Select the subdocument you want to copy and choose OK.

   The program copies the content of the subdocument into the new document.

8. On the Standard toolbar, click the Save button or, from the File menu, choose Save.

10 Creating Documents for Online Use

With *SWP, SW,* and *SNB,* you can produce documents for use online as well as in print. With Version 5, the variety of formats available for online use makes it easy to share your documents across platforms, installations, and systems, on a network or on the Web.

In the documents you create for online use, you can take advantage of hypertext to create links to information located inside your document or in other documents. This chapter explains how to structure and use hypertext links. It also explains how to create HTML files from your *SWP, SW,* and *SNB* documents and how to use *SWP* and *SW* to create typeset PDF files. The chapter also includes information about enhancing online .tex documents with popup notes and structuring your online content in a series of short .tex documents that are linked together in the sequence you specify.

With Internet access you can open the file at any Uniform Resource Locator (URL) address from inside *SWP, SW,* or *SNB.* If the file is a .tex or .rap document created with the program, the file opens as a read-only document in a new document window. If the information is in a different format, the program activates the appropriate program on your computer, such as your Web browser or PDF viewer, to access the location and open the file. Chapter 2 "Creating Documents" contains more information.

Using Hypertext Links

When you create information for use online rather than in print, the information doesn't have to be contained in a single linear document. Instead, from any place in your information, you can include *hypertext links,* or jumps, that point readers to key ideas, related topics, and supplementary material located inside or outside your document.

Creating Hypertext Links

You can create hypertext links to information located in the same document, in other *SWP, SW,* and *SNB* documents on the current system or network, or in documents on the Web. Hypertext links have two parts: the link and the target. The link creates a pointer to a target and defines how that pointer appears in your document. By default, text for hypertext links appears in the document window in color and in print as ordinary text.

The target can be a file, including files on the Web, or an object in a file—such as a figure, a section, or equation in *SWP, SW,* or *SNB* documents—to which you've assigned an identifying key or marker. Specifically, you can create links from your document to

- A marker elsewhere in the current document.
- A different `.tex` document located on your computer or network, or a marker in that document.
- Any URL location or file on the Web.

The link specifies the address of the target. The form of the address differs depending on the target itself and following the model used in standard Web browsers:

The address	Links to
`here`	The marker *here* in the current document
`yourdoc.tex`	The document `yourdoc.tex` in the current directory
`yourdoc.tex#here`	The marker *here* in the document `yourdoc.tex`
`c:\other\yourdoc.tex`	The document `yourdoc.tex` in the `other` directory on the local `c:` drive
`http://www.site/doc.htm`	The document at the URL *http://www.site/doc.htm*
`http://www.site/doc.htm#here`	The marker *here* at the URL *http://www.site/doc.htm*

Hypertext links are intended for use online rather than in print. If you print your document without typesetting it, any hypertext links appear in print just as they appear in the document window. However, if you typeset your document, the formatter changes the appearance of the links. Some modifications are required if you want to use *SWP* or *SW* to typeset documents containing hypertext links. See Making Typesetting Adjustments for Hypertext Links later in this chapter.

▶ **To create a hypertext link**

1. Place the insertion point where you want the link to appear.

2. From the Field toolbar, click the Hypertext Link button or, from the Insert menu, choose Hypertext Link.

3. In the Screen Text box, enter the link as you want it to appear online:

- If you want the link to appear as text or text and mathematics, type the information.
- If you want the link to appear as a graphic or you want to add a graphic to the text, from the File menu, choose Import Picture and select the graphic.

4. In the Target box, enter the address of the target using the appropriate format; see page 280 for address formats.

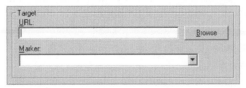

- If you want to create a link to a target outside the current document, enter the complete document address in the URL box.

- If you want to create a link to a target inside the current document, enter the marker for the target in the Marker box. Don't enter the pound sign (#).
  To see a list of all markers defined for the current document, click the arrow next to the Marker box.

- If you want to create a link to a numbered object that doesn't yet have a marker, enter the key you will assign to the item in the Marker box.

5. Choose OK.

The program creates the link.

▶ **To create a marker in an SWP, SW, or SNB document**

1. Open the target document and place the insertion point where you want the marker.

2. On the Field toolbar, click the Marker button ⬚ or, from the Insert menu, choose Marker.

3. In the Key box, enter a unique key for the item.

   Click the arrow to the right of the box to see a list of the keys already defined for the document.

4. Choose OK and then save the document.

Jumping with Hypertext Links

Using hypertext links, you can jump immediately to a *target* elsewhere in your document, in another online document, or on the Web. If the location is a .tex or .rap document created with *SWP, SW* or *SNB* and located on your system or network or on the Web, the program opens the target document in a new document window. If the location is a document with a different format, the appropriate program on your system is activated to open the document.

When the mouse pointer is over a hypertext link in a *SWP, SW* or *SNB* document, the pointer appears as ⬚ . The process of jumping from the link to the target depends on how the document has been saved. See Chapter 2 "Creating Documents" for more information about saving documents.

▶ **To jump to the target of a hypertext link**

- Place the insertion point in the link so that the pointer appears as 👆 and then, from the Tools menu or the Context menu, choose Action.
  or

- Hold down the CTRL key and click the link.
  or

- In a document saved as read-only, click the link.

If the target is a marker, the program moves the insertion point to the specified marker. If the target is a document, the program opens the document and moves the insertion point to the top of the document, linking to the Web if necessary.

Making Typesetting Adjustments for Hypertext Links

Although documents that contain hypertext links are intended for use online, you may occasionally want to print them. The way you produce a printed document determines the appearance of any links it contains. Specifically, if you're using *SNB* or if you don't typeset your document in *SWP* or *SW*, the appearance of links in print will reflect their appearance in the document window. Each link will appear as the specified screen text or graphic.

However, if you typeset the document in *SWP* or *SW*, the formatter generates information that changes the printed appearance of the links. It replaces the link information you see in the document window with information related to the target. If the target has an automatic number, such as a section or table number, the formatter replaces the specified screen text or graphic with that number. If the target doesn't carry an automatic number, the formatter replaces the specified screen text or graphic with a blank. However, the replacement works only within the current document, so if the target is another document or a location on the Web, the formatter replaces the screen text information with question marks, like this **??**. If you add the *hyperref* package, as described on page 288, you can create live links to other documents in typeset PDF documents.

In other words, the way a link appears online may not be appropriate in a typeset document without some modifications. Consider the statement

Click here to find more information about derivatives,

where the words *Click here* are the screen text for a link to the document's section 4, which has the marker *derive*. The link works well online, taking the reader right to the additional information in section 4. However, when the document is typeset, the formatter replaces the screen text for the link *(Click here)* with the number of the target *(4)*, so the printed sentence looks like this:

4 to find more information about derivatives,

which has no meaning.

If you have *SWP* or *SW*, you can use the Hypertext Link dialog box to specify what you want to appear in place of the screen text or graphic when you typeset. For example, you might specify that before the link (to its left) you want the words *See*

Section followed by a space. You might also specify that after the link (to its right) you want the text *of this document* preceded by a space. These specifications appear in the Hypertext Link dialog box as shown below. What you see in the document window is unchanged:

Click here to find more information about derivatives,

but when the document is typeset, the formatter replaces the link itself with the number of the section, 4, and places the number between the right and left text you specified, so that in print the sentence reads:

See Section 4 of this document to find more information about derivatives.

What you see in the typeset version of the document then points readers to the information appropriately.

In *SWP* and *SW*, you can specify the right and left text when you create the link or when you edit the link at a later time. The right and left text boxes don't appear in the dialog box in *SNB*.

▶ **To specify the typeset appearance of a link**

1. Double-click the link, or place the insertion point to its right and choose Properties to open the Hypertext Link dialog box.

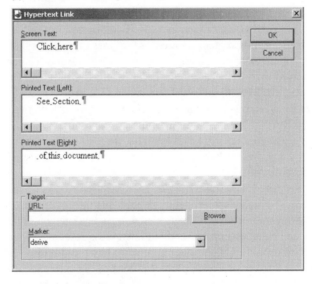

2. In the Printed Text (Left) area, enter the text and any necessary spaces that you want to appear to the left of the link itself.

3. In the Printed Text (Right) area, enter the text and any necessary spaces that you want to appear to the right of the link itself.

4. Choose OK.

Creating HTML Documents

Exporting your *SWP*, *SW*, or *SNB* documents as HTML files provides a way for others to view your documents on a variety of platforms via the Internet. The HTML export feature in Version 5 provides a fast way to create accurate HTML versions of your *SWP*, *SW*, or *SNB* documents. The files can be viewed with recent versions of the most popular browsers. Several export formats are available.

When you export documents as HTML files, the program uses default formats for graphics used to represent mathematics, plots, and graphics. The defaults are adequate for nearly all documents, and most users won't need to change them. However, you can specify different settings if necessary. By default, the filter converts any instances of mathematics and mathematics plots in your document to PNG graphics. Other graphics formats are available. Mathematics exported as a graphic isn't "live" and you can't perform computations with it. Alternatively, you can export mathematics as Mathematics Markup Language, or MathML. Note, however, that currently not all browsers support MathML. If you choose to export plots as graphics, the program applies a single format to all plots. If not exported as graphics, plots are not exported.

Also by default, the filter exports any graphics contained in your document as PNG files, saving them to a subdirectory of the directory containing the HTML file. Other graphics formats are available, but not all browsers support all graphics formats. You can use the default, or you can leave graphics in the original format, export them in the format you select, or not export them. Although you will probably specify a single format for all graphics, you can specify different formats for different types of graphics, such as raster or vector graphics, or for types of graphics that you group together in sets. A graphics file type can appear in more than one set. The program applies the selected export formats to the sets in the order in which the sets are listed in the **HTML Graphics Export Options** dialog; you can change the order. In addition to choosing the export formats, you can choose naming schemes for exported graphics.

When you export to HTML, the program automatically creates ALT text for each graphic in your document. By default, the ALT text is the full path name of the graphic. If you want more descriptive ALT text, change the name of the graphics frame as described on page 116.

Because HTML files are designed for use online instead of in print, the HTML filter doesn't create those document elements that are automatically generated when you typeset your document. Those elements, which include indexes, tables of contents, section and equation numbers, and internal cross-references, don't appear in the HTML file you export. The HTML filter completes any cross-references in the document with the key for the cross-reference target instead of the automatically generated number for the target. Therefore, what appears in the document window as

Section ref discussion discusses Eqn. (ref basic) and....

where ref discussion is a cross-reference to section 4 of your document and ref basic is a cross-reference to your first equation, will be typeset as

Section 4 discusses Eqn. (1) and....

But when you export the document to HTML, you will see

Section discussion discusses Eqn. (basic) and....

Choose key names with care if you use cross-references in documents that you plan to export to HTML. Note that cross-references in your document don't become links in the resulting HTML file. Therefore, when you plan to export a document as an HTML file, create jumps in the document using hypertext links instead of cross-references. You can choose to have any .tex extensions in hypertext links converted to .htm extensions when you export.

To make certain that the content of your document converts correctly to HTML, we urge you to develop the document without regard for its typeset form and appearance. By default, the filter creates a Cascading Style Sheet (.css file) that reflects the appearance of your document in the document window; that is, the .css file creates a document appearance similar to that created when you produce your document without typesetting.

You can insert HTML commands in fields in your document. The program ignores the commands, but the HTML filter interprets them when you export the document.

▶ To include HTML commands in your document

1. Place the insertion point where you want the commands to occur.

2. From the Insert menu, choose HTML Field.

3. Type a name for the object to identify it.

4. In the entry area, enter the HTML commands and choose OK.

▶ To export a document as an HTML file

1. Open the document.

2. Format the document so that its appearance in the document window is as you want it to appear online.

   If you change the tag properties as you format, you must save the .cst file in order for your changes to be reflected in the .css file that is generated when you export.

3. From the File menu, choose Export Document.

4. Select a location for the file.

5. In the box labeled File name, type a name for the document.

6. In the box labeled Save as type, specify the format you want and choose Save.

▶ To specify export settings for an HTML file

1. From the Tools menu, choose Export Settings.

2. Choose the HTML Document Export Options tab.

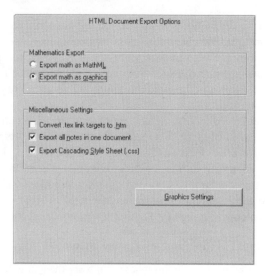

3. In the **Miscellaneous Settings** area,

- Check **Convert .tex link targets to .htm** to have any .tex extensions in hypertext links converted to .htm extensions when you export.
  Remember to export the linked .tex documents to HTML so the converted links work correctly.

- Check **Export all notes in one document** to have any popup notes contained in the document combined in a single file rather than separate files.
  This is the default setting. See Creating Popup Notes on page 291 for more information.

- Check **Export Cascading Style Sheet (.css)** to create a .css file that creates a document appearance in HTML similar to that in the document window.
  This is the default setting. The format of the document changes depending on the browser settings for the system on which the file is opened.

4. In the **Mathematics Export** area, select the format for exporting any mathematics in your document.

   Note The settings in the **Mathematics Export** area don't affect mathematics plots.

   a. Check **Export math as MathML** to convert all mathematics to MathML.
      or
      Check **Export math as graphics** to convert all mathematics to graphics.
      The default is to export mathematics as PNG graphics. The **Export as Picture** settings apply; see page 124 for more information.

   b. If you want to designate a different graphics format for exported mathematics,
      i Choose **Graphics Settings**.

      ii In the **Export of Mathematics as Graphics** area, specify the graphics format.

      iii If you want to designate a naming scheme for all exported mathematics, choose **Math File Naming Options**, select the scheme you want, and choose **OK**.

      iv Choose **OK**.

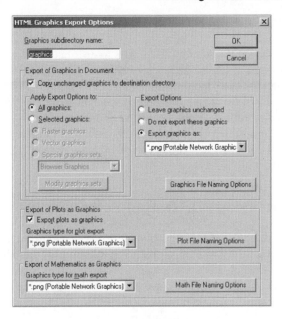

5. If you want to change the export settings for plots,

   a. Choose **Graphics Settings** from the **HTML Document Export Options** tab and check **Export plots as graphics**.

   b. Select a graphics format, designating a naming scheme if desired.

   c. Choose **OK**.

   Remember   If plots are not exported as graphics, they are not exported at all.

6. If you want to change the export settings for graphics, choose **Graphics Settings** from the **HTML Document Export Options** tab.

   a. If you want to change the directory in which to save the exported graphics and plots, enter the name of the subdirectory you want to use.
   If you leave the **Graphics subdirectory name** blank, all graphics and plots will be exported to a subdirectory of the directory containing the exported document.

   b. If you want the program to place in the target directory a copy of all graphics whose format is left unchanged during the HTML conversion, check **Copy unchanged graphics to destination directory**.
   Be sure to check this box if you expect to place your document on the Web.

   c. If you want to specify formats and naming schemes for graphics types and sets, change the export settings as described on page 33.

   d. When all selections are complete, choose **OK**.

7. Choose **OK**.

Creating PDF Documents

In addition to creating HTML files to distribute your work to a wide audience, you can use PDFLATEX to create typeset PDF files from your *SWP* and *SW* documents. Typeset PDF files can support some features that typeset DVI files can't. In particular, if you add the *hyperref* package to your document, the PDF compilation process changes any cross-references in the document to hypertext links. If the typesetting specifications call for a table of contents, the process creates a table of contents linked to the body of the document. Chapter 7 "Previewing and Printing" discusses both LATEX and PDFLATEX typesetting in detail.

Specifying PDF Output Settings

Before you typeset your document, you can choose an output option to indicate whether you want DVI or PDF output. The system uses the option to prepare the file and any mathematics, plots, and graphics it contains for DVI or PDF output. The default is DVI output. Regardless of the setting, however, the system produces successful DVI or PDF files when you typeset your document. If you're creating a PDF file and you change the default to PDF output, the program creates the PDF file and preserves any temporary files created during the typesetting process. If you don't change the default to PDF output, the program still creates a PDF file, but it doesn't preserve the temporary files. For most users, this isn't a consideration, but if you're creating a PDF file of a master document and subdocuments, you must specify PDF output settings for the master document, then reopen and save each subdocument before you typeset.

▶ **To select options for typesetting**

1. From the Typeset menu, choose Output Choice.

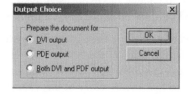

2. Click the option you want and choose OK.

The system has default settings for typesetting PDF files containing plots and graphics. The defaults are adequate for nearly all documents, and most users won't need to change them. However, you can specify different settings if necessary. See Chapter 7 "Previewing and Printing" for details.

Using the Hyperref Package

The *hyperref* package extends the options for ordinary cross-references, changing them to active links in the PDF file and enabling the placement of an automatic identifier, such as *section, page,* or *chapter,* before the reference. When you create the typeset

PDF file from your document, the cross-reference is changed to a link preceded by the identifier. The package also extends the hypertext possibilities of your .tex document, automatically creating bookmarks, linked headings, and thumbnails. If the typesetting specifications for your document include a table of contents, typesetting the document with PDFLATEX produces a table of contents linked to the body of the document. The package isn't supported by Style Editor styles or by the TrueTEX formatter.

When you add the *hyperref* package to your document, move it to the bottom of the list of packages in the **Packages in Use** list. See Chapter 8 "Formatting Documents" for more information about adding a package to your document.

Extensive information about the hyperref package and about the process of converting .tex files to PDF files appears in the package documentation. See also *Typesetting Documents in Scientific WorkPlace and Scientific Word*.

▶ **To create a hypertext reference**

1. Add the *hyperref* package to your document, following the instructions on page 226.

2. Place the insertion point where you want the reference to occur, then from the **Insert** menu, choose **Typeset Object**.

3. Choose **Hypertext Reference** to open the dialog box shown on the next page.

4. In the **Text** box, enter the link as you want it to appear online in the document window and when you print, either with or without typesetting:

   • If you want the link to appear as text, type the text.

   • If you want the link to appear as a graphic or you want to include a graphic with the text, import the graphic.

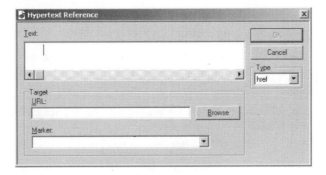

5. In the **Type** area, select the type of reference you want.

   The href option is appropriate in most cases. Two other options—hyperref and hyperlink—are available; see the package documentation for more information.

6. If you want to create a link to a target inside the current document, enter the marker for the target.

7. If you want to create a link to a target outside the current document, enter the address of the target in the **URL** box and, if necessary, the **Marker** box.

8. Choose **OK**.

Hypertext targets, like other markers, indicate a location in your document. Ordinarily, they aren't intended to appear in print. However, the *hyperref* package provides the option to identify the target with text. If you specify text, it appears both in the document window and in print, whether you typeset your document or not. If you don't specify text, the target behaves like other markers in the program.

▶ **To create a hypertext target**

1. Place the insertion point where you want the link to occur and, from the Insert menu, choose Typeset Object and then choose Hypertext Target.

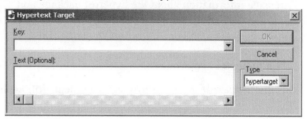

2. In the Type area, select the type of reference you want.

   In most cases, the hypertarget option is appropriate. Another option, hyperdef, is also available. Refer to the package documentation for information about these options.

3. In the Key box, enter the key for the target.

4. If you want the target to appear on screen as text rather than as a shaded box, enter the text information in the Text area.

5. Choose OK.

▶ **To create a cross-reference in a hyperref document**

1. Place the insertion point where you want the link to occur.

2. On the Typeset Object toolbar, click [image] or, from the Insert menu, choose Typeset Object and then choose Cross Reference to open an expanded Cross Reference dialog box:

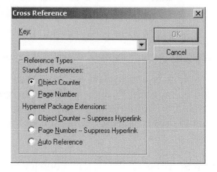

3. Enter the key of the marked item.

4. Select the type of reference you want to create:

- Check one of the **Standard References** to create a cross-reference to a numbered item or to a page in the current document.
  or

- Check **Object Counter – Suppress Hyperlink** or **Page Number – Suppress Hyperlink** to suppress hyperlinks in PDF files.
  or

- If you want to expand the link with an automatic identifier, such as *section, page,* or *chapter,* before the reference, check **Auto Reference**.

Refer to the package documentation for information about these options. Remember to check the PDF document carefully to make sure the automatically generated information is appropriate.

5. Choose **OK**.

Using .tex and .rap Documents Online

In addition to creating HTML and PDF files for a wide audience, you can also use your *SWP, SW,* or *SNB* (.tex or .rap) documents online. When you place a .tex or .rap document on the Web, nothing in the document changes. Any graphics in the document appear online unchanged, and LaTeX elements appear online as they do in the document window. The file is available as a read-only document. Any mathematics in the document is "live," so that if the .tex or .rap document is saved locally on a system on which *SWP* or *SNB* is installed, you can compute with the mathematics.

You can enhance online .tex or .rap documents by placing information in popup notes that are activated by the reader. The program displays the information only when the reader opens the notes. Also, instead of creating a single, lengthy online document, you can structure your information as a series of short, *related documents* that are linked together in the sequence you think most appropriate for your readers.

Creating Popup Notes

Intended for use in read-only online documents, popup notes can provide supplementary material such as additional explanations, solutions to quiz questions, hints for students, and other information. Popup notes can contain text, graphics, and mathematics. The availability of popup notes depends on the shell you use to create your document.

The information in popup notes appears on screen only when the note is activated. Otherwise, the note appears in the document as a predefined icon or as text, according to your specifications. In an online document containing mathematics problems, for example, you may want to provide hints to help students solve the problems. You can place the hint for each problem in a popup note signaled by an icon, as in this example:

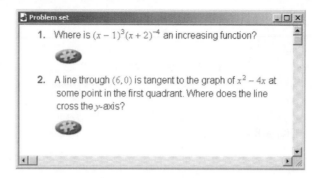

The hint itself doesn't appear until the student clicks the icon to activate the note, when the program displays it in a **Note** box, something like this:

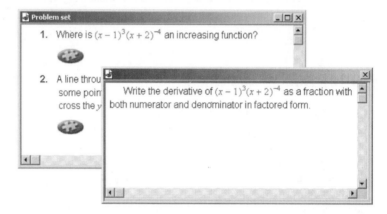

If you typeset your document in *SWP* or *SW*, the information contained in popup notes appears as margin notes, according to the typesetting specifications. No reference to the notes appears in the text. If you produce your document without typesetting it or in *SNB*, popup notes appear in the text according to the print options. If you export your document as HTML, popup notes appear in the HTML document as they do in the document window. The information in the notes is saved in separate documents or collected in a single document, depending on the export settings for HTML documents. See page 285.

▶ **To enter a popup note**

1. On the Field toolbar, click the Note button ▤ or, from the **Insert** menu, choose Note.

2. Choose the type of popup note you want to enter.

    The available options are determined by the shell.

3. In the entry area at the top of the dialog box, enter and format the note contents.

    Notes can contain text, graphics, and mathematics.

4. In the **Screen Appearance** area, specify how you want the note to appear online.

The note appears as a predefined icon unless you change its screen appearance.

- If you want the note to appear as text or as text and mathematics, choose **Show Text** and enter the information you want.

- If you want the note to appear as a graphic or you want to include a graphic with the text:

  i Make sure you have chosen **Show Text**.

  ii On the Editing toolbar, click or, from the **File** menu, choose **Import Picture**, and select the graphic you want.

  iii Edit the graphic properties as necessary.

- If you want to return to the predefined icon, choose **Show Icon**.

5. Choose **OK**.

▶ **To activate a popup note**

- Hold down the CTRL key and click the note.
  or

- Select the note and, from the **Tools** menu, choose **Action**.
  or

- In a document saved as read-only, click the note.

Creating Related Documents

Lengthy online documents, such as books, are easier to view when you divide them into a series of short *related* documents, each of which corresponds to a single section or subsection, fits approximately on a single screen, and can be read with a minimum of scrolling. You can guide readers through related documents in the sequence you think best by creating links to other documents in the series. Your readers can then jump from one short, online document to the next rather than scrolling through a single large document. You can also link related documents to information that they are likely to share, such as the publisher and copyright information or the index and bibliography.

For example, you can create an online book as a series of short documents beginning with a *top* document containing general information about the book and a link to the *contents* specifying the sequence of the documents. The text of a *parent* document might specify the sequence of all sections in a given chapter from the *beginning document* to the *end document*. Also, you might link all the related documents to the same appendixes.

The online Help contains a version of *Getting Started with Scientific WorkPlace, Scientific Word, and Scientific Notebook* created as a series of related documents. To read sequentially through the entire online book, begin with the top document, moving through the chapters and sections in sequence by clicking the Next Document button, and returning to previous sections as necessary with the Previous Document button.

This feature is very useful for creating presentations and slide shows. You can create a presentation as a series of short documents, each one a "slide" and each containing a link to the next slide in the series. You can move smoothly through your presentation by pressing the Next button to jump from slide to slide, as described on page 295.

In each related document, you can create links for these relations:

Relation	Links to
Author	Information about the author
Beginning Document	The first document in the current sequence
Bibliography	The bibliography for the document
Contents	The table of contents containing the document
Copyright	The copyright information for the document
Disclaimer	Information related to any associated disclaimers
Editor	Information about the editor
End Document	The last document in the current sequence
Glossary	The glossary for the document
Index	The index for the document
Next Document	The next document in the current sequence
Parent Document	The document one level higher than the current document
Previous Document	The previous document in the current sequence
Publisher	Information about the publisher
Top Document	The root document for the entire document structure
Trademark	Trademark information

Once links have been defined for a group of related documents, you can jump from document to document in the series with the commands on the Go Links menu and the buttons on the Link toolbar.

▶ **To create a link to a related document**

1. From the File menu, choose Document Info and then choose the Links tab shown on the next page.

2. In the Relation box, select the relation for which you want to specify a link.

3. In the File Selection box, type the address of the target: a document, an Internet location, or a marker in a document or Internet location.

4. Choose Link.

5. Repeat steps 2–4 for all other relations you want to specify.

6. Choose OK.

   The program establishes the links, which become active on the Links toolbar and the Go Links menu.

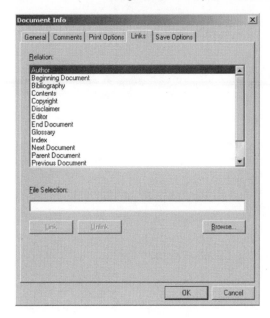

To remove a link to a related document

1. From the File menu, choose Document Info and then choose the Links tab.

2. In the Relation box, select the relation whose link you want to remove.

3. Choose Unlink.

4. Repeat steps 2–3 for all other links you want to remove and then choose OK.

To jump to a related document

- Click the Link toolbar button for the related document you want:

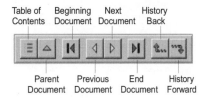

or

- From the Go menu, choose Links, and then choose the item for the related document you want.

Relations that have been defined for the document are active in the Links menu and on the Links toolbar. Relations that haven't been defined are dimmed.

11 Managing Documents

You can use document management techniques to simplify working with *SWP*, *SW*, and *SNB* documents and their associated files. For each document file, the program maintains basic information and stores comments and other data outside the body of the document.

With the Document Manager, you can handle subdocuments and graphics correctly when you copy, delete, or rename a document. Also, the Document Manager helps you clean up the auxiliary files generated by the typesetting process. Perhaps most importantly, the Document Manager simplifies working with files you send or receive by email or on diskette.

Maintaining Document Information

For each document you create, the program maintains a body of information called the Document Info. The Document Info contains general information about your document, including when it was created, how it is stored, and how it looks when you print it without typesetting. The **Document Info** dialog box contains these tab sheets:

- The **General** tab sheet contains the file name and directory location. It stores the date the document was created (if the document originated as an *SWP*, *SW*, or *SNB* document) and the date of the most recent revision. Once you've performed a spelling check on the document, the tab sheet stores the specified language for the document. If the document was created with the **New** command, the tab sheet stores the name of the document shell. You can use the tab sheet to specify the text that appears on the title bar of the document window when the document is open. If you don't specify a title, the program displays the file name. Note that specifying a title for the title bar doesn't change the file name.

- The **Comments** tab sheet stores notes about the document that you may want to preserve. You can have the notes appear at the beginning of the LaTeX document and in the tab sheet. Comments aren't printed, but you can use Document Info to view them.

- The **Print Options** tab sheet contains the settings used when you print your document without typesetting it. These settings govern the appearance of invisibles, helper lines, input boxes, index entries, markers, and gray boxes. If you have a color printer, these settings enable color printing of lines, text, and backgrounds. The tab sheet also contains a setting for the zoom factor used to scale output printed without typesetting, independent of the zoom factor used in the document window. Chapter 7 "Previewing and Printing" contains more information about the print options.

- The **Links** tab sheet contains links, if any, to related documents. The links you establish on this tab sheet are reflected in active buttons on the Link toolbar and in active commands on the Go Links menu. See Chapter 10 "Creating Documents for Online Use" for more information about related documents.

- The Save Options tab sheet contains the settings for graphics and view information to be saved with the document and for saving the document for quick loading. See Chapter 2 "Creating Documents" for more information.

▶ **To view or change the Document Info**

1. From the File menu, choose Document Info.

2. Choose the tab sheet you want.

3. Enter the information or settings you want in the tab sheet and then choose OK.

▶ **To add notes about a document in the Document Info**

1. From the File menu, choose Document Info.

2. Choose the Comments tab sheet.

3. In the Comments area, enter comments that you want to appear in the document preamble.

4. In the Description area, enter other comments that you want save with the document.

5. Choose OK.

You can enter comments in the body of your document with the Comment (TeX field) fragment. When you typeset your document, comments entered this way are ignored. When you produce your document without typesetting it, the comments appear in print according to the print option settings. See Chapter 7 "Previewing and Printing" for more information about the print options.

▶ **To change the text on the title bar**

1. From the File menu, choose Document Info.

2. Choose the General tab sheet.

3. In the Title area, type the text you want to appear on the title bar when the document is open.

   The title you specify doesn't affect the file name of the document.

4. Choose OK.

Using the Document Manager

In addition to the document file itself, your document is associated with many other files, such as backup files, graphics files, and quick-load files. In *SWP* and *SW*, the files may also contain subdocuments or typesetting information, or they may be files such as index files, bibliography files, or tables of contents that are generated when the document is typeset. *Generated files* have the same name as your document but a different file extension. The program retains some of these generated files for use the next time you typeset the document and retains others for use in maintaining information about program operation or in diagnosing problems. The list that follows describes the types of files most commonly used by the program and associated with your document.

Extension	File Type
.aaa....aaz	Temporary file format of an open file
.aut	Quick-load backup file
.aux*	File generated by LaTeX for cross-references, etc.
.bak	Backup of a .tex file
.bbl*	Bibliography generated by BIBTeX
.bib*	BIBTeX database file
.blg*	Report file generated by BIBTeX
.cdx	Quick-load document file
.dvi*	Device-independent file generated by LaTeX; required to typeset
.idx*	Index file created by LaTeX
.ind*	Index file created by MakeIndex
.lof*	List of figures generated by LaTeX
.log*	Report file generated by LaTeX
.lot*	List of tables generated by LaTeX
.tex	*SWP, SW,* or *SNB* document, TeX or LaTeX file
.toc*	Table of contents generated by LaTeX

* not used in *SNB*

In addition, you may save or export your document to create files with extensions including .qiz, .rap, .rtf, .pdf, and .htm. These other types of files are also commonly used by the program, but they aren't associated with a specific document:

Extension	File Type
.bst*	BIBTeX style file
.cfg	LaTeX package configuration file
.clo*	LaTeX document class options file
.cls*	LaTeX document class file
.cst	File controlling the screen appearance and nontypeset print appearance of a document
.dtx*	Precompiled documentation for an .sty file
.fmt*	TeX format file
.frg	Fragment file
.hlp	Online help file for the Document Manager
.ini	Initial settings file
.ins	Initial settings file; LaTeX install file
.lic	License file
.mu	MuPAD file
.reg	Registry file.
.shl	Document shell file
.sty*	LaTeX typesetting specifications
.tfm*	TeX font metric file
.ttf	True Type font file

* not used in *SNB*

Depending on the file type, the program may not store the associated files in the same directory that holds the document file.

The files associated with your document must be treated correctly when you perform operations such as copying, renaming, or deleting a document, or sending it to another location. The Document Manager simplifies this process. With the Document Manager, you can correctly copy and rename documents and you can delete those documents you no longer need, including documents that have generated files, subdocuments, and references to graphics files. You can also use the Document Manager to *wrap* documents and their associated files so they can be sent to another location by email or on diskette, and to *unwrap* documents that have been wrapped. To ensure that all files associated with your *SWP, SW,* and *SNB* documents are treated correctly, use the Document Manager to perform these operations:

Operation	Effect
Copy	Copy a document and all its associated files to a new location
Delete	Delete a document and all associated auxiliary, graphic, and subdocument files
Rename	Rename a document, subdocument, or graphics file and correct all references to the renamed file
Cleanup	Delete auxiliary and generated files that are no longer needed
Wrap	Gather in a single text file all files that accompany a document file
Unwrap	Break a wrapped file into separate files again
View	Display the first part of the selected file in ASCII form

▶ **To start the Document Manager**

- From outside the program:

  a. From the Windows **Start** menu, choose **Programs**.
  b. Choose the *SWP, SW,* or *SNB* submenu.
  c. Choose the Document Manager to open the **Document Manager** window.

  or

- From inside the program, choose **Document Manager** from the **Tools** menu to open the **Document Manager** window.

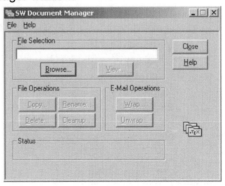

▶ **To specify a document for a Document Manager operation**

- In the File Selection box, enter the complete path name (including the drive, directory, and name) of the document file.
  or

- Choose Browse to display the Open dialog box, then select the drive, directory, and name of the document file.

▶ **To choose a Document Manager operation**

- Click the button for the operation you want.
  or

- Press TAB to select the button for the file or email operation you want and then press ENTER or the spacebar to open the associated dialog box.

Remember The Document Manager dialog box has tab sheets. When you choose OK to accept the settings in any tab sheet, you accept the settings in *all* tab sheets in the dialog box. Similarly, when you choose Cancel to discard the settings in any tab sheet, you discard the settings in *all* tab sheets in the dialog box.

The Document Manager focuses on *SWP, SW,* or *SNB* files and their current or destination location. When you wrap or unwrap a document, the tab sheets also reflect the location of the files containing the associated typesetting specifications.

Using Directory and File Lists

Document manager operations affect the document and subdocument files, any associated graphics, and, in *SWP* and *SW,* the typesetting specification files. The tab sheets for each Document Manager operation list the files associated with the document you select. Each tab sheet is organized in two panels, as this example shows:

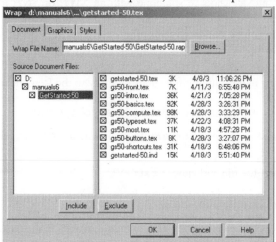

One panel indicates the drive and directory location of the files associated with the specified document and needed for the selected operation; the other indicates the files themselves. Subdirectories are indicated with indention. When you select a directory from

the panel on the left, the panel on the right lists any files in that directory that are associated with the specified document. The file names are listed along with their size, date,
and time of the last modification. The panels on the Document, Graphics, and Style
tab sheets operate the same way for all Document Manager operations.

Including and Excluding Files

By default, all possible files associated with the selected document are included in each
Document Manager operation, as shown by the check mark in the box next to the file
and directory names. The check boxes in the file panel reflect the selection status of the
files themselves. The check boxes in the directory panel reflect the selection status of all
the files in the directory. A checked box next to a directory name indicates that all files
in the directory will be included in the operation. A partially checked box, used only in
the directory panel, indicates that some of the files in the directory and its subdirectories
will be included. An unchecked box indicates that none of the files in the directory will
be included; that is, they will all be excluded from the operation.

Description		Effect on Directory	Effect on File
☒	Checked	All files in the directory are included in the operation	File is included in the operation
☒	Partially checked	Some but not all files in subdirectories are included in the operation	Not used
☐	Unchecked	No files in the directory are included in the operation	File is excluded from the operation

You may want to exclude certain files from Document Manager operations, especially if you're wrapping files to send to someone who also has an *SWP, SW,* or *SNB*
installation. For example, snapshots of plots can be very large. If you're sending a file
containing snapshots to someone with an *SWP* or *SNB* installation, the plots can be
recreated in that installation. Similarly, if you're working in *SWP* or *SW,* you may
want to exclude standard typesetting specifications.

After you've selected a document and chosen a Document Manager operation, you
can exclude files on a file-by-file basis or you can exclude all files in a selected directory.
Including and excluding files doesn't apply to the Rename operation.

▶ **To exclude a file from a Document Manager operation**

- Uncheck the check box next to the file name in the panel on the right.
  or

- Select the file and choose Exclude.

▶ **To exclude multiple files at once**

- Uncheck the check box next to the file names in the panel on the right.
  or

- Hold down the CTRL key while you select multiple files, and then choose Exclude.

or

- Select the first file in a range, press SHIFT and select the last file in the range, and then choose Exclude.

▶ To exclude all files in a directory

- Uncheck the check box next to the directory name in the panel on the left.
  or
- Select the directory and choose Exclude.

▶ To include all the files in a directory

- Check the check box next to the directory name in the panel on the left.
  or
- Select the directory and choose Include.

Working with Graphics Files

The dialog box associated with the Copy, Delete, Wrap, and Unwrap operations has a Graphics tab sheet, organized just like the Document tab sheet, that lists the directories and files of graphics associated with the document file. You can exclude them just as you exclude document files.

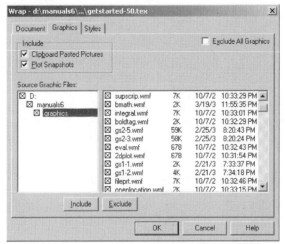

Note that clipboard pasted pictures that haven't been given a name and plot snapshots are stored in files with names that are meaningful only to the program. These file names are *not* displayed in the file list. You can exclude them from a Document Manager operation by clearing the check boxes (or include them by checking the boxes) next to Clipboard Pasted Pictures and Plot Snapshots. The box labeled Exclude All Graphics overrides any other settings on the Graphics tab sheet and disables all the controls. If the box is checked, no graphics files are included in the operation.

Working with Typesetting Specification Files

The dialog box associated with the Wrap and Unwrap operations has a Styles tab sheet. Organized just like the Document and Graphics tab sheets, the Styles tab sheet lists the directories and files containing the typesetting specifications necessary to compile the document for typesetting. The box labeled **Exclude All Style Files** overrides any other settings on the tab sheet and disables all the controls. If the box is checked, no typesetting specification files are included in the operation.

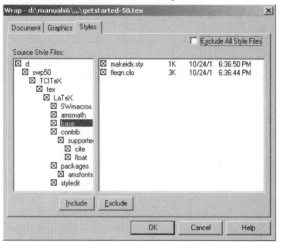

Changing Destination Directories

When you copy or unwrap a document, you can choose the destination of the document and its associated files. The Document Manager then restructures the destination directories of all associated files so that all graphic and subdocument files are located in the same directory as the document or in subdirectories within that directory. If you designate a new directory, the Document Manager will create it when you choose **OK** to begin the copy or unwrap operation.

Important   The Document Manager doesn't actually create directories or copy files until you choose **OK** to begin the copy or unwrap operation.

▶ **To change a file or directory destination**

1. From the files panel in the **Copy** or **Unwrap** dialog box, select the file or directory for which you want to change the destination.

2. Choose **Change Destination**.

   The program opens the **Move Files** or **Move Directory** dialog box and displays the default file destination in the **Folders** box.

3. If you want to choose an existing directory as the destination, double-click its name in the directory list, or select the name and choose OK.

4. If you want to create a new directory as the destination:

   a. Select an existing directory to contain the new directory and choose Create.
   b. Enter a new name for the directory and choose OK.
   c. Select the new directory and choose OK.

   The tab reflects the directory you select as the destination for the selected file or directory.

Copying Documents

Use the Document Manager to copy a document and all its associated files to a new location. You can't rename a document with the Copy operation. If you need to specify new names for files, use the Rename operation.

▶ **To copy a document**

1. Start the Document Manager.

2. In the File Selection box, select the document you want to copy.

   The document file name must have a .tex extension.

3. Choose Copy.

4. In the Copy To dialog box, select the drive and the directory to which you want to copy the document, creating a new directory if necessary.

   If you're working on a network, you may need to connect to a different network directory.

5. In the Copy dialog box, exclude any associated document and graphics files you don't want to copy.

6. If you want to change the destination of any associated files, choose Change Destination and select or create a new location.

7. In the Copy dialog box, choose OK to begin the operation.

8. If the destination directory contains a file of the same name as one of the files being copied, the program asks if you want to overwrite it.
   - Choose Yes to overwrite the file.
   - Choose Yes to All to overwrite all files that have duplicate names.
   - Choose Skip to exclude the file from the operation.
   - Choose Cancel to return to the Copy dialog box.

   A message box indicates when the operation is complete.

9. Choose OK and choose Close to leave the Document Manager.

Deleting Documents

When you no longer need a document, you can delete it. Because your documents can contain subdocuments and references to graphics files, you should use the Document Manager to delete a document and all associated files.

▶ **To delete a document and its associated files**

1. Start the Document Manager.

2. In the File Selection box, select the document you want to delete.

3. Choose Delete.

   The Document Manager opens the Delete dialog box and selects for deletion the document file (.tex) and all associated files with these extensions: .aux, .bak, .bbl, .blg, .cdx, .dvi, .idx, .lof, .log, .lot, and .toc.

4. From the Document and Graphics tab sheets, exclude any files that you don't want to delete.

5. Choose OK to delete the document and the associated files.

6. When the operation is complete, choose OK and then choose Close to leave the Document Manager.

Renaming Files

Use the Rename operation to change the name of a file. Use the Copy operation to rename directories. When you rename a file with the Document Manager, the program corrects all references to that file that occur in associated files.

▶ **To rename a file**

1. Start the Document Manager.

2. In the File Selection box, select the document that you want to rename.

   The document file name must have a .tex extension.

3. Choose Rename to open the Rename dialog box shown on the next page.

4. Select the file you want to rename and choose Rename.

5. In the Rename File dialog box, specify a different file name for the selected file and choose OK.

   In the file section of the Rename dialog box, the original name is shown in parentheses next to the renamed file, like this:

newname.tex(oldname.tex)   2K   3/15/5

6. Choose OK and choose Close to leave the Document Manager.

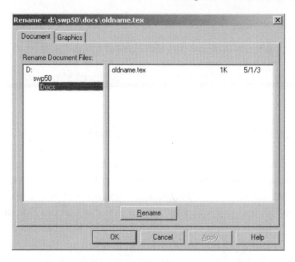

Cleaning Up Generated Files

You can delete files generated for your document when you no longer need them. Generated files have the same name as the document file but different file extensions.

▶ **To clean up generated files**

1. Start the Document Manager.

2. In the File Selection box, select the document you want to clean up.

3. Choose Cleanup.

   The program opens the Cleanup dialog box and selects for deletion all associated files with these extensions: .aux, .bak, .bbl, .blg, .cdx, .dvi, .idx, .lof, .log, .lot, and .toc.

4. Exclude any files that you don't want to delete and choose OK.

5. When the program indicates that the operation is complete, choose OK and then choose Close to leave the Document Manager.

Viewing the ASCII Form of a File

You can use the Document Manager to view the ASCII form of the first part of a document.

▶ **To view the ASCII form of a document**

1. Start the Document Manager.

2. In the File Selection box, type the name of the file.

3. Choose **View**.

The program displays the ASCII form of the first part of the file in a dialog box.

4. Choose **Close** twice to leave the Document Manager.

Wrapping and Unwrapping Documents

When you need to send a document to another location by email or on diskette, *wrap* the document; that is, gather together in a single text file the document file and all the files that must accompany it. The person who receives your file can *unwrap* it; that is, break the text file into separate files again. You can use the Document Manager to wrap and unwrap files.

You can wrap a document with the Document Manager or with the **Save As** or **Export Document** commands on the **File** menu. Using the Document Manager offers greater control and more features. When you work from the **Save As** or **Export Document** commands, the style and typesetting specification files are excluded from the wrapping operation. The options to exclude graphics and plot snapshots are not available, nor are master documents wrapped with their subdocuments.

The **Send** command on the **File** menu also automatically wraps documents. Wrapped documents have the same name as the original document but a file extension of .rap. Documents that have been saved with the Portable LATEX filter will be wrapped as Portable LATEX files. Other types of files can't be wrapped.

Documents that have been wrapped by this or earlier versions of the program can be unwrapped with the Document Manager or with the **Open** command on the **File** menu. If you need to unwrap a document, choose the format for the system on which the file was wrapped.

Use this format	To unwrap a file that was created by
Wrap (*.rap)	*SNB* or Version 3 or later of *SW* or *SWP*
Wrap created by SW/SWP 2.5 (*.msg)	Earlier versions of *SW* or *SWP*

If the program isn't available, documents can be unwrapped using a text editor and compiled on a system that runs LATEX.

▶ **To wrap a document with the Document Manager**

1. Start the Document Manager.

2. In the **File Selection** box, select the document you want to wrap.

3. Choose **Wrap**.

The Document Manager opens the **Wrap** dialog box; displays a default name for the wrapped document; and selects all associated files, graphics, and typesetting specification files to be wrapped with the document.

4. If you want to change the name of the wrapped file, enter the name you want.

5. If you want to change the type of wrapped file:

   a. Choose the **Browse** button next to the box labeled **Wrap File Name**.

   b. In the box labeled **Save as type**, choose the type of wrap file appropriate for the *SWP*, *SW*, or *SNB* system on which the document will be unwrapped.

   c. Choose **Save**.

6. Exclude any files you don't want to wrap with the document.

Remember that snapshots of plots can be very large. If you're sending your document to someone who has *SWP* or *SNB*, you don't need to include the snapshots, because they can be recreated when the document is opened on the other system. Similarly, you may want to exclude standard typesetting specifications if you're sending your document to someone who has *SWP* or *SW*.

7. Choose **OK**.

The program creates a file that contains your document, all selected associated files, and instructions for using a text editor to recreate the original files, in case the recipient doesn't have *SWP*, *SW*, or *SNB*. The wrapped file has the name you specified and the extension for the type of wrapped file you selected.

8. When the program indicates that the operation is complete, choose **OK** and then choose **Close** to leave the Document Manager.

If you export a document as a wrapped file, the program copies the current document to a new .rap file, but doesn't open the new file. The original file remains open so you can continue working in it. If you save a document as a wrapped file, the program saves the current document as a .rap file and leaves it open. The original document is closed.

▶ **To wrap a document from the File menu**

1. From the **File** menu, choose **Save As**.

2. In the box labeled **Save as type**, select **Wrap (*.rap)**.

3. Choose **Save**.

or

1. From the **File** menu, choose **Export Document**.

2. In the box labeled **Save as type**, select **Wrap (*.rap)**.

3. Choose **Save**.

Remember that certain associated files (style and typesetting specifications, graphics, and subdocuments) are excluded from the wrapping operation when you use **Save As** or **Export Document**.

▶ **To unwrap a document with the Document Manager**

1. Start the Document Manager.

2. In the File Selection box, select the file you want to unwrap.

3. Choose Unwrap.

4. Make any necessary changes to the destination directories.

5. Exclude any files you don't want to unwrap. By default, the program excludes the typesetting specifications files listed on the Styles tab sheet.

6. Choose OK.

   The program unwraps the document, automatically placing each file in the correct directory.

7. When the program indicates that the operation is complete, choose OK and then choose Close to leave the Document Manager.

▶ **To unwrap a document from the File menu**

1. On the Standard toolbar, click the Open button 📂 or, from the File menu, choose Open.

2. Select the wrapped file and choose Open.

   The program unwraps the file, automatically placing the associated files in the correct directories.

▶ **To unwrap a document with an ASCII editor**

1. Open the wrapped file with the editor.

2. Follow the instructions contained in the file header.

Sending Documents by Email

You can send a .tex document created with the program to another location using your email program. If your mail program supports the MAPI protocol, as do Microsoft Mail and Microsoft Internet Mail, you can send your document from *SWP, SW,* or *SNB* with the Send command on the File menu.

The document must be wrapped before it is sent to include the document itself and any associated files, such as graphics, that it requires. If you use the Send command, the program wraps the file automatically. It creates a file with an extension of .rap, and opens a new mail message with the file as an attachment. If you don't use the Send command to email your document, you must wrap the document yourself before you send it by email.

The person who receives the document must unwrap the file before it can be read in *SWP, SW,* or *SNB.* See Wrapping and Unwrapping Documents earlier in this chapter.

Important   Be sure to choose the wrapped file format appropriate for the system on which the file will be unwrapped.

▶ To send a document by email from inside the program

1. Open the document you want to send.

2. From the File menu, choose Send.

   The program wraps the document if it needs to and creates a file with an extension of .rap. If the document has no associated files, the program uses the .tex file.

3. When the mail dialog box opens, complete the mail form according to the instructions for your mail program.

   The wrapped document appears as an attachment to your message.

12 Customizing the Program

SWP, SW, and SNB are easy to use because of their straightforward approach to creating documents. They are even more convenient when you customize the program to suit the way you work. This chapter explains how to customize the program window and toolbars, the individual document windows, and the function key assignments. It also explains how to use the commands on the Tools menu to set the defaults for general program operations, for computations, and for document exports. It outlines the default options available for typesetting in SWP and SW and for computation in SWP and SNB. Many of your customized settings can be saved and restored as you need them.

Customizing the Program Window

In addition to varying the size of the program window, you can choose which toolbars and symbol panels appear in the window and where in the window they appear. You can customize the symbol panels and the symbol cache.

Sizing the Program Window

You can size the program window to your liking with standard Windows techniques.

▶ **To change the size of the program window**

- Use the Maximize ⬜ or Minimize ▬ button on the right end of the title bar for the program window.
  or

- Use the Maximize or Minimize commands in the Control box on the left end of the title bar.
  or

- Double-click the title bar to enlarge the program window to fill the screen.
  or

- Use the mouse to drag the edges of the window to the size you want.

▶ **To restore the program window to its previous size and location**

- On the title bar for the program window, click the Restore button ⧉ .
  or

- Double-click the title bar for the program window.
  or

- From the Control box on the title bar, choose Restore.

Using the Toolbars

To customize your workplace, you can display, hide, or reshape any toolbar; move it to a new location; *dock* it in a permanent position around the edges of the program window; or let it *float* anywhere on the screen, even outside the program window. The program retains the toolbar arrangement from session to session. If you hide and later display a toolbar, it will appear in its most recent location and shape.

▶ **To display or hide the toolbars**

1. From the View menu, choose Toolbars.

2. In the Toolbars dialog box, check the name of each toolbar you want to display and uncheck the name of each toolbar you want to hide.

3. Choose Close.

▶ **To return to the original toolbar display**

1. From the View menu, choose Toolbars.

2. Choose Reset and then choose Close.

▶ **To dock a toolbar in the program window**

1. Place the mouse pointer anywhere in the gray area surrounding the toolbar buttons.

2. Drag the toolbar to a new location in the gray area at the top, bottom, or sides of the program window.

   The program drags a light outline of the toolbar to the new location. When the outline reaches a possible docking location, it snaps into place. Toolbars containing lists, such as the Tag toolbar, can be docked only on the top or bottom of the program window.

▶ **To float a toolbar on the screen**

1. Place the mouse pointer anywhere in the gray area surrounding the toolbar buttons.

2. Drag the toolbar to a new location in the entry area of the program window or outside the program window.

   The program drags a heavy outline of the toolbar to the new location and displays the toolbar with a title bar.

▶ **To reshape a toolbar**

- Float the toolbar on the screen, and then drag any side of the toolbar to reshape it.

▶ **To close a floating toolbar**

- In the upper-right corner of the toolbar, click the Close button ☒ .

You can change the size of the toolbar buttons and turn off and on the display of the tooltips that describe each button's function. The tooltips for the symbol panels display the LaTeX name of each character or symbol; the Status bar at the bottom of the program window displays a fuller description.

The Status bar also displays messages concerning the current command or operation. It displays the names of graphics and hypertext targets and information about Internet activity and calculations. You can toggle on and off the display of the Status bar.

▶ **To display large buttons on the toolbars**

1. From the View menu, choose Toolbars.

2. Check Large Buttons and choose Close.

▶ **To toggle the display of tooltips on and off**

1. From the View menu, choose Toolbars.

2. Check or uncheck Show ToolTips and choose Close.

▶ **To display a tooltip**

- When the display of tooltips is turned on, hold the mouse pointer over a toolbar button for several seconds until the tooltip appears.

▶ **To display or hide the Status bar**

- From the View menu, check or uncheck Status Bar.

Displaying and Modifying the Symbol Panels

The symbol panels are available from the Symbol Panels toolbar. For faster access to symbols and characters, you can leave the panels open and float them anywhere you want. As with toolbars, the program retains the way you arrange the panels from session to session.

You can reorder the symbols on the panels and remove from the panels any character that you don't want. You can reset the panels to the full complement of characters at any time.

▶ **To display a symbol panel**

- On the Symbol Panels toolbar, click the button for the symbol panel you want.

▶ **To float an open symbol panel on the screen**

1. Place the mouse pointer on the title bar of the symbol panel.

2. Drag the panel to a new location on the screen.

▶ **To close a symbol panel**

- In the upper-right corner of the symbol panel, click the Close button ☒ .
  or

- On the Symbol Panels toolbar, click the button for the open symbol panel.

▶ **To move a symbol within a panel**

- Hold down the SHIFT key, select the symbol, and drag it to a new location on the panel.

▶ **To remove a symbol from a panel**

- Hold down the SHIFT key, select the symbol, and drag it off the panel.

▶ **To restore a panel to its original configuration**

- Click the right mouse button in the toolbar and choose Reset to Defaults.

Tailoring the Symbol Cache Toolbar

The Symbol Cache toolbar can be completely customized. You can customize the cache to suit your work by adding as many symbols as you need and removing those you don't need. You can reset the symbol cache to its original configuration at any time.

▶ **To add a symbol to the cache**

1. Open the symbol panel containing the symbol you want.

2. Select the symbol and drag it to any location on the Symbol Cache toolbar.

▶ **To remove a symbol from the cache**

- Hold down the SHIFT key, select the symbol, and drag it off the toolbar.

You can also add and remove symbols by clicking the right mouse button in the toolbar, choosing Customize, and adding or removing symbols using the Customize Toolbar dialog box.

▶ **To restore the cache to its original configuration**

- Click the right mouse button in the toolbar and choose Reset to Defaults.

Customizing Document Windows

Multiple document windows can be open in the program window at the same time (see Chapter 2 "Creating Documents"). You can arrange them to your liking. You can size or maximize a document window, or minimize it so that it appears as a small title bar in the program window. And you can customize the size and characteristics of the display in each document window. Occasionally, the view may not quite keep up with your changes, so you may want to refresh it.

▶ **To refresh the active view**

- From the View menu, choose Refresh.
  or

- Press ESC or SHIFT+ESC.

Sizing Document Windows

You can arrange document windows any way you want using standard Windows techniques. If you maximize one window, any other open windows remain open behind it.

▶ **To change the size of a document window**

- Use the Maximize ☐ or Minimize ▬ button on the right end of the title bar for the document window.
  or

- Use the Maximize or Minimize commands in the Control box on the left end of the title bar.
  or

- Double-click the title bar of document window to enlarge it to fill the program window.
  or

- Use the mouse to drag the edges of the document window to the size you want.

    When you maximize a document window to fill the program window, the Control box and the sizing buttons for the maximized window appear on the Menu bar. When you minimize a document window, the program creates a small title bar containing the path and file name of the document, a Control box, and sizing buttons, like this:

If you later maximize another document window, the title bar icon is hidden behind it.

▶ **To restore a maximized window to its previous size and location**

- On the right end of the Menu bar, click the Restore button ⎀ .
  or

- From the Control box on the Menu bar, choose Restore.

▶ **To restore the display of a minimized document window**

- Double-click the icon for the minimized window.
  or

- Click the icon and then, from the popup menu, choose Restore.
  or

- In the icon, click the Restore button ⎀ .
  or

- From the Window menu, choose the title of the minimized document or type the number to its left.

Arranging Multiple Document Windows

▶ **To arrange the open document windows**

- With the mouse, drag the title bar of a window to position it conveniently.
  or
- From the Window menu:
  - Choose Cascade to arrange the windows one in front of the other.
  - Choose Tile Horizontally to arrange the windows one above the other.
  - Choose Tile Vertically to arrange the windows side by side.

▶ **To arrange the icons for minimized windows**

- From the Window menu, choose Arrange Icons.

▶ **To move from window to window**

- From the list of open windows on the Window menu, double-click the window you want or type the number next to the window you want.
  or
- Click the title bar of the document window you want.
  or
- Press CTRL+TAB.

Changing the Magnification in a Document Window

You can reduce or magnify the view of the document in each window. Increasing the magnification is useful if you have difficulty discerning text at normal size or if you want to do detailed work in a complex mathematical expression. Decreased magnification can be helpful when dealing with very long mathematical expressions or tables. Regardless of the size of the text, the program always breaks lines to fit the screen window, so there is no need to scroll horizontally. The one exception is when an unbreakable object is too large for the current window at the current view size.

You can display your document at normal size or at twice normal size, or you can set the percentage of magnification (from 50% to 400%) you want the program to apply to the normal size. Normal size is an arbitrarily chosen size that most people use for ordinary work. When you open a document, the program displays it using the magnification currently in effect, unless the view percent has been saved with the document. If you have several document windows open, you can set a different display size for each window.

The program stores the defaults as you most recently set them if you check the Store View Percent in File option in the Document Info dialog box before you save your document. See Chapter 2 "Creating Documents."

You can set the print options to print at normal size, to reflect the view percent in effect, or to reflect a different view percent, as described in Chapter 7 "Previewing and Printing."

▶ **To change the display size of the information in the active document window**

- From the View menu
  - Choose 100% or 200%.
    or
  - Choose Custom and then, in the View Setting dialog box, set the percentage of magnification you want and choose OK.

  or

- On the Standard toolbar, click the Zoom Factor box [100% ▼] and set the percentage of magnification you want:
  - Click the arrow on the right of the box and select the percentage you want from the list.
    or
  - Type a magnification setting from 50% to 400% and press ENTER.

Modifying the Characteristics of the View

With the commands on the View menu, you can display or hide the following nonprinting characters and guidelines that facilitate the entry of text and mathematics:

- *Invisibles,* or nonprinting characters, in text. Invisibles indicate the ends of paragraphs and the spaces between words, like this:

  Paragraph marks and spaces appear when invisibles are displayed. ¶

- Lines that indicate the input boxes in mathematical structures. Input boxes indicate an empty place in a mathematical template where you can enter characters, symbols, or other mathematical objects. For example, the input boxes for the numerator and denominator in a fraction template appear like this:

  $$\frac{\square}{\square}$$

- Lines that indicate the rows and columns in tables, matrices, and column vectors, and the borders of displayed mathematics and multiline equations. Normally, the program shows a nonprinting grid of table, matrix, and vector cells to assist you in entering and editing content. The grid looks like this:

  Mathematical displays and multiline equations are boxed with nonprinting lines:

  $$\begin{array}{|l|} \hline x = a + b \\ \hline < c + d \\ \hline \end{array}$$

- Shaded boxes for markers and index entries. Shaded boxes appear like this:

  index View Menu commands

Turning the nonprinting elements on can be helpful when you're creating or editing a document, but you may want to turn them off when you're more interested in reading a document than making changes to it.

▶ **To display or hide guidelines and boxes**

- On the View menu, check the elements you want to display and uncheck the elements you want to hide.

▶ **To display or hide spaces and paragraph marks**

- On the Standard toolbar, click the Show/Hide Nonprinting button ⟨¶⟩ or, from the View menu, choose Invisibles.

You can set the view characteristics independently for each document window. When you open a new document, the program displays it using the view settings you used most recently. Some dialog boxes retain the view characteristics as they were set the last time you saved the document. In those cases, the nonprinting elements that appear in the dialog box may not be the same as those that appear in the document window.

The view settings, in combination with the Print Options, also affect the appearance of your document when you print it without typesetting. Invisibles, grids, input boxes, and shaded boxes may or may not appear depending on the settings you make. See Setting Print Options on page 163 for information.

The program stores the file with the defaults as you most recently set them if you check the Store View Settings in File option in the Document Info dialog box before you save your document.

Customizing the Assignment of Function Keys to Tags

You can assign the function keys on your keyboard to item, section, and text tags so you can apply the tags more quickly. Initially, the function keys have these global tag assignments; that is, the assignments are in effect for all documents:

Key	Tag	Key	Tag
F2	Remove Item Tag	F7	Numbered List Item
F3	Body Text	F8	Bullet List Item
F4	Normal	F9	Typewriter
F5	Bold	F11	Section
F6	Emphasized	F12	Subsection

In addition to being saved globally, tag assignments can be saved with the style information in the .cst file. If you change the key assignments for a style, the new assignments are in effect for all other documents of the same style. (See Chapter 8 "Formatting Documents" for more style information.) When a function key has different global and style assignments, the assignment for the style takes precedence. You can change the settings as often as you want.

▶ **To change a function key assignment**

1. From the Tag menu, choose Function Keys to open the Tag Key Assignments dialog box:

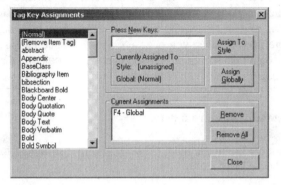

2. From the list of tags, select the tag to which you want to assign a function key.

3. Place the insertion point in the **Press New Keys** box.

4. Press the function key you want to assign to the tag, using *modifiers* such as CTRL, ALT, and SHIFT, alone or in combination, if necessary.

5. Choose either Assign to Style or Assign Globally, and then choose Close.

   If the function key is already assigned to a tag in the environment you selected, the program clears the old assignment and makes the new one, displaying it in the **Current Assignments** box. If the function key is assigned to a tag in the other environment, that assignment remains unchanged. The program indicates any existing style and global tag assignments for the function key you pressed:

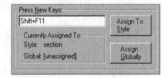

▶ **To remove a tag assignment**

1. From the Tag menu, choose Function Keys.

2. From the list of tags, select the tag whose assignment you want to clear.

3. If you want to clear one of several assignments for the tag, select the assignment from the **Current Assignments** box and choose Remove.

   or

   If you want to clear all assignments for the tag, choose Remove All.

4. Choose Close.

Customizing the Program Defaults

The User Setup command on the Tools menu opens a tabbed dialog box that contains the controls for customizing the global defaults related to the document, text, and mathematics interface; start-up document shell; graphics; file storage; and font mapping.

Remember   When you choose OK in a tabbed dialog box, you accept the settings made on all tab sheets. When you choose Cancel, you discard the settings made on all tab sheets.

▶ **To customize a program default**

1. On the Editing toolbar, click the User Setup button 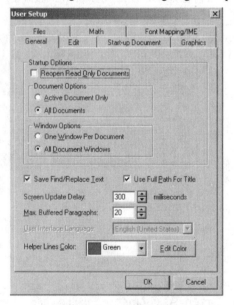 or, from the Tools menu, choose User Setup.

2. Choose the tab for the kind of default you want to set.

3. Specify the settings you want, and choose Close.

Setting the General Defaults

Use the General tab sheet to change defaults relating to general program properties.

Default	Effect
Startup Options	
Reopen Read Only Documents	Restore read-only documents the next time the program is started
Document Options	Set which read-only documents are to be restored
Window Options	Set the number of document views to be restored

(Continued)

Default	Effect
Miscellaneous Options	
Save Find/Replace Text	Retain text of find and replace search patterns between sessions
Use Full Path For Title	Display the full path of a document in the title bar
Screen Update Delay	Increase or reduce frequency with which the screen is updated
Max. Buffered Paragraphs	Set number of paragraphs kept ready for display in memory
User Interface Language*	Set the language in which strings in dialogs and menus appear in the program window.
Helper Lines Color	Set the display color for nonprinting elements
Edit Color	Edit the Helper Lines color

* For localized versions of the program only

If you refer to read-only documents as you work, you can use the Startup Options to open and display read-only documents the next time you start the program. Document Options control the number of read-only documents restored. Window Options control the number of document views restored. The two sets of options work together.

If you check both	On the next startup, the program
Active Document Only and One Window Per Document	• Reopens in a single document window the read-only document that was active when you last exited the program • Displays the part of the document that was displayed before in the active document view • Places and sizes the document window the same way as before
Active Document Only and All Document Windows	• Reopens the read-only document that was active when you last exited the program in as many views of the document as were open at that time • In each document view, displays the part of the document that was displayed before • Places and sizes all document views the same way as before
All Documents and One Window Per Document	• Reopens all read-only documents that were open when you last exited the program, each in its own window • Displays the part of each document that was displayed before in the view most recently active for the document • Places and sizes the document windows according to the most recently active view for each document
All Documents and All Document Windows	• Reopens all read-only documents that were open when you last exited the program, each in as many views as were open then • In each document view, displays the part of each document that was displayed before • Places and sizes all views of all documents as before

▶ **To restore the state of read-only documents the next time you start the program**

1. On the Editing toolbar, click the User Setup button or, from the Tools menu, choose User Setup.

2. Choose the General tab and check Reopen Read Only Documents.

3. Check the Document Options and Windows Options you want and check Close.

Setting the Edit Defaults

Use the Edit tab sheet to change defaults relating to drag-and-drop operations, certain mouse and keyboard operations, table and matrix sizes, and automatic substitution.

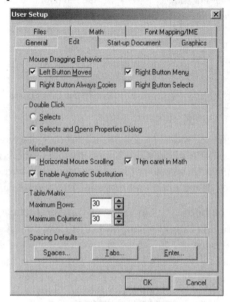

Default	Effect
Mouse Dragging Behavior	
Left Button Moves	Drag with left mouse button moves a selection
Right Button Always Copies	Drag with right mouse button copies a selection
Right Button Menu	Click with right mouse button displays the Context menu; drag with right mouse button displays the Context menu after button is released
Right Button Selects	Drag with right mouse button makes a selection
Double Click	
Selects	Double-click to select an object
Selects and Opens Properties Dialog	Double-click to select an object and open the corresponding Properties dialog box
Miscellaneous	
Horizontal Mouse Scrolling	Scroll horizontally when dragging the mouse past the left or right edge of the window
Enable Automatic Substitution	Enable automatic substitution (also from the Tools menu)
Thin caret in Math	Use thin caret to indicate the insertion point in mathematics
Table/Matrix	
Maximum Rows	Set maximum number of rows allowed in a table or matrix; the maximum number of cells is 10,000
Maximum Columns	Set maximum number of columns allowed in a table or matrix; the maximum number of cells is 10,000

(Continued)

Default	Effect
Spacing Defaults	
Spaces	Set the default for handling two spaces in succession
Tabs	Set the default for handling a TAB keypress in text
Enter	Set the default for handling an ENTER keypress at the beginning of a paragraph

Because the spacing in documents depends on the style and typesetting specifications, adding an extra space between words, adding an extra line between paragraphs, or using the TAB key to indent isn't necessary. When you type an extra space or press TAB in text, the program can either ignore the keypress or enter the space, depending on the spacing defaults you set. Also, you can set the default to be in effect at all times or you can choose each time whether to ignore or insert the space.

▶ **To change a spacing default**

1. On the Editing toolbar, click the User Setup button ![icon] or, from the **Tools** menu, choose **User Setup,** and then choose the **Edit** tab.

2. In the **Spacing Defaults** area, select the button for the kind of spacing you want to specify.

   The program opens the corresponding dialog box:

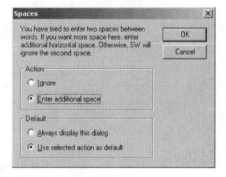

3. In the **Action** area, select **Ignore** to ignore the spacing command or **Enter additional space** to enter the space you typed.

4. In the **Default** area, select **Always display this dialog** to open the dialog box every time you enter an extra space or **Use selected action as default** to follow the default set in the **Action** area.

5. Choose **OK.**

6. If you chose to enter additional space, select the default space you want to insert when the **Horizontal Space** or **Vertical Space** dialog box opens, and choose **OK.**

7. Choose **Close.**

Setting the Start-up Document Defaults

Starting the program automatically opens an empty start-up document based on a default shell. The shell has typesetting specifications, a style, page setup specifications, and print options. Use the Start-up Document tab sheet to set the default document shell.

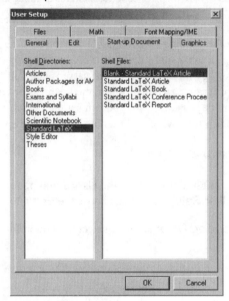

Default	Effect
Shell Directories	Set the default document type
Shell Files	Set the default document shell

▶ **To change the start-up document default shell**

1. On the Editing toolbar, click the User Setup button ⚒ or, from the Tools menu, choose User Setup, and then choose the Start-up Document tab.

2. From the Shell Directories list, choose the type of document you want as the default.

3. From the Shell Files list, choose the shell you want as the default.

4. Choose Close.

Setting the Graphics Defaults

Use the Graphics tab sheet to set the defaults for importing, sizing, and placing new graphics and graphics frames.

The Global Settings define the maximum amount of memory available for storing graphics used by the program and the number of inactive graphics allowed at any time. The default settings are appropriate for most installations.

When you paste a graphic or create a plot snapshot, the program stores temporary graphics files on your hard drive. When you delete a graphic, the program keeps it on the hard drive until the maximum number of inactive graphics is exceeded. The program then clears out all inactive graphics. Thus you can adjust the number of inactive graphics allowed so that the hard drive is cleared out more or less often.

The defaults that apply to new graphics affect only those graphics imported to the document after the settings are changed. The Screen Attribute settings affect all graphics in all open documents for which the Use Model option is selected on the Layout tab sheet of the Graphic Properties dialog box.

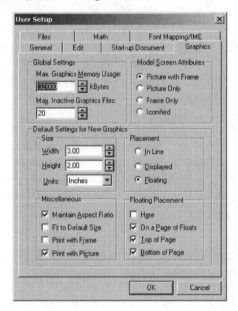

Default	Effect
Global Settings	
Max. Graphics Memory Usage	Set an upper limit on memory used by the program to to store graphics
Max. Inactive Graphics Files	Set the maximum allowable number of inactive graphics files
Model Screen Attributes	Set the default for the screen appearance of all graphics:
Picture with Frame	Display both the picture and the frame outline
Picture Only	Display only the picture
Frame Only	Display only the frame outline
Iconified	Minimize the picture so that it appears as an icon

(Continued)

Default	Effect
Size	(Applies only when Fit to Default Size is checked)
Width	Set the frame width for newly imported graphics to this dimension
Height	Set the frame height for newly imported graphics to this dimension
Units	Set the default unit of measure for frames of newly imported graphics
Miscellaneous	For all newly imported graphics:
Maintain Aspect Ratio	Maintain proportions of image when sizing
Fit to Default Size	Fit image to the default size specified rather than using the original size of the graphic
Print with Frame	Print image with a frame outline
Print with Picture	Print image without a frame outline
Placement	
In Line	Place all new graphics in the current line
Displayed	Center all new graphics on a separate line
Floating*	Allow all new graphics to float
Baseline	(Appears only when In Line Placement is checked)
Offset from Bottom of Frame	Align the bottom of the frame in relation to the baseline of the surrounding text
Floating Placement	(Appears only when Floating Placement is checked)
Here*	Place graphics where the frame is in the document file
On a Page of Floats*	Place graphics on a separate page of floating objects
Top of Page*	Place graphics at the top of a page
Bottom of Page*	Place graphics at the bottom of a page

* not available in *SNB*

If you check **Floating Placement** in *SWP* or *SW,* floating graphics are positioned according to the options you check in the **Floating Placement** area. See Chapter 5 "Using Graphics and Tables."

Setting the Files Defaults

Use the **Files** tab sheet to set the defaults for working with files and directories. In particular, these settings govern automatic saving, the creation of backup files, the length of the Recent List, and many aspects of opening and saving documents. You can set the format for the default file type in which to save and open files. The defaults are reflected in the **Save As** and **Open** dialog boxes.

By default, the program saves all files as LaTeX files with a .tex file extension. If you're using *SWP* or *SW,* you can choose to save documents as Portable LaTeX (.tex) files. Also, if you need to send your document to a different location, you can save it as a wrapped (.rap) file; read about wrapped files in Chapter 11 "Managing Documents."

The program uses default subdirectories in your installation for storing fragments, shells, styles, Help files, reference files, temporary files, and, MuPAD libraries.

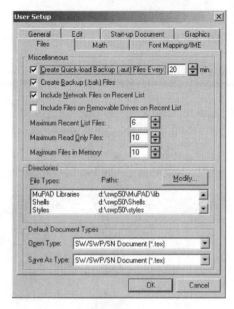

Default	Effect
Miscellaneous	
Create Quick-load Backup (.aut) Files	Set the frequency of regular saving
Create Backup (.bak) Files	Create backup files when the document is saved
Include Network Files on Recent List	Include on the Recent List documents that reside on network drives
Include Files on Removable Drives on Recent List	Include on the Recent List documents that reside on removable drives
Maximum Recent List Files	Set the maximum number of documents that can be included on the Recent List
Maximum Read Only Files	Set the maximum number of read-only documents that can be open at one time
Maximum Files in Memory	Set the maximum number of files that can be open in virtual memory at one time before the least recently used file is moved to the hard drive; a higher number uses more virtual memory but improves performance
Directories	
File Types / Paths	Display the drive and directory locations of file types used by the program
Modify	Modify drive and directory locations
Default Document Types	
Open Type	Set the type of file listed in File Open dialog box
Save As Type	Set the type of file used for the Save As operation

You can change the default directories used for BIBTₑX databases and styles with the **Expert Settings** command on the **Typeset** menu. To change other default directories, use the following instructions.

▶ **To change the default file directories**

1. On the Editing toolbar, click the User Setup button  or, from the **Tools** menu, choose **User Setup**, and then choose the **Files** tab.

2. Double-click the file type whose directory you want to change, or select the file type and choose **Modify** to display the **Modify Location** dialog box.

3. Set the new directory and choose **OK**.

   You can choose a directory on your network.

4. Choose **Close**.

Setting the Math Defaults

You can customize the way you toggle between text and mathematics by setting the IN-SERT key as the toggle; setting the program to force the entry of mathematics when you press the spacebar twice within text; or removing the toggle function from the CTRL+T and CTRL+M key sequences. You can set options for numbered equations, fractions, radicals, and math names.

Mathematics displays that contain a single equation created on multiple lines are treated differently depending on how you produce your document. When you typeset, LATₑX determines the appearance of the equation according to the typesetting specifications. When you don't typeset, the equation appears in a display whose right and left edges are indented a fixed distance from the margins of the page. You can use the box labeled **Margins for AMS Multi-line Displays** to set the indention.

The program also has built-in defaults that govern the appearance of mathematics in the document window. In the **Tag Appearance** dialog box, you can turn off these defaults and specify the mathematics screen appearance settings you want.

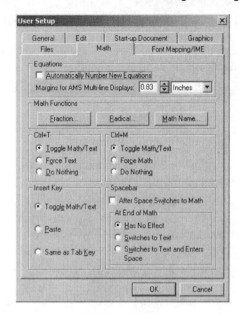

Default	Effect
Equations	
Automatically Number New Equations	Automatically create an equation number for each new equation
Margins for AMS Multi-line Displays	Set the distance from left and right margins for a single equation displayed on multiple lines
Math Functions	
Fraction	Set the size and line type for fractions
Radical	Set whether or not new radicals have roots
Math Name	Set placement of limits in functions; automatically add newly defined math names to list of math names
Ctrl+T and Ctrl+M	Use the key sequence to:
Toggle Math/Text	Toggle between mathematics and text
Force Text or Force Math	Change to text or to mathematics
Do Nothing	Do nothing
Insert Key	Use the INSERT key to:
Toggle Math/Text	Toggle between mathematics and text
Paste	Paste the current selection
Same as Tab Key	Have the same effect as the TAB key
Spacebar	
After Space Switches to Math	Set the second of two spacebar keypresses to toggle to mathematics
At End of Math	Set spacebar keypress at end of mathematics to:
Has No Effect	Have no effect
Switches to Text	Switch to text
Enters Space and Switches to Text	Enter a space and switch to text

Customizing Font Mapping/IME Defaults

The Font Mapping defaults determine the way the program maps characters and symbols to fonts available on your system, including the fonts tci1–4, which are installed with the program. The tci1–4 fonts contain the mathematical and other special symbols that aren't available in the standard Windows fonts.

- Use Symbol Font Mapping.

  The program uses characters from the Windows Symbol font in place of the same characters from the Default fonts. Use this option if you prefer the appearance of the characters in the Windows Symbol font to that of the same characters from the Default fonts.

- Use Default Font Mapping.

  The program uses characters from the tci1–4 fonts. Note that if you uncheck this option, most mathematical symbols won't appear.

- Use Accent Font Mapping.

  Wherever possible, the program uses combination characters to display accents. For example, the character $\ddot{u}$ is available as a single combination character. In many cases, however, combination characters don't exist, so the program must accent these characters by displaying a separate accent character in the appropriate position. On some systems, such as Japanese Windows, separate accents aren't available in the standard Windows fonts. Therefore, when you choose Use Accent Font Mapping, the program takes these separate accent characters from the tci1–4 fonts. The resulting accent may not match the typeface in use. You may find that the accents match the character style better and the printed results are more pleasing if you uncheck the box.

The choices in the Font Mapping dialog box take effect from top to bottom. That is, if you choose both Symbol and Default font mapping, Symbol font mapping takes precedence. You may notice a difference when you display Greek characters. Some Greek characters are available in the Symbol font and all are available in the tci1–4 fonts. When you choose both of these defaults, all of the Greek characters in the Symbol font will be used, and the remaining Greek characters will come from the tci1–4 fonts.

When you install the program, the settings in the Font Mapping dialog box are set to the most conservative values. With these settings, some of the extended Latin characters may not always display or print correctly on your system if you use Windows 95, Windows 98, or Windows Me. Provided your computer has correctly functioning screen and print drivers, you can fix these problems by installing Windows Multilanguage Support. Without it, some characters, especially those with accents, will be missing, and ligatures won't appear properly when you preview or print. For example, words like *first, flow,* and *difficult* will be missing the *fi, fl,* and *ffi,* respectively.

The Input Method Editor (IME) allows the entry of multibyte characters, as used in Japanese and other multibyte languages. If you're working in a multibyte language, you may want to enter text using multibyte characters but enter mathematics using single-byte characters, as for standard mathematics. The IME Behavior default settings determine when multibyte characters are allowed.

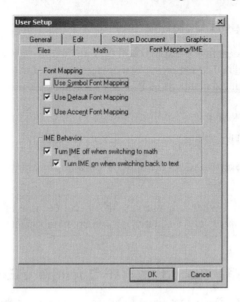

Default	Effect
Font Mapping	
Use Symbol Font Mapping	Use characters from the Windows Symbol font
Use Default Font Mapping	Use characters from the tci1–4 fonts
Use Accent Font Mapping	Take separate accent characters from the tci1–4 fonts when necessary
IME Behavior	
Turn IME off when switching to math	Don't allow multibyte characters in mathematics
Turn IME on when switching back to text	Allow multibyte characters in text

▶ **To install Windows Multilanguage Support (Windows 95, 98, and Me)**

1. From the Windows Start menu, choose Settings, and then choose Control Panel.

2. Choose Add/Remove Programs and choose the Windows Setup tab.

   If Multilanguage Support isn't available, obtain an installable version of it from Microsoft, install the support, and then continue with these instructions.

3. Check the box for Multilanguage Support.

4. If prompted, insert your Windows CD and follow the instructions on the screen.

5. When the installation is complete, restart Windows.

▶ **To change the Font Mapping defaults**

1. On the Editing toolbar, click the User Setup button ![icon] or, from the Tools menu, choose User Setup.

2. Choose the Font Mapping/IME tab, check or uncheck the options, as necessary, and choose Close.

Customizing the Export Defaults

The tab sheets in the Export Settings dialog box contain the controls for customizing defaults related to exporting or copying graphic images of your text and mathematics and exporting documents as RTF or HTML files.

▶ **To customize an export setting**

1. From the Tools menu, choose Export Settings.

2. Choose a tab and set the options as you want, and then choose OK.

Important   When you choose OK or Cancel in a tabbed dialog box, you accept or discard, respectively, the settings made on all tab sheets.

Setting the Export as RTF Document Export Options

Use the RTF Document Export Options to customize the way you export mathematics, plots, and graphics when you export your documents to RTF. In most cases, the default settings are adequate and no changes are necessary. However, you can specify formats for graphics at a fine level if you choose Graphics Settings and follow the instructions in Chapter 2 "Creating Documents."

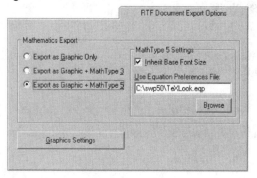

Option	Effect
Mathematics Export	
Export as Graphic Only	Export each instance of mathematics in the document as a graphic
Export as Graphic + MathType 3	Export each instance of mathematics in the document as a graphic and a MathType 3 object
Export as Graphic + MathType 5	Export each instance of mathematics in the document as a graphic and MathType 5 object
MathType 5 Settings	(Available only when Export as Graphic + MathType 5 is checked)
Inherit Base Font Size	Create MathType 5 objects that inherit their size from the surrounding text
Use Equation Preferences File	Specify an Equation Preferences file for use with MathType 5 objects
Graphics Settings	Specify formats for graphics, mathematics, and plots

Setting the HTML Document Export Options

Use the HTML Document Export options to customize the way you export mathematics, plots, and graphics when you export your documents to HTML. In most cases, the default settings are adequate and no changes are necessary. However, you can specify formats for graphics at a fine level if you choose Graphics Settings and follow the instructions in Chapter 10 "Creating Documents for Online Use."

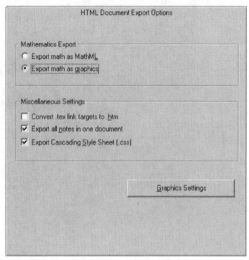

Option	Effect
Mathematics Export	
Export math as MathML	Export each instance of mathematics in the document as MathML
Export math as graphics	Export each instance of mathematics in the document as a graphics file
Miscellaneous Settings	
Convert .tex link targets to .htm	Convert .tex extensions in hypertext link target addresses to .htm extensions
Export all notes in one document	Combine any popup notes contained in the document in a single file rather than in separate files
Export Cascading Style Sheet (.css)	Create a .css file that creates a document appearance in HTML similar to that in the document window
Graphics Settings	Specify formats for graphics, mathematics, and plots

Setting the Export as Picture Options

Use the Export as Picture options to set the appearance of a selection when you copy or export it as a picture. The options are similar to the print options (see page 163) except that they apply to graphic images instead of documents as a whole. Note that the settings apply both when you use the Copy Picture command on the Edit menu or the Export as Picture command on the File menu. The settings also apply to mathematics graphics created when you export to HTML.

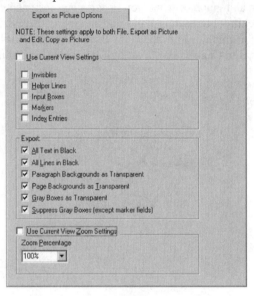

Option	Effect
Use Current View Settings	Show or hide invisibles, helper lines, input boxes, index entries, and markers only if they are turned on in the View menu
Invisibles	Show or hide invisibles despite View menu setting
Helper Lines	Show or hide helper lines despite View menu setting
Input Boxes	Show or hide input boxes despite View menu setting
Markers	Show or hide markers despite View menu setting
Index Entries	Show or hide index entries despite View menu setting
Export	
All Text in Black	Show text in black despite color specified for the tag
All Lines in Black	Show lines in black despite color specified
Paragraph Backgrounds as Transparent	Show no background color for paragraphs
Page Backgrounds as Transparent	Show no background color for pages
Gray Boxes as Transparent	Show no background color for gray boxes
Suppress Gray Boxes (except markers)	Show no gray boxes except index entries and markers
Use Current View Zoom Settings	Use the zoom factor in effect
Zoom Percentage	Set the zoom percentage

Customizing the Typesetting Defaults

The program has both general and expert typesetting defaults available from the **Typeset** menu. The general settings relate to typesetting with both LaTeX and PDFLaTeX and to creating portable LaTeX files. The expert settings are for specific formatters and preview and print drivers.

Important   Don't attempt to modify the expert settings unless you know TeX and LaTeX very well.

Specifying the General Settings

When you typeset, the program can use the auxiliary files created during previous compilations of your document. The default is to use the .aux files, which saves time during subsequent compilations. Similarly, the program issues a warning any time you attempt to typeset a document with a file name that restricts the document's portability, as described on page 32. You can turn off both defaults. In addition, your program installation specifies default directories for BIBTeX databases and styles. You can change the default directories.

When you create typeset PDF files and portable LaTeX files, you can change the way the program treats graphics and plots. The options are described in Chapter 2 "Creating Documents." In most cases the defaults are adequate and no changes are required.

▶ **To customize the general typesetting options**

1. From the **Typeset** menu, choose **General Settings**.

2. If you want to change the default directories for the BIBTeX database and style files, specify the directories you want to use.

3. Check or uncheck the options according to your preferences.

4. Choose **OK**.

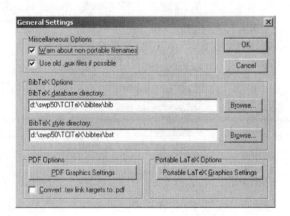

Option	Effect
Miscellaneous Options	
Warn about non-portable filenames	Display a warning before beginning to typeset if the file name or directory name includes a space or a character that has a special meaning to TEX
Use old .aux files if possible	Save the .aux files generated for the document during typesetting for subsequent use
BIBTEX *Options*	
BIBTEX database directory	Specify the directory for storing BIBTEX databases
BIBTEX style directory	Specify the directory for storing BIBTEX style files
PDF Options	
PDF Graphics Settings	Specify the settings to be used for exporting plots and graphics in PDF files
Convert .tex link targets to .pdf	Convert hypertext links to files with a .tex extension to files with a .pdf extension when typesetting with PDFLATEX
Portable LATEX Options	
Portable LATEX Graphics Settings	Specify the settings to be used for exporting plots and graphics in portable LATEX files

Setting the PDF Options

When you typeset a document with PDFLATEX, you can use the PDF option settings to specify formats for graphics created from plots and graphics. See Chapter 7 "Previewing and Printing" for more information.

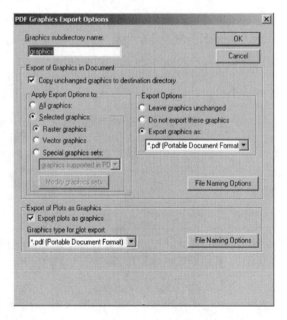

Option	Effect
Graphics subdirectory name	Specify the subdirectory in which you want to save the exported graphics and plots. The program creates a subdirectory with the name in each directory into which you save a PDF file
Export of Graphics in Document	
Copy unchanged graphics to destination directory	Place in the target directory a copy of all graphics whose format is left unchanged during export
Apply Export Options to:	Select a type or set of graphics to which you want to apply an export option
Modify graphics sets	Modify, add, or remove a set of graphics
Export Options	Select a formatting option for the selected type or set of graphics
Graphics File Naming Options	Designate a file naming scheme for exported graphics
Export of Plots as Graphics	Select a formatting option for exported plots
Plot File Naming Options	Designate a file naming scheme for exported plots

Setting the Portable LaTeX Options

When you export a document as a Portable LaTeX file, you can use the Portable LaTeX option settings to make your plots and graphics more portable to other installations. Chapter 2 "Creating Documents" contains details.

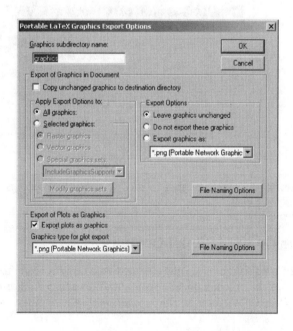

Option	Effect
Graphics subdirectory name	Specify the subdirectory name in which you want to save the exported graphics and plots. The program creates a subdirectory with the name in each directory into which you save a Portable LaTeX file
Export of Graphics in Document	
Copy unchanged graphics to destination directory	Place in the target directory a copy of all graphics whose format is left unchanged during export
Apply Export Options to:	Select a type or set of graphics to which you want to apply an export option
Modify graphics sets	Modify, add, or remove a set of graphics
Export Options	Select a formatting option for the selected type or set of graphics
Graphics File Naming Options	Designate a file naming scheme for exported graphics
Export of Plots as Graphics	Select a formatting option for exported plots
Plot File Naming Options	Designate a file naming scheme for exported plots

Specifying the Expert Settings

TrueTeX is the LaTeX system installed with *SWP* and *SW*. It includes support for PDFLaTeX. The program defaults to the TrueTeX formatter, preview driver, and print driver. You can use a different formatter or drivers if you are knowledgeable about TeX, LaTeX, and the formatter and drivers in question. See Chapter 7 "Previewing and Printing" for more information.

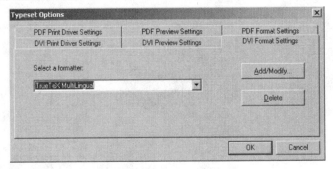

Important Don't attempt to modify the expert settings unless you know TeX and LaTeX very well.

Customizing the Computational Defaults

The Computation Setup and Engine Setup options customize the way you use the features of the computational engine in *SWP* and *SW*. For details about computing in *SWP* and *SW*, refer to *Doing Mathematics with Scientific WorkPlace and Scientific Notebook*.

Specifying the Computation Setup Defaults

In *SWP* and *SNB*, you can customize defaults related to displaying mathematics and mathematical functions, saving and restoring mathematical definitions, selecting a computational engine, displaying frames containing mathematics plots, displaying 2- and 3-dimensional plots, and creating plot snapshots.

▶ **To set a computational default**

1. From the Tools menu, choose Computation Setup.

2. Choose the tab sheet you want.

3. Change the default settings and choose OK.

Setting the General Computation Defaults

Use the General tab sheet of the Computation Setup dialog box to set defaults for displaying mathematics and mathematical functions.

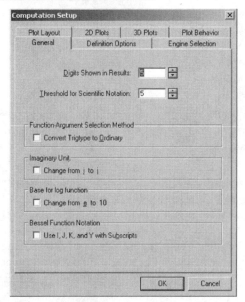

Default	Effect
Digits Shown in Results	Determine the number of digits put on the screen as the result of a numerical computation
Threshold for Scientific Notation	Limit the number of digits that leads to a response in scientific notation; cannot exceed the value for Digits Shown in Results
Function-Argument Selection Method	Place parenthesis around arguments of trigonometric functions
Imaginary Unit	Select i or j as the imaginary unit
Base for Log Function	Change the base for log functions from e to 10
Bessel Function Notation	Activate Bessel function notation

Setting the Definition Option Defaults

Use the Definition Options tab sheet of the Computation Setup dialog box to set defaults for saving and restoring mathematical definitions when a document is saved or opened. The default for each new document is Always Save and Always Restore.

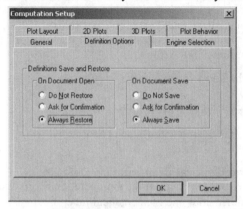

Default	Effect
On Document Open:	
Do Not Restore	Do not restore any definitions
Ask for Confirmation	Ask whether or not to restore saved definitions
Always Restore	Activate any definitions stored with the current document
On Document Save:	
Do Not Save	Discard all the currently active definitions
Ask for Confirmation	Ask whether or not to save currently active definitions
Always Save	Store all currently active definitions in the working copy of the current document

Selecting the Computational Engine

The computational engine provided with *SWP* and *SNB* is MuPAD. The Maple engine is still supported, so you can use it if you bought a previous version of *SWP* or *SNB* that contained the Maple engine. You can use the Engine Selection tab sheet of the Computation Setup dialog box to select the computational engine you want to use.

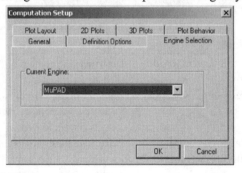

▶ **To select a different computational engine**

    1. From the Tools menu, choose Computation Setup.

    2. Choose the Engine Selection tab.

3. Select the engine you want from the pull-down list.

4. Choose OK.

Because computations require a lot of virtual memory, you can use the available memory more efficiently by turning off the computational engine when you don't need it or by turning it off and then back on.

► **To turn off the computational engine**

1. From the Tools menu, choose Computation Setup and then choose the Engine Selection tab.

2. From the pull-down list, select None and choose OK.

Setting the Plot Layout Defaults
Use the Plot Layout tab sheet of the Computation Setup dialog box to set defaults for screen attributes of frames containing mathematical plots.

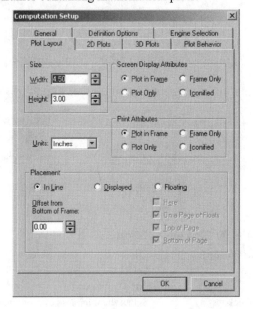

Default	Effect
Size	Specify the size of the frame for plots
Units	Specify the unit of measure for plot size
Screen Display Attributes	Specify whether plots will be displayed with or without a frame, as an empty frame, or as an iconified frame
Print Attributes	Specify whether plots will be printed with or without a frame, as an empty frame, or as an iconified frame
Placement	Specify whether plots will be in line, displayed, or floating
Offset from Bottom of Frame	(Active only when In Line Placement is checked) Align the bottom of the frame in relation to the baseline of the surrounding text

(Continued)

Default	Effect
Floating Placement	(Active only for typesetting with Floating Placement checked)
Here*	Place graphics where the frame is in the document file
On a Page of Floats*	Place graphics on a separate page of floating objects
Top of Page*	Place graphics at the top of a page
Bottom of Page*	Place graphics at the bottom of a page

* not available in SNB

Setting the Plot Defaults

Use the 2D Plots and 3D Plots tab sheets of the Computation Setup dialog box to set defaults for the style, display, and attributes of 2- and 3-dimensional plots.

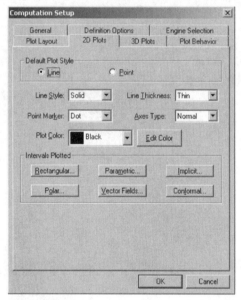

Defaults for 2D Plots	Effect
Default Plot Style	Choose line or point plots
Line Style	Select the appearance of plot lines as solid, dotted, dashed, or a combination
Line Thickness	Select the thickness of plot lines
Point Marker	Select the style of point markers
Axes Type	Select the type of axes
Plot Color	Select the color of plot lines
Edit Color	Select an unlisted color for plot lines
Intervals Plotted	Specify the default plotting intervals and sample size for the selected plot interval (rectangular, parametric, implicit, polar, vector fields, or conformal)
Specify Discontinuity Behavior*	Determine whether or not the engine adjusts for discontinuities

* Engine dependent

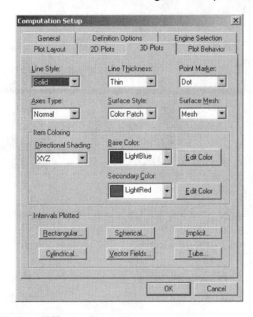

Defaults for 3D Plots	Effect
Line Style	Select the appearance of plot lines as solid, dotted, dashed, or a combination
Line Thickness	Select the thickness of plot lines
Point Marker	Select the style of point markers
Axes Type	Select the type of axes
Surface Style	Control the way the grid points are connected (by small patches of polynomial surfaces, straight line segments on a transparent or opaque surface, or by points only)
Surface Mesh	Control the type of curves that are drawn on the surface (show only a colored surface, or show the images of horizontal lines, vertical lines, or both)
Item Coloring	Determine the base and secondary colors and directional shading (based on coordinates) used in 3D plots*
Edit Color	Select an unlisted base or secondary color
Intervals Plotted	Specify the default plotting intervals and sample size for the selected plot interval (rectangular, spherical, implicit, cylindrical, vector fields, or tube)

* Directional shading begins with the base color and shades to the secondary color

Setting the Plot Behavior Defaults

Use the Plot Behavior tab sheet of the Computation Setup dialog box to set defaults for plot properties and recomputation, and for automatic generation of plot snapshots.

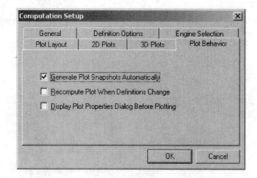

Default	Effect
Generate Plot Snapshots Automatically	Create a corresponding snapshot file for each new plot
Recompute Plot When Definitions Change	Automatically replot when mathematical definitions change.
Display Plot Properties Dialog Before Plotting	Instead of using default settings, allow specification of options for each plot.

Specifying the Engine Setup Defaults

In *SWP* and *SNB*, you can customize certain defaults for the selected computational engine from the Engine Setup dialog box:

Tab Sheet	Defaults relating to
General	Global operation of the computational engine
Error Handling	Error logging and notification

▶ **To set a default**

1. From the Tools menu, choose Engine Setup and choose the tab sheet you want.

2. Specify the default settings and choose OK.

Saving and Restoring User Preferences

You can save your customized user setup in a Windows Registry (.reg) file so that you can revert to it in the future. Saved settings include:

- Editing preferences.
- Mouse behavior preferences.
- Helper lines color.
- Default graphics and plot behavior.
- Default start-up document shell.
- Toolbar configurations.

If you save preferences that you find particularly useful, you can change the settings temporarily, and then quickly restore your favorite settings later. Restoring preferences requires a program restart, so you must close all open documents, saving them where necessary, before you restore the settings.

▶ **To save user preferences**

1. From the Tools menu, choose Save User Preferences.

2. In the Save As dialog box, select a file name for the preferences.

   The program automatically adds the .reg file extension.

3. Choose Save.

▶ **To restore user preferences**

1. Save and close all open documents.

2. From the Tools menu, choose Restore Saved Preferences.

3. In the Open dialog box, select the preferences file you want to use and choose Open.

4. When the program displays an exit message, choose OK to leave the program.

5. Restart the program to restore the selected preferences.

A Toolbar Buttons and Menu Commands

Compute Toolbar

SWP and *SNB* only.

Button	Menu / Command
=?	Compute / Evaluate
#?	Compute / Evaluate Numerically
x?	Compute / Solve / Exact
x+x=2x	Compute / Simplify
	Compute / Expand
	Compute / Plot 2D
	Compute / Plot 3D
f(x)_	Compute / Define / New Definition
f(x)	Compute / Define / Show Definitions

Exam Toolbar

SWP and *SNB* only.

Button	Menu / Command	Use
	none	View the quiz resulting from the document
EB	Tools / Exam Builder	Open the Exam Builder

Editing Toolbar

Button	Menu / Command	Use
N	Tag / Apply / (Normal)	Apply the Normal tag to the selection or the next character(s) typed
B	Tag / Apply / Bold	Apply the Bold tag to the selection or the next character(s) typed
I	Tag / Apply / Italic	Apply the Italic tag to the selection or the next character(s) typed
E	Tag / Apply/ Emphasized	Apply the Emphasized tag to the selection or the next character(s) typed
ᗡA	Tag / Appearance	Clone styles and tags; modify the appearance of tags in the document window and when you produce the document without typesetting
🔍	Edit / Find	Search for words, mathematics, or tags
🔍	Edit / Replace	Replace words, mathematics, or tags
e.m	Insert / Spacing / Horizontal Space	Insert thick, thin, required, or other horizontal spacing
🖼	File / Import Picture	Import a graphic image
🛠	Tools / User Setup	Customize defaults for files, text, mathematics, shells, graphics, and fonts

Field Toolbar

Button	Menu / Command	Use
▤	Insert / Note	Create a footnote, margin note, or note for an online document
🖊	Insert / Marker	Create a marker
▤	Insert / Hypertext Link	Create a hypertext link to any marker or any object with a key in the active document, in a different document, or on the Internet
d=rt	Insert / Formula	Enter a formula for use in generated exams

Fragments Toolbar

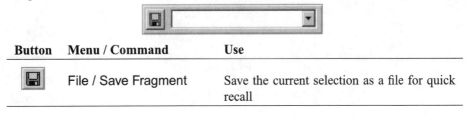

Button	Menu / Command	Use
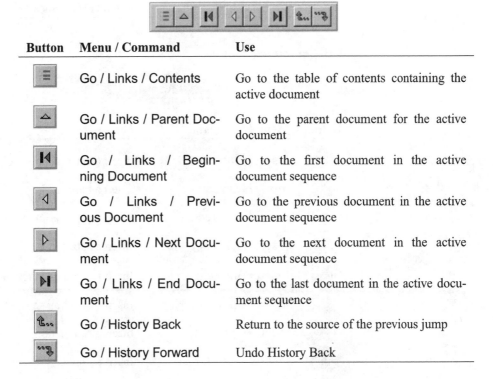	File / Save Fragment	Save the current selection as a file for quick recall

History Toolbar

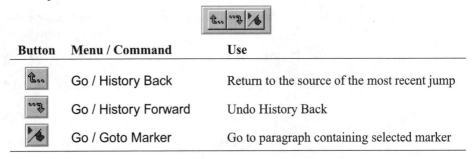

Button	Menu / Command	Use
	Go / History Back	Return to the source of the most recent jump
	Go / History Forward	Undo History Back
	Go / Goto Marker	Go to paragraph containing selected marker

Link Toolbar

Button	Menu / Command	Use
	Go / Links / Contents	Go to the table of contents containing the active document
	Go / Links / Parent Document	Go to the parent document for the active document
	Go / Links / Beginning Document	Go to the first document in the active document sequence
	Go / Links / Previous Document	Go to the previous document in the active document sequence
	Go / Links / Next Document	Go to the next document in the active document sequence
	Go / Links / End Document	Go to the last document in the active document sequence
	Go / History Back	Return to the source of the previous jump
	Go / History Forward	Undo History Back

Math Objects Toolbar

Button	Menu / Command	Use
≡	Insert / Display	Insert a mathematical display
Σ∫	Insert / Operator	Insert mathematical operators such as summations, integrals, and products
()[]	Insert / Brackets	Insert expanding brackets and enclosures in matched or unmatched pairs
▦	Insert / Matrix	Insert a matrix or vector
sin cos	Insert / Math Name	Insert a mathematical function (e.g., sin, lim)
(ₐᵇ)	Insert / Binomial	Insert binomials or generalized fractions
⊟	Insert / Label	Insert labels for expressions or formulas
⇆	Insert / Decoration	Insert a bar, arrow, or brace over or under expressions; box an expression, or insert boxes around expressions

Math Templates Toolbar

Button	Menu / Command	Use
⊟	Insert / Fraction	Insert a vertical fraction
√◻	Insert / Radical	Insert a radical
N^x	Insert / Superscript	Insert a superscript
N_x	Insert / Subscript	Insert a subscript
(◻)	Insert / Brackets	Insert expanding parentheses
[◻]	Insert / Brackets	Insert expanding square brackets
Σ	Insert / Operator	Insert a summation operator
∫	Insert / Operator	Insert an integral operator
ft lb	Insert / Unit Name	Insert a computable unit of measure

Navigate Toolbar

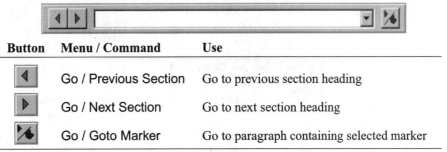

Button	Menu / Command	Use
◀	Go / Previous Section	Go to previous section heading
▶	Go / Next Section	Go to next section heading
↘	Go / Goto Marker	Go to paragraph containing selected marker

Standard Toolbar

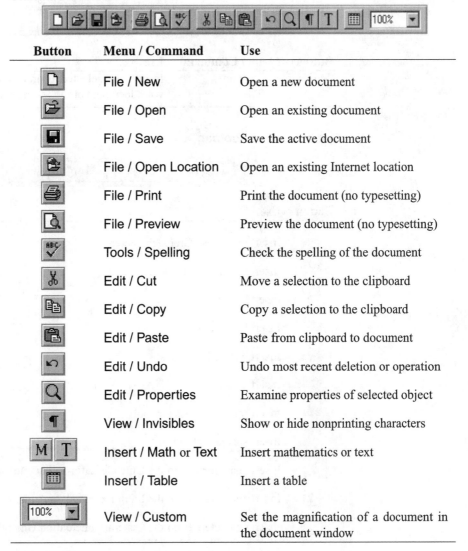

Button	Menu / Command	Use
🗋	File / New	Open a new document
🗁	File / Open	Open an existing document
🖫	File / Save	Save the active document
🗐	File / Open Location	Open an existing Internet location
🖶	File / Print	Print the document (no typesetting)
🔍	File / Preview	Preview the document (no typesetting)
ABC✓	Tools / Spelling	Check the spelling of the document
✂	Edit / Cut	Move a selection to the clipboard
🗐	Edit / Copy	Copy a selection to the clipboard
📋	Edit / Paste	Paste from clipboard to document
↶	Edit / Undo	Undo most recent deletion or operation
🔍	Edit / Properties	Examine properties of selected object
¶	View / Invisibles	Show or hide nonprinting characters
M T	Insert / Math or Text	Insert mathematics or text
▦	Insert / Table	Insert a table
100% ▼	View / Custom	Set the magnification of a document in the document window

Stop Toolbar

Button	Menu / Command	Use
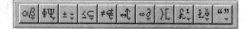	none; use CTRL+BREAK	Halt a computation or cancel an attempt to link to the Internet

Symbol Cache Toolbar

The Symbol Cache toolbar can be customized; the default toolbar appears here.

Button	Menu / Command	Use
Varies	none	Inserts the selected character or symbol in your document at the insertion point

Symbol Panels Toolbar

Button	Use
αβ	Insert lowercase Greek characters
ΦΨ	Insert uppercase Greek characters
± ÷	Insert binary operations
≤⊆	Insert binary relations
≠∉	Insert negated relations
↔↥	Insert arrows
∞∂	Insert miscellaneous symbols
)[	Insert special delimiters
£¹	Insert characters from the Unicode Latin-1 character set
Łĕ	Insert characters from the Latin Extended-A character set
" "	Insert characters from the General Punctuation Unicode character set

Tag Toolbar

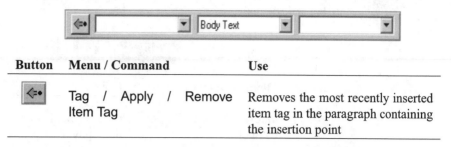

Button	Menu / Command	Use
	Tag / Apply / Remove Item Tag	Removes the most recently inserted item tag in the paragraph containing the insertion point

Typeset Toolbar
SWP and *SW* only.

Button	Menu / Command	Use
	Typeset / Print	Print the DVI file for the document, compiling first if necessary
	Typeset / Preview	Preview the DVI file for the document, compiling first if necessary
	Typeset / Compile	Process a document with LaTeX to produce a DVI file
	Typeset / Print PDF	Print the PDF file for the document, compiling first if necessary
	Typeset / Preview PDF	Preview the PDF file for the document, compiling first if necessary
	Typeset / Compile PDF	Process a document with PDFLaTeX to produce a PDF file
	Typeset / Front Matter	Enter or modify front matter for the document
	Typeset / Options and Packages	Add, remove, or modify LaTeX document classes and packages

Typeset Object toolbar

SWP and *SW* only.

Button	Menu / Command	Use
"	Insert / Typeset Object / Citation	Create a citation for an item listed in the bibliography
	Insert / Typeset Object / Index Entry	Create an index entry
	Insert / Typeset Object / Cross Reference	Create a reference to a document page number or part
	Insert / Typeset Object / TeX Field	Insert a field for TeX commands
	Insert / Typeset Object / Subdocument	Create a subdocument within a master document
	Insert / Typeset Object / Bibliography	Insert a BibTeX bibliography in a document

B Keyboard Shortcuts

These instructions assume the program defaults haven't been changed.

Scrolling and Editing

Working with Files

To	Press
Open a file	CTRL+O
Close a file	CTRL+F4
Print	CTRL+P
Exit	ALT+F4
Open Help contents	F1

Scrolling

To move	Press
To the left	LEFT ARROW
To the right	RIGHT ARROW
Up	UP ARROW
Down	DOWN ARROW
To start of the line	HOME
To end of the line	END
To next screen	PAGE DOWN
To previous screen	PAGE UP
To document start	CTRL+HOME
To document end	CTRL+END
To next field inside a template	TAB or ARROW KEYS
To previous field inside a template	SHIFT+TAB or ARROW KEYS
To outside a template	SPACEBAR or RIGHT ARROW or LEFT ARROW (repeated)
To the word to the right of the insertion point	CTRL+RIGHT ARROW
To the word to the left of the insertion point	CTRL+LEFT ARROW
Between open documents	CTRL+TAB

Editing

To	Press
Copy the selection to clipboard	CTRL+C
Cut the selection to clipboard	CTRL+X
Paste from clipboard	CTRL+V
Edit Properties	CTRL+F5
Undo the last deletion	CTRL+Z
Delete the word to the right	CTRL+DELETE
Delete the word to the left	CTRL+BACKSPACE
Delete	DELETE
Negate the character to the left	CTRL+N
Find	CTRL+Q
Replace	CTRL+W
Refresh the screen	ESC or SHIFT+ESC

Selecting

To select	Press
The following screen	SHIFT+PAGE DOWN
The previous screen	SHIFT+PAGE UP
The word to the right of the insertion point	CTRL+SHIFT+RIGHT ARROW
The word to the left of the insertion point	CTRL+SHIFT+LEFT ARROW
The object or symbol to the left of the insertion point	SHIFT+LEFT ARROW
The object or symbol to the right of the insertion point	SHIFT+RIGHT ARROW
Everything in the document	CTRL+A
Everything between the insertion point and the start of the line	SHIFT+HOME
Everything between the insertion point and the end of the line	SHIFT+END
Everything between the insertion point and the start of the document	CTRL+SHIFT+HOME
Everything between the insertion point and the end of the document	CTRL+SHIFT+END
To choose a command	ALT+the Accelerator keys (the underlined letters for the menu and command)

Entering Mathematics and Text

Toggling Between Mathematics and Text

To	Press*
Toggle math/text	CTRL+M or CTRL+T or INSERT

*Assumes default user settings

Entering Mathematical Objects and Punctuation

To enter	Press		
Fraction	CTRL+F	or CTRL+/	or CTRL+1
Radical	CTRL+R	or CTRL+2	
Superscript	CTRL+H	or CTRL+3	or CTRL+UP ARROW
Subscript	CTRL+L	or CTRL+4	or CTRL+DOWN ARROW
Summation	CTRL+7		
Integral	CTRL+I	or CTRL+8	
Parentheses	CTRL+9	or CTRL+0	or CTRL+(
		or CTRL+)	
Square brackets	CTRL+[	or CTRL+]	or CTRL+6
Angle brackets	CTRL+<		
Braces	CTRL+{	or CTRL+}	or CTRL+5
Display	CTRL+D		
Absolute value	CTRL+\		
Norm	CTRL+| (CTRL+SHIFT+\)		
Required space	SHIFT+SPACEBAR		
Nonbreaking space	CTRL+SPACEBAR		
Thin space	CTRL+,		
Thick space	CTRL+SHIFT+SPACEBAR		
" (double open quote)	Single open quote (') twice		
" (double close quote)	Single close quote (') twice		
- (intraword dash or hyphen)	Hyphen (-)		
– (en dash)	Hyphen (-) twice		
— (em dash)	Hyphen (-) three times		
- (Discretionary hyphen)	CTRL+– (CTRL + hyphen twice)*		
¿ (inverted question mark)	? followed by '		
¡ (inverted exclamation point)	! followed by '		

*Visible only when Invisibles are displayed

Entering Symbols and Characters

To enter	Press CTRL+S then press	To enter	Press CTRL+S then press
$\rightarrow$	1	$\subset$	c or &
$\uparrow$	2	$\vee$	v
$\leftarrow$	3	$\bullet$	b
$\downarrow$	4	∇	n
$\supseteq$	5	$\Downarrow$	$
$\cap$	6	$\Rightarrow$	!
$\subseteq$	7	$\Uparrow$	@
$\cup$	8	$\Leftarrow$	#
$(\Box)$	9 or 0 or (or)	$\supset$	%
$\equiv$	-	$\cong$	$\overline{+}$
$\neq$	=	$\pm$	
$\approx$	w	$\aleph$	W
$\in$	e	$\notin$	E
$\sqrt{\Box}$	r or R	∞	I
$\otimes$	t or T	$\wp$	P
$\int$	i	$\{\Box\}$	{ or }
$\emptyset$	o	$\forall$	A
$\prod$	p	$\oplus$	S
$[\Box]$	[or]	$\diamond$	D
$\angle$	a	$\div$	X
$\sum$	s	$\cdot$	C
∂	d	$\wedge$	V
$\frac{\Phi}{\Box}$	f or F	$\neg$	N
$\alpha^{\Box}$	h or H	$\leq$	<
$\alpha_{\Box}$	l or L	$\geq$	>
$\times$	x	$\exists$	z
Last matrix created	m	$\begin{array}{cc}\Box & \Box \\ \Box & \Box\end{array}$	M

The symbols are mapped to U.S. keyboards like this:

Uppercase

Lowercase

Entering Mathematical Accents

To enter accents	Press
$\hat{a}$	CTRL+^ (CTRL+SHIFT+6)
$\tilde{a}$	CTRL+~ (CTRL+SHIFT+`)
$\acute{a}$	CTRL+'
$\grave{a}$	CTRL+`
$\dot{a}$	CTRL+.
$\ddot{a}$	CTRL+" (CTRL+SHIFT+')
$\bar{a}$	CTRL+_
$\vec{a}$	CTRL+-

Entering Greek Characters

To enter		Press CTRL+G then press	To enter		Press CTRL+G then press
alpha	α	a	pi	π	p
beta	β	b		Π	P
gamma	γ	g		ϖ	v
	Γ	G	rho	ρ	r
delta	δ	d		ϱ	R
	Δ	D	sigma	σ	s
epsilon	ε	e		Σ	S
	ϵ	E		ς	T
zeta	ζ	z	tau	τ	t
eta	η	h	upsilon	υ	u
theta	θ	y		Υ	U
	ϑ	Z	phi	ϕ	f
	Θ	Y		Φ	F
iota	ι	i		φ	j
kappa	κ	k	chi	χ	q
	$\varkappa$	K	psi	ψ	c
lambda	λ	l		Ψ	C
	Λ	L	omega	ω	w
mu	μ	m		Ω	W
nu	ν	n	digamma	$\digamma$	I
xi	ξ	x			
	Ξ	X			

Greek characters are mapped to U.S. keyboards like this:

Uppercase

Lowercase

Entering ANSI Characters

The ANSI codes depend on the Windows code page in use. The sequences in the table below are for U.S. Windows systems.

▶ **To enter an ANSI character**

1. Hold down the ALT key.

2. On the numeric keypad, enter **0** and the number for the ANSI character you want.

3. Release the ALT key.

To enter	Type 0 +	To enter	Type 0 +	To enter	Type 0 +
space	160	À	192	à	224
¡	161	Á	193	á	225
¢	162	Â	194	â	226
£	163	Ã	195	ã	227
¤	164	Ä	196	ä	228
¥	165	Å	197	å	229
¦	166	Æ	198	æ	230
§	167	Ç	199	ç	231
¨	168	È	200	è	232
©	169	É	201	é	233
ª	170	Ê	202	ê	234
«	171	Ë	203	ë	235
¬	172	Ì	204	ì	236
—	173	Í	205	í	237
®	174	Î	206	î	238
¯	175	Ï	207	ï	239
°	176	Ð	208	ð	240
±	177	Ñ	209	ñ	241
²	178	Ò	210	ò	242
³	179	Ó	211	ó	243
´	180	Ô	212	ô	244
µ	181	Õ	213	õ	245
¶	182	Ö	214	ö	246
·	183	×	215	÷	247
¸	184	Ø	216	ø	248
¹	185	Ù	217	ù	249
º	186	Ú	218	ú	250
»	187	Û	219	û	251
¼	188	Ü	220	ü	252
½	189	Ý	221	ý	253
¾	190	Þ	222	þ	254
¿	191	ß	223	ÿ	255

Entering Units of Measure

Amount of Substance

To enter	Unit symbol	In Math, type
Mole	mol	$umol$

Area

To enter	Unit symbol	In Math, type
Acre	acre	$uacre$
Square foot	ft^2	uft (insert superscript)
Square inch	in^2	uin (insert superscript)
Square meter	m^2	ume (insert superscript)

Current

To enter	Unit symbol	In Math, type
Ampere	A	uA
Microampere	μA	$umcA$
Milliampere	mA	umA
Nanoampere	nA	unA

Electric Capacitance

To enter	Unit symbol	In Math, type
Farad	F	uF
Microfarad	μF	$umcF$
Millifarad	mF	umF
Nanofarad	nF	unF
Picofarad	pF	upF

Electric Charge

To enter	Unit symbol	In Math, type
Coulomb	C	uCo

Electric Conductance

To enter	Unit symbol	In Math, type
Kilosiemens	kS	ukS
Microsiemens	μS	$umcS$
Millisiemens	mS	umS
Siemens	S	uS

Electric Resistance

To enter	Unit symbol	In Math, type
Gigaohm	GΩ	*uGohm*
Kiloohm	kΩ	*ukohm*
Megaohm	MΩ	*uMohm*
Milliohm	mΩ	*umohm*
Ohm	Ω	*uohm*

Electrical Potential Difference

To enter	Unit symbol	In Math, type
Volt	V	*uV*

Energy

To enter	Unit symbol	In Math, type
British thermal unit	Btu	*uBtu*
Calorie	cal	*ucal*
Electron volt	eV	*ueV*
Erg	erg	*uerg*
Gigaelectronvolt	GeV	*uGeV*
Joule	J	*uJ*
Kilocalorie	kcal	*ukcal*
Megaelectronvolt	MeV	*uMeV*
Microjoule	μJ	*umcJ*
Millijoule	mJ	*umJ*
Nanojoule	nJ	*unJ*

Force

To enter	Unit symbol	In Math, type
Dyne	dyn	*udyn*
Newton	N	*uN*
Pound	lb	*ulb*

Frequency

To enter	Unit symbol	In Math, type
Exahertz	EHz	*uEHz*
Gigahertz	GHz	*uGHz*
Hertz	Hz	*uHz*
Kilohertz	kHz	*ukHz*
Megahertz	MHz	*uMHz*
Petahertz	PHz	*uPHz*
Terahertz	THz	*uTHz*

Illuminance

To enter	Unit symbol	In Math, type
Footcandle	fc	ufc
Lux	lx	ulx
Phot	phot	$uphot$

Length

To enter	Unit symbol	In Math, type
Angstrom	Å	uan
Attometer	am	uam
Centimeter	cm	ucm
Femtometer	fm	ufm
Foot	ft	uft
Inch	in	uin
Kilometer	km	ukm
Meter	m	ume
Micrometer	μm	$umcm$
Mile	mi	umi
Millimeter	mm	umm
Nanometer	nm	unm
Picometer	pm	upm

Luminance

To enter	Unit symbol	In Math, type
Stilb	sb	usb

Luminous Flux

To enter	Unit symbol	In Math, type
Lumen	lm	ulm

Luminous Intensity

To enter	Unit symbol	In Math, type
Candela	cd	ucd

Magnetic Flux

To enter	Unit symbol	In Math, type
Maxwell	Mx	uMx
Weber	Wb	uWb

Magnetic Flux Density

To enter	Unit symbol	In Math, type
Gauss	G	uGa
Tesla	T	uTe

Magnetic Inductance

To enter	Unit symbol	In Math, type
Henry	H	uHe

Mass

To enter	Unit symbol	In Math, type
Atomic mass unit	u	uu
Gram	g	ugr
Kilogram	kg	ukg
Microgram	μg	$umcg$
Milligram	mg	umg

Physical Quantity

To enter	Unit symbol	In Math, type
Becquerel	Bq	uBq
Curie	Ci	uCi

Plane Angle

To enter	Unit symbol	In Math, type
Degree	°	$udeg$
Microradian	μrad	$umcrad$
Milliradian	mrad	$umrad$
Minute	′	$udmn$
Radian	rad	$urad$
Second	″	uds

Power

To enter	Unit symbol	In Math, type
Gigawatt	GW	uGW
Horsepower	hp	uhp
Kilowatt	kW	ukW
Megawatt	MW	uMW
Microwatt	μW	$umcW$
Milliwatt	mW	umW
Nanowatt	nW	unW
Watt	W	uWa

Pressure

To enter	Unit symbol	In Math, type
Atmosphere	atm	$uatm$
Bar	bar	$ubar$
Millibar	mbar	$umbar$
Pascal	Pa	uPa
Torr	torr	$utorr$

Solid Angle

To enter	Unit symbol	In Math, type
Steradian	sr	usr

Temperature

To enter	Unit symbol	In Math, type
Celsius	°C	$ucel$
Fahrenheit	°F	$ufahr$
Kelvin	K	uK

Time

To enter	Unit symbol	In Math, type
Attosecond	as	uas
Day	d	uda
Femtosecond	fs	ufs
Hour	h	uhr
Microsecond	μs	$umcs$
Millisecond	ms	ums
Minute	mn	umn
Nanosecond	ns	uns
Picosecond	ps	ups
Second	s	use
Year	y	uy

Volume

To enter	Unit symbol	In Math, type
Cubic foot	ft^3	uft (insert superscript)
Cubic inch	in^3	uin (insert superscript)
Cubic meter	m^3	ume (insert superscript)
Gallon (U.S.)	gal	$ugal$
Liter	l	uli
Quart	qt	uqt

Entering TEX Commands

▶ **To enter TEX commands**

1. Hold down the CTRL key.

2. Type the command name.

   Available commands are categorized following these instructions.

3. Release the CTRL key.

Spaces and Breaks

To	Hold CTRL then type
Permit a line break at this point	allowbreak
Begin a new line at the break and justify text	linebreak
Enter approximately $\frac{7}{32}$" between lines	mathstrut
Enter approximately $\frac{3}{8}$" between lines	medskip
Enter a space the width of $-\frac{1}{6}$ em	negthinspace
Begin a new line at the break	newline
Begin a new page and a new paragraph	newpage
Prevent a line break at this point	nolinebreak
Begin a new page	pagebreak
Enter a space the width of MM (2-em space)	qquad
Enter a space the width of M (em space)	quad
Enter approximately $\frac{5}{16}$" between lines	smallskip
Enter approximately $\frac{3}{16}$" between lines	strut
Enter a space the width of $\frac{1}{6}$ em	thinspace

Decorations

To enter	Hold CTRL then type	To enter	Hold CTRL then type
$\boxed{a}$	fbox	$\underbrace{a}$	underbrace
$\boxed{a}$	frame	$\underleftarrow{a}$	underleftarrow
$\overbrace{a}$	overbrace	$\underleftrightarrow{a}$	underleftrightarrow
$\overleftarrow{a}$	overleftarrow	$\underline{a}$	underline
$\overleftrightarrow{a}$	overleftrightarrow	$\underrightarrow{a}$	underrightarrow
$\overline{a}$	overline	$\widehat{a}$	widehat
$\overrightarrow{a}$	overrightarrow	$\widetilde{a}$	widetilde

Big Operators

To enter	Hold CTRL then type	To enter	Hold CTRL then type
∩	bigcap	∐	coprod
∪	bigcup	∫ ⋯ ∫	idotsint
⊙	bigodot	∫∫∫∫	iiiint
⊕	bigoplus	∫∫∫	iiint
⊗	bigotimes	∫∫	iint
⊔	bigsqcup	∫	int
⊎	biguplus	∮	oint
∨	bigvee	∏	prod
∧	bigwedge	∑	sum

Other Objects

To enter	Hold CTRL then type
$\frac{\square}{\square}$	frac

Lowercase Greek

To enter	Hold CTRL then type	To enter	Hold CTRL then type	To enter	Hold CTRL then type
α	alpha	μ	mu	υ	upsilon
β	beta	ν	nu	ε	varepsilon
χ	chi	ω	omega	$\varkappa$	varkappa
δ	delta	ϕ	phi	φ	varphi
ϵ	epsilon	π	pi	ϖ	varpi
η	eta	ψ	psi	ϱ	varrho
γ	gamma	ρ	rho	ς	varsigma
ι	iota	σ	sigma	ϑ	vartheta
κ	kappa	τ	tau	ξ	xi
λ	lambda	θ	theta	ζ	zeta

Uppercase Greek

To enter	Hold CTRL then type	To enter	Hold CTRL then type
Δ	Delta	Π	Pi
F	digamma	Ψ	Psi
Γ	Gamma	Σ	Sigma
Λ	Lambda	Θ	Theta
Ω	Omega	Υ	Upsilon
Φ	Phi	Ξ	Xi

Binary Operations

To enter	Hold CTRL then type	To enter	Hold CTRL then type	To enter	Hold CTRL then type
∐	amalg	∪	cup	▷	rhd
&	And	⋎	curlyvee	⋌	rightthreetimes
∗	ast	⋏	curlywedge	⋊	rtimes
⊼	barwedge	†	dagger	\	setminus
○	bigcirc	‡	ddagger	∫	smallint
▽	bigtriangledown	◇	diamond	╲	smallsetminus
△	bigtriangleup	÷	div	⊓	sqcap
⊡	boxdot	⩲	divideontimes	⊔	sqcup
⊟	boxminus	∔	dotplus	⋆	star
⊞	boxplus	⩞	doublebarwedge	×	times
⊠	boxtimes	⊤	intercal	◁	triangleleft
•	bullet	⋋	leftthreetimes	▷	triangleright
∩	cap	◁	lhd	⊴	unlhd
⋒	Cap	⋉	ltimes	⊵	unrhd
·	cdot	∓	mp	⊎	uplus
▪	centerdot	⊙	odot	∨	vee
∘	circ	⊖	ominus	⊻	veebar
⊛	circledast	⊕	oplus	∧	wedge
⊚	circledcirc	⊘	oslash	≀	wr
⊝	circleddash	⊗	otimes		
⋓	Cup	±	pm		

Binary Relations

To enter	Hold CTRL then type	To enter	Hold CTRL then type	To enter	Hold CTRL then type
≈	approx	⋛	gtreqless	⌢	smallfrown
≊	approxeq	⪌	gtreqqless	⌣	smallsmile
≍	asymp	≷	gtrless	⌣	smile
϶	backepsilon	≳	gtrsim	⊏	sqsubset
∽	backsim	∈	in	⊑	sqsubseteq
⋍	backsimeq	⋈	Join	⊐	sqsupset
∵	because	≤	leq	⊒	sqsupseteq
◊	between	≦	leqq	⋐	Subset
◀	blacktriangleleft	⩽	leqslant	⊂	subset
▶	blacktriangleright	⪅	lessapprox	⊆	subseteq
⋈	bowtie	⋖	lessdot	⫅	subseteqq
≏	bumpeq	⋚	lesseqgtr	≻	succ
≎	Bumpeq	⪋	lesseqqgtr	⪸	succapprox
≗	circeq	≶	lessgtr	≽	succcurlyeq
≅	cong	≲	lesssim	⪰	succeq
⋞	curlyeqprec	≪	ll	≿	succsim
⋟	curlyeqsucc	⋘	lll	⊃	supset
⊣	dashv	|	mid	⋑	Supset
≐	doteq	⊨	models	⊇	supseteq
≑	doteqdot	∋	ni	⫆	supseteqq
⋕	eqcirc	∥	parallel	∴	therefore
≂	eqsim	⊥	perp	≈	thickapprox
⋝	eqslantgtr	⋔	pitchfork	∼	thicksim
⋜	eqslantless	≺	prec	⊴	trianglelefteq
≡	equiv	⪷	precapprox	≜	triangleq
≒	fallingdotseq	≼	preccurlyeq	⊵	trianglerighteq
⌢	frown	⪯	preceq	∝	varpropto
≥	geq	≾	precsim	△	vartriangle
≧	geqq	∝	propto	◁	vartriangleleft
⩾	geqslant	≓	risingdotseq	▷	vartriangleright
≫	gg	∣	shortmid	⊨	vDash
⋙	ggg	∥	shortparallel	⊩	Vdash
⪆	gtrapprox	∼	sim	⊢	vdash
⋗	gtrdot	≃	simeq	⊪	Vvdash

Negated Relations

To enter	Hold Ctrl then type	To enter	Hold CTRL then type
⪊	gnapprox	∤	nshortmid
⪈	gneq	∦	nshortparallel
⪈	gneqq	≁	nsim
⋧	gnsim	⊄	nsubseteq
⪈	gvertneqq	⊈	nsubseteqq
⪉	lnapprox	⊁	nsucc
⪇	lneq	⋡	nsucceq
⪇	lneqq	⊅	nsupseteq
⋦	lnsim	⊉	nsupseteqq
⪇	lvertneqq	⋪	ntriangleleft
≇	ncong	⋬	ntrianglelefteq
≠	neq	⋫	ntriangleright
≱	ngeq	⋭	ntrianglerighteq
≱	ngeqq	⊬	nvdash
⩾̸	ngeqslant	⊮	nVdash
≯	ngtr	⊭	nvDash
⇍	nLeftarrow	⊯	nVDash
↚	nleftarrow	⪹	precnapprox
↮	nleftrightarrow	⪵	precneqq
⇎	nLeftrightarrow	⋨	precnsim
≰	nleq	⊊	subsetneq
≰	nleqq	⊊	subsetneqq
⩽̸	nleqslant	⪺	succnapprox
≮	nless	⪶	succneqq
∤	nmid	⋩	succnsim
∉	notin	⊋	supsetneq
∦	nparallel	⊋	supsetneqq
⊀	nprec	⊊	varsubsetneq
⋠	npreceq	⊊	varsubsetneqq
⇏	nRightarrow	⊋	varsupsetneq
↛	nrightarrow	⊋	varsupsetneqq
∤	nshortmid		

Arrows

To enter	Hold CTRL then type	To enter	Hold CTRL then type
↺	circlearrowleft	⟼	longmapsto
↻	circlearrowright	⟹	Longrightarrow
↶	curvearrowleft	⟶	longrightarrow
↷	curvearrowright	↫	looparrowleft
←--	dashleftarrow	↬	looparrowright
--→	dashrightarrow	↰	Lsh
⇓	Downarrow	↦	mapsto
↓	downarrow	⊸	multimap
⇊	downdownarrows	↗	nearrow
⇃	downharpoonleft	↖	nwarrow
⇂	downharpoonright	⇒	Rightarrow
↩	hookleftarrow	→	rightarrow
↪	hookrightarrow	↣	rightarrowtail
⟺	iff	⇁	rightharpoondown
⟸	impliedby	⇀	rightharpoonup
⟹	implies	⇄	rightleftarrows
⤳	leadsto	⇌	rightleftharpoons
⇐	Leftarrow	⇉	rightrightarrows
←	leftarrow	⇝	rightsquigarrow
↢	leftarrowtail	⇛	Rrightarrow
↼	leftharpoondown	↱	Rsh
↽	leftharpoonup	↘	searrow
⇇	leftleftarrows	↙	swarrow
⇔	Leftrightarrow	↞	twoheadleftarrow
↔	leftrightarrow	↠	twoheadrightarrow
⇆	leftrightarrows	⇑	Uparrow
⇋	leftrightharpoons	↑	uparrow
↭	leftrightsquigarrow	⇕	Updownarrow
⇚	Lleftarrow	↕	updownarrow
⟸	Longleftarrow	↿	upharpoonleft
⟵	longleftarrow	↾	upharpoonright
⟺	Longleftrightarrow	⇈	upuparrows
⟷	longleftrightarrow		

Delimiters

To enter	Hold CTRL then type	To enter	Hold CTRL then type
⌈	lceil	⌉	rceil
⟨	langle	⟩	rangle
⌊	lfloor	⌋	rfloor
┌	ulcorner	┐	urcorner
└	llcorner	┘	lrcorner

Miscellaneous Symbols

Note Not all symbols are available in all font schemes.

To enter	Hold CTRL then type	To enter	Hold CTRL then type
ℵ	aleph	♡	heartsuit
∠	angle	ℏ	hslash
‵	backprime	ℑ	Im
\	backslash	ı	imath
𝕜	Bbbk	∞	infty
ℶ	beth	ȷ	jmath
★	bigstar	ƛ	lambdabar*
◆	blacklozenge	{	lbrace
■	blacksquare	[	lbrack
▲	blacktriangle	. . .	ldots
▼	blacktriangledown	¬	lnot
⊥	bot	◊	lozenge
· · ·	cdots	✠	maltese
¢	cents	∡	measuredangle
✓	checkmark	℧	mho
®	circledR	∇	nabla
Ⓢ	circledS	♮	natural
♣	clubsuit	∄	nexists
∁	complement	∂	partial
†	dag	£	pounds
⅂	daleth	′	prime
‡	ddag	}	rbrace
⋱	ddots	]	rbrack
╲	diagdown	ℜ	Re
╱	diagup	♯	sharp
◊	Diamond	♠	spadesuit
◊	diamondsuit	◁	sphericalangle
. . .	dots	□	square
ℓ	ell	√	surd
∅	emptyset	™	texttrademark
ð	eth	⊤	top
€	euro	△	triangle
∃	exists	▽	triangledown
⅃	Finv	∅	varnothing
♭	flat	⋮	vdots
∀	forall	‖	Vert
⅁	Game	℘	wp
⅂	gimel	¥	yen
ℏ	hbar		

*available in REVTEX4 only

Latin-1

Note   Not all symbols are available in all font schemes.

To enter	Hold CTRL then type	To enter	Hold CTRL then type
Å	AA	¬	lnot
å	aa	±	pm
Æ	AE	£	pounds
æ	ae	ß	ss
¢	cents	¡	textexclamdown
©	copyright	·	textperiodcentered
°	degree	¿	textquestiondown
Ð	DH	®	textregistered
ð	dh	Þ	TH
÷	div	þ	th
«	guillemotleft	×	times
»	guillemotright	¥	yen

Latin Extended

Note   Not all symbols are available in all font schemes.

To enter	Hold CTRL then type
Đ	DJ
đ	dj
ı	imath
Ŋ	NG
ŋ	ng
Œ	OE
œ	oe

General Punctuation

To enter	Hold CTRL then type
—	emdash
–	endash
‹	guilsinglleft
›	guilsinglright
'	lq
„	quotedblbase
‚	quotesinglbase
'	rq
"	textquotedblleft
"	textquotedblright

C Commands in Version 5

The commands listed below are available in Version 5. The menu on which each command appears is noted at the end of the description. The commands on the Compute menu in Version 5 of *SWP* and *SNB* are not included in this list. See the online Help and *Doing Mathematics with Scientific WorkPlace and Scientific Notebook* for more information.

The command sets differ slightly from product to product. In *SW*, the Computation Setup and Engine Setup commands on the Tools menu and the commands on the Compute menu aren't available. In *SNB*, the commands on the Insert / Typeset Object menu and the commands on the Typeset menu aren't available.

About
Display the program version and build number and a copyright notice. (Help)

Action
Activate a hypertext jump. (Tools)

Appearance
Change the tag properties in the style. (Tag)

Apply
Apply tags to portions of your document. (Tag)

Arrange Icons
Arrange the icons of minimized documents. (Window)

Author
Link to information about the author of a linked document. (Go / Links)

Automatic Substitution
In mathematics, substitute expressions for sequences of letters and numbers. (Tools)

Beginning Document
Go to the first document in the sequence containing the active document. (Go / Links)

Bibliography
Insert a BIBTEX bibliography in a document. (Insert / Typeset Object)

Bibliography
Go to the bibliography for the linked document. (Go / Links)

Bibliography Choice
Choose a manual bibliography or an automatic bibliography. (Typeset)

Binomial
Insert a binomial or generalized fraction. (Insert)

Brackets
Insert matched or unmatched pairs of brackets or enclosures. (Insert)

Break
Insert a page break or line break. (Insert / Spacing)

Cascade
Arrange the document windows one in front of the other. (Window)

Citation
Create a citation for an item listed in the bibliography. (Insert / Typeset Object)

Close
Close the active document. (File)

Close All
Close all open documents. (Window)

Compile
Process a document with LaTeX to produce a typeset device independent (DVI) file. (Typeset)

Compile PDF
Process a document with PDFLaTeX to produce a typeset Portable Document Format (PDF) file. (Typeset)

Computation Setup
Customize global defaults for computations. (Tools)

Computing Techniques
Open the index of information about computing in *SWP* and *SNB*. (Help / Index)

Contents
Link to all program information available online. (Help)

Contents
Go to the table of contents containing the active linked document. (Go / Links)

Copy
Copy the selection to the clipboard. (Edit)

Copy as Internal Format
Copy the selection to the clipboard as internal format. (Edit)

Copy Picture
Copy to the clipboard the formatted image of selected text and mathematics. (Edit)

Copyright
Go to the copyright information for the active linked document. (Go / Links)

Cross Reference
Create a reference to a document page or part. (Insert / Typeset Object)

Custom
Size the document display as specified. (View)

Cut
Cut the selection to the clipboard. (Edit)

Decoration
Insert a bar, arrow, or brace over or under an expression. (Insert)

Delete
Delete the selection. (Edit)

Delete Columns
Delete the selected matrix or table columns. (Edit)

Disclaimer
Go to the information about any disclaimers related to the active linked document. (Go / Links)

Display
Insert a mathematical display. (Insert)

Document Info
Open a collection of information about the document. (File)

Document Manager
Copy, delete, wrap, and unwrap documents. (Tools)

Editor
Go to information about the editor of the active linked document. (Go / Links)

End Document
Go to the last document in the sequence containing the active linked document. (Go / Links)

Engine Setup
Select defaults for the computational engine. (Tools)

Exam Builder
Open the Exam Builder. (Tools)

Exit
Leave the program. (File)

Expert Settings
Modify TEX options and settings related to compiling, previewing, and printing your document with LATEX and PDFLATEX. (Typeset)

Export as Picture
Capture and export the formatted image of text and mathematics. (File)

Export Document
Export the document as an HTML (.htm or .xhtml), shell (.shl), quiz (.qiz), wrap (.rap), or Rich Text Format (.rtf) file. (File)

Export Settings
Customize the defaults for exporting graphics and for exporting HTML and RTF documents. (Tools)

Find

Find occurrences of specified mathematics or text. (Edit)

Formula

Enter a formula for use in generated exams. (Insert)

Fraction

Insert a vertical fraction. (Insert)

Front Matter

Enter title page/area, abstract, table of contents, and related information. (Typeset)

Function Keys

Assign tags to function keys. (Tag)

General Information

Open the index of general information about working with the program. (Help / Index)

General Settings

Modify options related to BIBTEX databases and styles, to PDF and portable LATEX output, and to typesetting in general. (Typeset)

Glossary

Go to the glossary for the active linked document. (Go / Links)

Helper Lines

Toggle on and off the display of matrix, table, and vector lines. (View)

History Back

Return to the source of the previous jump. (Go)

History Forward

Undo History Back. (Go)

Horizontal Space

Add horizontal space. (Insert / Spacing)

HTML Field

Create an HTML field. (Insert)

Hypertext Link

Create a hypertext link to any marker or to any object with a key in the active document, in a different document, or on the Internet. (Insert)

Hypertext Reference

Create a hypertext reference (href, hyperref, or hyperlink) for use with the *hyperref* package. (Insert / Typeset Object)

Hypertext Target

Create a hypertext target (hypertarget or hyperdef) for use with the *hyperref* package. (Insert / Typeset Object)

Import Contents

Import a document into the active document. (File)

Import Fragment
Paste a previously saved fragment at the insertion point or over the current selection. (File)

Import Picture
Import a graphic into a frame. (File)

Index
Go to the index for the active linked document. (Go / Links)

Index
Access three online Help indexes. (Help)

Index Entries
Toggle on and off the display of index entries. (View)

Index Entry
Create an index entry. (Insert / Typeset Object)

Input Boxes
Toggle on and off the display of template input boxes. (View)

Insert Column(s)
Insert a specified number of columns at a specified position in a matrix or table. (Edit)

Insert Row(s)
Insert a specified number of rows at a specified position in a matrix or table. (Edit)

Invisibles
Toggle on and off the display of symbols for spaces and paragraphs and other non-printing characters. (View)

Label
Insert a labeled expression. (Insert)

Launch Exam Builder
Open the Exam Builder. (Exam toolbar)

License Information
Display information about registering your software and obtaining a license. (Help)

Links
Go to the document indicated by the selected link. (Go)

MacKichan Software Website
Open the MacKichan Software, Inc. home page on the Internet. (Help)

Marker
Create a marker for a document page or part. (Insert)

Markers
Toggle on and off the display of markers. (View)

Math
Insert mathematics. (Insert)

Math Name
Insert a mathematical function. (Insert)

Matrix
Insert a matrix or vector. (Insert)

Merge Cells
Merge the selected cells of a table. (Edit)

New
Create a new file. (File)

New Window
Open another window containing the active document. (Window)

Next Document
Go to the next document in the sequence containing the active document. (Go / Links)

Next Section
Go to the next section heading. (Go)

Note
Create a footnote, margin note, or note for an online document. (Insert)

Open
Open an existing file. (File)

Open Location
Open an Internet location. (File)

Operator
Insert a mathematical operator. (Insert)

Options and Packages
Modify the typesetting specifications and LaTeX packages in use for your document. (Typeset)

Output Choice
Indicate the kind of file you want to produce when you typeset so the program can prepare the file appropriately for DVI or PDF output. (Typeset)

Page Setup
Set the margins, headers, footers, and page numbers for the document when not using typesetting. (File)

Parent Document
Go to the parent document for the active linked document. (Go / Links)

Paste
Paste cut or copied material from the clipboard to the insertion point. (Edit)

Paste Special
Specify the format in which text is pasted into your document. (Edit)

Preamble
Add LaTeX code before the **begin{document}** statement in your document. (Typeset)

Preview

Display the document as it will appear in print without typesetting. (File)

Preview

Preview the typeset device independent (DVI) file for the document, compiling first if necessary. (Typeset)

Preview PDF

Open your PDF viewer to preview the typeset Portable Document Format (PDF) file for the document, compiling first if necessary. (Typeset)

Previous Document

Go to the previous document in the sequence containing the active document. (Go / Links)

Previous Section

Go to the previous section heading. (Go)

Print

Print the document without typesetting. (File)

Print

Print the typeset device independent (DVI) file for the document, compiling first if necessary. (Typeset)

Print PDF

Open your PDF viewer to print the typeset Portable Document Format (PDF) file for the document, compiling first if necessary. (Typeset)

Properties

Edit the properties of the first object in the selection or of the object to the left of the insertion point. (Edit)

Publisher

Go to the information about the publisher of the active linked document. (Go / Links)

Radical

Insert a radical. (Insert)

Reference Library

Open the index of mathematics and science information. (Help / Index)

Refresh

Refresh the view. (View)

Register

Register your software and request a license. (Help)

Replace

Replace specified occurrences of mathematics or text with new content. (Edit)

Restore Saved Preferences

Restore previously saved customized settings from a Windows Registry file. (Tools)

Rule

Add a rule (line) in your document. (Insert / Spacing)

Run BibTeX
Run the BibTeX program independent of a LaTeX or PDFLaTeX compilation. (Typeset / Tools)

Run MakeIndex
Run the MakeIndex program independent of a LaTeX or PDFLaTeX compilation. (Typeset / Tools)

Save
Save the active file and keep the file open. (File)

Save All
Save all open files and keep the files open. (File)

Save As
Save the active file under a new name or in a new directory, as a protected file, or as a wrapped (.rap) or portable LaTeX file and keep the file open. (File)

Save Fragment
Save the current selection as a file for quick recall. (File)

Save User Preferences
Save customized settings in a Windows Registry file. (Tools)

Search
Search for a help topic. (Help)

Select All
Select the entire text of the active document. (Edit)

Send
Wrap and send a file by email. (File)

Set Alignment
Align the current line of a multiline display with other lines in the display. (Edit)

Spacing
Insert horizontal or vertical space, rules, or breaks. (Insert)

Spelling
Check the spelling of the active document. (Tools)

Split Cells
Split the selected cells of a table. (Edit)

Status Bar
Toggle on and off the display of the Status bar. (View)

Stop Operation
Cancel an attempt to link to the Internet or halt a computation in progress. (Stop toolbar)

Style
Set or change the screen style of the document. (File)

Style Editor
Open the Style Editor. (Tools)

Subdocument
Create a subdocument within a master document. (Insert / Typeset Object)

Subscript
Insert a subscript. (Insert)

Superscript
Insert a superscript. (Insert)

System Features
Show a list of available features; change the serial number for your installation. (Help)

Table
Insert a table. (Insert)

TeX Field
Insert a field for $\TeX$ or $\LaTeX$ commands. (Insert / Typeset Object)

Text
Insert text. (Insert)

Tile Horizontally
Arrange the document windows horizontally. (Window)

Tile Vertically
Arrange the document windows vertically. (Window)

To Marker
Go to a designated marker. (Go)

To Paragraph
Go to a designated paragraph. (Go)

Toolbars
Toggle on and off the display of toolbars and tooltips and the use of large or small toolbar buttons. (View)

Tools
Run $\text{B{\small IB}}\TeX$ or MakeIndex independent of a $\LaTeX$ or $\text{PDF}\LaTeX$ compilation. (Typeset)

Top Document
Go to the root document for the entire active linked document. (Go / Links)

Trademark
Go to trademark information for the active linked document. (Go / Links)

Typeset Object
Insert an object to hold a citation, cross-reference, index entry, $\TeX$ command, or other document element generated by $\LaTeX$ or $\text{PDF}\LaTeX$. (Insert)

Undo
Return the last deletion to the document or undo the last operation. (Edit)

Unit Name
Insert a unit of measure. (Insert)

User Setup

Customize the defaults. (Tools)

Vertical Space

Add vertical space. (Insert / Spacing)

View History

Display the list of jumps made. (Go)

View Quiz

View the quiz resulting from the current document. (Exam toolbar)

100%

Size the document display at the normal size (100%). (View)

200%

Size the document display at twice the normal size (200%). (View)

Index

Software

 ### Scientific WorkPlace®

Scientific WorkPlace makes writing, sharing, and doing mathematics easier than you ever imagined possible. This scientific word processor increases your productivity because it is easy to learn and use. You can compose and edit your documents directly on the screen, without being forced to think in a programming language. With a simple click of a button, you can typeset your document in LaTeX. You can also compute and plot solutions with the included computer algebra system. With *Scientific WorkPlace*, both professional and support staff can produce stunning results quickly and easily, without knowing TeX™, LaTeX, or computer algebra syntax. ***Contact us for a free 30-day trial version.***

 ### Scientific Word®

The Gold Standard for mathematical publishing since 1992, *Scientific Word* makes writing and sharing scientific documents straightforward and easy. With over 150 LaTeX styles included, *Scientific Word* ensures your documents will be beautiful. This means you can concentrate on the content, not the appearance. It has been estimated that support staff using *Scientific Word* experiences a doubling or tripling of productivity over the use of straight LaTeX. Also, MacKichan Software provides free, prompt, and knowledgeable technical support. ***Contact us for a free 30-day trial version.***

 ### Scientific Notebook®

Scientific Notebook makes word processing and doing mathematics easy. With this complete word processor, you can enter text and mathematics quickly, without having to use an inefficient equation editor. The built-in computer algebra system lets you solve and plot equations without having to learn a special syntax. After creating your scientific documents and exams in *Scientific Notebook*, you can publish them in print and on the World Wide Web. ***Contact us for a free 30-day trial version.***

 ### MuPAD® Pro

MuPAD Pro is a modern, full-featured computer algebra system in an integrated and open environment for symbolic and numeric computing. Its domains and categories are like object-oriented classes that allow overriding and overloading methods and operators, inheritance, and generic algorithms. The *MuPAD* language has a Pascal-like syntax and allows imperative, functional, and object-oriented programming. A comfortable notebook interface includes a graphics tool for visualization, an integrated source-level debugger, a profiler, and hypertext help. ***Contact us for a free 30-day trial version.***

MacKichan
SOFTWARE, INC.

Additional Software

MathTalk™/Scientific Notebook®

MathTalk/Scientific Notebook, created by Metroplex Voice Computing, provides voice input for *Scientific Notebook*. With this program, you can enter even the most complex mathematics using voice commands. You can use it in conjunction with the keyboard and mouse to speed the entry of text and mathematics, or to completely replace the keyboard and mouse. *MathTalk/Scientific Notebook* requires *Dragon NaturallySpeaking®*, which is not included.
Visit *www.mathtalk.com* for more information.

Duxbury Braille Translator

Duxbury Systems leads the world in software for braille. Their *Duxbury Braille Translator* converts *Scientific Notebook* files into braille. Create your print or large print math, save, then open your *Scientific Notebook* file and go to braille. Used with *MathTalk/Scientific Notebook*, the *Duxbury Braille Translator* provides dramatic new power to visually impaired students and professionals.
Visit *www.duxburysystems.com* for more information.

Books

Doing Mathematics with Scientific WorkPlace® and Scientific Notebook®, Version 5
By Darel W. Hardy and Carol L. Walker

Doing Mathematics with Scientific WorkPlace and Scientific Notebook describes how to use the built-in computer algebra system to do a wide range of mathematics, without having to deal directly with the computer algebra syntax.

Creating Documents with Scientific WorkPlace® and Scientific Word®, Version 5
By Susan Bagby

Creating Documents with Scientific WorkPlace and Scientific Word gives you an overview of the process of creating beautiful documents using these two powerful software programs. It covers basic editing and entering of mathematical expressions as well as tables, graphics, lists, indexes, cross-references, tables of contents, and large document management. If you are using *Scientific WorkPlace* or *Scientific Word* to prepare documents for publication, this book is highly recommended.

(Continued)

TO ORDER: Visit our webstore, fax, email, or phone us.
Website: www.mackichan.com ♦ Fax: 360-394-6039 ♦ Email: info@mackichan.com ♦ Toll-free: 877-724-9673
19307 8th Avenue NE ♦ Suite C ♦ Poulsbo, WA 98370

Books (cont.)

Typesetting Documents in Scientific WorkPlace® and Scientific Word®, Third Edition
By Susan Bagby and George Pearson

Typesetting Documents in ScientificWorkPlace and Scientific Word is an aid to choosing and customizing the typeset appearance of your documents. The manual explains how to work from within these two programs to tailor the typeset appearance of a document; how to choose and add document shells; and how document shells use LaTeX document classes, class options, and packages. The manual also documents many of the LaTeX packages that accomplish specific formatting tasks.

A Gallery of Document Shells for Scientific WorkPlace® and Scientific Word®, Version 5
By Susan Bagby and George Pearson (In PDF format on the program CD-ROM)

A Gallery of Document Shells for Scientific WorkPlace and Scientific Word helps you choose document shells that are appropriate for your typesetting purposes. It illustrates and briefly describes the characteristics of almost 200 shells provided with these two programs.

Doing Calculus with Scientific Notebook®
By Darel W. Hardy and Carol L. Walker

Take the mystery out of doing calculus with this must-have companion to the *Scientific Notebook* software. This book provides activities to complete with *Scientific Notebook* that will help develop a clearer understanding of calculus. Think of *Scientific Notebook* as a laboratory for mathematical experimentation and *Doing Calculus with Scientific Notebook* as a lab manual of experiments to perform.

An Interactive Introduction to Mathematical Analysis
By Jonathan Lewin (Cambridge University Press)

This book is a sequel to *An Introduction to Mathematical Analysis*. It includes an on-screen hypertext version that you can read with *Scientific Notebook*. This on-screen version contains alternative approaches to material, more fully explained forms of proofs of theorems, sound movie versions of proofs of theorems, interactive exploration of mathematical concepts using the computing features of *Scientific Notebook*, automatic links to the author's website for solutions to exercises, and more. It can be ordered at any bookstore.

(Continued)

TO ORDER: Visit our webstore, fax, email, or phone us.
Website: www.mackichan.com ♦ Fax: 360-394-6039 ♦ Email: info@mackichan.com ♦ Toll-free: 877-724-9673
19307 8th Avenue NE ♦ Suite C ♦ Poulsbo, WA 98370

MacKichan
SOFTWARE, INC.

Books (cont.)

Precalculus with Scientific Notebook®
By Jonathan Lewin (Kendall Hunt Publishing Company)

This book contains a standard printed version and an on-screen hypertext version designed for interactive reading with *Scientific Notebook*. The on-screen version includes links to solutions to exercises that reside on the author's website. It can be ordered at any bookstore.

Exploring Mathematics with Scientific Notebook®
By Wei-Chi Yang and Jonathan Lewin (Springer-Verlag)

This book is supplied both in printed form and in an on-screen hypertext version for interactive reading with *Scientific Notebook*. It contains a sequence of modules from a variety of mathematical areas and, in each, demonstrates how the editing, Internet, and computing features of *Scientific Notebook* can be combined to deepen the reader's understanding of mathematical concepts. It can be ordered at any bookstore.

MuPAD® Pro Computing Essentials, Second Edition
By Miroslav Majewski (Springer-Verlag)

Intended for teachers of mathematics and their students, *MuPAD Pro Computing Essentials* presents basic information about doing mathematics with *MuPAD Pro*. It includes basic instructions useful in various areas of mathematics that are facilitated by *MuPAD Pro*. Chapters 1 through 7 focus on the basics of using *MuPAD Pro*: Syntax, programming control structures, procedures, libraries, and graphics. Chapters 8 through 13 focus on applications in geometry, algebra, logic, set theory, calculus, and linear algebra. Each chapter includes examples and programming exercises.

TO ORDER: Visit our webstore, fax, email, or phone us.
Website: www.mackichan.com ♦ Fax: 360-394-6039 ♦ Email: info@mackichan.com ♦ Toll-free: 877-724-9673
19307 8th Avenue NE ♦ Suite C ♦ Poulsbo, WA 98370

Workshops

Scientific WorkPlace®, Scientific Word®, and Scientific Notebook®
By Professor Jonathan Lewin, Ph.D.

Seminars, workshops, and training sessions by Jonathan Lewin are available at professional conferences and, by arrangement, at individual campuses of high schools, colleges, and universities.

Scientific Notebook: This presentation introduces the editing, Internet and computing features of *Scientific Notebook* documents. It also covers the publication of mathematical material on websites and how *Scientific Notebook* can be used as an electronic whiteboard in the classroom.

Scientific WorkPlace and Scientific Word: This presentation introduces the editing and typesetting features of *Scientific WorkPlace* and *Scientific Word*. Participants will be trained in the production of documents that will be printed as professional quality hard copy or submitted to an editor for publication.

Each participant will be given a CD containing sound movies that review the material covered in the workshops. Contact Jonathan Lewin for details at *lewins@mindspring.com* or 770-973-5931.

Scientific WorkPlace® and Scientific Notebook®
By Professor Bill Pletsch, Ph.D.

Bill Pletsch has been using computer algebra systems since the early 1980s. He is available for workshops and training sessions on the use of *Scientific WorkPlace* and *Scientific Notebook* as a research and teaching aid.

The workshops and training sessions begin with a demonstration of the capabilities of *Scientific WorkPlace/Notebook*. The introductory demonstration is followed by a thorough nuts and bolts hands-on session on the basics. Participants learn how to compute numerically and symbolically, graph, and manipulate data. Also included are word-processing, Internet techniques, and utilizing other resources. More advanced topics include the use of *Scientific WorkPlace/Notebook* in the classroom and in the preparation of computer classroom lectures and demonstrations.

An overview of computer algebra systems and why every teacher of mathematics should own a copy of *Scientific Notebook* will accompany the presentation. Included in the workshops will be a CD on the electronic delivery of mathematics instruction. No prior computer experience is required. Contact Bill Pletsch for details at *bpletsch@tvi.edu* or 505-224-3672.

(Continued)

TO ORDER: Visit our webstore, fax, email, or phone us.
Website: www.mackichan.com ♦ Fax: 360-394-6039 ♦ Email: info@mackichan.com ♦ Toll-free: 877-724-9673
19307 8th Avenue NE ♦ Suite C ♦ Poulsbo, WA 98370

Scientific Notebook®
By Professor John H. Gresham, Ph.D.

John Gresham has been using *Scientific Notebook* since 1997 to prepare materials for classroom instruction. He is available for workshops and training sessions on *Scientific Notebook*, including the use of *Scientific Notebook*'s Exam Builder to generate both objective and free-response test forms. Workshop participants will receive hands-on step-by-step instruction in using *Scientific Notebook* as a mathematics word processor to prepare class notes, overhead transparencies, and exams. *Scientific Notebook* will also be used to view and prepare web materials, including HTML files. Participants will become familiar with the capability of *Scientific Notebook*'s computer algebra system to perform numeric and symbolic computations, solve equations, and generate graphs and tables. Participants will receive printed materials and a floppy disk with sample files. No prior experience with *Scientific Notebook* is required, but familiarity with basic Windows commands will be helpful. For details, contact John Gresham at jgresham@ranger.cc.tx.us or 254-647-3234.

TO ORDER: Visit our webstore, fax, email, or phone us.
Website: www.mackichan.com ◆ Fax: 360-394-6039 ◆ Email: info@mackichan.com ◆ Toll-free: 877-724-9673
19307 8th Avenue NE ◆ Suite C ◆ Poulsbo, WA 98370